WITHDRAWN

JOHN SMIBERT, PAINTER

Library of American Art

JOHN SMIBERT, PAINTER

WITH A DESCRIPTIVE CATALOGUE OF PORTRAITS
AND NOTES ON THE WORK OF NATHANIEL SMIBERT

BY HENRY WILDER FOOTE

Kennedy Galleries, Inc. • *Da Capo Press*
New York • *1969*

This edition of *John Smibert, Painter* is an unabridged re-publication of the first edition published in Cambridge, Massachusetts, in 1950. It is reprinted by special arrangement with Harvard University Press.

Library of Congress Catalog Card Number 78-87537

Published by
Kennedy Galleries, Inc.
20 East 56th Street, New York, N.Y. 10022
and
Da Capo Press
A Division of Plenum Publishing Corporation
227 West 17th Street, New York, N.Y. 10011

JOHN SMIBERT *Painter*

Self-Portrait, Detail from the "Bermuda Group"

JOHN SMIBERT *Painter*

WITH A DESCRIPTIVE CATALOGUE OF

PORTRAITS · AND NOTES ON THE

WORK OF NATHANIEL SMIBERT

HENRY WILDER FOOTE

HARVARD UNIVERSITY PRESS · CAMBRIDGE

1950

Printed in the United States of America

Preface

MORE THAN TWENTY YEARS AGO, AS THE INEVITABLE CONSEQUENCE of my search for traces of the elusive Colonial portrait painter Robert Feke, I found myself confronted with many puzzling problems in trying to determine what known or unknown artists could have painted the increasing number of eighteenth-century portraits which came to my notice. Not many persons in the nineteenth century had taken any interest in such matters; the names of only a few painters were handed down by tradition; and to those few were frequently attributed, often regardless of historical probability, any old portraits which had survived the neglect to which they were then so commonly subjected.

In New England only two painters who had worked there before the Revolution were well remembered—John Smibert and John Singleton Copley—for, although it was realized that a few portraits were signed "J. Blackburn," nothing was known of him and he was miscalled "Jonathan" instead of Joseph, and not even Feke's name was known to more than a very few persons. Since John Smibert, the Scot who came to America with Dean George Berkeley, was an older contemporary of Feke's who worked in the same locale in New England, it was to be expected that the older should have influenced the younger man (to a greater degree than I realized when I wrote about Feke) and that in some cases it should have been difficult to decide to which of the two a given portrait should be attributed.

My attention being thus drawn especially to Smibert I quickly discovered how little was really known about him, although William Dunlap gave some information in his valuable *History of the Rise and Progress of the Arts of Design in the United States* (1834), and in 1866 William H. Whitmore discussed Smibert and Peter Pelham before the Massachusetts Historical Society, where, in 1878, he was followed by Augustus T. Perkins in a paper listing a considerable number of portraits which he attributed to Smibert or Blackburn. There was, however, no adequate account of Smibert until the publication of Professor Theodore Sizer's brief biographical sketch of

him in the *Dictionary of American Biography* in 1936. I had begun
the following study of Smibert and his work several years before
that date, as an avocation, but the work, both then and in more recent years, went very slowly, with many long interruptions due to
the pressure of professional occupations. My biographical sketch of
him was, indeed, substantially completed long ago, but the Descriptive Catalogue of Portraits has been a prolonged and tedious task,
requiring much time to search out and examine portraits, and in very
many cases to weigh the evidence as to the identification of the sitters
and the correctness of the attribution. The delay in completing the
work, however, has had the compensation of bringing to light new
items of information or portraits which had previously been overlooked. It is unlikely that further investigation will uncover any
important facts about Smibert's life, but it is probable that other portraits will be found which I have failed to discover, especially in
Great Britain where his work has been almost completely overlooked.

My approach to the subject has been that of the biographer and
historian rather than that of the technical expert in painting, which I
make no claim to be. I have sought to depict the life of a European
artist coming to New England in the first half of the eighteenth century, how he fared, and what his influence was. Conditions of life in
New England make the story a quite different one from that of a
painter in the Middle and Southern Colonies, such as John Wollaston
who followed Smibert to America after an interval of some twenty
years.

The portraits by Smibert which are known or supposed to be still
in existence in Great Britain are few in number, and of these few I
have seen but three—the portrait of George Berkeley in the National
Portrait Gallery, and those representing Mrs. Ferne and Henry Ferne
—but I have no doubt that there are scores of others as yet unidentified.
I have seen all the known American portraits which, in my opinion,
it seems reasonable to attribute to him except in cases where it is
noted that the portrait is lost or its present location is unknown, or
where it is stated that judgment is based on a photograph. I have not
attempted to see all the portraits in the long list of questionable attributions, because in many cases reproductions, or the biographical
data concerning the subject represented, made it sufficiently evident
that the attribution was a mistaken one.

So many of Smibert's American portraits have been reproduced,
some of them repeatedly, in publications easily accessible to the
student of art (as indicated in the Descriptive Catalogue) that I have
felt that the general reader would be better served by a few full-page
reproductions of his best portraits in appropriate places in the text

than by a much larger number shown in smaller size in an appendix. The Self-Portrait was the inevitable frontispiece, and the "Bermuda Group," though many times reproduced, was clearly called for. The other five portraits by John Smibert have been chosen from among the less well known but most vigorous of his works, and one by Nathaniel Smibert is included to illustrate the young man's characteristic style.

I owe a debt of gratitude to many persons who have helped me: to the owners of portraits who in every case have courteously permitted me to see their pictures; to Miss Margaret Morrison of Edinburgh for furnishing the record of Smibert's baptism and data as to his family connections; to the staffs of the Newport Historical Society, of the Museum of Fine Arts, Boston (especially Mrs. Haven Parker), and of the Frick Art Reference Library in New York, for invaluable assistance; to several authorities on colonial portraiture, the late John Hill Morgan, Miss Louisa Dresser of the Worcester Art Museum, Mr. Alan Burroughs, Mr. J. T. Flexner, Prof. Oskar Hagen, and Prof. Theodore Sizer, and I have tried to make due acknowledgment in the footnotes for information derived from these and other sources.

I owe a special debt of gratitude to Mr. John Marshall Phillips of the Yale University Art Gallery for arranging the exhibition of Smibert's portraits which opened there on October 8, 1949, with a conference of experts in the field of colonial painting who were of great assistance to me.

Not infrequently my opinions have differed from those of other writers on colonial portraiture, as is inevitable in a field as yet only partially explored. Where disputed questions are involved I have sought to give both sides. It is not to be expected that readers will accept my conclusions at every point, and it is quite certain that growing knowledge will invalidate some of my views. I can only claim that I have sought to give as complete a picture of John Smibert and his works as present resources permit.

HENRY WILDER FOOTE

Cambridge, Massachusetts

Contents

ILLUSTRATIONS

CHAPTER I

Early Years

JOHN SMIBERT [1] WAS BORN IN EDINBURGH, SCOTLAND, ON MARCH 24
(New Style), 1688.[2] Eight days later he was baptized. The record is
to be found in the Register of Births and Baptisms for the Parish of
Edinburgh. It reads:

First of Aprill 1688
John Smibert, Litster and Alison Bell a s.n.
John. W John Gardyn, Merchant: Capt.
Patrick Chalmers, Deacon of the Wrights, Archibald
Paterson and James Barrowman, John Liveington
and Joseph Young —————————————————— s.w.

Being interpreted this entry means that his parents were John Smibert
and Alison Bell. "Litster" is an old provincial synonym for dyer. The
letters *s.n.* signify a "son named" John. *W* signifies witnesses. The

---

[1] In early Scottish records of the sixteenth and seventeenth centuries the family name
appears as Smeithberd, Smythbeard, Smeberd, Smeebert, Smibeard, Smibaird, Sme-
bard, and Smiebeard. George Fraser Black, in *Surnames of Scotland* (New York,
1946), p. 734, derives it from "smooth beard" and cites a William Smeithberd as a
member of the Edinburgh town council in 1530. Smibert is a relatively modern form.
The name is a rare one, found only in Edinburgh and neighboring southeastern
Scotland, perhaps limited to one family. In the Harvard University Library it is
found only on cards referring to John Smibert and his sons Williams and Nathaniel,
with the single exception of the Scottish writer, Thomas Smibert (1810–1854), who
edited a book on *The Clans of the Highlands*. This would indicate both the rarity
of the name and a certain lack of distinction among those who bore it. John Smibert's
contemporary, George Vertue, on one page of his *Note Books* (Walpole Society,
1930–1947) spelled the name both Smibert and Smybert, though generally using the
second spelling. Dunlap is chiefly responsible for giving currency to "Smybert," having been misinformed by Professor C. A. Goodrich of Yale, who had written to him
"So he [Smibert] spelled his name on the picture of Dean Berkeley and family now at
Yale College." Goodrich evidently neglected to verify his statement by taking a look
before he wrote at the signature so clearly painted on the picture. Tuckerman and
others perpetuated this error. The painter, however, in all his known signatures,
whether written or painted, spelled his name with an *i* and not with a *y*, and so it
appears in his advertisements and in the obituary notices in the Boston newspapers.
[2] Appendix 1.

letters *s.w.* indicate the Southwest Parish of Edinburgh which, in 1688, worshipped in what is now known as Old Greyfriars Church. The six witnesses to the baptism were, no doubt, friends of the infant's father. "The Wrights," of which Captain Chalmers was deacon, were the guild of carpenters and joiners.

John Smibert, the father, came from a family of artisans settled at the hamlet of Middletown, in the parish of Borthwick, about twenty miles southeast of Edinburgh, some miles beyond Dalkeith on the road to Galashiels. No less than seven young men of this family name, coming from Middletown, appear as apprentices in the Edinburgh records of the seventeenth century, the names John and William each occurring three times. No records of births, marriages, or deaths appear to have been kept at Borthwick prior to 1700, so that the relationships cannot be clearly determined, but the father of the painter must have been one of two Johns (presumably cousins) one of whom is recorded as "son of the late John Smibert in Middletown, apprenticed with George Clerk, litster, 20 July, 1664," while the other was "son of the late William Smibert in Middletown, apprentice with George Gilmour, litster, 18 January, 1665." The second of these two Johns was probably the father of the painter. If so, he was the grandson of an earlier John Smibert of Middletown. As fourteen years was the usual age for entering upon an apprenticeship he must have been born in 1650 or soon after. In the Edinburgh marriage register is an entry, under date of April 5, 1678, of his marriage to Alison Bell, of South Leith, an adjacent hamlet now included within the city limits. Four daughters and two sons were born to the couple, of whom the future painter was the fifth child and younger son.[3]

The father had his dye shop on the south side of the Grassmarket and no doubt lived in the same building, above the shop, after the custom of the time. The Grassmarket is an open square in a hollow on the southern slope of Castle Rock. Its buildings of the seventeenth century have long since been demolished, and the exact site of John Smibert's shop cannot now be determined, but the dyers and brewers lined its southern side to avail themselves of the excellence of the well water found there. The Grassmarket had an important place in Scottish

---

[3] Edinburgh Parish Record of Births, children of John and Alison (Bell) Smibert:

Jan.	19, 1679, daughter,	Alison
Aug.	28, 1681, son,	William
July	15, 1683, daughter,	Janet
Aug.	31, 1686, daughter,	Elizabeth
April	1, 1688, son,	John
July	29, 1690, daughter,	Euphan [?]

In the case of John the date is that of baptism, and so, probably, with the others also.

history because, after the Restoration, it was the place of execution and there most of the Covenanters who suffered martyrdom in Edinburgh for conscience's sake between 1661 and 1688—about a hundred in all—were put to death. They were buried in Greyfriars Churchyard, just round the corner from the Grassmarket.

On February 16, 1681, John Smiebard, litster, was enrolled as a burgess "gratis on supplication," and in the Greyfriars record of interments there is a note of the burial of a John Smibaird, litster, on January 29, 1690. It is uncertain whether either or both of these entries refer to the father of the future painter or to his contemporary cousin of the same name. It is probable, however, that at least the record of burial is that of the cousin, since its date is six months earlier than the record of birth (or baptism) of the youngest child of the painter's father, who would, according to custom, have been recorded as the daughter of the "umquhile" John Smibert had her father been dead. When, however, the future painter's oldest sister Alison was married to Thomas Moffatt, on February 5, 1702, she was recorded as the "daughter of deceased John Smibert, litster, burgess." No record of the death of the painter's mother has been found and there is no reason to suppose that she may not have lived for many years after his birth. The father is said to have been a deacon, or a lay member of the church council; and an old man in Boston, who in his youth had known the painter, long years afterwards reported that the painter had told him that he had been intended for the ministry, but that the intention had been abandoned because he showed no inclination to letters, but was always drawing. In due time young John was apprenticed to a house painter and plasterer. His father's trade, and that of the master whom he served as apprentice, made him familiar from his early youth with the use of color and the ways of handling it.

When his apprenticeship was up young Smibert obeyed the impulse which has come to many another ambitious Scotsman and struck out for London. If we assume that he had been apprenticed at fourteen, and served the customary seven years, he might have reached London by the late spring or early summer of 1709. George Vertue,[4] who is our ultimate authority for Smibert's early life in

---

[4] Vertue, c.1684–1756, was an engraver who was the familiar associate of the London artists during the first half of the eighteenth century. For nearly forty years he kept notebooks in which he assiduously jotted down memoranda about them and their doings. These notebooks, most of which are now in the British Museum, are the best source of information about the artistic life of London of the period, and almost our only source of knowledge of Smibert's career previous to his emigration. After Vertue's death about forty of them came into the possession of Horace Walpole who used them as the basis for his *Anecdotes of Painting in England*. But Walpole

London, and who presumably got the facts from Smibert himself, says that he had long "had a strong inclination to drawing and studying, but no opportunity to improve." [5] He had many difficulties at first, but found employment in coach painting. The coaches of the period were, of course, all hand-painted, and the private coaches and sedan chairs of noblemen and people of wealth were often elaborately decorated. This work was one of the minor arts which might well serve as a steppingstone to more ambitious work. From coach painting he turned to copying pictures for dealers, for three or four years, though without any instruction. At any rate he found work with his brush, and saved his money like a canny Scot for the great ambition which he had in mind.

Vertue goes on to say that Smibert "never copied any thing from the life, till he came to the academy haveing never drawn from plaister." It has been commonly assumed that the academy in which Smibert had his first lessons was the one opened by James Thornhill in James Street, near his own house in Covent Garden, in 1724. But Smibert was then thirty-six years old, had had three years of study and travel in Italy, and was already a portrait painter of established reputation in London. The school in which Smibert worked must, therefore, have been the earlier one which was founded by a group of London artists, including Thornhill, on October 18, 1711, and which occupied a dilapidated mansion on Great Queen Street, where it lasted for a number of years. About a dozen of the better known artists were elected directors, and Sir Godfrey Kneller was chosen governor, an office which he held until St. Luke's Day, 1716.[6] Vertue, who was one of the earliest pupils in this academy, writes: "The subscription was a guinea for each person, paid down; the place for drawing, a large room, ground floor, in the great house in the middle of Great Queen Street, near Lincoln Inn Fields, where formerly many great noblemen had lived and once a land-bank was kept there, but gone to decay and uninhabited." [7] Here, no doubt, Smibert first met not only Vertue but also many of the artists included in his London acquaintance.

Vertue recorded that Smibert "after this went to Edenborough

did not utilize all of Vertue's materials. Nearly all of the Vertue notebooks in the British Museum have been published, 1930–1947, admirably edited, by the Walpole Society (see Bibliography).
[5] Vertue, III, 14.
[6] For an account of this academy of 1711 see William T. Whitley: *Artists and Their Friends in England, 1700–1799.* I, 7–15.
[7] Vertue, I, 8.

there first tryd to paint faces, after came to London and set out to Italy." [8] This visit to Edinburgh must have occurred early in 1717. There is no evidence that he had returned home at any earlier date, and the supposition which has been advanced that he was involved in the Jacobite rising of 1715 does not appear to have a shred of evidence to support it. It seems clear that he had long had in mind the project of a journey to Italy, the goal of every ambitious artist of his time in the northern countries of Europe, and that he had been saving up his money for the purpose. First, however, he paid a dutiful visit at home and Vertue may well have based his statement that Smibert's first essays at portraiture were made at this time on information furnished by Smibert himself. In London a painter with as little experience and training as Smibert had then had would have found no sitters, but in Scotland the situation was different. Aside from William Aikman, who was then working in Edinburgh, there was little competition, for the Scottish school of artists had hardly come into being,[9] but on the other hand there was small demand even for portraits, the only form of art to which any attention was paid, and in the general poverty then prevailing there were few people who could afford them. A tradition of American origin reports that Smibert's "first essay in colours is said to have been the portrait of a young negro, brought

[8] *Ibid.*, III, 14.
[9] Very little pictorial art earlier than the seventeenth century survives in Scotland. Before the union with England (1608) the court of the Stuarts had no foreign artists of repute attached to it, like those gathered at the court of Henry VIII and his successors in England, none of whom ever came north of the Tweed. The country was poor; dependent on agriculture, with little commerce and few industries; torn by political and religious dissensions; and after the union the removal of the court drew many of the richer nobles to England. The earliest native-born Scottish painter of any distinction was George Jamesone (1587–1644), many of whose portraits remain in Scotland. The next was John Michael Wright (1625–1700), but he painted mostly in England. Both of these artists paid visits to Italy. The Scougalls, father and son, painted portraits before and after 1700. The foreign-born Sir John Medina (half Spaniard, half Fleming) worked in Edinburgh from about 1690 until his death in 1710. He was known as "The Kneller of the north," and followed that artist's picture-factory methods in the execution of his commissions. It is not at all likely that the youthful Smibert had any acquaintance with him. The most notable Scottish painter in the first quarter of the eighteenth century was William Aikman (1682–1731), a man of good family, being nephew of Sir John Clerk of Penicuik. He had visited Italy, Constantinople, and the East between 1707 and 1712. He returned to Edinburgh in 1712 and painted many portraits there until his removal in 1723 to London, where he remained until his death. The work of all these men was in portraiture, there being no demand for other forms of art until near the end of the eighteenth century. But even in this field the demand was not great, and noblemen who had the means to frequent London preferred to be painted by the fashionable artists there. See James Lewis Caw, *Scottish Painting Past and Present* (Edinburgh, 1908), introd. and chap. i, ii.

from Martinique to Scotland." [10] This tradition, like that of Smibert's
noting the resemblance of the Indians to the Siberian Tartars, may be
founded on some statement made by Smibert when he was in Newport. It is not inconsistent with Vertue's statement, since it implies
that the negro was in Scotland when painted. In any event it is certain
that during this visit Smibert painted an oval portrait, dated 1717,
of Lady Grant, the wife of Sir Francis Grant of Monymusk, afterwards Lord Cullen. On his second visit to Edinburgh, after his return
from Italy in 1720, he painted Lord Cullen, and a large group showing
twelve persons of his family.

It also seems clear that on this earlier visit Smibert painted the first
of his two portraits of Allan Ramsay, the poet. Allan Ramsay was a
lifelong friend of Smibert, who was seventeen months his junior.
Although Ramsay was a great-grandson of the laird of Cockpen who
was a brother to Lord Dalhousie, he was brought up as a shepherd
boy in Lanarkshire, his father having died early and his mother having
married the peasant proprietor of a small, rugged farm. His stepfather
seems to have treated him fairly, and as generously as his scanty means
permitted, but when, in his fifteenth year, his mother died, Ramsay
was glad to escape from the farm by being apprenticed to a wigmaker in Edinburgh. By 1707 he was master of his own shop on the
High Street "at the sign of the Mercury, opposite Niddry's Wynd."
He had never read any poetry until he was twenty, but, having been
introduced to it, tried his hand at turning out popular verses, humorous or satirical, on topics of the day. He quickly acquired a local
reputation and became a sort of poet laureate for the Easy Club, a
group of a dozen congenial spirits who met at a tavern to drink, to
read papers and poems, and to discuss literary topics.[11] Between 1713
and 1720 no less than thirty-four issues (including reprints) of Ramsay's verses were printed, most of them penny broadsides or slender
pamphlets. In the latter year Thomas Ruddiman printed for him the
first octavo edition of his collected *Poems*. In 1721 the *Poems* appeared
in a quarto subscription edition of four hundred copies. The Edinburgh *Evening Courant* contained the following advertisement:

The Poems of Allan Ramsay is a large quarto volume, fairly printed,
with notes, and a complete Glossary (as promised to the subscribers),
being now finished; all who have generously contributed to the carrying

[10] Wilkins Updike, *A History of the Episcopal Church in Narragansett Rhode
Island* (Boston, 1907), I, 523.
[11] It was originally a semisecret Jacobite organization and was broken up after the
suppression of the rebellion of 1715. Oliphant Smeaton, *Allan Ramsay* (1896), pp.
45-53.

on of the design, may call for their copies as soon as they please, from the author, at the Mercury, opposite to Niddry's Wynd, Edinburgh.

The dedication of the book "To the most Beautiful the Scots Ladies," is dated July 14, 1721, and is followed by an imposing alphabetical list of some two hundred subscribers beginning with "His Grace, the Duke of Argyle and Greenwich," and including a large number of Scottish and English nobles, gentry, writers, and merchants, among whom "John Smibert *Painter*" is the only artist except William Aikman. In 1728 a second quarto edition of the *Poems* appeared, identical with the first in format, but with a "Dedication to the Patrons who subscribed for the first and this Volume," followed by a list of subscribers similar to the first, though with some names omitted and others added. In this second list Smibert appears as "Mr. John Smibert Painter." In both volumes Smibert's *second* portrait of Ramsay is reproduced as the frontispiece, engraved in 1721 by Vercruysse, in 1728 by George Vertue. Smibert's own copy of the handsome edition of 1728, with his autograph, "Smibert's," in the upper corner of the title page, is now in the Sterling Memorial Library at Yale University. Vertue's engraving has been covered with water-color paints, presumably by a child after the book had passed into later hands.

Between these two editions of *Poems* the indefatigable Ramsay published, in 1725, his best-known work, the pastoral comedy called *The Gentle Shepherd*, which brought him a widespread and lasting fame. It has been called "the first genuine pastoral after Theocritus," and the enthusiastic author of his "Life," prefixed to the edition of his *Poems* published in 1800, calls it "one of the finest pastorals in any language." [12]

Encouraged by his success Ramsay had abandoned wig-making for bookselling and in 1726 moved his shop to the Luckenbooths and opened the first lending library in Scotland.

In 1736 he built and opened a playhouse, which was promptly suppressed by the magistrates. Scotland at this time was just emerging from the desolate period of turmoil which had lasted during two centuries following the Reformation and during which art and letters all but disappeared. Ramsay was one of the earliest of the notable group of Scottish men of letters who made the eighteenth century illustrious. But even his literary activities aroused opposition. He was attacked in a pamphlet entitled *The Flight of Religious Piety from Scotland, upon the account of Ramsay's lewd books, and the hell-bred*

[12] *The Poems of Allan Ramsay,* with a biographical sketch by George Chalmers.

playhouse comedians, who debauch all the faculties of soul of our rising generation. The fact is that some of his earlier poems were written in a broad vein of humor that is at times decidedly coarse, and that some of the books imported from London for his lending library gave such offense to the pious that his bookshop was searched at least once for indecent literature. No one, however, seems to have accused him of loose living, and he survived to the age of seventy-two, a leading figure among the wits and men of letters in Edinburgh. Smibert must have gone to London about the time that Ramsay began to write verse, and he can never have been a member of the Easy Club, but the portraits, Ramsay's poem addressed to Smibert in Florence, and his letter of 1736, quoted later, are evidence that the friendship was a close and lasting one, and we may surmise that Smibert was a congenial spirit in Ramsay's circle.

It has long been common knowledge that Smibert painted *one* portrait of Ramsay, from which the frontispiece to the *Poems* of 1721 and 1728 was engraved, though the portrait itself has long been lost, but the fact that Smibert painted *two* portraits of Ramsay, showing him in different positions, appears to have been generally overlooked. The author of the unsigned "authentic life" of Ramsay prefixed to the 1808 edition of *The Gentle Shepherd* was, however, necessarily aware of the existence of two portraits, since in that book the earlier of the two was, for the first time, reproduced as the frontispiece. It is labeled: "Drawn by A. Carse from the Original Family Picture in New Hall House & Eng^d by A. Wilson." Alexander Carse was a Scottish painter who worked in Edinburgh early in the nineteenth century, and his sepia drawing from which the engraving was made is now in the possession of the National Scottish Portrait Gallery. The phrase, "the original family picture," refers to the fact that this portrait remained in the possession of Ramsay and then in that of his eldest surviving daughter, Miss Jane Ramsay, until the latter's death in 1804, when it was transferred to Newhall House, where it remained until that property was sold in 1925, when it was given to the National Scottish Portrait Gallery.

This first portrait of Ramsay was painted by Smibert during his visit to Edinburgh in 1717, and shows Ramsay's face in profile. It is far from complimentary, portraying all too truthfully his heavy jowl and large upturned nose. It is of this portrait that Caw says:

Smibert's friendship with Allan Ramsay, like Aikman's, is perpetuated in a portrait, and it must have taken a good deal of friendship on the poet's part to stand the strain of that record of his appearance. It hangs among other interesting portraits by Aikman and the younger Ramsay in "Pennicuik's Parlour" in the Newhall House, the district around which is so intimately connected with the "Gentle Shepherd." [13]

In the engraving Ramsay's bust is shown three-quarters front, the head turned right nearly in profile. The shirt is unbuttoned at the neck, and the short hair of the head is covered by a thick woolen cap. The head and bust are enclosed in a draped tartan, with a mask above. The picture is as uncomplimentary as Caw intimated it to be, but the accuracy with which the features are drawn is corroborated by other, though suaver, pictures of Ramsay. Ramsay was himself aware that his features were homely, and more than once dealt humorously with the subject, saying, "I am a little unhappy in the mould of my face, which is not quite so long as it is broad," and one of his biographers says of the portrait, "The picture from which the prefixed engraving was taken precisely agrees with descriptions by himself and others, as to expression, complexion and features." [14] Furthermore it is probably to this portrait that Oliphant Smeaton refers in his *Life of Allan Ramsay* when he says, "Of Ramsay we have only two portraits remaining that are of any real value, that painted by his son Allan, and that by Smibert, the poet's life-long friend. The latter represents him in youth, the former in age, both being considered at the time of execution striking likenesses." [15]

Smibert's second portrait of Ramsay (No. 2 in the Descriptive Catalogue) was the one from which the frontispiece in the *Poems* of 1721 was engraved. The engraving is marked in the lower left-hand corner, *I.S.p.*, and in the lower right, *T. Vercruysse, s.*[16] Ver-

---

[13] Caw, *Scottish Painting*, p. 28. Aikman's portrait of Ramsay, referred to by Caw, was painted in 1723 and is a good deal suaver but probably less realistic as a likeness. Apparently it was not used for any of the engraved frontispieces which adorn many of the numerous editions of Ramsay's works. Several different pictures of Ramsay appear in these engravings, but in the later editions the frontispiece is frequently a reproduction of the somewhat idealized drawing made by Ramsay's son Allan, who became a noted painter in his day. Newhall House, a few miles out of Edinburgh, was, in the first half of the eighteenth century, a countryseat of the Forbes family, and a place where Ramsay "met a clever set of men with a taste for letters, who gathered in a chamber called the 'Clubroom,' Pennicuik's Parlour, adorned with portraits of its members from the skillful hand of William Aikman, the laird of Cairney." See Henry Grey Graham, *Scottish Men of Letters in the Eighteenth Century* (London, 1901), p. 14. (Quotation from Caw courtesy of T. Nelson & Sons Ltd., Edinburgh.)
[14] *Poems of Allan Ramsay* (1800), pp. 20, 22.
[15] Smeaton, p. 120.
[16] The name of the engraver is known in many variant forms—Ver Cruys, Verkruis, Verkruys—and in some of his engravings done in Florence it is translated into della Croce. His given name was Theodor. He is said to have been born c.1646 and to have died after 1723. Nagler lists twenty-five engravings by him of paintings in the Grand Ducal Gallery in Florence, but omits two of his finest ones of marines by Salvator

cruysse was, in all probability, the Dutch engraver of whom very little is known beyond the fact that he worked in the first (and second ?) decades of the eighteenth century in Florence, where he made many engravings of pictures in the Grand Duke's collection. He might still have been there at the time of Smibert's visit. Aside from this engraving of Smibert's portrait of Ramsay no evidence is available that Vercruysse visited Great Britain, but it is possible that he went to London in his old age and that Smibert secured him to do this job. Inasmuch as there is no frontispiece in the small octavo edition of Ramsay's *Poems* in 1720, it is perhaps safe to assume that the portrait was painted in that year, during Smibert's second visit to Edinburgh, and that it was done to give Ramsay's readers a more favorable impression of the author than they would have received from the earlier portrait. It shows Ramsay full face, dressed in Scottish costume, and, while he cannot by any stretch of the imagination be called handsome, the face is attractive in its expression of keen intelligence and humor. In the 1728 quarto of *Poems* the same portrait is again used for the frontispiece, enclosed in an identical frame showing a masonry wall, but the engraving is better done by Smibert's London friend George Vertue, which would indicate that Smibert then had the portrait in London.

Three other engravers also reproduced this portrait as frontispiece in later editions of the *Poems*, the latest in 1733, after which engravers resorted to No. 1 instead. The explanation may be that Smibert had had the portrait shipped to him in Boston, as we know that others of his pictures were sent out to him. In any case a portrait of Allan Ramsay by Smibert was owned by the latter's nephew, Dr. Thomas Moffatt, many years later, because Moffatt, in his will dated August 5, 1786, after his return to London from America, bequeathed "to George Chalmers of Berkeley Square" (who later wrote the "Life of Ramsay" prefixed to the 1800 edition of *The Poems of Allan Ramsay* as noted above), among other pictures, one of "Allen [*sic*] Ramsay by Smibert." This can hardly have been any other than portrait No. 2. Since Moffatt's Newport house was sacked in the Stamp Act riots of 1765, and he lived a troubled life thereafter, it would seem probable

---

Rosa, and several others. Oskar Hagen in *Birth of the American Tradition in Art* (New York, 1940), reproduces, facing p. 42, the engraving by Vercruys to refute the statement that it bears the inscription, "The Scottish Hogarth." Theodore Bolton, in his article on John Smibert in *The Fine Arts* (August, 1933), p. 12, had already pointed out that this was not the case, but had mistakenly attributed the phrase to Lionel Cust's sketch of Smibert in the *DNB* instead of to T. Bayne's sketch of Allan Ramsay. Hagen correctly points out that in 1721 the phrase would have been meaningless because Hogarth was still an unknown young man who had not yet become a portrait painter.

that he had acquired the portrait (with at least two other pictures from Smibert's studio) [17] before 1765, either by gift or bequest from his uncle, or by purchase after Smibert's death. Nothing is known of this portrait of Allan Ramsay after it passed into the hands of George Chalmers.

When his visit of 1717 in Edinburgh was done Smibert proceeded to Italy in fulfillment of the plan which he must long have had in mind. No doubt he had saved up his money for the journey, and he found some profitable employment while in Italy, so that he was able to prolong his sojourn there till 1720. Presumably, being Scottish, he lived frugally, but later gossip in Boston had it that he had "spent a fortune in travel and study." The only definite information which exists about his Italian sojourn is found in Vertue's notes, but it is confirmed by Allan Ramsay's poem addressed to Smibert while the latter was in Florence, with such added inferences as may be drawn from the poem by Mather Byles about Smibert's exhibition in Boston in 1730 (quoted, pp. 54–55) and from the contents of Smibert's studio as reported by visitors in later years. Vertue says that "when he [Smibert] came to Florence there from ye great Dukes pictures he copyd several particularly the Card. Bentivoglio of Vandyke & many other heads making his whole study after Titian Raphael Rubens, &c. At Rome he painted several persons from the life. Naples, &c." [18]

There was at this time a great vogue for frescoes in the Italian manner, decorating public buildings and the great houses of noblemen. Hagen, in his *Birth of the American Tradition in Art*, assumes that Smibert went to Italy to learn the art, which was much more profitable than portrait painting. Other writers have assumed that while studying under Thornhill he had assisted his master in designing huge frescoes. Neither assumption has any support in Vertue's notes, but Professor Hagen thinks that Vertue "was surely insufficiently informed" as to Smibert's ambitions and procedure. Aside, however, from the high probability that Vertue got his information from Smibert's own lips after his return from Italy, what he says is, at least in part, corroborated by Allan Ramsay's poem, which must have been written in 1718 and which is clearly a response to a letter from Smibert giving an account of his doings in Florence and of his plans for a subsequent visit to

[17] Thomas Moffatt was something of an art collector and, although he lived in Newport throughout the period of Smibert's sojourn in Boston, it is clear that the relations between them continued to be close and affectionate. Moffatt's bequest included also the "Bermuda Group" (the small copy of or study for the large painting), and "St. Peter's head being the present of the Duke of Tuscany to Smibert." Smibert might have given these two to his nephew on leaving Newport for Boston.
[18] Vertue, III, 14.

Rome. The poem, entitled "To a Friend at Florence, on his way to Rome," is as follows:

Your steady impulse foreign climes to view,
To study nature, and what art can shew,
I now approve, while my warm fancy walks
O'er Italy, and with your genius talks;
We trace, with glowing breast and piercing look,
The curious gall'ry of th' illustrious duke,
Where all those masters of the arts divine,
With pencils, pens, and chisels greatly shine,
Immortalizing the Augustine age,
On medals, canvass, stone, or written page,
Profiles and busts originals express,
And antique scrolls, old e'er we knew the press.
For's love to science, and each virtuous Scot,
May days unnumber'd be great Cosmus' lot.
    The sweet Hesperian fields you'll next explore,
'Twixt Arno's banks and Tiber's fertile shore.
Now, now I wish my organs could keep pace,
With my fond muse and you these plains to trace;
We'd enter Rome with an uncommon taste,
And feed our minds on every famous waste;
Amphitheatres, columns, royal tombs,
Triumphal arches, ruins of vast domes,
Old aerial aqueducts, and strong pav'd roads,
Which seem to've been not wrought by men but gods.
    These view'd, we'd then survey, with utmost care,
What modern Rome produces fine or rare,
Where buildings rise with all the strength of art,
Proclaiming their great architect's desert,
Which citron shades surround and jessamine,
And all the soul of Raphael shines within;
Then we'd regale our ears with sounding notes,
Which warble tuneful thro' the beardless throats,
Join'd with the vib'rating harmonious strings,
And breathing tubes, while soft eunuch sings.
    Of all those danties [sic] take a hearty meal;
But let your resolution still prevail:
Return, before your pleasure grows a toil,
To longing friends, and your own native soil:
Preserve your health, your virtue still improve,
Hence you'll invite protection from above.[19]

[19] Allan Ramsay, Poems (1800), II, 375–376, but the verses are incorrectly dated 1721, and Smibert, named in the footnote as the "Friend in Florence," is mistakenly said to have instructed the younger Allan Ramsay in painting.

The lines, "For's [for his] love to science, and each virtuous Scot, May days unnumber'd be great Cosmus' lot," indicate that Smibert had reported his favorable reception by Cosimo III, who perhaps had happy recollections of his visit to England many years earlier which inclined him to welcome British artists. Three other straws also indicate that he had the Grand Duke's patronage. The first is that he copied the head and bust of Van Dyck's famous portrait of Cardinal Bentivoglio, which, as Professor Hagen has pointed out, then hung in the Grand Duke's private apartments and could have been seen and copied only by special permission. The second is the bequest in the will of Thomas Moffatt, already referred to, of "St. Peter's head being the present of the Duke of Tuscany to Smibert." Obviously, this was a picture which the Grand Duke bestowed upon Smibert as a mark of favor. The third is the tradition that Cosimo employed him to paint two or three Siberian Tartars whom the Czar had sent to the Grand Duke as a present, the pictures being sent back to the Czar by way of acknowledgment. This episode is not mentioned by Vertue but is associated with the American tradition that when Smibert first saw the Narragansett Indians he was struck by their resemblance to the Tartars whom he had painted for the Grand Duke.

Ramsay's poem gives no indication that Smibert intended to visit Venice, where many important frescoes were to be seen, nor do Vertue's notes give any hint that he did so, but both indicate that he spent his time chiefly in Florence and Rome, copying the works of the great masters and devoting himself to the study of portraiture. The collection of copies which Smibert brought to America supports this theory. Among them were copies of Raphael's Madonna dell' Impannata and his Madonna della Sedia; of Titian's Venus and Cupid; of Van Dyck's portrait of the youthful princes Charles and James Stuart; and of the picture, called "gloting monks" in the poem by Mather Byles celebrating Smibert's Boston exhibition of 1730, which Professor Hagen believes to have been Magnasco's Landscape with Monks at Prayer. The originals of all these pictures were then in Florence.

Among the other items which Smibert brought to America were "landskips," which may have been either copies of works by Italian painters or originals, pictures of "Roman views," and casts of Homer's Head and of the Venus de' Medici—"The breathing Statue and the living Bust," of Mather Byles' poem. His copy of Poussin's "Continence of Scipio" was sent to him later from London. It was admired by colonial visitors, was called "a good copy" by Gilbert Stuart, and is now owned by Bowdoin College. His copy of Van Dyck's Bentivoglio has an interesting history. The original was painted when Van Dyck was in his early twenties, during his visit to Italy from 1621 to 1625. While in Venice Van Dyck was greatly influenced by the portraits of Titian and Tintoretto, an influence which is reflected in the portrait of Bentivoglio, though transformed somewhat in his later years in Flanders and England. Through the copy which Smibert made of the head and bust of Van Dyck's picture he was the channel by which, at third hand and much diluted, a little trickle of this influence was brought into early American painting. Smibert's copy hung for many years in his Boston studio where Copley took some hints from it and where it was copied in turn, a generation after Smibert's death, by the youthful John Trumbull, who later gave to Harvard College the copy which he had made.

In view of the favors which Smibert had received from Cosimo III it would seem improbable that the drawing which caricatures the senile Grand Duke, now at Bowdoin College, is really from his hand. It is one of three drawings in that collection which were formerly attributed to him. Two of them are clearly by other and earlier hands. The third is a biting caricature in profile, showing the large open mouth, hooked nose, and retreating chin of the bigoted and imbecile old man. On the sheet on which it is mounted is an inscription reading, "Cosmo the 3rd, Grand Duke of Tuscany, from the life, by John Smibert," written in the small and elegant handwriting of the late eighteenth or early nineteenth century, certainly not by Smibert himself. It is unlikely that he, when in Florence, would have cared, or perhaps dared to produce so harsh a caricature of his benefactor. Professor Hagen gives a plausible explanation of it as in reality a copy made by Smibert of an original sketch by Alessandro Magnasco, who was in Florence at the time. His explanation, however, is rendered questionable by the fact that another very similar, or duplicate, drawing was in the Bowdoin Collection and was sold many years ago. Both versions of the drawing may have been owned by John Smibert and have been purchased by James Bowdoin when Smibert's pictures were sold long after his death, but whether they were actually his original drawings, or were copied by him from Magnasco, or are by another hand altogether, are questions to which we now have no answer. It is not possible to identify any pictures which Smibert painted in Rome, but Vertue's statement that while "in Rome he painted several persons from the life" should be noted. Probably the sitters were English visitors there, and George Berkeley may well have been one of them, as will presently appear. No doubt Smibert sold also some of his copies to traveling Englishmen of wealth who desired more vivid and exact reproductions of famous pictures than those furnished by black-and-white engravings. But he kept a good many of them, and brought them to America, where they figured in his early exhibition of 1730, in his sale of 1735, and in the collection which made his studio a little art gallery for Boston for nearly half a century.

Aside from the knowledge of art and the technical skill which Smibert acquired in Italy, one other thing occurred which was destined profoundly to affect his career: he met George Berkeley. Berkeley was one of the most remarkable men of the eighteenth century. He was three years older than Smibert, having been born on March 12, 1685, at Dysart Castle, near Thomastown, Kilkenny County, Ireland. Dysart Castle, or Tower, was the remnant of a monastic ruin, the habitable part of which amounted to hardly more than a substantial farmhouse. George Berkeley's line of descent is obscure, but there was an acknowledged relationship with Lord Berkeley of Stratton and with Earl Berkeley, the head of the English branch of the family. He matriculated at Trinity College, Dublin, took his B.A. in 1704, his M.A. in 1707, and became a fellow of Trinity in the latter year. He made a reputation as a brilliant student, published his *Essay Towards a New Theory of Vision* in 1709, and his *Treatise Concerning the Principles of Human Knowledge* in 1710. About the same time he was ordained deacon in the Anglican Church. In April 1713, he appeared in London in the company of Dean Swift, who had known him in Ireland. Swift's introduction, with his own reputation as a scholar and his great personal charm, gave him an immediate entry into literary circles, Steele, Addison, and Arbuthnot becoming his close friends. The testimony to his extraordinary combination of charm in conversation, great intellectual ability, broad-mindedness, modesty, and unaffected piety, is universal. Swift, presenting him to Earl Berkeley said, "My lord, here is a young gentleman of your family. I can assure your lordship that it is a much greater honor to you to be related to him, than to him to be related to you." The earl later introduced him to Bishop Atterbury, who had asked to have him presented. After George Berkeley had left, the earl asked, "Does my cousin answer your lordship's expectations?" To which the bishop replied, "So much understanding, so much knowledge, so much innocence and such humility, I did not think had been the portion of any but angels until I met this gentleman." Even Alexander Pope appreciated him, counted him a friend, accepted his literary criticism, and, twenty-five years later, after George Berkeley had become Bishop of Cloyne, wrote:

E'en in a Bishop I can spy desert;
Secker is decent, Rundle has a heart:
Manners with candour are to Benson given,
To Berkeley every virtue under heaven.[20]

Swift also introduced George Berkeley to the Earl of Peter-borough, who, in October 1713, was sent as ambassador extraordinary to the Kingdom of Sicily. Berkeley went with him as his chaplain and secretary, returning to London in August 1714. He went back to the continent in the autumn of 1716, as traveling tutor to St. George Ashe, son of the Bishop of Clogher, and remained there, mostly in Italy, until well on in the year 1720. His letters give evidence of his un-bounded curiosity in the fields of natural history, art, and architecture. Furthermore, while in Rome he had lodging in the Piazzi di Spagna, at the south end of which still stands the Palazzo di Propaganda Fidei, the great training school for Roman Catholic missionaries in foreign lands. The daily spectacle of these young seminarians is said to have given birth in Berkeley's mind to his idea of founding a college in the American colonies for the education of missionaries to the Indians who should counteract the Roman Catholic influence upon them, exerted through Canada and Louisiana.

At some time in the course of this sojourn he met Smibert, who fell under his spell. Professor Oskar Hagen says that Smibert met Berkeley and Ashe in Florence and that they "stayed together and returned to England together." [21] I have found no evidence to sup-port this statement. Vertue only says that they met "in Italy." Berke-ley, who had been in Rome from January to March, 1717, and again April to November, 1718, does not appear to have visited Florence until July 1720, by which time Smibert was probably on his way home. Smibert's name does not appear in Berkeley's correspondence of this period, but there are two passages which may perhaps refer to him. Writing from Rome, November 13, 1718, to his good friend Lord Percival, Berkeley says:

. . . we are now proposing to set out from hence in a day or two, which makes me fear I shall not have time to enquire about the medals and other things your Lordship mentioned in your last. But I design to leave directions with a friend here to inform himself as to the price of them and where they may be had. He is one who having an excellent genius for painting designs to continue a year longer in Rome, and will gladly serve me in anything that lies in his power.

[20] *Epilogue to the Satires*, Dialogue II, 70 (1738).
[21] *Birth of the American Tradition in Art*, p. 52.

And writing again from Florence on July 20, 1720, Berkeley says:

I hoped to have been able to send you this advice about the medals long since, having employed an English gentleman who passed this way to Rome (for my friend whom I left there was returned to England.) [22]

It is at least possible that this friend with "an excellent genius for painting" may have been Smibert, whom Berkeley, eight years later, employed in London to arrange for the sale of pictures which he had inherited, and that Smibert may also have been the same friend who, in July 1720, "was returned to England."

Smibert painted Berkeley at least three times in later years. Fraser, in his *Life and Letters of Dr. George Berkeley* (vol. IV, Clarendon Press ed. of *Works*, 1871), gives an inaccurate and incomplete list of the extant portraits of Berkeley, but he includes, as the earliest of his list, one said to have been painted in Italy. This picture is now in the possession of George F. A. Berkeley, Esq., of Hanwell Castle, Banbury. It shows Berkeley as a young man wearing a blue coat, and on the back of the frame is an inscription in ink reading, "George Berkeley Bishop of Cloyne painted at Rome before he had taken orders." [23] The question naturally suggests itself as to whether this picture might not have been one of those which Smibert, according to Vertue, painted "from the life" while in Rome. It is not impossible that such may have been the case, and that it was the first fruits of Smibert's acquaintance with Berkeley. Their ways separated for a time, but eight years later Smibert became one of Berkeley's associates in the latter's American adventure, and thus it came about that he ultimately settled in Boston.

[22] Benjamin Rand, *Berkeley and Percival* (Cambridge University Press, 1914), pp. 174–175. John Percival, or Perceval, b. 1683; succeeded to a baronetcy in 1691; Baron Percival, 1715; Viscount Percival, 1723; Earl of Egmont, 1733. He assisted Oglethorpe's project for the settlement of Georgia and was the first president of the trustees incorporated by royal charter, June 1732, for the establishment of the colony. On the margin of a letter, written to him about Berkeley, Lord Percival made the following note: "Mr. Berkeley, fellow of Dublin College, now Bishop of Cloyne, 1736. A man of the noblest virtues, best learning I ever knew."
[23] Probably written by the grandfather of the present owner. As a matter of fact Berkeley had taken orders before going to Rome. Presumably his secular attire gave rise to the error.

CHAPTER II

Life in London

WHEN SMIBERT RETURNED TO ENGLAND IN 1720 AFTER HIS LONG
sojourn on the Continent there were nowhere in Great Britain any
native-born painters of much distinction, and this was to remain true
for most of his lifetime. The portrait painters William Dobson, in
the reign of Charles I, and Robert Walker, during the period of the
Commonwealth, had long since died, and the men who were to make
the second half of the eighteenth century illustrious in British art had
not yet risen above the horizon. The earliest of them—Joseph Highmore, William Hogarth, and Thomas Hudson—were, indeed, all start-
ing their careers in the period of Smibert's residence in London, but
they were from four to a dozen years younger than he was and still
had their mark to make. The later painters—Allan Ramsay, Jr.,
Reynolds, Gainsborough, Romney, and Raeburn—had hardly begun
to paint and the latest of them had not been born when Smibert died.

In this dearth of native talent the German-born Sir Godfrey
Kneller completely dominated the field. He came of a land-owning
family of good social and economic status seated at Lübeck in North
Germany. A precocious youth, he had taken full advantage of opportunities to study art in Italy and Holland, so that when he arrived in
England in 1675 as a young man of twenty-nine he came with an
already established reputation as a painter. His immediate predecessor
in the long line of Continental artists who had sought the patronage
of English sovereigns, ever since Hans Holbein the Younger had
journeyed to England with a letter of introduction from Erasmus to
Sir Thomas More, was Peter Lely. But Lely by that time was an old
man, and after his death in 1680 Kneller had no serious rivals. To
the end of his long life he remained unquestionably the best-trained
painter in England and was regarded as without a peer. He was handsome in person, inordinately vain, avaricious, astute in cultivating the
friendship of persons of importance among men of letters as well as

in the titled aristocracy, and a successful courtier who gained wealth, celebrity and a baronetcy.

The product of his studio was enormous, for he had far more commissions from persons in the great world, from the king down, than he could execute singlehanded, so that his studio became a picture factory in which much of the painting was done by assistants and pupils. Except to portraits of the most highly placed of his patrons Kneller gave little personal attention. His usual method was to visit a client at his or her own house and to sketch the head and shoulders in crayon. He then painted these without further sittings and turned the picture over to his assistants, who specialized on draperies, backgrounds, or accessories, so that his portraits frequently are the work of several hands, little more than the head being actually the work of Kneller himself. Lord Killanin [1] gives an account of several of his chief assistants, some of whom, such as his pupils Highmore and Jervas, became artists of distinction on their own account, but there were doubtless many others who sought employment under him that they might learn to paint in the manner which he had made so fashionable and so profitable. There is no evidence that Smibert was one of them.

As a result of these methods and of some forty-five years of active practice in England, there are several thousand portraits in Great Britain attributed to Kneller. When, in 1723, he reluctantly relinquished the acclaim of fashion and the elegance of his town house and of his country seat at Whitton for the uncertain joys of a mansion in the skies, with no belief that the exchange would be to his advantage, he left to his widow about eight hundred pictures, finished or incomplete, with instructions that they were to be sold at his regular prices after his assistant Edward Byng had finished the incomplete ones. [2] Of all his portraits perhaps a hundred represent his best work—especially his portraits of men, for his women are more often fashion plates—and his work at its best was very good, but the great majority of the pictures attributed to him fall into varying degrees of mediocrity and it is often impossible to tell to what extent they are from his hand or from those of his assistants, are copies by others of an original by him, or are only imitations of his style. Certainly in his later years his dominance had a depressing effect on English art, as other artists long continued to imitate him, especially in matters of pose and costume. One can trace his influence in the American portraits by Smibert and in the few portraits painted in Virginia between 1735 and 1740 by the almost unknown artist Charles Bridges, of whom

[1] *Sir Godfrey Kneller and his Times, 1646–1723* (1948), chap. vii.
[2] Killanin, p. 94.

tradition reports that he had been an assistant of Kneller's, though he is not mentioned as such by Lord Killanin.

Michael Dahl, the Swede, was the best-known artist after Kneller in the London of the period, and Highmore was the best of the rising native-born painters, but there were a number of other men, now nearly forgotten, who contended for the crumbs of patronage which Kneller disdained. When they could they followed Kneller's example and painted only faces, employing drapery painters to aid them in the parts of the work which they either felt it beneath their dignity or were incompetent to carry out. Hogarth and Highmore did not need such assistance,[3] and if Smibert ever employed drapery painters he certainly did without them when painting in Scotland and in Boston until after the arrival of his nephew John Moffatt, who probably served as his assistant during the last decade of his active career.

Smibert, on his return to England, journeyed again to Edinburgh, primarily, no doubt, to see his kinsfolk and friends. Aikman was still the portrait painter in possession of that field, such as it was, but Sir Francis Grant of Monymusk, Lord Cullen, whose wife Smibert had painted on his previous visit, again employed him, this time to paint a large family group, including twelve figures, and a portrait of himself of which an engraving was made many years later as an act of filial devotion. In addition Smibert must at this time have painted his second portrait of Allan Ramsay, already discussed, and, quite possibly, a few other pictures the existence of which is not recorded.

Then he went back to London and settled down as a professional portrait painter. Vertue, in his earliest note on Smibert, November 1722, wrote:

> John Smibert a Scotsman born
> Studyed in the Academy several years,
> born went to Italy [1717], return'd after three years
> 1688 stay there.   a good ingenious man paints and
> draws well [Vertue crossed out the word "well"
> and substituted "handsomely"]

and again,

> at his return already several good heads especially men. the Lord Carpenter in Arm° ½ lenght very well (but since that I do not see any so well) An old Lady sitting in a chair admirably well done. several other very good portraits one large peice being a Club of Virtuosi or a group of Rosa Coronians [4]

[3] Whitley, *Artists and Their Friends in England*, I, 52–55.
[4] III, 14. The words in parentheses crossed out by Vertue.

The Lord Carpenter referred to in this note was a noted British general of the period, whom Smibert painted in a fancy suit of armor, such as was still worn by officers on ceremonial occasions. Smibert must have seen many such portraits in Italy. Rubens' great portrait of Thomas Howard, Earl of Arundel, in a glorious suit of armor, now in the Gardner Museum in Boston, was then in England, and Walker had painted Oliver Cromwell similarly accoutered. Early in the eighteenth century successful warriors still enjoyed being thus depicted. Smibert painted such a picture of Jean Paul Mascarene in Boston in 1730. The portrait of Lord Carpenter is presumably still in existence, but has not been located. Unfortunately the other portraits are so indefinitely noted by Vertue that they cannot be identified.

His reference to Smibert's "large peice being a Club of Virtuosi or a group of Rosa Coronians" gives us a glimpse into the artist's London associations. The word "virtuosi" had come into English use in the preceding century to designate lovers or practitioners of painting and music, and in Vertue's day there were at least two clubs of virtuosi in London.[5] One was the "Society of Virtuosi of St. Luke" (St. Luke being the patron saint of painters), the members of which liked to trace its origin to Van Dyck because he had occasionally invited a group of artists and connoisseurs to meet at his house. The meetings had lapsed with his death, had been revived by Sir Peter Lely and had lapsed again, but in 1689 the group formed an organization which for more than half a century thereafter met regularly to dine in a tavern. Vertue belonged to it, and was very proud of it, calling it "the tip-top club of all." Smibert was not a member. The other club was the "Rosa Coronians"; probably playfully so called because the members met at the Rose and Crown Tavern. Vertue was a member of this club also, having been admitted as early as 1704. Smibert must have joined it before 1723, since he included himself in this group picture which he "designed and begun" in that year. Vertue, in a later entry of 1724, refers again to the picture as follows:

In the large painting peice of the Virtuosi of London designed and begun by Mr. Smibert are the following persons: its divided into three groupes. in the Middle. Harvey. painter bald head .... Wotton .... Gibson ..... on the left Keller setting. at the Harpsichord ..... Kinkead setting looking up backwards .... Cope standing with a fiddle in his hand leaning .... Baraudi behind him. on the right side .... Vertue holding a print .... Bird looking in .... Smybert behind & Poit .... pointing up .... Lens on the Easel a profil,[6]

[5] For information about these clubs see Whitley, I, 7, 68, 74–75.
[6] Vertue, III, 24.

Vertue illustrated his note with a thumbnail outline showing the position of the figures.

Unfortunately the picture is lost, but Vertue's description of it is of especial interest because it records the names of Smibert's cronies in London. John Harvey was an "architect painter," and was steward of the Society of Virtuosi of St. Luke in 1726. "Wotton" was John Wootton, the leading painter of horses and sporting pictures. Thomas Gibson had been active in directing the Academy of 1711, and Smibert inquired after him in his letter to Arthur Pond of April 6, 1749. Godfrey Keller [7] was a musician. Kinkead is reported in Vertue III, 43, to have brought from Paris "a curious . . . set of prints," but is otherwise unidentified. Baraudi has not been identified. Anthony Cope was an art connoisseur and musician. Vertue was, of course, the engraver and antiquarian. Francis Bird was a sculptor. "Poit" is uncertain; [8] one would like to interpret it as a misreading for "Pond," namely, Arthur Pond, the etcher, dealer, and connoisseur, from whom Smibert in later years ordered his supplies to be sent out to Boston. Bernard Lens painted in water colors and, like Gibson and Wootton, had belonged to the group which organized the Academy of 1711.

Vertue refers to this group portrait elsewhere in his notebooks. In 1723 he listed "Names of Living painters of Note in London and their pictures by whom painted," [9] and included, among others, "Mr Gibson portrait by himself in a Wigg—by Smybert in the large picture," and

---

[7] Killanin, p. 23, writing of portraits representing Kneller, says: "Smibert, the portrait painter who later took the art of English portraiture to America by way of the West Indies [sic] . . . included him in a *Group of Virtuosi* in 1724, but this was painted after Kneller's death." Since the only known contemporary reference to Smibert's group picture is that found in Vertue's notes quoted above, Lord Killanin's statement is presumably based on the supposition that Vertue carelessly wrote "Keller" when he intended to write "Kneller." Aside from the probability that the careful Vertue would have corrected such an arror, it would have been quite inappropriate to place the famous Kneller at one side sitting at a harpsichord. There is no reason to suppose that he was ever a member of the Rosa-Coronians. The high and mighty Sir Godfrey was a complete snob, who consistently sought company advantageous to him, and is little likely in his old age and at the height of his prestige to have condescended to join a club of younger men, none of whom had wealth or high social position or, at that time, had achieved any great reputation.

[8] The name is so read by the editors of the *Vertue Note Books*, but Vertue's minute and crabbed handwriting makes it so difficult to decipher the last two letters that Worthington C. Ford, in his article on "The Smibert-Moffatt Letters" in M.H.S. *Proc.*, XLIX, 28-30, in which the page is reproduced, read the name as "Post." There is no known individual named either Poit or Post who is likely to have been a member of the group. I admit the difficulty of reading Vertue's scribble as "Pond," but the suggestion that he so intended it at least has in its favor the fact that a well-known person of that name was a friend of Smibert's and must certainly have been acquainted with the other Rosa-Coronians.

[9] Vertue, III, 12.

in the large painting piece of the Virtuosi. of London

1724 designed & begun by Mr Soubert.

are the following persons.

As divided into three groupes

in the Middle . Harvey. painter bald head
. Wotton. — Gibson .

on the left Keller setting. as the
Harpsicord. — Kinkead setting. looking
up backward. — Cope standing with
a fiddle in his hand leaning. ... Bertolucci
behind him. on the right side
—... Vertue holding - print. ... Bird
. looking on .... Smybert behind &
.... Port. pointing up. ... Lens
on the Easel a profil.

a whole len. cloth

Page in Vertue's Notebook, Showing Sketch of the "Virtuosi"

as late as 1733 he records that a portrait of himself was painted by Gibson in 1723 and that he was also "painted amongst the Virtuosi by Mr Smybert." [10]

In his list of "Names of Living Painters of Note" he also included

Mr Wotton . . . . 1723 Aeta 45 Smybert
Mr Harvey . . . . J. Smybert 1723 aeta 42

without indicating whether he is referring to their inclusion "in the large picture" or to separate portraits, though the former is more probable. Wootton was included in a similar group of twelve virtuosi, perhaps another club, painted by Gawen Hamilton in 1735,[11] and Whitley points out that yet another such group, painted about 1739, now hangs in the National Gallery.[12]

Vertue adds to his list the name of

Mr Enoch Seeman . . . . Mr Smybert.

Seeman, or Zeeman, was a painter, but is not included in the Rosa-Coronian group. Nothing further is known of this portrait.

One further entry by Vertue throws light on Smibert's activities about 1723–1724. He abruptly jotted down: "of many pictures of Mr Smybert's doing a head done of C. Dubosc Engraver. on a Kit-Cat. well disposed. strongly painted tho clear. the action mightily well disposed & like him." [13] One can but lament that he did not take the trouble to record the subjects of the other "many pictures of Mr Smybert's doing."

In 1732 Vertue wrote down a list of the artists then working in London (except "Mr Smibert abroad in Boston, New England"), with his rating of them.[14] The three foremost, whom he terms "the old masters," are (Charles) Jervas (Principal Painter to the King), (Jonathan) Richardson (Senior), and (Michael) Dahl (the Swedish

[10] Vertue, III, 69. It should be noted that Vertue, writing in 1724, spoke of this picture of the Virtuosi as "designed and begun." Lionel Cust, in his account of Smibert in the Dictionary of National Biography, LII, 405, says that the picture was never completed but gives no authority for that statement. Smibert certainly had ample time to finish it before he left London four years later, and the fact that in 1733 Vertue refers to his inclusion in the group would seem to indicate the completion of the picture. Whether such was the case cannot be proved because the picture is now either lost or destroyed.
[11] Vertue, III, 71.
[12] Whitley, I, 68.
[13] Vertue, III, 28. Claude Du Bosc (1682–1745), French engraver in London. A kit-cat was a portrait measuring 36 by 28 inches, so-called because a set of portraits of members of the Kit-Cat Club was painted in that size to be hung in the room in which the club dined, the ceiling of which was too low to permit the hanging of the more usual half-length portraits.
[14] Vertue, III, 54.

portrait painter). Then follows a list of those of the "next Class": "Those (generally) that studied in the Academy here under Sir Godfrey Kneller, Sheron [Cheron], Laguerre and Thornhill." The list of these "next Class" artists runs as follows:

Mr. Gibson [Thomas]
Mr. Vanderbank [John]
Mr. Hyssing [Hans Huyssing, a Swedish pupil of Dahl's]
Mr. Highmore [Joseph]
Mr. Dandridge [Bartholomew]
Mr. Smibert, abroad, in Boston, New England
Mr. Hogarth, small figures,
Two Zeemans [Enoch and Isaac, painters]
Mr. Joseph Goupy, water-colour
Mr. Bernard Lens, water-colour
Mr. Fred Zincke, enameller [Frederick, a German miniaturist and enameler, patronized by George II]

Aside from Hogarth, who at that period had not begun to paint full-size portraits, and Highmore, whose work today receives renewed recognition, most of these persons have passed into obscurity. Smibert's inclusion among them as an artist of the second class is a not unfair estimate of his abilities. These notes, however, prove that he had attained a reasonable amount of recognition in London, and he must have found enough work to support himself, which means that he can hardly have painted fewer than fifteen to thirty portraits a year between 1720 and 1728, unless he was employed in other ways as well. Many of these pictures are, no doubt, still extant, unidentified as his work either because unsigned or because heedlessly attributed to other painters. I have seen only two of his portraits of this period, representing an old lady, Elizabeth Ferne, and a middle-aged man, Henry Ferne of London. Both are clearly signed by Smibert and dated 1724 and 1727 respectively, yet both, even though dated after Kneller's death, were, until recently, attributed to the latter painter.

Aside from his early portrait of Sir Francis Grant, Lord Cullen, which was engraved in 1744, and his two portraits of Allan Ramsay, each of which was reproduced as the frontispiece in certain of the many editions of that author's works, as already noted, no engravings appear to be extant reproducing any of Smibert's portraits painted in Great Britain. This would indicate that most of his sitters were relatively inconspicuous and unimportant people. By extreme contrast, it is estimated that at least four hundred of Kneller's portraits were reproduced by at least forty engravers.[15] Of course no other artist

15 Killanin, p. 57.

of this period ever attained more than a small percentage of that number of engraved reproductions of his work; probably no other British artist has ever equaled that figure, save, possibly, Sir Joshua Reynolds. The mezzotint was a form of engraving which had been invented in the middle of the seventeenth century and had quickly become popular on the Continent and in England, since, down to the development of photography, it was much the best way of reproducing inexpensively and in multiple form the likenesses of well-known individuals. At this period the makers of mezzotints in London did a thriving business, which the painters were glad to encourage because the appearance of their names at the foot of the engravings was obviously useful as advertising. Six of Smibert's portraits painted in Boston, four of them of ministers, were engraved in this country by Peter Pelham, and a copy of another painted here was engraved by T. Kelley.

There are two other straws which indicate the measure of success which Smibert attained in London within a few years of his return from Italy. The first indicates his reputation as a painter; the second that he was not cramped for money. The first is found in what I think must certainly be a reference to him in an effusively eulogistic unsigned poem which appeared in 1725 entitled "A Session of Painters Occasioned by the Death of Sir Godfrey Kneller." [16] In the poem, which consists of an introduction and twenty stanzas, the god Apelles descends from heaven to choose a successor to the now "vacant crown" which had been worn by Kneller. A crowd of claimants appears, most of them to be dismissed in short order, and at the end Apelles declares none of them to be worthy of Kneller's crown. The rival claimants are described in terms which, no doubt, enabled their contemporaries to identify them, but which are lost on us, or their names are indicated by a few letters which, in some cases, make identification possible. In stanza eleven the author speaks more kindly of the candidates before him than in most cases:

> The God's piercing eye soon Smy—t saw
>   With Dy—r by his side.
> Thy merit Smy—t hust [hushed? just?] applause will draw,
>   Apelles smiling cried
> In Dy—r both the sister arts agree
> To please in painting, and in poetry.

There can hardly have been any artist other than John Smibert who could have been referred to as "Smy—t." Presumably "Dy—r" was John Dyer (c.1700–1758), a minor poet and painter.

[16] Printed in full in Killanin, pp. 91–94.

The second bit of evidence that he enjoyed at least a modest measure of prosperity at this period is his appearance as *Mr.* John Smibert in the aristocratic list of subscribers to Alexander Gordon's handsome and costly *Itinerarium Septentrionale*, an account of Roman antiquities in Scotland and in northern England, published in London in 1726, illustrated with engravings. Gordon was a Scottish antiquary and painter, four years younger than Smibert, who for a time enjoyed the patronage of Sir John Clerk of Penicuick.[17] It is reasonable to assume that Smibert was acquainted with him, either in Edinburgh or in London, but the appearance of his name as a subscriber to Gordon's book indicates not only friendship for the author but that he had money to spare for minor luxuries.

These various bits of evidence, and the fact that he resided in Covent Garden, "the rendezvous of the most celebrated artists," afford ample proof that Smibert, in the eight years of this period of his residence in London, found sufficient employment to support himself at least reasonably well, and attained a recognized standing as an artist of good abilities, though not of the first rank, which was reserved for the more immediate associates and successors of Kneller.

While Smibert was thus engaged in London George Berkeley, now Dr. Berkeley, Dean of Derry, reappeared on his horizon. Berkeley, like Smibert, had returned to England in 1720, and had again entered the best London society. He found England in the depths of the financial depression which followed the collapse of that gigantic speculation, the South Sea Bubble. Many fortunes had been lost; political corruption was rife; and there was a marked decline in morality and religion. "The growth of atheism and profaneness and immorality" was the common complaint of the clergy. Berkeley's highly idealistic nature was profoundly disturbed. He wrote his *Essay Towards Preventing the Ruin of Great Britain*, which he published in 1721, with some good advice to the nation: "Let us be industrious, frugal, and religious if we are to be saved at all." In August 1721, the Duke of Grafton was appointed Lord Lieutenant of Ireland, and Berkeley went as one of his chaplains, a position little to his taste which he did not hold long. Trinity College, of which he was now Senior Fellow, in November granted him the degrees of Bachelor and Doctor of Divinity, and made him a lecturer. In 1722 he was appointed Dean of Dromore, a pure sinecure, but the appointment

---

[17] Alexander Gordon (1692–1754?) was after 1726 engaged in various literary activities, at which he failed to make a living. In August 1741, he emigrated to Charleston, South Carolina, as secretary to Governor James Glen. There he acquired land and prospered. In his will, probated July 23, 1755, he bequeathed his portrait, painted by himself, to his son Alexander, of Charleston (see *DNB*).

was contested and he was never inducted into office nor enjoyed its emoluments. In its place he was appointed, in May 1724, Dean of Derry, one of the best places of preferment in the Irish Church. The income was £1250 a year, out of which he had to pay four curates and meet certain other charges, leaving him a net income of £900.

In the meantime a fantastic turn of fortune had brought him a handsome bequest. The story of Dean Swift's ambiguous relations with the two young women who sought his hand, and whom he called Stella and Vanessa, is well known. Vanessa was a Miss Esther Vanhomrigh, who had followed him to Ireland and had made a will leaving all her property to him. But in 1723, when Swift refused to tell her whether or not he had secretly married her rival, Stella, she tore up the will in her anger and grief, and made another dividing her property equally between Berkeley and another man. Not long after, she died, and Berkeley was amazed to find himself the heir to a property of some £4000. He protested that he had never even met Miss Vanhomrigh,[18] but it appeared that she had once, several years before, dined in a company of which he was a member. The bequest brought him some troublesome lawsuits, but Swift bore him no grudge, and when the estate was settled Berkeley found himself in possession of what was for the times a comfortable independent income.

He had already formulated his plan of emigrating to Bermuda and establishing there a college for the education and conversion of the American Indians for, in a letter to Lord Percival, dated March 4, 1722/23, he wrote, "It is now about ten months since I have determined with myself to spend the residue of my days in the Island of Bermuda, where I trust in Providence I may be the means of doing some good to mankind."[19] In his letter he went on to outline his scheme for a college, and enlarged on the advantages of Bermuda as a site.

His inheritance of a modest private fortune, followed by his appointment as Dean of Derry, gave him sufficient financial independence to push the project, which seemed fanciful enough to his contemporaries, for it was evident that if he really should go to Bermuda to settle he would have to relinquish the lucrative deanship. In September 1724, he left Ireland to gain English support for his plan. His staunch friend, Dean Swift, wrote a letter to Lord Carteret, newly appointed Lord Lieutenant of Ireland in succession to the Duke of

[18] Writing to Percival, immediately after her death, Berkeley did not even get her name correctly, calling her "Hester van Omry."
[19] Rand, *Berkeley and Percival*, p. 203.

Grafton, which discloses a mingling of admiration for Berkeley with amazement at his plan.

[Dublin] September 3, 1724

There is a gentleman of this kingdom just gone for England. It is Dr. George Berkeley, Dean of Derry, the best preferment among us, being worth £1100 a year . . . I sent him Secretary and Chaplain to Sicily with my Lord Peterborough; and, upon his lordship's return, Dr. Berkeley spent above seven years in travelling over most parts of Europe, but chiefly through every corner of Italy, Sicily, and other islands. When he came back to England, he found so many friends that he was effectually recommended to the Duke of Grafton, by whom he was lately made Dean of Derry . . . He is an absolute philosopher with regard to money, titles and power; and for three years past has been struck with the notion of founding a University at Bermudas, by a charter from the Crown. He has seduced several of the hopefullest young clergymen and others here, many of them well provided for, and all in the fairest way of preferment; but in England his conquests are greater and I doubt will spread very far this winter. He showed me a little tract which he designs to publish; and there your Excellency will see his whole scheme . . . of a College founded for Indian scholars and missionaries; where he most exorbitantly proposes a whole hundred pounds a year for himself, fifty pounds for a Fellow, and ten for a Student. His heart will break if his Deanery be not taken from him, and left to your Excellency's disposal. I discouraged him by the coldness of courts and ministers, who will interpret all this as impossible and a vision; but nothing will do. And therefore I humbly extreat your Excellency either to use such persuasions as will keep one of the first men in the kingdom for learning and virtue quiet at home, or else assist him by your credit to compass his romantic design; which, however, is very noble and generous, and directly proper for a great person of your excellent education to encourage.[20]

Berkeley printed in February 1724/25 his pamphlet advocating the project, entitled *A proposal for the better supplying of churches in our foreign plantations, and for converting the Savage Americans to Christianity, by a college to be erected in the Summer Islands, otherwise called the isles of Bermuda*. Armed with this pamphlet and his own persuasive personality, he sought to obtain from the government a charter for the college and the grant of a large sum of money, a task which would have seemed impossible to one of a less idealistic nature. It was in the course of this campaign that he wrote the poem containing the famous line, "Westward the course of empire takes its

[20] Alexander Campbell Fraser, *Life and Letters of George Berkeley, D.D.* (vol. IV of *The Works*, 1871), pp. 102–103.

way." The earliest mention of the poem occurs in a letter which he wrote to Percival from London, February 10, 1725/26.[21]

> You have annexed a poem wrote by a friend of mine with a view to the scheme. Your Lordship is desired to shew it to none but of your own family, and to suffer no copy to be taken of it.

America or the Muse's Refuge
A Prophecy.

> The muse, offended at this age, these climes
>   Where nought she found fit to rehearse,
> Waits now in distant lands for better times,
>   Producing subjects worthy verse;
> In happy climes where from the genial sun
>   And virgin earth fair scenes ensue,
> Such scenes as shew that fancy is outdone,
>   And make poetic fiction new;
> In happy climes, the seat of innocence,
>   Where nature guides and virtue rules,
> Where men shall not impose for truth and sense
>   The pedantry of Courts and Schools.
> There shall be sung another golden age
>   The rise of Empire and of arts,
> The good and great inspiring epic rage,
>   The wisest heads and noblest hearts.
> Not such as Europe breeds in her decay,
>   Such as she bred when fresh and young,
> When heavenly flame did animate her clay,
>   By future poets shall be sung
> Westward the course of Empire takes its way,
>   The first four acts already past
> A fifth shall close the drama with the day;
>   The world's great effort is the last.[22]

There is no indication at what stage in the development of his project Berkeley renewed his acquaintance with Smibert, begun in Italy six years earlier. The first mention of the painter in his correspondence is found in a letter written to his friend Thomas Prior, dated August 24, 1726, in which he says, "I have quitted my old lodging, and desire you to direct your letters to be left for me with

---

[21] Rand, *Berkeley and Percival*, p. 230.
[22] Note that Berkeley does not claim authorship of these verses "wrote by a friend of mine," but they were included as his in his "Miscellany," published in 1752, the year before his death, under the title, "Verses on the Prospect of planting Arts and Learning in America."

Mr. Smibert, painter, next door to the King's Arms tavern, in the little piazza, Covent Garden," [23] which seems to indicate that Berkeley made Smibert's lodgings his London headquarters. Three months later he wrote again, referring apparently to some paintings which had come to him with Miss Vanhomrigh's property:

December 1, 1726.
I shall take care the pictures be sold in an auction. Mr. Smibert, whom I know to be a very honest, skilful person in his profession, will see them put into an auction at the proper time, which he tells me is not till the town fills with company, about the meeting of parliament. [24]

And once more he wrote to Prior:

London, Feb. 27, 1726/7
The pictures were all sold for forty-five pounds, at an auction which was held last week in Covent Garden, at the house of one Mr. Russell, a painter. They were sold publicly and fairly among several other pictures. The truth of it is, that of late years the taste lies so much towards Italian pictures, many of which are imported daily, that Dutch pictures go off but heavily. Mr. Smibert did not think they would have brought so much.

In view of this evidence of Berkeley's renewed acquaintance with Smibert we may take it for granted that the Bermuda project was talked over between them, and that sooner or later Berkeley proposed that Smibert should accompany him as professor of art and architecture in the proposed college. Berkeley's plans were slow in maturing, because it took several years for him to persuade an unwilling government to give him the grant of £20,000 for which he asked. The opposition was based upon the argument that an island several hundred miles from the mainland of North America was not a suitable place for a college, and upon the reluctance of the ministry to vote good money for what they deemed a visionary project. While he was working towards his goal he raised several thousand pounds by private subscription. At length his persuasiveness triumphed, and Parliament, with only a few dissenting voices, voted the grant, to be paid out of the proceeds of crown lands, in St. Christopher's Island in the West Indies, which were to be sold to settlers there. Berkeley naïvely assumed that the success of his plan was assured and pro-

[23] Fraser, p. 132. The Piazza, Covent Garden, was, according to Vertue "the rendezvous of the most celebrated artists," and again he wrote in his *Note Books* (III, 30; 1726), "Covent Garden Piazza is inhabited by Painters (a credit to live there)" going on to name several, among them "Sr J. Thornhill . . . Smybert . . . Zincke." Kneller lived there before removing to Great Queen Street.
[24] Fraser, p. 139.

ceeded to assemble his companions and arrange for the charter of a ship to transport his party and their supplies. These negotiations must have occupied many months, and we may assume that Smibert must have had Berkeley's invitation to join him under consideration for a year or more before the party actually sailed in September 1728.

Until recently it has been assumed that Smibert remained at work in London until his departure for America, for there is no record of his having paid a farewell visit to Edinburgh. However, in 1927 two portraits came to light which, if they are his work, indicate that he went to Italy late in 1727 or early in 1728. These two portraits are further described in the Descriptive Catalogue as "John Smibert(?) so-called Self-Portrait No. 1" and "No. 2." Both were said to have come from "an old court in Kent" when acquired by Christie, Manson and Woods, who sold them in London, June 27, 1927. No. 1 was listed in the sales catalogue as "No. 126. Portrait of a gentleman in a brown dress, pointing to a pyramid," with neither identification of the subject nor attribution to an artist. It was bought for ten guineas by Leger & Son, who soon after shipped it to this country. That it might be a self-portrait by Smibert was my guess, when I saw it in New York.

No. 2 was purchased by a dealer named Feldman, and later also came into the hands of Leger who shipped it to New York where I saw it at the same time I saw No. 1. It had then been relined, and on the back, in black letters, and resembling other signatures by Smibert, was painted

Jo. Smibert pinxit
Romae, 1728.

Mr. Sidney Leger, who showed me the pictures, declared that this inscription was carefully copied from one which he himself had seen on the back of the original canvas. The picture is a curious one, evidently intended to be jocose. No painter would have portrayed a patron in such guise, but Smibert in Italy might have thus represented himself for the entertainment of his Rosa-Coronian friends. The face sufficiently resembles that of Smibert shown in the "Bermuda [or Berkeley] Group" for Alan Burroughs to say of it: "The style agrees fairly well with the . . . *Berkeley Group*, and the smiling features agree sufficiently with the serious face at the left of the group, which has been considered a portrait of Smibert himself." [25] I may add that it was also the resemblance of the features of the man shown in No. 1 to those of Smibert in the "Bermuda Group," allowing for

[25] *Art in America*, XXX, 112-113.

the difference made by the wig which he wears and certain other details, which led me to surmise that No. 1 might also be a self-portrait of the artist, painted during the same visit to Rome.

Both attributions have been regarded by competent critics as very doubtful, but the existence of the two portraits should be recorded, since it is at least possible that they may be Smibert's work. It is true that there is no record that he made a second trip to Italy, but there is no reason why we should expect one unless Vertue had happened to make a note of it. At least there was ample time for him to have spent several months in Rome, early in 1728, getting back to London by summer, and he may well have sought to avail himself of an opportunity which would never come again. At present writing the acceptance of either or both pictures as self-portraits of Smibert remains an open question, but they offer at least some ground for thinking that Smibert may have made a second journey to Italy, and that while in Rome he painted them, one in a serious, the other in a jocose mood, for friends at home.

It must have been after his return to London—assuming that he had left it—that he painted his portrait of Berkeley, dated 1728, now in the National Portrait Gallery. If the early portrait of Berkeley, painted in Rome, is not by Smibert, then this portrait of 1728 is the first of the series which Smibert painted of Berkeley in the next year or two. It is not a very successful picture. The face is not so pleasing as in his later portraits and the figure is uncomfortably seated in too small an armchair. The right arm and hand are badly drawn, with the forefinger awkwardly pointing across Berkeley's body to a distant view, a gesture which Smibert frequently used. It is the last picture of which we have any record that Smibert painted before sailing for America.

CHAPTER III

The Voyage to America

BERKELEY ASSEMBLED HIS PARTY IN LONDON PREPARATORY TO SAILING in September 1728. A month earlier, on August 1, having long evaded the matrimonial snares artfully laid for him by interested relatives, he had taken to himself a wife of his own selection. She was Anne, daughter of John Forster, Recorder of Dublin, Chief Justice of Common Pleas, and Speaker of the Irish House of Commons. She is reported to have been an attractive and accomplished woman, of a deeply religious nature, a reader of mystical writers, especially of Fénelon and of Madame Guyon. She also brought her husband a dowry of £2000. She was accompanied on the American adventure by a friend, Miss Handcock, probably a daughter of Sir William Handcock, who had been Recorder of Dublin.

The young clergymen of whom Swift wrote to Lord Carteret in his letter of 1724 as intending to go with Berkeley to Bermuda had apparently faded out of the picture, having, no doubt, settled down to other work in the four years which had elapsed. Berkeley's associates, besides Smibert, consisted of Richard Dalton of Lincolnshire and John James of Bury St. Edmunds, afterwards Sir John James, Bart. Presumably these two were to occupy professorial chairs in the proposed "College of St. Paul" in Bermuda. Smibert's nephew, Dr. Thomas Moffatt[1] of Edinburgh, a young man recently returned from studying medicine at Leiden, was to have accompanied them, but fell ill, and sailed later, joining the party at Newport in 1729.

Berkeley had chartered for his party a ship under command of a Captain Cobb, who proved to be a poor navigator. Berkeley seems to have slipped quietly away for America, without formal farewells

[1] In the Edinburgh Parish Record of Births, immediately below the record of the birth (or baptism) of Alison, eldest child of John and Alison (Bell) Smibert, and on the same date, January 19, 1679, is the entry: "Thomas Moffatt, flesher, Marjorie Hardy, a s. n. Thomas" These infants, baptized (?) on the same day, were married twenty-three years later, the entry in the Marriage Records reading, "Moffatt, Thomas, burgess, married Alison Smibert, daughter of deceased John Smibert, litster, burgess, 5 Feb. 1702." Their eldest son, Thomas, was probably born late in the same year. A younger son, John Moffatt, joined his uncle John Smibert in Boston about 1740, and was his associate and successor in his shop there.

and without many people knowing that he was actually leaving. On September 3, he wrote to Lord Percival:

Greenwich, 3rd Sept. 1728.

. . . Tomorrow we sail down the river. Mr. James and Mr. Dalton go with me. So doth my wife, a daughter of the late Chief Justice Forster, whom I married since I saw your Lordship. I chose her for the qualities of her mind and her unaffected inclination to books. She goes with great cheerfulness to live a plain farmer's life, and wear stuff of her own spinning wheel, and for her encouragement have assured her that from henceforth there shall never be one yard of silk bought for the use of myself, herself, or any of our family.

. . . If your Lordship should at any time favor me with a line, please direct to Dean Berkeley at Rhode Island, near Boston, and enclose the letter in a cover to Thomas Corbett, Esq., at the Admiralty Office in London, who will further it by the first opportunity.[2]

The ship did not get away on the fourth, however, for on the fifth she was still at Gravesend, and Berkeley wrote again to his friend Thomas Prior:

Gravesend, Sept. 5, 1728.

Tomorrow, with God's blessing, I set sail for Rhode Island, with my wife and a friend of hers, my lady Hancock's daughter, who bears us company. I am married since I saw you to Miss Forster, daughter of the late Chief Justice, whose humour and turn of mind pleases me beyond anything that I know in her whole sex. Mr. James, Mr. Dalton, and Mr. Smibert go with us on this voyage. We are now all together at Gravesend, and are engaged in one view.[3]

The *Historical Register* for 1728 also noted his departure, "in a ship of about 250 tons which he hired. He took several tradesmen and artists with him. Two gentlemen of fortune are gone, with their effects, to settle in Bermuda."[4] Smibert was the "several tradesmen and artists" of this loose statement, and the two "gentlemen of fortune" were, of course, James and Dalton.

Smibert's willingness to take part in this romantic adventure had occasioned surprise and remonstrances among his friends, and Vertue proceeded to comment upon it at some length in terms which read as though he had himself talked it over with Smibert, and which also reveal his estimate of Smibert's character:

In a few days after [crossed out and "Just after this" substituted] Mr Smibert left England. to go to the West Indies, New York, or Bermudas

2 Rand, *Berkeley and Percival*, p. 236.
3 Fraser, p. 151.
4 *Historical Register*, XIII, 289.

taking all his pictures Effects entending there to Settle. according to a Scheme propos'd by Dean Barclay. to lay the foundation of a College for all sorts of Literature on Bermudas. & professors of several sciences. to Instruct the European and Indian children in the Christian faith, & other necessary educations. to which end the Dean had made great Solicitations at Court in the last reign. & had obtained grant of 20000 pound from some of the plantation revenues, to be employ'd in making a settlement there. of a College & several fellows, to which design the Dean had engag'd, or perswaded several gentlemen of fortune & Substance to join with him in this project. 3 or four of them. sett out with ye Dean & Mr Smibert. Mr Smybert had a very good business here. a great many friends generally all of them dissuaded him from leaving here a certainty. for an uncertainty. but he was warm'd with imaginations of the great success of such a design, & the pleasures of a finer Country & Air more healthfull he being often a little inclined to indispositions. or hip. or Vapours ^{5} . . . & also having a particular turn of mind towards honest, fair & righteous dealing—he could not well relish, the false selfish griping, overreaching ways too commonly practiz'd here. nor was he prone to speak much in his own praise. nor any violent ways but a decent modesty. which he thought such a retirement, as at Bermudas he might live quietly & for small expence. & make a great advantage. by ready money declaring he rather sought repose, than profitt. he was a good like man ^{6} born at Edenburgh and now about 45 or 6—furthermore it is said that the Dean & Smibert took with them two young Gentlewomen. of good fortune. both sisters. & married one to ye Dean and ye other to Smibert.^{7}

Horace Walpole gave a page to Smibert when, many years later, he compiled his *Anecdotes of Painting in England* from Vertue's notebooks, and made a quizzical comment on the project. But Horace Walpole was, presumably, acquainted with the not very straight-forward tactics said to have been employed by his father, Sir Robert Walpole, in balking the success of Berkeley's plan after the latter was safely out of the way in America.

The voyage was a long and tedious one. As indicated in his letter to Percival, Berkeley never intended going directly to Bermuda, but sailed for Newport,^{8} where he planned to acquire a farm from which supplies should be shipped to Bermuda, having, apparently, the idea that the island itself would not supply adequate provisions and that

^{5} "Hip" was a common abbreviation for hypochondria, supposed to be caused by injurious exhalations or "vapours" developed within the body and leading to a morbid depression of spirits. We still speak of a person as being "hipped."
^{6} We should say "a good sort," or "a likeable man."
^{7} Vertue III, 36. Smibert was, in fact, in his forty-first year. Vertue later carefully ran his pencil through the last five words of this entry.
^{8} Miss Handcock, one of several daughters of "my lady Handcock," is said to have

Newport was the most convenient point on the mainland from which they could be shipped to him. His course was also guided by the knowledge that, once settled in Bermuda, he would be obliged to resign as Dean of Derry within a year, a step which it would have been imprudent to take before the government's grant for the college was actually in hand. That is the explanation of his prolonged sojourn at Newport.

There has been a tradition that the large picture now at Yale University, representing Berkeley and his associates and called by them the "Bermuda Group," though more recently known as Dean Berkeley and his Entourage, was painted on the voyage. While it may have been planned, and some small sketches may have been made for it, it would have been quite impossible for so large a canvas to have been painted on board a small vessel. Furthermore the picture includes Thomas Moffatt, who did not come out until the following summer, and the child, Henry Berkeley, who was born in Newport. Smibert is also said to have given Mrs. Berkeley instruction in painting during the voyage, which may well have been the case, since she practiced the art, to her husband's satisfaction, in later years. That, however, is hardly sufficient ground for calling Mrs. Berkeley, as some writers have done, "one of the earliest women artists in America."

The incompetent captain seems not to have known how to find Newport, and made his landfall off the Virginia coast early in January after a four-month voyage. The ship must have come into Chesapeake Bay, and gone up either the James or the York Rivers, for Berkeley visited Williamsburg. Five months later Col. William Byrd wrote to Lord Percival:

> Virginia, 10th June, 1729.
> About two months ago [sic] Dean Berkeley put into this country, on his way to Rhode Island, where he is gone to purchase some lands that may supply his college at Bermudas with provisions. I had not the pleasure of seeing him by reason his stay was exceeding short. He only dined with the Governour [William Gooch] and went out of town in the evening. However, he visited our College [William and Mary], and was very well pleased with it. When the Dean's project was first communicated to me by your Lordship, I took the liberty to call it a very romantic one.[9]

been closely related to the Coddington family, then prominent and prosperous in Newport. It is possible that her presence on the ship may have influenced the choice of destination, or, knowing that Newport was the intended haven, she may have embarked not so much to provide Mrs. Berkeley with female companionship as with an eye to matrimonial possibilities in the new world where her cousins could give her a good introduction.

[9] Rand, *Berkeley and Percival*, p. 244.

Byrd went on, with a combination of trenchant wit and sound common sense, to point out to Percival the impracticability of Berkeley's plan of a college in Bermuda to convert the Indians of the mainland, though his views were somewhat biased by his desire to have the college established in one of the Southern colonies and by his dissatisfaction at having Berkeley's base of supplies located in Rhode Island instead of in Virginia.

From Virginia the captain, having presumably received accurate sailing directions, made a quick run to Rhode Island. Berkeley wrote to Percival, announcing his arrival at Newport:

> Newport in Rhode Island, 7th Feb. 1728/9
> We came last from Virginia, where I received many unexpected as well as undeserved honours from the Governour and principal inhabitants. The same civil, kind treatment attends us here. We were a long time blundering about the ocean before we reached Virginia, but our voyage from thence hither was as speedy and prosperous as could be wished.[10]

The actual date of arrival at Newport was January 23, as is shown by an item in the *Boston Gazette* of Monday, January 27, 1729, which noted:

> By letters from Newport, we have an account of the 24th instant, that Captain Cobb arrived there from London the day before, but last from Virginia, having Dean Berkeley on board, etc., who were 4 months and 16 days before they got there, and five months to Rhode Island from London.

A similar notice in the *New England Weekly Courier* of February 3, 1729, added a description of Berkeley

> Newport, January 24, 1729.
> Yesterday arrived here Dean Berkeley of Londonderry, in a pretty large ship. He is a gentleman of middle stature, of an agreeable, pleasant, and erect aspect. He was ushered into the town with a great number of gentlemen, to whom he behaved himself after a very complaisant manner. 'Tis said he proposes to tarry here about three months.

A much more detailed though not wholly accurate account of Berkeley's arrival is to be found in the chapter by Henry Bull on Trinity Church, Newport, which is included in Updike's *History of the Episcopal Church in Narragansett*. He writes:

> [Dean Berkeley arrived] in Newport by a circumstance purely accidental. He, with other gentlemen, his associates, were bound to the island of Bermuda, with the intention of establishing there a college for the

[10] Rand, *Berkeley and Percival*, p. 238.

education of the Indian youth of this country—a plan, however, which wholly failed. The captain of the ship in which he sailed could not find the island of Bermuda and having given up the search after it, steered northward until he discovered land unknown to him, and which he supposed to be inhabitated only by savages. On making a signal, however, two men came on board from Block Island, in the character of pilots, who on enquiry, informed him that the harbour and town of Newport were near and that in the town there was an Episcopal Church, the minister of which was Mr. James Honyman.[11] On which he proceeded for Newport, but an adverse wind caused him to run into the west passage, where the ship came to anchor. The Dean wrote a letter to Mr. Honyman, which the pilots took on shore at Conanicut island, calling on Mr. Gardiner and Mr. Martin, two members of Mr. Honyman's church, and informing them that a great dignitary of the Church of England, called Dean, was on board the ship, together with other gentlemen passengers. They handed them the letter from the Dean, which Gardiner and Martin brought to Newport, in a small boat, with all possible dispatch. On their arrival, they found Mr. Honyman was at church, it being a holyday on which divine service was held there. They then sent the letter by a servant, who delivered it to Mr. Honyman in his pulpit. He opened it, and read it to the congregation, from the contents of which it appeared the Dean might be expected to land in Newport at any moment. The church was dismissed with the blessing and Mr. Honyman, with the wardens, vestry, and congregation, male and female, repaired immediately to the ferry wharf, where they arrived a little before the Dean, his family, and friends.[12]

It will be observed that this account, written a century or more after the event, is in error in stating that Berkeley's arrival in Newport was accidental, and it omits any reference to the earlier landing in Virginia. But the description of his landing in Newport may be accepted as substantially correct. Smibert shared in this ceremonious reception of the Dean, but James and Dalton did not, having decided to come overland from Virginia. On April 11, 1729, Berkeley wrote to Dr. Benson, Prebendary of Durham, "James is not yet arrived from Virginia. Dalton hath been here some time, he and Smibert are now at Boston where they propose passing a few daies." [13] Evidently they had gone thither at that early date to spy out the land.

[11] Rev. James Honyman had come to Newport in 1704 as an Anglican missionary sent out by the Society for the Propagation of the Gospel in Foreign Parts. He long resided there, and owned a farm about three miles outside the town which included the height still called Honyman's Hill. At the time of Berkeley's visit he was rector of Trinity Church, which had been erected a few years earlier and which still stands practically unchanged.

[12] Wilkins Updike, *A History of the Episcopal Church in Narragansett* (2nd ed., 1907), II, 155–156.

[13] Quoted by permission from an autograph letter now owned by the Fellows of Berkeley College, Yale University.

Berkeley resided for a time at the house of Mr. Honyman. He promptly took steps, however, to acquire a farm. In the letter to Dr. Benson he goes on:

Your little friend [i.e., himself] hath been much embarrassed in dealing with a Quaker of this island for the hire of his farm. This affair is one of the greatest eclat and importance that for many years hath been transacted in this Rhodian Government the principal persons of the State having all interposed therein.[14] I have purchased a pleasant farm of about one hundred acres with two fine groves and a winding rivulet upon it. Till such times as I hear of my associates being arrived with his Majesty's bounty money at Bermuda I do not think I cou'd be so useful in any part of the world as in this place.

The farm in question was purchased from Joseph Whipple[15] on February 18 and consisted of ninety-six acres of land in the valley just beyond Honyman's Hill. Its price was £2500 "in current money of New England." In the deed the property is described as containing "one Dwelling House, Stable and Crib and a certain Tract of Land to the same adjoining and belonging containing about ninety-six acres." The "dwelling house" must have been promptly replaced by the house which Berkeley called Whitehall, for a year later on March 9, 1730/31, he wrote to his friend Thomas Prior: "I live here upon land I have purchased and in a farm-house I have built in this island. It is fit for cows and sheep and may be of good use for supplying our college in Bermuda."[16]

Whitehall is a roomy, comfortable, and convenient dwelling of the best New England farmhouse type. Save for an exceptionally fine doorway and a massive chimney off center it has no unusual features either of design or structure. It seems reasonable to assume that Smibert drew the plans, and that this residence and the original Faneuil Hall in Boston constitute his contribution to architecture in America. Fortunately the house stands unchanged since Berkeley's day, and no

[14] This probably refers to the difficulty caused by the ruling that only freemen of the Colony of Rhode Island and Providence Plantations could own land. Berkeley was admitted freeman on May 6, 1729, after a much shorter stay in the colony than was customarily required, but some adjustment must have been made by the authorities to enable him to purchase the Whipple farm on the preceding February 18.

[15] Land Evidence, Newport, vol. IX. The deed was recorded on February 26. The tradition that Berkeley bought his land from Capt. John Anthony, whose daughter afterwards married Gilbert Stuart, the snuff grinder, and became the mother of the painter of the same name, is unfounded.

[16] Benjamin Rand, *Berkeley's American Sojourn* (Cambridge, Mass., 1932), p. 21. Some recent writers have held that Whitehall had been erected and occupied for several years before Berkeley's purchase of the property. See Theodore Sizer, article on John Smibert, *DAB*. Others have accepted Barnaby's statement about "the indifferent wooden house" built by Berkeley. The letter quoted above seems decisive.

other spot, in Great Britain, Ireland, or America is more intimately associated with his memory.

In May 1729, Berkeley, accompanied by Smibert and Col. Updike of Newport, paid a visit to "the Narragansett Country" on the west shore of the bay. The expedition was in part, no doubt, to enable him to have his first sight of the "American savages" whom he had come out to convert; in part to visit Rev. James McSparran, the missionary in charge of St. Paul's Church of Narragansett. McSparran was a vigorous person, of Scotch-Irish descent, who had first come to Massachusetts as a Presbyterian and who, after a brief and somewhat unhappy experience, had returned to England, taken Anglican orders, and been sent in 1721 to Narragansett by the Society for the Propagation of the Gospel. The next year he was married by Mr. Honyman to "handsome Hannah," daughter of William Gardiner, and in 1726 he bought the house which had been built by her parents about 1690. It was thereafter known as "The Glebe," and still stands, though now long deserted and in ruinous condition. It was a simple but comfortable residence shut off from the road by great lilac hedges, between which passes a pathway of stone flags, while behind are the remnants of an orchard. The location, however, was not a good one, being cold in winter and cut off in summer by the heights of McSparran's Hill from the prevailing southwesterly breezes, so that McSparran wrote that he was alternately "frying or freezing."

To reach it from Newport was not much of an expedition. Granted a fair wind, a sailboat could cross the bay to the South Ferry on the west shore in less than an hour. Thence it was only a couple of miles over the ridge and down into the valley of the Pettaquamscutt River, a tidal estuary which broadened out into a little lake of brackish water in front of "The Glebe." [17] The date of this visit can be accurately determined because Fraser prints outlines of twelve sermons which Berkeley preached in the course of his American sojourn, with Berkeley's annotations as to the date and place of delivery of several of them. The first of them was preached in Trinity Church, Newport, on January 26, the first Sunday after his arrival, and also "In the Narragansett Country, May 11, 1729." [18]

The little church in which Berkeley preached for McSparran was

[17] Only a mile or so above The Glebe there falls into the lake the small stream upon which about 1750 Dr. Thomas Moffatt built his snuff mill, designed and managed for him by Gilbert Stuart the snuff grinder, whom Moffatt had imported from Scotland for the purpose. In the modest house above the mill Stuart's son and namesake, the great portrait painter, was born in 1755. A few months later the child was baptized by Dr. McSparran.

[18] Fraser, pp. 629-631.

then located about two and a half miles from "The Glebe," within a walled burial ground now known by the curious name of "The Platform." It was in the open country, which was taken up with the fairly large plantations of country gentry who lived more like the Virginia planters than did other New Englanders. They were proud of their horses—the then famous "Narragansett pacers"—and were slave owners, McSparran himself owning one or two.[19] St. Paul's Church was built in 1707, and is a rectangular, white-clapboarded edifice, without tower or organ, with the entrance on the middle of one long side, while the pulpit stood opposite. It is of the plain, meetinghouse type, but with a simple dignity, and its box pews and gallery on three sides would hold a good many people. In 1800 it was moved several miles from its isolated position to the town of Wickford, where it still stands in good condition and is occasionally used. One can imagine that on that Sunday in May, when the pulpit was occupied by the highest dignitary of the Anglican Church who had ever visited this coast, it was filled to the doors with the Narragansett gentry whose families occupied the pews, while perhaps some Negro slaves and a few stolid Indians were in the rear gallery.

It must have been in the course of this visit to "The Glebe" that Smibert painted his portraits of Mr. and Mrs. McSparran. Smibert, having returned from his brief visit to Boston, accompanied Berkeley to see the encampments of Narragansett Indians who lived not far beyond the church, and to this expedition we owe Smibert's comment on the resemblance of the Indians to the two or three Siberian Tartars whose portraits he had painted in Florence for the Grand Duke. The anecdote is recorded by Ezra Stiles, who in a sermon preached in 1785, says:

The portrait painter, Mr. Smibert, who accompanied Dr. Berkeley, then Dean of Derry, and afterward Bishop of Cloyne, from Italy [sic] to America in 1728, was employed by the Grand Duke of Tuscany, while at Florence, to paint two or three Siberian Tartars, presented to the Duke by the Czar of Russia. This Mr. Smibert, upon landing at Narragansett Bay with Dr. Berkeley, instantly recognized the Indians here

---

[19] Berkeley bought three Negro slaves soon after his arrival, and on June 11, 1731, had them baptized in Trinity Church, Newport, as Philip Berkeley, Anthony Berkeley, and Agnes Berkeley, although there was a prejudice against the baptism of slaves, presumably based on the feeling that it was inconsistent to hold fellow Christians in slavery. After his return to London he spoke, in a sermon before the Society for the Propagation of the Gospel, of the condition of the thousand Negroes and fifteen hundred Indians in Rhode Island, and procured a legal opinion in favor of the reception of Negroes in the church, copies of which he sent to the colonies for distribution. Rand, *Berkeley's American Sojourn*, p. 28.

to be the same people as the Siberian Tartars whose pictures he had taken.[20]

Inasmuch as Ezra Stiles had become minister of the Second Congregational Church in Newport as early as 1755, when many people still vividly remembered Berkeley's sojourn there, the tradition appears well founded.

This visit in May 1729 appears to be the only one into "the Narragansett country" for which there is any evidence, although Updike says that Berkeley repeatedly visited Narragansett, accompanied by Smibert, Col. Updike, and Dr. McSparran, to examine into the condition and character of the Narragansett Indians. It is quite likely that Berkeley made several such visits, of which no record survives, in the course of the two and a half years of his Newport residence. Smibert may also have gone again in the course of the summer of 1729, to complete his portraits of Mr. and Mrs. McSparran, as he remained in Newport until the autumn of that year. In her declining years, after her husband's death at Oxford, Mrs. Berkeley was wont to dilate upon these hazardous and arduous expeditions, for such they no doubt appeared to her to be. She wrote, "When the season and his health permitted, he visited the Continent [i.e., crossed from Newport on Rhode Island to the mainland], not only its outward skirts, but penetrated far into its recesses." [21] Considering that these expeditions could not, at the utmost, have been longer than a day or two's ride on horseback along forest trails to visit encampments of quite tame Indians not many miles from the shores of Narragansett Bay, we are perhaps justified in feeling that the good lady's ignorance of "the recesses" of the American continent was equaled only by her admiration for her husband.

Smibert remained with Berkeley in Newport some six months longer, while the latter was awaiting news that his grant of £20,000 from the government had become available. In the course of this period he must have executed his large "Bermuda Group" which includes all Berkeley's associates in his proposed enterprise. It is signed and dated

Jo. Smibert fecit 1729
[Newport?]

[20] Ezra Stiles, *The United States elevated to Glory and Honor, A Sermon, preached before his Excellency Jonathan Trumbull, Esq. L. L. D. etc.* (Worcester, 1785), pp. 16–17, quoted in Benjamin Smith Barton's *New Views of the Origin of the Tribes and Nations of America* (Philadelphia, 1797), p. xvi, note. Ledyard, the American traveler, when in Siberia in the opening years of the nineteenth century, made the same comparison.
[21] Fraser, p. 161.

It includes, besides Berkeley and his wife and child, Miss Handcock, Mr. James, Mr. Dalton, Smibert himself, and Thomas Moffatt, who, meantime, had reached Newport. The child, Henry Berkeley, was born in May or June,[22] and was baptized in Newport, September 1, 1729. He is not shown as an infant, looking rather as though he were a year or two old, but it seems to have been the custom so to represent very small children, and an X-ray of the picture gives no ground for the theory that he was painted into the picture, or repainted, two years later, while Berkeley and his family were in Boston before the return voyage to England.[23]

This picture of the "Bermuda Group" is the largest and best-known work by Smibert in America. It was not, however, Smibert's first portrayal of a group of persons, since, as already stated, he had in 1720 painted for Lord Cullen in Scotland a family group of twelve individuals, as well as the group of the Rosa-Coronian Club. Both must have been large canvases. The erroneous statement that the "Bermuda Group" was the first picture painted in the colonies which included more than one figure has been often repeated. That is not the case. There are at least two pictures showing a mother and child, and one showing the Three Mason Children, painted in New England in the seventeenth century, and others with two figures dating from the first quarter of the eighteenth century. And in 1722 Gustavus Hesselius is supposed to have painted for St. Barnabas' Church, Queen Anne's Parish, Maryland, an altarpiece showing "Our Blessed Saviour and ye Twelve Apostles at ye Last Supper," probably adapted from an Italian painting, although both the provenance of the painting and the attribution to the artist appear open to some doubt.

But, if Smibert's conversation piece was not the earliest colonial portrayal of more than a single figure on an artist's canvas, it assuredly was an artistic tour de force such as the colonies had not seen before. It remained on exhibition in his studio during his lifetime and for many years after his death, and its influence on young colonial painters is discussed in Chapter VIII. It is by far the most interesting and important picture of his entire career, and shows the high-water mark of his artistic ability. It set a new standard for colonial painting and is a valuable historical document on account of the individuals represented. Although the two women are purely conventional figures with little individual expression, as is the case in many of his portraits

[22] Berkeley wrote to Percival on June 27, "For my amusement I have got a little son, whom my wife nurses."
[23] Alan Burroughs, *Art in America*, XXX, 115.

The "Bermuda Group"

of women, and the child is a doll figure, the men are strongly individualized and vigorously painted, giving a clearcut impression of Berkeley's associates on his expedition to America. Smibert was at the height of his powers; he knew his subjects well; and he had every incentive to do his best. Not many of Smibert's later portraits of individuals are as good.

This important picture remained in Smibert's studio in Boston for nearly eighty years after Smibert's settlement there, and for more than thirty years after the death in 1777 of John Moffatt, the last survivor of his household. Following that event the studio was rented to a succession of young painters, the last of whom was John Johnston (1752–1818), who occupied it for a considerable period, down to at least 1808, when the picture was still there and was his property. Presumably he had purchased it when the contents of the studio were sold. In 1808 it was bought from Johnston by Isaac Lothrop of Plymouth and, after Johnston had cleaned it, was sent by ship to President Dwight as a present to Yale College. These facts were not recorded at the time in the Yale archives, and after Dwight's death Professor Chauncey A. Goodrich, writing to William Dunlap, could only report the romantic legend which had sprung up that Dwight had "discovered" the picture about 1800 "in the southeastern part of Massachusetts," in poor condition and in the hands of persons who placed small value on it. After Dunlap had printed this legend in his *History of the Arts of Design* in 1834, Judge John Davis, of Boston, who had been an agent for Mr. Lothrop in making the purchase, wrote to Goodrich to give him a true account of the transaction, but his letter and those of other persons to the same effect were buried in the Yale archives and have only recently been unearthed, unfortunately too late for the correction to have been made in Bayley and Goodspeed's revised edition of Dunlap in 1918.

In Smibert's group Dean Berkeley stands at the side of the picture on the spectator's right, wearing a white wig, black cassock and girdle, and white bands. He is looking upward, and, in some accounts of the picture, has been described as dictating his book *Alciphron.* That book, however, was not written until some months after Smibert had left Newport for Boston. Before Berkeley is a table covered with a bright Turkey cloth or rug, of the type first introduced into England in the sixteenth or seventeenth century by the Venetian trade. With his right hand he holds upright a large leather-bound book, which tradition has described as "his favorite Plato," but the label is illegible and the volume represented is certainly not the copy of *Opera*

Platonis which belonged to Berkeley and is now owned by the Berkeley Divinity School.[24]

Behind the table and next to Berkeley sits his wife, facing full front, with dark hair and eyes, dressed in yellow and holding in her lap their eldest child, Henry, who is dressed in white and is sitting up with a peach in his right hand. Next to Mrs. Berkeley sits Miss Handcock, dressed in blue, her face turned left to look at Mrs. Berkeley and the child, her left arm and hand held rather awkwardly across her body pointing in the other direction.

Between and behind the two women stands John James of Bury St. Edmunds, leaning forward over a chair rail. He has a prominent hooked nose, and wears a gray wig, a brown coat, and a long steenkirk tie, the end of which is tucked through a buttonhole of the coat. James went from Newport to Boston with Smibert and Dalton, and apparently remained in America until after his father's death in 1736, as a letter to him from Berkeley, then Bishop of Cloyne, dated June 30, 1736, speaks of his succession to the baronetcy, of his expected return to "our hemisphere," and of not knowing whether he is "still sailing on the ocean or already arrived." [25] James died in 1741 and the baronetcy became extinct.

At the end of the table opposite Berkeley, in a chair lined with green cloth, sits Richard Dalton of Lincolnshire, in some accounts miscalled Sir James Dalton. He is shown in profile, his right side towards the spectator, and is posed as though in the act of writing from Berkeley's dictation, his quill pen poised on the page of a large book, his eyes lifted to look expectantly at Berkeley. He has short black hair and an intelligent face with a rather heavy chin. He wears a brown velvet coat and breeches, and white ruffles, while a red cloak is thrown over his left shoulder and brought round his lower body.

Behind him stands Smibert's nephew, Dr. Thomas Moffatt, who had been prevented by illness from sailing with the party but had joined it at Newport sometime during the summer. In some accounts he has been erroneously identified as John Moffatt, his younger brother, who came to Boston sometime before 1740 to assist his uncle. He is shown half front, his right hand on the back of Dalton's chair. He wears a gray wig and a gray-green coat with ruffles.

Thomas Moffatt matriculated at the University of Edinburgh on April 3, 1721, but there is no further record of him as a student there. Later he studied medicine under the famous physician, Boerhaave, at

---

[24] Theodore Sizer, "Bishop Berkeley as a Patron of Art," an address before the Berkeley Divinity School, January 23, 1929, manuscript.
[25] *The Gentleman's Magazine*, CI, 99 (February 1831).

Leiden. Presumably he was selected as one of Berkeley's party that he might teach medicine in the proposed college at Bermuda. After Berkeley's return to England he remained in Newport but failed to achieve much success in the practice of medicine, and turned to other activities. He was for a time librarian of the Redwood Library and later one of its board of directors. When the Scottish traveler, Dr. Alexander Hamilton, visited Newport in 1744 he recorded that Moffatt, "a fellow student of mine," showed him the town and took him to visit the painter Robert Feke. Moffatt had something of a taste for the fine arts, and is said to have owned, beside paintings and drawings, fifty or more prints "framed and glazed." [26] It was Moffatt who conceived the idea of manufacturing snuff in Newport and who imported Gilbert Stuart, father of the painter, to set up and operate a snuff mill. His later years were unhappy. He took office under the obnoxious Stamp Act in 1765, was burned in effigy, and had his house sacked. He left Newport for England, and a year later was appointed comptroller at New London, Connecticut. While in New London he sought compensation for the destruction of his property and the General Assembly was ordered to pay him £1000, but he never received anything. At the outbreak of the Revolution he sought refuge with the British troops under General Gage in Boston, and eventually returned to London, where he was granted an annual pension of £200.

That he did not lose all his property in Newport, but was able to retrieve and carry to England at least part of his collection of pictures, seems clear from his will dated August 5, 1786. The will begins:

In the name of God, Amen. I Thomas Moffatt of Charlotte Street Pimlico Doctor of Physics being sound of mind, but weak of body think proper to make my last *Will* as follows, viz. . . .
Fourthly,—I bequeath . . . to George Chalmers of Berkeley Square the following pictures—The Bermuda Group painted by Smibert, a naked man painted by Carrach, St. Peter's head being the present of the Duke of Tuscany to Smibert, The Marquis of Montrose by Jamieson, Allen Ramsay by Smibert, a small picture of Salvator Rosa, being a present from Mr. Richard Cumberland. [27]

The portrait of "Allen" Ramsay and "St. Peter's head" have been already discussed. The "Bermuda Group" must, I think, certainly have been the small copy now in the National Gallery of Ireland in Dublin, or perhaps a study for the original picture. Smibert may well have painted this in Newport before going to Boston, and have

26 W. T. Whitley, *Gilbert Stuart* (Cambridge, Mass., 1932), p. 4.
27 Ms. copy of records in Somerset House, London, in possession of Mr. Maurice P. van Buren, New York.

given it to his nephew as a memento of his membership in the party. Moffatt died in London in March 1787.[28]

In the background at the extreme left of the "Bermuda Group" stands the retiring figure of Smibert himself, as though reluctant to intrude upon the society of his betters. He has no wig, his dark brown hair falling to his shoulders, and he wears a brown coat with ruffles. His right hand holds a partly unrolled scroll with what looks like the sketch of a tree on it. His face is turned right, three quarters front, with dark eyes, rather full lips, and a long pointed nose. The face is the pleasing one of a modest and unaggressive man, such as Vertue described. It is the only likeness of Smibert which can be accepted as certainly representing him.

Besides this group Smibert painted, during his nine months' residence in Newport, another bust portrait of Berkeley on commission for Henry Collins, the wealthy and public-spirited citizen of Newport. William Hunter, in an address before the Redwood Library, Newport, in 1847, says, "Collins was fortunate enough to engage his [Smibert's] earliest labours not for his own portrait only, but likewise for those of the venerable Clapp, and the worthy and pious Callender, and, above all, of Berkeley himself."

The portrait of Henry Collins is still extant, a fine picture in the possession of Countess Lâszlo Széchényi, to whom it passed by descent through the Flagg family. The portrait of Berkeley is probably the one listed in the Descriptive Catalogue as Dean George Berkeley, No. 3, now owned by the Massachusetts Historical Society. Hunter, however, was mistaken in attributing to Smibert the pictures of Clapp and Callender. The portrait of Rev. Nathaniel Clapp must have been painted at a later period than that of Smibert's brief sojourn in Newport and is too crude a piece of work to be his. It may possibly be an early painting by Robert Feke, to whom the much finer and later portrait of Rev. John Callender is certainly to be assigned.[29]

[28] The Gentleman's Magazine for 1787 has a brief obituary notice of him, concluding with the epitaph on his gravestone in the burying ground of St. George's, Hanover Square:

Here is laid
THOMAS MOFFATT, M.D.
21 March, 1787:
who left his gratitude
to the King and British nation,
his prayers to the Loyalists,
and pardon to the Rebels
of America.

The obituary is unsigned but may perhaps be from the pen of Rev. Samuel Peters, who preached a discourse on Moffatt's death.
[29] See H. W. Foote, Robert Feke, Colonial Portrait Painter (Cambridge, Mass., 1930), pp. 38, 63, 64, 131–132, 135–136.

The only other portraits by Smibert which can with assurance be assigned to the period of his stay in Newport are those supposed to represent Joseph Wanton and Mrs. Wanton; the one representing David Cheseborough, and the portrait of Rev. Samuel Johnson, who twenty-five years later became the first president of King's College, now Columbia University, New York. Johnson, at the time of Berkeley's stay in Newport, was the rector of the Episcopal church in Stratford, Connecticut. In his autobiography he states that he took an early opportunity to go to Newport to meet Berkeley, and his apparent age in the picture as well as the manner in which it is painted support the conjecture that it was executed by Smibert sometime between April and October, 1729.

While Smibert was still in Newport the London gossip that he had married Miss Handcock, which Vertue had recorded—though he later carefully crossed out the item—crossed the Atlantic in a letter from Percival to Berkeley, who was probably far from pleased by it. Percival wrote, in a letter dated "Charlton, 20th Sept. 1729": "There is a report that Mr. Smibert is married to the lady who accompanied Mrs. Berkeley, but if so I suppose you would have said something of it." Berkeley replied, on March 29, 1730: There is no truth in what your Lordship heard of Mrs. [Mistress] Handcock's being married, or about to marry.[30]

Meantime Smibert, finding no further opportunities for portrait painting in Newport, had removed to Boston. In the letter of March 29, 1730, quoted above, Berkeley had written to Percival:

We have passed the winter in a profound solitude at my farm on this Island, all my companions having been allured five or six months ago to Boston, the place of pleasure and resort in these parts, where they still continue. After my long fatiguing business this retirement is very agreeable to me; and my wife loves the country life so well as to pass her days contentedly and cheerfully.

In a letter of March 9 to Thomas Prior he had also written:

Mr. James, Dalton, and Smibert etc. are at Boston, and have been there for several months. My wife and I abide by Rhode Island, preferring quiet and solitude to the noise of a great town not withstanding all the solicitations that have been used to draw us thither. [And in a postscript he adds] as to what you ask about my companions, they are all at Boston and have been there these four months, preferring that noisy town to this peaceful retreat which my wife and I enjoy in Rhode Island. Being in a hurry I have writ the same thing twice.[31]

There is no record as to what financial arrangements Berkeley had made with him, but presumably Smibert had had free passage to

[30] Rand, *Berkeley and Percival*, pp. 257, 262. [31] Fraser, p. 173.

America, with the promise of a fixed stipend when the college in Bermuda should be established. Perhaps he soon guessed that Berkeley's dream was not likely to be fulfilled; the inactivity at Newport which Berkeley found so pleasant may have been irksome to him; and in any event it was necessary for him to earn money. Boston offered the most promising field in the colonies, for, although between about 1675 and 1725 a considerable number of portraits had been painted in Boston by painters few of whom can now be identified with any certainty, there were, at the time of Smibert's arrival, only two painters there, neither of whom could be regarded as a serious competitor. The elder of these was Peter Pelham, who had reached Boston from London probably in the spring of 1727, but Pelham was primarily an engraver, and as such proved an ally rather than a rival by virtue of his mezzotints reproducing Smibert's portraits of popular divines and military heroes. The younger man was Nathaniel Emmons, a native New Englander, presumably self-taught, who was capable of fairly good work, and was well thought of locally, but whose reputation was very small compared to Smibert's.

From Berkeley's rather loose statement, it is evident that Smibert must have reached Boston by November 1729. It was, no doubt, in the course of his journey overland from Newport that Smibert stopped to see the Dighton Rock and to copy the pictographs cut thereon. Dighton Rock is a large, sandstone boulder standing in the stream of a tidal estuary known as Taunton Great River, a few miles below the city of Taunton, Massachusetts. It is covered with ancient pictographs which have long puzzled archeologists. The earliest copy of these pictographs was made in 1680 by Rev. John Danforth. Public attention was drawn to the Rock by Cotton Mather in a communication to the Royal Society written in 1712. The next extant drawing of the Rock was made in 1730, by Isaac Greenwood. Smibert's draw-in, which has disappeared, must have been made a year earlier; it was seen in the winter of 1767–1768 by Pierre Eugène Du Simitière,[32] who in his memoranda of his visit to New England noted:

There was in the collection of Doctor Smibert at Boston, an accurate drawing of the Supposed inscription at Taunton, done by his father John Smibert an eminent portrait painter that came over to America with Dean Berkeley, and afterwards settled in Boston.

This memorandum is attached to a longer one about Dean Berkeley, as follows:

[32] Pierre Eugène Du Simitière was born in the "Republic of Geneva" during the first quarter of the eighteenth century and was trained as an artist. He went to the West Indies about 1750, where he spent ten years painting and collecting shells, botanical specimens, and historical documents for a history of the islands. He reached

The learned Dean Berkeley resided near the last mentioned place [Newport] about the year 1732. He visited the Rock at Taunton and had begun an Elaborate dissertation upon the Supposed inscription, when a farmer in its neighborhood, observing the Dean one day employed in copying the unknown caracters informed him, that, that rock had been used formerly by the Indians that resorted thither to Shoot Ducks, and dart fish, to wett and sharpen the points of their arrows and darts on the Stone which was the cause of the curious hollow lines and figures found thereon. However, it seems that the Opinion of the learned of this day in New England is, that the above mentioned inscription or some other, in that part of the continent is really of the highest antiquity.

Eugene Burke Delabarre, in his volume on Dighton Rock, quotes three witnesses to the effect that Berkeley had visited the Rock while living in Newport.[33] The testimony of all three was given long after the event, and does not appear wholly reliable, but Berkeley's curiosity about all sorts of natural objects makes the story not altogether improbable. At that time, however, the Rock was difficult of access. It lay more than twenty miles off the road then followed from Newport to Boston, in a very sparsely settled region, and a boat was required to reach it. That Smibert sought it out, either on his trip to or from Boston in April or when he went thither again about the beginning of November, 1729, is hardly open to question in view of du Simitière's report of the drawing, but it is certainly questionable whether Berkeley did so, since it would have involved a rather arduous trip lasting four or five days. If he ever did visit the Rock it was probably with Smibert early in November, for when he came again that way, two years later, he was accompanied by his family, and was pressed for time. It is a misfortune that Smibert's drawing has been lost, both because it was an interesting item in the record of his American sojourn, and because of its importance as one of the earliest representations of the Rock.

New York in 1764 or 1765 and Philadelphia in 1766. He visited Boston for a short period, 1767–1768. He was elected a member of the American Philosophical Society, Philadelphia, in 1768, and was later one of its curators. The College of New Jersey (now Princeton University) made him an honorary Master of Arts in 1781. He died in 1784, leaving a mass of miscellaneous manuscripts in which he had noted down items regarding the natural history, economic conditions, location of portraits of outstanding persons, and other matters of interest in the country. His manuscripts were purchased by the Library Company of Philadelphia at a sale of "the American Museum collected by the late Pierre Eugène du Simitière," and are now mounted in twelve volumes. For an account of Du Simitière see the *Pennsylvania Magazine*, XIII, 341–375, article by William John Potts, on "du Simitière, Artist, Antiquary, and Naturalist." See also *DAB*. du Simitière also painted portraits and may be regarded as the founder of the first museum in the colonies.

[33] *Dighton Rock* (New York, 1928), p. 36.

CHAPTER IV

Settlement in Boston

SMIBERT ARRIVED IN BOSTON, PERHAPS ACCOMPANIED BY JOHN JAMES and Richard Dalton, not later than early November, 1729. He is said to have lodged for a time at the house in Green Lane which belonged to James Gooch, whose portrait he afterwards painted. Some tidings of his reputation must have already preceded him and he must have formed some acquaintanceships during his earlier brief visit in April. He was the first London artist with a background of study and work in Italy who had ever visited these shores, and he had the prestige of being a member of Dean Berkeley's party. Berkeley's coming to America had been heralded by letters to a number of prominent people from Henry Newman, who, after graduating from Harvard, had become secretary to the Society for Promoting Christian Knowledge in London, and the Dean's arrival in Newport was a notable event.

It is probable that the only person in Boston whom Smibert had known previous to his emigration was Peter Pelham,[1] the engraver, who had emigrated in 1727. Inasmuch as Pelham had worked in London for at least six years previously as an associate of the painters and engravers there, it is hardly possible that he and Smibert should not have known each other. Pelham was the earliest maker of mezzotints to come to the Colonies, but, though his work was excellent, the de-

[1] Peter Pelham was born in England (baptized September 25, 1697), and died in Boston before December 14, 1751, on which date his burial is noted in the records of Trinity Church. He was married and working in London as an engraver as early as 1720, the date of his earliest known print. His son Peter was baptized in St. Paul's, Covent Garden, on December 17, 1721, and his son Charles in the same place on December 9, 1722. He emigrated to Boston in the spring of 1727 and the same year painted and engraved the portrait of Cotton Mather. His son William was baptized in Boston on February 22, 1729. On May 22, 1748, he married as his third wife the widow Mary Singleton Copley, by whom he had a son, Henry, half-brother of John Singleton Copley. Stauffer, *American Engravers*, II, 406–410, lists twenty-three English plates by him, and fifteen portraits and a view of Louisburg engraved by him in this country.

mand for it was far too small to support him and he resorted to various other occupations, such as teaching school, where the subjects included dancing and music, to make a living. He painted a few portraits here, but apparently only for the purpose of reproducing them in mezzotints. As he engraved several portraits by Smibert,[2] and sold many of his prints at Smibert's shop, it is clear that they were friendly collaborators.

Smibert at once found work in Boston and in the next three months painted portraits of the aged Chief Justice Samuel Sewall, of Nathaniel Byfield, of Jean Paul Mascarene[3] in armor, and probably of several others as well. Inasmuch as Sewall died on January 1, 1729/30, after a month's illness, it seems clear that his portrait must have been painted during the month of November, at the latest.

In the course of the winter, certainly not later than early March, 1729/30, Smibert held an exhibition at which not only these portraits were shown, but also the copies of pictures which he had made in Italy and brought with him to America. The evidence for this is found in a highly interesting poem written by an enthusiastic admirer in Boston. The poem was printed anonymously here, but no trace of its publication has been found. Perhaps it was issued as a broadside, or it may have appeared in the *Boston Gazette* of March 31–April 6, no copy of which, or of the issue of April 7–13, is known to exist. The poem promptly found its way to London, sent probably either by Smibert or by the author, and appeared in the *Daily Courant* for April 14, 1730. Vertue noted its appearance, writing: "Mr Smybert painter being settled at Boston New England.—a Friend of his there inscribed a Poem to Mr Smibert on the subject of his pictures. which was transmitted here & published in The Courant Apr 1730. it begins . . ." and he went on to quote fifteen lines from it.[4] The whole poem deserves attention. The *Daily Courant* introduces it as follows:

[2] Namely, those of: Rev. Benjamin Colman, 1735; Rev. William Cooper, 1743 (issued May 1, 1744); Sir William Pepperell, 1747; Governor William Shirley, issued July 27, 1747; Rev. Henry Caner, 1750; Rev. Joseph Sewall, n.d.
[3] In a letter written by Mascarene to his daughter "Margritt" from Annapolis Royal in 1740, after he had become Lieutenant-Governor of Nova Scotia, he described in detail his "appartement" and way of life. He wrote that, in what he called "the great room . . . The white walls are hung in part with four large pictures of Mr. Smibert." There is no clue as to whom these four portraits represented, and all trace of them has been lost, unless one was the picture of himself "in arms," which passed down to descendants in Halifax, from the estate of the last of whom it was purchased and returned to Boston early in this century.
[4] Vertue, III, 42.

We are obliged for the following little Piece to a Gentleman of New-England where it was wrote and published; and we doubt not but it will be agreeably received here by our Readers of Taste.

Virginis est verae facies: quam vivere credas;
Et, si non obstet reverentia, velle moveri.
Ars, adeo latet arte suo.

Ovid, Met. Lib. X, v. 250.

To Mr. Smibert

on the sight of his Pictures.

Ages our Land a barb'rous Desert stood,
And Savage Nations howl'd in every Wood;
No laurel'd Art o'er the rude Region smil'd,
Nor blest Religion dawn'd amidst the Wild;
Dullness and Tyranny, confederate, reign'd,
And Ignorance her gloomy State maintain'd.
   An hundred Journeys now the Earth has run
In annual circles round the central Sun,
Since the first Ship th' unpolish'd Letters bore
Thro the wide Ocean, to the barb'rous shore.
Then infant Science made its early Proof,
Honest, sincere, tho unadorned and rough,
Still, thro' a cloud, the rugged Stranger shone,
Politeness, and the softer Arts unknown.
No heav'nly Pencil the free Stroke could give,
Nor the warm Canvas felt its Colors live.
No moving Rhet'rick rais'd the ravish'd Soul,
Flourish't in flames or heard its Thunders roll;
Rough, horrid verse, harsh, grated thro' the Ear,
And jarring Discords tore the tortur'd Air.
Solid, and grave, and plain the Country stood,
Inelegant, and rigorously good.
   Each Year succeeding the rude Rust devours,
And softer Arts lead on the following Hours;
The tuneful nine begin to touch the Lyre,
And flowing Pencils light the living Fire.
In the fair Page new Beauties learn to shine,
The Thoughts to brighten, and the Stile refine;
Till the great Year the finish'd Period brought,
A *Smibert* painted and a ——wrote.
   Thy Fame, O *Smibert*, shall the Muse rehearse,
And sing her Sister-Art in softer Verse.
   'Tis yours, Great Master, in just Lines to trace
The rising Prospect, or the lovely Face,

In the fair Round to swell the glowing cheek,
Give Thought to Shades, and bid the Colours speak.
Touch'd by thy Hand, how *Sylvia's* Charms engage,
And *Flavia's* Features smile thro' ev'ry Age!
In *Clio's* Face th' attentive Gazer spies
Minerva's reasoning Brow, and azure Eyes;
Thy blush, *Belinda,* future hearts shall warm,
And *Celia* shine in *Citherea's* form.
In hoary majesty, see *Sewall* here;
Fixt strong in thought there Byfield's Lines appear;
Here in full Beauty blooms the charming maid,
Here Roman ruins nod their awful Head:
Here gloting monks their am'rous rights debate,
Th' *Italian* master sits in easy state,
Vandike and *Rubens* show their Rival Forms,
And studious *Mascarene* asserts his Arms.
But cease, fond Muse, nor the rude Lays prolong,
A thousand Wonders must remain unsung;
Crowds of new Beings lift their dawning Heads,
In conscious Forms, and animated Shades.
What Sounds can speak, to ev'ry Figure just,
The breathing Statue, and the living Bust?
Landskips how gay! arise in ev'ry Light,
And fresh Creations rush upon the Sight.
Thro' fairy Scenes the roving Fancy strays,
Lost in the endless visionary Maze.
Still, wondrous Artist, let thy Pencil flow.
Still warm with Life, thy blended Colours glow,
Raise the ripe Blush, bid the quick Eye-balls roll,
And call forth every Passion of the Soul.
Let thy soft Shades in mimic Figures play,
Steal on the Heart, and call the mind away.
Yet, *Smibert,* on the kindred muse attend,
And let the Painter prove the Poet's Friend.
In the same Studies nature we pursue,
I the Description touch, the Picture you;
The same gay scenes our beauteous Works adorn
The flamy Evening, or the rosy Morn:
Now, with bold hand, we strike the strong Design,
Mature in Thought now soften ev'ry line,
Now, unrestrain'd, in freer Airs surprize,
And sudden at our Word new Worlds arise;
In gen'rous Passion let our Breasts conspire,
As is the Fancy's, be the Friendships' Fire;
Alike our Labour, and alike our Flame,
'Tis thine to raise the Shape, and mine the Name.

The youthful poet who composed these lines was Mather Byles, the precocious nephew of Cotton Mather, who had had a large part in his upbringing. His authorship is proved by the inclusion of the poem, in slightly altered form, in Byles' *Poems on Several Occasions* (1744), in which it appears addressed "To Picturio," and with classical names substituted for those of the Boston worthies.[5]

At the time of Smibert's exhibition Byles was twenty-four years old, and four years out of Harvard College. Two years later he became minister of the Hollis Street Church in Boston, a preacher of distinction who was even more renowned as an inveterate punster. In his youth he aspired to be a poet, and was hailed by one of his contemporaries as "Harvard's honour and New England's hope [who] Bids fair to rise and sing and rival Pope." He was, indeed, the leader of a little group in the young generation who were eager to see the introduction of art and letters into New England, and he was quite ready to lend a helping hand when "A Smibert painted and a . . . wrote."

That his rather cocky poem attracted attention is proved by the appearance in the *Boston Gazette*, in the missing issue of April 13, 1730, of a bit of satirical verse making fun of him.

> *To Mr. B—, occasioned by his verses to Mr. Smibert on seeing his Pictures.*
>
> Unhappy Bard! Sprung in such Gothic Times
> As yield no friendly muse, t' extol your Rhymes
> Hard is the Task you singly undergo
> To praise the Painter and the Poet too.
> But much I fear you raise a short-lived FAME
> Which lives but on the Pen from whence it came.
> Boast on, and take what fleeting Life can give,
> For when you cease to write you cease to live.
> If you to future Ages would be known,
> Make this Advice I freely give your own.
> Go to the Painter—for your Picture sit
> His art will long survive the Poet's wit.

[5] I am indebted to Miss Anne Allison for calling my attention to Byles' authorship. Byles was, of course, following the British fashion according to which poets, usually anonymous, hailed more or less distinguished painters in panegyric verse, claiming close kinship between art and poetry. Kneller received several such verbal bouquets while living, as well as eulogistic verses after his death (see Chapter II). The same fashion was followed by Francis Hopkinson a generation later when he wrote a similar poem to John Wollaston during the latter's visit to Philadelphia in 1758, and by "Dr. T. T." in Annapolis when Wollaston went thither.

No doubt Byles knew, as we do not, who was the author. Suspicion strongly points to Byles' contemporary and rival wit, Joseph Green, whose humorous face Copley later portrayed. Probably not much love was lost between them, for Green on at least two later occasions, and probably much more frequently, aimed some very pointed shafts of wit at Byles.[6] Jeremy Belknap, Jr., Byles' nephew, carefully copied out this counterblast in a memorandum book entitled "A Collection of Poetry, Begun November 6, 1764," which has eventually found its way, with other family papers, to the Massachusetts Historical Society.[7] Thus the verses have been preserved with the notation "BG, Ap. 13, 1730" to indicate their source, though no copy of the paper in which they appeared has survived. That the *Gazette* was willing to print it may be due to the fact that the publishers were in general opposed to the leadership of the Mather family in Boston affairs, and were not averse to taking a dig at one of the tribe, who, it must be admitted, had laid himself open to satire.

Mather Byles, for all his enthusiasm for Smibert's art, did not accept the advice to have his portrait painted by him, perhaps because to have done so would have seemed like an admission of the fleeting value of his own literary aspirations. Instead, in 1731, he had his portrait painted by Peter Pelham who made a small, undated mezzotint[8] of it, presumably in the same year. Now Pelham, in the course of the twenty-five years which he spent in Boston, made about a dozen mezzotints of older, well-known, and long-settled ministers from portraits painted by himself, Smibert or Greenwood, because there was a market for the prints among the parishioners whom the ministers served. But in 1731 Byles was still a young man who had not yet entered upon his first pastorate. The indication seems to be that he had sufficient means, and thought well enough of himself, to pay for the portrait and the plate, perhaps for free distribution of the mezzotints among the little clique of literary aspirants which he led.

To return to the poem by Mather Byles, besides the portraits of Sewall, Byfield, and Mascarene which Smibert had painted in the preceding four months, five ladies are mentioned,—Sylvia, Flavia, Clio, Belinda, and Celia,—but it is impossible to tell whether these are copies

---

[6] See H. W. Foote, *Three Centuries of American Hymnody* (Cambridge, Mass., 1940), pp. 71–73.
[7] It was printed in M.H.S. *Proc.*, LIII, 59 (December, 1919), but without any information about the occasion which called it forth, because at that time Byles' poem to Smibert was unknown.
[8] This is the scarcest of Pelham's mezzotints. The portrait is now owned by the American Antiquarian Society, Worcester, Mass. Byles was painted later by Copley, and later still by his young kinsman, Mather Brown.

of European pictures which Smibert had brought with him, or freshly painted portraits of Boston maids and matrons whose identity was veiled, for the sake of delicacy and according to custom, under classical names. The pictures which without doubt were copies, painted by Smibert in Italy—"Th' Italian master" (Raphael?), "Vandike and Rubens," the "gloting monks" and "Roman ruins," and the "landskips"—have been discussed in Chapter I.

In addition to the light which it throws on Smibert's little art collection, Byles' poem is of value as indicating the enthusiasm with which Smibert was welcomed in Boston in circles to which he looked for patronage. With such a flourish of trumpets, backed by the prestige of having come as Berkeley's professor of the fine arts, he was fairly launched on his American career. For more than a decade he had no serious rivals in Boston. It was not until 1740 or later that the two native-born painters, Joseph Badger and John Greenwood, entered the field, and both were far inferior to Smibert in skill and reputation. Robert Feke paid his first visit to Boston in 1741, and his second in 1748, when Smibert's career was drawing to a close. If, therefore, Smibert was looking for a place where there would be a good demand for his work and where he would be cock of the walk, he had found it. As Vertue put it in his notes, "He was not content to be on a level with some of the lesser painters, but desired to be where he might be looked on at the top of his profession—then and thereafter." [9] In London, as he must have known well, he would never have risen to a painter of the first rank, and no one would have addressed him in panegyric verse as "great Master" or "wondrous Artist." But in Boston that is how he appeared, and his reception must have gratified him. If, in our more sophisticated day, such an estimate of Smibert seems ridiculously exaggerated, we must remember that in the field of art (though not of letters, in which his education was very limited), he was beyond question the most cultivated man who came to America before the middle of the eighteenth century. He had been the associate of the London artists of his day, and Berkeley deemed him competent in knowledge and skill. The glamour of his sojourn in Italy counted, for although there was much passing of New Englanders to and from England, and occasionally to the Continent, there were few, aside from sailors, who visited Italy in the first half of the eighteenth century. It may well be doubted if in 1730 there was in Boston, or, for that matter, elsewhere in the colonies, anyone who had an acquaintance with that country comparable to Smibert's. [10]

[9] Vertue, III, 161.
[10] Professor Hagen, in the chapter on Robert Feke in his *Birth of the American*

Jane Clark

Smibert soon found other attractions in Boston, for on July 30, 1730, he married a young woman twenty years his junior, Mary, daughter of Dr. Nathaniel Williams. The minister who married them was Rev. Joseph Sewall of the Old South Church, of which Smibert had become a member less than three weeks earlier and with which his wife's family had long been connected, her grandfather having been a deacon there. Her father was the third of his name who had lived in Boston on what is now called Court Street, facing Scollay Square, his grandfather having bought the site in 1649. This grandfather had prospered as a dry-goods merchant, and Dr. Williams' father had married a daughter of the first Peter Oliver, a leading merchant. Dr. Williams, therefore, had inherited a substantial property, and he also made a good marriage, his wife being Anne Bradstreet, granddaughter of Governor Simon Bradstreet and his wife Anne, who was the earliest woman writer in the North American colonies and herself the daughter of Governor Thomas Dudley. Mary Williams, therefore, had an excellent social position and useful connections in the provincial town. A number of the persons whom her husband later painted, notably the members of the Oliver family, were related to her. Her father, Dr. Williams, had graduated from Harvard in 1693, and had been ordained in Cambridge in 1698 to preach the gospel in Barbados. Apparently his experience there was an unhappy one, except for his marriage, which took place in that colony. He and his wife returned to Boston in January 1700/01. In 1703 he was assistant to Master Cheever of the Boston Latin School, and he became master on the latter's death in 1708, with a salary which eventually amounted to £150. He was succeeded by John Lovell in 1734. He also preached occasionally, and practiced medicine. In 1723 he was elected Rector of Yale College, but declined the position. He died on January 10, 1737/38, universally respected, and left an estate of nearly £4500.[11] His daughter Mary brought Smibert a dowry of £400. It was a good match for Smibert, and no doubt she thought it a good match too, for she seems to have been a devoted wife.

Smibert's marriage indicates a decision to settle permanently in Boston, even before it became evident that Berkeley's visionary plan

---

Tradition in Art, maintains that Feke must have had a considerable sojourn in Italy and Spain studying art before he came to Boston in 1741. His surmise may be correct, although there are no recorded facts to support it, but Smibert's preëminence as regards acquaintance with Italy remains true for at least the first decade of his life in Boston.

[11] The inventory gives some idea of the household in which Mary Williams had been reared. It included house and land, £3000; books, £342; plate, £228; a Negro, £100; "shays and tackle, "£25; drugs, £40.

of a college at Bermuda was impracticable and that Smibert must either return to London or make a place for himself in New England. Some of his London associates, who had tried to dissuade him from embarking with Berkeley, wondered at his willingness to remain an exile in the American wilderness. Walpole says that Smibert either "found it convenient or had not resolution enough to proceed [i.e. to return to England] but settled at Boston in New England, where he succeeded to his wish, and married a woman with a considerable fortune." [12] The latter part of Walpole's statement is open to two interpretations, either that Smibert had here the success as an artist for which he wished, or that he had been successful in finding a wife with a fortune. If the latter is what Walpole meant, it is true that Smibert's marriage helped to give him a relatively much better position in the community than he could have hoped to achieve in London, although Mary Williams' dowry would have seemed a very modest "fortune" in the latter city.

Smibert may also have found in Boston a certain pleasurable resemblance to the Edinburgh of his youth. Boston was, indeed, only a provincial town of some fifteen thousand inhabitants, but the Edinburgh which Smibert knew was a much smaller city than it is now—not more than thirty-five or forty thousand people—closely confined to the narrow ridge which sloped down from the Castle to Holyrood. The whole section of the modern city which includes Princes Street and beyond was then open country. Boston has often been called the most English of American cities,[13] but in the eighteenth and early nineteenth centuries it was a good deal more like Edinburgh than like London. Of course it lacked the Castle, and the narrow wynds and courtyards with their crowded high-built stone houses which adjoined "the King's Mile," but it had its own narrow and winding streets, already closely built with wooden structures along the water front, with a good many handsome mansions and some churches of brick

[12] *Anecdotes of Painting in England* (ed. Wornum, 1862), II, 673. Walpole was indebted to Vertue's notes for the information which he included about Smibert, but he dressed his story in a more elegant literary form and added a few comments of his own.

[13] As early as 1718 Daniel Neal reported of Boston: "The Conversation in this Town is as polite as in most cities and towns of England; many of their Merchants having travell'd into Europe; and those that stay at home having the advantage of a free Conversation with Travellers, so that a Gentleman from London would think himself at home in Boston when he observes the Numbers of People, their Houses, their Furniture, their Table, their Dress and Conversation which is perhaps as splendid and showy, as that of the most considerable Tradesman in London . . . in the Concerns of Civil Life, as in their Dress, Tables and Conversation they affect to be as English as possible, there is no Fashion in London, but three or four Months is to be seen here at Boston." *History of New-England* (1747 ed.), II, 225.

in the more open parts of the town. And topographically the setting was not unlike Edinburgh's, with Beacon Hill rising beyond the town—as Arthur's Seat rose beyond Edinburgh—giving a then unobstructed and beautiful panorama of the bay with its islands and the sea beyond, of the rivers which encircled the city and its adjacent peninsulas, and of the wooded hills on the mainland.

There were few Scots in Boston, only a small group of mechanics who in 1728 had organized "The Church of the Presbyterian Strangers," in Long Lane, afterwards known as the Federal Street Church, now the Arlington Street Church. But the religious atmosphere was as Calvinistic as Edinburgh's, the Puritan clergy were dominant figures, and most of the people were as little favorable to episcopacy as the Scots had been when Jenny Geddes had flung her stool at the dean in St. Giles Cathedral with the cry "Wad ye say Mass at my lug?" The people, like those of Edinburgh, were independent, not easily controlled, assertive of their rights, constantly at odds with the royal governor, who, with a few other officers of the crown, represented the British government and maintained with some elegance at the Province House on week days and at King's Chapel on Sundays a petty semblance of court life.

The social habits of the people, in their virtues as well as in their pleasures or their vices, resembled those of Edinburgh more than of London. As in the former city, there was no theater, and not much dancing, but there were several bookshops [14] and a rather widespread intellectual interest, and social gatherings about the dinner table or in taverns. There were, to be sure, no clubs of "virtuosi" uniting patrons and practitioners of art, poetry, and music, but a revival of interest in music had begun in the decade preceding Smibert's arrival, so that he found better opportunities to enjoy or to take part in the performance of music than he had known as a youth in Edinburgh, though not equal to those in London. Peter Pelham appears to have promoted the first public concert ever given in the British North American colonies, for the following advertisement was published in the *Boston News-Letter* of December 16–23, 1731:

On Thursday the 30th of this instant December, there will be performed a "Concert of Music" on sundry instruments at Mr. Pelham's great

[14] "The Exchange is surrounded with Booksellers Shops, which have a good Trade. There are five Printing-Presses in Boston, which are generally full of Work, by which it appears, that Humanity and the Knowledge of Letters flourish more here than in all the other English Plantations put together; for in the City of New York there is but one little Bookseller's Ship [*sic*] and in the Plantations of Virginia, Maryland, Carolina, Barbadoes, and the Islands, none at all" (Neal, II, 225).

Room, being the House of the late Doctor Noyes near the Sun Tavern. Tickets to be delivered at the place of performance at "Five Shillings" each. The concert to begin exactly at Six o'clock, and no Tickets will be delivered after Five the day of performance.
N.B. There will be no admittance after Six.[15]

We may be pretty sure that Smibert was present on that occasion, and probably at several similar ones held in Boston before his death. It will not do to press too far the resemblance between Edinburgh and Boston, but probably Smibert could have found no town outside of Scotland which was so much like his native city as was the Boston of 1730.

While Smibert was thus establishing himself in his new home his great and good friend Berkeley was vainly waiting at Newport for news that the British government's grant of £20,000 had become available for the college at Bermuda. The lands at St. Christopher's were being sold, and eventually brought in £90,000, but George I, who had favored Berkeley's plan, had died, and Sir Robert Walpole, the Prime Minister, persuaded Parliament to vote away £80,000 of the proceeds of St. Christopher's as the dowry of the Princess Royal on her marriage to the Prince of Orange, and, later on, James Edward Oglethorpe, after having obtained Berkeley's consent, induced Parliament to devote the remaining £10,000 to the establishment of his colony in Georgia, in which Lord Percival was deeply interested.

Berkeley, in spite of his growing anxiety and disappointment, enjoyed his quiet life at Whitehall. He was made a freeman of the Colony of Rhode Island and Providence Plantations on May 6, 1729; he preached frequently in Trinity Church, Newport, to crowded congregations which included Baptists and Quakers, whose admiration he won by his tact and breadth of mind; and in the summer of 1730 he composed his *Alciphron*, written for the most part in a sheltered nook on the seashore near Whitehall, though not published until his return to England. In the same year a group of Newport men, including Col. Daniel Updike, Rev. Peter Bours, Rev. James Honyman, Rev. John Callender, William Ellery, Henry Collins, and Edward Scott, a great-uncle of Sir Walter Scott, all of whom must have been acquainted with Berkeley, organized the "Society for the Promotion

[15] H. W. Foote, "Musical Life in Boston in the Eighteenth Century," *Proc. American Antiquarian Society* (October 1939). It is worth noting that when Karl Theodor Pachelbel, a distinguished German organist, left Boston for Charleston, S. C., after a visit of some months in 1732–1733, he took with him as a pupil Peter Pelham, Jr. Peter returned after nine years, served briefly as organist of Trinity Church, and later as organist of Bruton Church, Williamsburg, Virginia.

of Knowledge and Virtue," of which the issue was the Philosophical Society and the Redwood Library. Berkeley's name does not appear in its membership, but his influence probably lay back of its formation. Smibert's nephew, Dr. Thomas Moffatt, was for a time its librarian.

Meantime Berkeley's friends in England were sending him discouraging news. Lord Percival wrote from Bath, on December 23, 1730:

> I own I do not see at present great reason to hope success, [in getting the £20,000] but who knows what sparks of fire may yet remain among the ashes. I discoursed it with the speaker, who though he approves it not —— yet thinks the honour of Parliament engaged ——. But on the other hand Sir Robert Walpole told Mr. Hutchinson in confidence, as he has undoubtedly sent you word, that the money would never be paid, so I confess I have very little hopes.[16]

An even more discouraging version of Walpole's attitude reached Berkeley in the statement that Walpole had said that as a minister of the crown it was his duty to say that the grant would be paid when convenient to the government, but that, speaking as a friend, he could not advise Dean Berkeley to expect it. Berkeley himself had apparently come to realize that Bermuda was not a really good location for his college and would gladly have established it at Newport, where the Episcopalians were eager to have it built. But he felt in honor bound to proceed to Bermuda if the grant were paid, or under the necessity of returning to England if it were not. The latter alternative was forced upon him by the information he received from England, and led him to reply to Percival as follows:

> Rhode Island, 2nd March, 1731.
> I have received such accounts on all hands, both from England and Scotland that I now give up all hopes of executing the design which brought me to these parts. I am fairly given to understand that the money will never be paid . . . This disappointment which long lay heavy upon my spirits I endeavor to make myself easy under, by considering that we even know not what would be eventually good or bad, and that no events are in our power. Upon the whole my thoughts are now set towards Europe, where I shall endeavour to be useful in some other way.[17]

His wife was expecting another child, so he stayed on at Whitehall through the summer. The child, Lucia, died soon after birth, on September 5, 1731, and lies buried in Trinity Church yard in Newport.

[16] Rand, *Berkeley and Percival*, pp. 269–270.
[17] Rand, *Berkeley and Percival*, p. 273.

Two days later Berkeley wrote to Rev. Samuel Johnson of Stratford, Connecticut, "I am now upon the point of setting out for Boston to embark for England." He left Newport with his family on September 9, and reached Roxbury the next day. Benjamin Walker of Boston noted in his diary: "Fryday, 10th [September] 1731: Dean George Berkeley with his wife and family came into town from Road Island by land to go to England in Carlin," [18] that is, in the ship commanded by Capt. Carlin. The journey from Newport must have been a fatiguing one, and neither Berkeley nor his wife were in good health, besides being burdened with sorrow at the loss of their child and the labors of removal from Whitehall. During their stay of ten days before sailing they were guests at Datchett House, the Roxbury mansion of Colonel Francis Brinley, which stood on high ground approximately on the site now occupied by the Church of the Redemptionist Fathers, about halfway from Boston to Cambridge by the road which ran out over the Neck and through what are now known as Brookline, Roxbury, and Brighton. Colonel Brinley was an officer of the crown and a member of King's Chapel, where he and his wife are buried. Smibert painted their portraits about the time of Berkeley's visit.

Berkeley's stay was probably a quiet one, to rest in anticipation of the voyage, but on Sunday, the twelfth, he preached in King's Chapel —not in the existing church, but in its small, wooden predecessor on the same site, though the pulpit in which Berkeley stood is still in use. Benjamin Walker went to hear him and recorded the text of his discourse: "On Lord's Day 12 [September, 1731] in ye morn Dean George Berkeley preacht in ye King's Chapel from ye 1st Epistle to Timothy 3rd Chap, Verse 16, and a fine sermon. A very great auditory."

Berkeley's sermon was from the same text and in all probability was the same discourse that he had delivered in Trinity Church, Newport, on August 3, 1729.[19] And on September 17 Rev. Joseph Sewall noted in his diary: "Dean Berkeley visited the College [Harvard]. Colonel Hutchinson and I overtook him at Mr. Brinley's." We may also be sure that Smibert saw something of Berkeley during these days and presented his wife to the Dean and Mrs. Berkeley.

[18] Manuscript in the library of the Massachusetts Historical Society, quoted by my father, Henry Wilder Foote the first, in his *Annals of King's Chapel*, II (1896), 49, and in Rand, *Berkeley's American Sojourn*, p. 44.
[19] It is the fourth of the twelve sermons of which the outlines are given in Fraser, pp. 629–649. It is annotated as having been preached at Newport, but not at Boston, but about half of the sermons, though apparently all were preached at Newport, are not annotated as to place or date of delivery.

Berkeley's departure was noted in the *Boston Weekly News-Letter* of September 16–23, 1731, as follows: "On Tuesday last [September 21] Capt. Carlin sailed from hence for London in whom embarked the Rev. Dean Berkeley and his family who lately came hither from Rhode Island for the purpose." And Benjamin Walker noted in his Diary, "Dean Berkeley saild in Carlin for London wi*th* family."

The homeward voyage was much speedier than the outbound one had been, for Berkeley reached London on October 30. Early in the next year he deeded Whitehall to Yale College, the income of the property to maintain "three bachelors chosen for excellence in Greek and Latin." These scholarships still exist at Yale, though the property has been disposed of on a lease for nine hundred and ninety-nine years and Whitehall is now maintained as a Berkeley Memorial by the Colonial Dames of Rhode Island. In 1733 Berkeley sent a gift of eight hundred books to Yale, the finest collection hitherto brought to this country. He also sent books to Harvard, and a gilded crown and miters to adorn the organ of Trinity Church in Newport.

Smibert was, no doubt, at the dock to see the last of the friends with whom he had been so closely associated for several years, and whose American adventure had had so fateful an influence upon his own career. He never saw them again. But Berkeley did not forget him. After his return to Ireland he was made Bishop of Cloyne and, three and a half years after their parting in Boston, he wrote to Smibert as follows:

Cloyne, May 31, 1735.

Dear Mr. Smibert:

A great variety and hurry of affairs, joined with ill state of health, hath deprived me of the pleasure of corresponding with you for this good while past, and indeed I am very sensible that the task of answering a letter is so disagreeable to you, that you can well dispense with receiving one of mere compliment, or which doth not bring something pertinent and useful. You are the proper judge whether the following suggestions may be so or not. I do not pretend to give advice, I only offer a few hints for your own reflection.

What if there be in my neighborhood a great trading city? What if this city be four times as populous as Boston, and a hundred times as rich? What if there be more faces to paint, and better pay for painting, and yet nobody to paint them? Whether it would be disagreeable to you to receive gold instead of paper? Whether it might be worth your while to embark with your busts, your prints, and your drawings, and once more cross the Atlantic? Whether you might not find full business in Cork, and live there much cheaper than in London? Whether all these things put together might not be worth a serious thought? I have one more question to ask, and that is, whether myrtles grow in or near Boston without pots, stoves, or greenhouses, in the open air? I assure you they do in my garden. So much for the climate. Think of what hath been said, and God direct you for the best. I am, good Mr. Smibert, your affectionate humble servant,

Geor. Cloyne.

P.S. My wife is exceedingly your humble servant, and joins in compliments both to you and yours. We should be glad to hear the state of your health and family. We have now three boys, doubtful which is the prettiest. My two eldest past well through the smallpox last winter. I have my own health better in Cloyne than I had either in old England or New.[20]

This letter implies that other correspondence had passed between them, and recognizes the fact that Smibert was a poor letter writer. Neither Smibert's reply nor any other of Berkeley's letters to him have been preserved, but it is easy to guess what Smibert's answer was. By his marriage he had given hostages to fortune, for Mary Smibert, who probably never journeyed so much as twenty miles from Boston, would have viewed with utter dismay the prospect of going to live in a foreign land. And Smibert himself was nearing fifty, too old to pull up stakes and start anew. His time for adventure and travel was over. He was well off where he was. For better or worse he had become a Bostonian.

[20] *The Gentleman's Magazine, and Historical Chronicle*, vol. CI (January–June 1831).

CHAPTER V

The Boston Citizen

THE HOUSE IN WHICH JOHN SMIBERT AND HIS WIFE TOOK UP THEIR residence after their marriage is located in the advertisement which he placed in the *Boston Gazette* for October 21, 1734, as "in Queen Street, between the Town House and the Orange Tree." After the Revolution Queen Street became Court Street, the name which it still bears. The "Town House" is now called The Old State House and still stands at the head of State Street. The "Orange Tree" was the tavern of that name which stood at the corner of Hanover and Sudbury Streets, one block north of Smibert's residence, from the end of the seventeenth to the end of the eighteenth century, and which from 1716 on was the point of departure for the stage coach running to Newport.

The site of Smibert's residence is now occupied by brick buildings erected in the earlier half of the nineteenth century and numbered 5, 7, and 9 Scollay Square, including also a subway entrance. They stand between Brattle Street and Cornhill, both of which have been cut through since Smibert lived there, slicing off strips of land from either side of his property. In the eighteenth century the center of the present Scollay Square was occupied by a long block called the Scollay Buildings, at the southern end of which was the Free Writing School. On each side of these buildings there was a narrow road, barely wide enough for two carts to pass, and it was not until the buildings were removed, leaving an open space, that that part of Court Street became known as Scollay Square. To the west, beyond the Scollay Buildings, the easternmost of the three peaks which gave the Boston peninsula the earlier name of Trimount rose sharply to the height of the roof of the present Courthouse, which stands upon its greatly reduced crest.

As already stated, the house had belonged to the Williams family for eighty years, and it was occupied by descendants of the first Nathaniel Williams until the death of John Smibert's last surviving

child, Dr. Williams Smibert. It must have been rather large, for it had
long been divided into two apartments, east and west. The west side
of the house had served as both residence and shop for Mary Williams'
great-grandfather and grandfather; the east side had generally been
occupied by married daughters of the family. Smibert and his wife
occupied the western half, which Dr. Williams bequeathed to Mary
Smibert at his death. The eastern half he left to his other daughter,
Anne, who, in 1736, married Dr. Belcher Noyes,[1] and who occupied
it until 1743, when Smibert bought it, no doubt to accommodate his
growing family and to give him space for the large painting room in
which he kept the collection of paintings and casts which he had
brought from Europe. The house was admirably located for his purpose, in what was the best residential part of the town, but near the
business and governmental district. For nearly thirty years after Smibert's death his art collection remained in his painting room, which,
after the death of his nephew and business associate John Moffatt, was
rented as a studio by a succession of young painters until early in the
nineteenth century. No other building in the colonies came so near
being what might be called an "art center" for the greater part of a
century.[2]

In this house Mary Smibert promptly began the task of rearing a
family, bearing her husband seven sons and two daughters in the less
than twenty-one years of their married life.[3] The tragically high infant
mortality of the period is illustrated in this family, for when Smibert
died in April 1751 only three sons survived him. His nephew, John
Moffatt, writing the following year to Arthur Pond, says, "He left a
Widow and three sons, the eldest is apprentice to a Merchant, the
second inclines to Painting and seems to me of a Promising Genius,

---

[1] Belcher Noyes was a nephew of Governor Belcher, and brother of Mather Byles'
second wife.

[2] The foregoing information about Smibert's residence is drawn from an article by
Walter K. Watkins, "The New England Museum and the Home of Art in Boston,"
Bostonian Society Publications, II (second series, 1917), 103–130.

[3] This is the number of children given in the draft of the epitaph sent by John
Moffatt to Arthur Pond to be cut upon the monument which it was proposed to
erect over Smibert's grave. In the Report of the Record Commissioners for the City
of Boston the record of births for the first half of the eighteenth century is very
incomplete and the births of only the first four of Smibert's children are recorded:
Alison, b. May 14, 1731 (named for Smibert's mother and oldest sister); William, b.
Jan. 29, 1732/33; John, b. Nov. 24, 1733; Nathaniel, b. Jan. 20, 1734/35. The names of
the five younger children are found in the Records of the West Church, New England
Hist. Gen. Society Register, Oct. 1937, as having been baptized, probably in each case
only a few days or weeks after birth, as follows: "April 23, 1738, John Son of John
and Mary Smibert"; "Oct 14, 1739, sam: smibert son of John and Mary"; "Nov. 8,
1741, Thomas son of John smibert and Mary"; "July 24, 1746. Thomas son of John and
Mary Smibert, Mary Anne Daughter of John and Mary smibert" (twins).

the youngest is at Grammar School." [4] The first mentioned of these sons was the one whose name appears in the birth records as William but who was later known as Williams.[5] After his apprenticeship had been served he took up the study of medicine and in the seventeen-fifties traveled to his father's native Edinburgh, where he took the degree of Doctor of Medicine in 1762. He came back to Boston and set up as a practicing physician, living in the ancestral residence with his cousin John Moffatt. He died unmarried in 1774, while still in middle age, and with him passed the last of the offspring of John and Mary Smibert. He bequeathed the house to Moffatt, "for his affection shown me all my life." [6] The second son, with an inclination to painting, was Nathaniel. He sought to follow in his father's footsteps, and a few portraits can be definitely assigned to him, but he died in 1756 before his twenty-second birthday.[7] The youngest, still "at Grammar School," was the second of the sons named John. Nothing more is heard of him and he probably died at an early age.

Smibert's nephew, John Moffatt, who played so important a part in the life of the family, was born in Edinburgh about 1704, or perhaps later. The date of his arrival in Boston is not recorded, but it was probably before 1740. That he assisted his uncle not only in managing the "colour shop," but in painting portraits seems at least possible because Williams Smibert, in his will dated 1770, describes him as "Mr. John Moffatt of Boston, Painter." Moffatt also thus described himself in the opening words of his will, "I, John Moffatt, Painter," and the same term is used by his executor, Belcher Noyes, in the inventory of his estate. Since the word "Painter" was in common use in England as the designation of a portrait painter, e.g., "John Smibert, Painter," the implication is that Moffatt regarded himself as a professional artist, rather than merely as a dealer in paints and artists' materials. It is possible that he may have had some training as a painter before coming to America, or Smibert may have trained him as an assistant. On the other hand Dr. Benjamin Waterhouse, writing in 1815 (nearly forty years after Moffatt's death) to President Dwight of Yale about Smibert's "Bermuda Group," said "Mr. John Moffatt was a dealer in

[4] See Smibert's epitaph, Chapter VII.
[5] See Appendix 2.
[6] John Moffatt, dying in 1777, bequeathed the house to his brother, Dr. Thomas Moffatt, provided he should return to America to claim it within three years. Thomas Moffatt, as noted in Chapter III, was an ardent Loyalist, who fled to England at the outbreak of the Revolution. He probably had no desire to return, nor would he have been permitted to do so in any case. Eventually the house passed to Suriah Waite, a widow, upon whose death in 1795 it was sold to William Smith. In 1818 it became the New England Museum. See Appendix 3.
[7] See Appendix 4.

paints, canvas and brushes, and, in that line the right hand man of Mr. Smibert," which indicates that he was not remembered as a professional artist. If he did assist Smibert in portrait painting such participation may explain the unevenness of style in some of Smibert's later portraits and also the existence of portraits which must have been painted after Smibert's death but which resemble his work save that they are not quite good enough to be his. It is at least possible that they may be from Moffatt's brush.

The painting of portraits doubtless occupied much of Smibert's time for the first three or four years after his settlement in Boston, for persons who could afford them naturally took advantage of the presence of the most distinguished artist who had ever lived in Boston. Although Smibert signed and dated the Ferne portraits and the picture of Berkeley which he painted in England, and probably all his portraits painted there, as well as the large canvas of the "Bermuda Group" painted after his arrival at Newport, it does not appear that he either signed or dated any of his later pictures here. His signature has not been found on a single one of the other portraits painted in Newport, or on those painted after he came to Boston which can be accepted as unquestionably his, though some bear a later inscription by which they can be dated. It is true that a number of portraits bearing an alleged signature and a date later than 1729 have come to light in the last twenty years, but unfortunately the authenticity of every one of them is open to doubt (see Descriptive Catalogue, Section E). Perhaps he felt that, although in England it had been desirable to sign his paintings to distinguish them from the work of other men, here the absence of rivals made his signature seem superfluous. As a result the date of many of his American portraits can be determined only approximately, by the apparent age of the subject, or when the date of the subject's death or the reproduction of the portrait in a dated mezzotint gives us the latest possible date of painting.

There is a rather large group of portraits, in addition to those of Samuel Sewall, Byfield, and Mascarene, already mentioned, which must have been executed either in 1730 or in the next two or three years. Thus the fine portrait of Samuel Browne of Salem must have been done before the subject's death in 1731. It ranks with the portrait of Browne's brother-in-law, Judge Benjamin Lynde, Sr., painted six or seven years later, as among Smibert's finest pieces, in marked contrast to his full-length portrait of Samuel's son William Browne, done in 1744. But Smibert was at his best in portraying at half-length elderly men of distinction, and at his worst in full-length pictures. The portraits of Daniel Oliver and his wife must also have been done

Daniel Oliver

before the former's death in April 1732, and the second portrait of Mrs. Oliver as a widow must have been done soon afterwards. Daniel Oliver is shown as a gaunt old man, and Lawrence Park has called it "one of the best Smiberts, particularly in the characterization of the face." The figure is unusually well posed and has dignity. The group showing Daniel Oliver's three sons, Daniel, Andrew, and Peter, must also have been painted in 1730 or 1731. Although the painting is characteristic of Smibert, there has been some doubt as to whether it could be his work because the younger Daniel had died of smallpox in London in 1727, three or four years before the earliest possible date at which Smibert could have painted the picture. His inclusion in the group is, however, easily explained. The young man before his death had had a miniature of himself painted in London to be sent home to his parents. This miniature (now owned by W. H. P. Oliver, Esq.), when compared with the figure of Daniel, Jr., in the group portrait, indicates that Smibert reproduced in life size the pose and features shown in the miniature—though he altered somewhat the style of the wig—thus meeting the desire of the parents that their dead son should be included with the living ones in the group.

The portrait of Daniel Oliver, Sr., like that of Samuel Browne and others, includes one item of costume which may be mentioned here, as it is very characteristic of Smibert's portraits of elderly men. It is the long steenkirk tie with fringed ends, hanging down over the coat. It is to be seen in the portraits of Sewall, Byfield, and Benjamin Lynde, Sr., and in those of Charles Chambers, Francis Brinley, and Richard Waldron: the loose ends are drawn through a button hole in the coat or waistcoat, perhaps to keep them from falling into the chowder when the wearer was dining. The name and fashion of the loose steenkirk tie are said to have come from the battle of Steenkirk at which the French nobles went into action having dressed in too great a hurry to tie their cravats. In the seventeen-thirties elderly gentlemen in Boston still wore the steenkirk, but among the younger generation, more concerned to follow the latest fashions, it was giving way to the ruffles down the shirt front which are typical of the portraits of men in the succeeding decades. All of the above-mentioned group of portraits are finely executed pictures.

The existence of a full-length portrait of Governor Jonathan Belcher has hitherto been unrecorded, but that Smibert executed such a commission is clear from a letter written by John Boydell of Boston to John Yeamans, then in London. In this letter, dated Boston, March 1, 1730/31, Boydell describes the refusal of the General Court to settle the Governor's salary and goes on to say: "His [Governor

Belcher's] Picture is a Drawing at full length to answer the King and Queen's it's Supposed he intended it as a present to the General Court if they had fixed his Salary. Mr. Smibert the Painter has £80 for drawing it." [8] Boydell was in a position to be well informed about the political situation.[9] His statement seems to indicate that either he or someone of his acquaintance had actually seen the portrait, and is so explicit that there is no reason for rejecting it. The price which Smibert received seems a very high one, but it is figured in "New England currency" (paper), which in 1730 was worth only a little more than one fourth the value of sterling. £80 "old tenor" would, therefore, have been equivalent to about £20 sterling, a price which Smibert might well have charged the Governor for a full-length portrait.[10]

Belcher never gave his portrait to the General Court, with which he had a standing quarrel throughout his governorship. In 1746 he was appointed governor of New Jersey, where he had a happier time. He interested himself in the foundation of the College of New Jersey (now Princeton University) to which, shortly before his death, he gave a full-length portrait of himself. Unfortunately this portrait was destroyed during the Revolution, and the name of the painter is not recorded, but in all probability it was Smibert's.

One of the best of all Smibert's portraits is that which he painted of Chief Justice Lynde, Sr., of Salem. It portrays with skill and vigor the old man's fine, intelligent face, and would be a credit to any artist. Augustus T. Perkins, in the communication about Smibert which he made in 1878 to the Massachusetts Historical Society, stated that in England Smibert had been "patronized by the learned and eccentric Earl of Bristol, by whom he was probably introduced to his cousin, Chief Justice Lynde, of Salem. . . . Soon after his arrival, he visited as a guest his friend, Chief Justice Lynde, whose portrait he painted." [11] This information would be interesting if it were well founded. I have, however, found no earlier confirmation for Perkins'

[8] Ms. letter in the Massachusetts Historical Society, Boston.
[9] He was Registrar of Probate for Suffolk County as early as 1723, postmaster 1732–1734, and publisher of the Boston Gazette 1732–1739. He had been close to Governor Shute and apparently had a hand in managing Shute's property interests in Boston after Shute returned to England. Yeamans had married a daughter of Colonel Shrimpton and was Shute's nephew.
[10] The value of the colonial paper money declined to a still lower figure, so that in December 1734 a man in Boston noted that he had bought a bill of exchange on London for £100 for which he had had to pay £525 "New England currency." The financial depression in Boston at that period gives point to the question in Berkeley's letter to Smibert of May 31, 1735, inviting him to settle in Ireland, when he asks "whether it would be disagreeable to you to receive gold instead of paper."
[11] Proceedings of the Massachusetts Historical Society, XVI, 392, 396.

painters who immediately followed Smibert in New England, Robert Feke and Joseph Blackburn.

Smibert was commonly less successful in his portraits of women than with his men, but several of them, dating from the first half of this decade, deserve mention. One of them is the picture of Mary Williams, who became his wife. Presumably it was painted about the time of their marriage, for it shows a pleasing young woman of fresh complexion, though no outstanding beauty. In spite of his personal interest in the subject the portrait, like most of those in which he represented young or middle-aged women, lacks the vigorous realism shown in many of his portraits of men and repeats the fashionable formula of sloping shoulders, elongated neck, and overlarge "doe eyes" which make his women subjects look pretty much alike. The portrait of Mrs. Thomas Bulfinch, one of his best, illustrates the same conventional pattern, but the subject seems more of a person, perhaps because of her greater maturity.

Perhaps the finest of all his portraits of women is that showing Mrs. John Erving, an upstanding woman of character and charm, about thirty years of age. The noble portrait of Mrs. Stephen Sewall, now at the Essex Institute at Salem, Massachusetts, has much of the vigor and individuality which characterize Smibert's portraits of older men. Mrs. Sewall is portrayed seated in an armchair, holding a very large open Bible, from which she has looked up. The austere figure has much dignity and the face of this mother of ten children shows strength of character and the serenity of old age at the end of a fruitful life. Though it lacks the superb technique and decorative quality of Whistler's "Portrait of my Mother," painted about a hundred and thirty-five years later, this picture of an old New England matron may be regarded as a not unworthy prototype of that celebrated painting. Another of these portraits of women by Smibert is his delightful little idyl of Mary Pemberton painted about 1734 when she was sixteen or seventeen years old. It is as pleasing a representation of graceful girlhood as his portrait of Mrs. Sewall is of dignified old age.

After the first few years of Smibert's residence in Boston the number of commissions seems to have slackened. At least there are fewer portraits which can be assigned to the period 1735–1740. And with the passage of years, the lack of competition, and poor health, including deterioration of eyesight, Smibert grew more careless except when some unusual situation caused him to exert himself, and his portraits painted after 1740 are commonly less successful than those of his first decade in Boston. After all, Boston, although probably at that time the best single field in the colonies for a portrait painter, was still too small a town to keep an artist fully occupied. Furthermore, times were hard, and the paper money was at a heavy discount.

With spare time on his hands, and with the increasing expenses of a growing family, Smibert was faced with the alternative of becoming an itinerant artist, like other European painters who visited the colonies, or of opening a shop to keep himself busy and to add to his income. The uncertainties, discomforts, and hazards which were the inevitable lot of an itinerant painter would have caused him to consider such a career only as a last resort. He had already worked in Newport. The only other towns near Boston where commissions were at all likely were Salem and Portsmouth. Salem could be reached in half a day, Portsmouth in two days, and Smibert may have gone to either place to execute his portraits of women living there, or persons in these towns who wanted to have their pictures painted could come to Boston for the purpose. But to go to New York and Philadelphia involved a long journey with uncertain results, and to secure the patronage of the planters in Virginia or South Carolina meant even longer absences from home and greater discomfort in travel. It is true that a number of portraits of persons resident in New York or Philadelphia have been attributed to Smibert, generally by an unfounded family tradition, but if he painted any of them, it must be assumed that the subjects journeyed to Boston and were painted there.

Since he was very comfortably situated at home, with space in his own house which had formerly been used as a shop, it was quite natural that, when the first rush of commissions following his arrival slackened, he should have set up the first "colour shop" in Boston, instead of venturing further afield. His advertisement in the *Boston News-Letter* for October 10–17, 1734, and the *Boston Gazette* for October 14–21, reveals his decision. It reads:

JOHN SMIBERT, PAINTER, sells all Sorts of Colours, dry or ground, with Oils, and Brushes, Fans of Several Sorts, the best Mezotints, Italian, French, Dutch and English Prints, in Frames and Glasses, or without, by Wholesale or Retail at Reasonable Rates: at his House in Queen Street, between the Town-House and the Orange Tree, Boston.[14]

[14] Quoted from G. F. Dow, *Arts and Crafts in New England* (1927), p. 3. Smibert was not, however, the earliest printseller in Boston. In 1712 some pictures taken from a prize ship were sold at public vendue. As early as 1721 William Price advertised in the *Gazette* "a Choice parcel of the best Sort of Prints & Maps lately brought from London," with similar advertisements as late as 1750. He also sold music books, musical instruments, and furniture. See Dow, cited above. It does not appear, however, that he sold colors or other artists' materials.

Although the opening words of this advertisement may mean that he was prepared to sell paints and brushes suitable for house-painting and similar work,[15] there is at least the suggestion that there were in Boston persons who would patronize a shop where artists' materials were obtainable. The offering of fans indicates that the daughters of the Puritans were not averse to such aids to cool flirtation. And prints were the only form of picture available for domestic decoration, except painted portraits. They had, of course, to be imported, except for the mezzotints of local celebrities which Peter Pelham was producing from time to time.

Smibert's shop was maintained long after his death by his widow and his nephew, John Moffatt. Either, however, it was not at first as profitable as he had hoped, or he found himself encumbered with the art collection which he had brought from Europe. Whichever the cause, seven months later he advertised a sale of a part of his collection in the *Boston News-Letter* of May 15–22, 1735. The advertisement ran:

JOHN SMIBERT. To be Sold, at Mr. Smibert's, in Queen Street, on Monday, the 26th Instant, A Collection of valuable PRINTS, engrav'd by the best Hands, after the finest Pictures in Italy, France, Holland, and England, done by Raphael, Michael Angelo, Poussin, Rubens, and other the greatest Masters, containing a great Variety of Subjects, as History, etc, most of the Prints very rare, and not to be met with except in private Collections: being what Mr. Smibert collected in the above-mentioned Countries, for his own private Use & Improvement: The Price of each single Print or Book to be mark'd upon 'em, and to be the same, which Mr. Smibert, who bought 'em at the best Hand, himself gave for them.

At the same Time, there will be Sold a Collection of Pictures in Oil Colours; the price of each Picture, to be mark'd upon it.
N.B. The Sale will last from Monday morning till the Saturday Evening following, and no longer: Those Prints that shall remain then unsold, will be sent to England.

A fortnight later, in the *News-Letter* of June 5–12, he advertised a continuation of the sale.

---

[15] Mr. John Marshall Phillips reports the following entries in the account book of Andrew Belcher at the Massachusetts Historical Society.

1747? To p^d Jno Smibert in part for oil & paints &c for Warehouse & New Garden Fence at Milton p Rect on Back of his Acct.   41.4
1750
Apr. 2 Cash p^d Smibert and Moffat for linseed oil & Sundry Paints for Second paint^g of the Open Garden Fence Front Battery etc.   31.10

JOHN SMIBERT. At the Desire of several Gentlemen who were hindered the last week from being present at Mr. Smibert's Sale, it will be continued till Saturday next; and those Prints that shall then remain unsold, will be sent to England.[16]

Evidently the prints, which were more marketable, were the chief items in this sale, the paintings being subsidiary, and there is ample evidence that Smibert retained a considerable collection of his own copies of Italian paintings.

Smibert's literary education had not gone far. Aside from the two volumes of Allan Ramsay's *Poems* and Alexander Gordon's *Itinerarium Septentrionale* to which he had subscribed while in England and presumably brought with him to this country, we know the titles of only three books owned by him. Of these one was a copy of Captain John Smith's *Generall Historie of Virginia, New England, and the Summer Isles* (Bermuda), of 1624, which we may well believe he purchased in London while considering Berkeley's proposal to emigrate to America, and which has somehow found its way to the Archives Building at Halifax, Nova Scotia, with his name in it. The other two books were Campbell's pamphlet, *The Apostles no Enthusiasts*, and Pricke's *Perspective*, which he asked Arthur Pond of London to send out to him. But he must have had some other books, besides "books of prints," since the inventory of his estate includes a "library" of rather low valuation.

Probably he was not much of a reader, and it is clear that letter writing was a labor. Bishop Berkeley implies as much in his letter of May 1735, already quoted. But Smibert did make some effort to keep in touch with his friends in Great Britain. His heart must have been warmed by a letter he received in 1736 from the friend of his youth, Allan Ramsay.

Edinburgh, May 10. 1736.
My dear old Friend,
    Your health and happiness are ever ane addition to my satisfaction. God make your life ever easy and pleasant—half a century of years have now row'd o'er my pow, that begins now to be lyart [liard, gray]; yet, thanks to my Author, I eat, drink, and sleep as sound as I did twenty years syne; yes, I laugh heartily too, and find as many subjects to employ that faculty upon as ever; fools, fops, and knaves, grow as rank as formerly; yet here and there are to be found good and worthy men, who are ane honour to humane life. We have small hopes of seeing you again in our old world; then let us be virtuous, and hope to meet in heaven. My good auld wife is still my bed-fellow; my son

[16] Dow, p. 3.

Allan [17] has been pursuing your science since he was a dozen years auld—was with Mr. Hyffidg,[18] at London, for some time about two years ago: has been since at home, painting here like a Raphael—set out for the seat of the Beast, beyond the Alps, within a month hence— to be away about two years.—I'm sweer to part with him, but canna stem the current, which flows from the advice of his patrons, and his own inclinations. I have three daughters, one of seventeen, one of sixteen, one of twelve years old, and no re-waly'd draggle among them, all fine girls. These six or seven years past I have not wrote a line of poetry; I e'en gave o'er in good time, before the coolness of fancy that attends advanced years should make me risk the reputation I had acquired.

> Frae twenty-five to five-and-forty
> My Muse was nowther sweer nor dorty;
> My Pegasus wad break his tether,
> E'en at the shagging of a feather,
> And throw ideas scour like drift,
> Streaking his wings up to the lift:
> Then, then my saul was in a low,
> That gart my numbers safely row,
> But eild and judgment gin to say,
> Let be your sangs, and learn to pray.

I am, Sir, your friend and servant,
Allan Ramsay.[19]

We have occasional glimpses of Smibert's activities as a householder and citizen. In 1734 he was excused, "for reasons given by him," from duty as constable, which able-bodied male citizens were supposed to take in rotation. In 1735 he gave £15 to the workhouse. In

[17] Allan Ramsay, Jr., born Edinburgh 1713, died Dover 1784. He went to London about 1731, and studied for two years under Hans Huyssing. He returned to Edinburgh, where he began painting portraits. In the spring of 1736 he set out for Italy, reaching Rome in October, and remaining in Italy for some three years. He was back in Edinburgh about 1740, and painted many portraits there until 1754 or later, when he removed to London. He was very successful there, especially with his portraits of women, his work being more in demand than even that of Reynolds. He succeeded Shackleton as Painter-in-Ordinary to George III. The latter enjoyed giving away portraits of himself, as marks of royal favor, and Ramsay spent much of his time producing these likenesses, with the aid of a staff of assistants. Late in life he went again to Italy, and died at Dover on his way home.
[18] The copyist or typesetter for The Gentleman's Magazine evidently misread Ramsay's handwriting. The person referred to was Hans Huyssing, a Swede born in Stockholm, who came to London about 1700 as pupil and assistant to Michael Dahl, whose style he imitated and to whose practice he succeeded. Huyssing painted many portraits, and was under royal patronage. He was not a great painter, but Allan Ramsay, Jr., could not have had a better initiation into the career of a popular artist.
[19] The Gentleman's Magazine, LIV, 672 (September 1784).

1740 he was a member of a committee appointed to report on the feasibility of placing a battery on Long Wharf. In 1747 he was a member of another committee "to consider what will be most for the advantage of the Town to do with the dirt in the streets."

In January 1736/37, Smibert was one of seventeen persons from six of the churches in Boston who met to organize a new religious society, the West Church. They proceeded to erect a small, wooden meetinghouse on what was then the northwestern edge of the town. The only known picture of the building, which it is possible Smibert may have designed, is taken from a sketch of the Battle of Bunker Hill made by a British officer from the northern slope of Beacon Hill, looking across the Charles River to the Charlestown shore. The roof and pleasing open spire of the church are shown in the foreground.[20] The spire was soon after demolished by the British who suspected that it had been used for signaling to the Revolutionary Army. The church itself was replaced in 1809 by the brick edifice on the same site, on what is now Cambridge Street, west of Bowdoin Square, a building which still stands but is now used as a branch of the Public Library.

The new church was considerably further from Smibert's residence than was the Old South, and, in view of that fact and of the long connection of his wife's family with the older church, the only plausible explanation of Smibert's action in transferring his membership is that he found the excellent Rev. Joseph Sewall's theology too conservative. From its beginning and throughout the eighteenth century the West Church was the most liberal in the town. Its first minister, who baptized Smibert's last five children, was Rev. William Hooper, whose Arminian tendencies involved him in controversy with some of the other ministers. In 1746 Hooper scandalized his flock by abruptly sailing for England to seek Anglican ordination, returning later to become the first rector of Trinity Church in Boston. His successor at the West Church was Rev. Jonathan Mayhew, who for nearly twenty years was an eloquent and courageous leader of liberal religious and political thought. In January 1750, fourteen months before Smibert's death, young Mr. Mayhew preached a series of three sermons against arbitrary rule which stirred Boston to the depths and which John Adams later called "the opening gun of the Revolution." Smibert's transfer of membership from the Old South to the West Church may indicate the trend of his own thinking in religion and politics.

His church membership did not prevent him from becoming a

[20] Woodcut reproduction in *The West Church, Boston, Commemorative Services* (1887), p. 56.

Mrs. John Erving

slave owner. The rise of antislavery sentiment in New England was, indeed, beginning, and as early as 1700 Judge Samuel Sewall had published a broadside of protest entitled *The Selling of Joseph*, but in the first half of the eighteenth century a good many Negro slaves were kept for domestic service in New England, and by clergymen as well as by laymen. A Negro girl named "Phillis" is included in the inventory of Smibert's estate, and that he owned at least one other slave is proved by the following advertisement in the *Boston Gazette* for October 3–10, 1737:

JOHN SMIBERT. Ran-away on the 26th of this Instant September, from Mr. John Smibert of Boston, Painter, a Negro man Servant named Cuffee, who formerly belonged to Capt. Prince, and understands something of the business of a sailor, he is about 22 Years of Age, and speaks good English, a pretty tall well shap'd Negro with bushy Hair, has on a large dark colour'd Jacket, a pair of Leather Breeches stain'd with divers sorts of paints, and a pair of blue stockings. Whoever shall take up said Runaway and him safely convey to his aforesaid Master in Boston, shall have Three Pounds Reward and all necessary Charges paid. All Masters of Vessels are hereby warned against carrying off said Servant on penalty of the Law in that Case made and provided.

It does not appear that Cuffee was ever restored to his master, and we may be permitted to hope that he made good his escape.

More to Smibert's credit was his employment as architect for Faneuil Hall, which the wealthy and generous Peter Faneuil in 1740 offered to build in Dock Square as a gift to the town, to house the public market which had until then been held there in the open air. The gift was gratefully accepted, as was the proposal to include a much needed hall for public meetings on the floor above the market. The building was "completed in a most substantial and elegant manner in September, 1742, after a design by Mr. Smibert," as Charles Bulfinch noted in a memorandum written sixty-five years later.

The first public meeting in the hall was held on September 13 of that year, at which a committee of distinguished citizens was appointed to wait upon Mr. Faneuil and to convey to him the town's vote of thanks. The meeting also voted "That in testimony of the town's gratitude to Peter Faneuil, Esq., and to perpetuate his memory, that the Hall over the Market Place, be named Faneuil Hall, and at all times hereafter, be called and known by that name. And as a further testimony of respect, it was voted, that Mr. Faneuil's picture be drawn at full length, at the expense of the town, and placed in the Hall." [21]

[21] Abram E. Brown, *Faneuil Hall and Faneuil Hall Market* (1900), pp. 85–86.

Smibert was employed to paint the portrait, the history of which is traced in later votes of the town's Board of Selectmen.[22] At a meeting on March 30, 1743, soon after Faneuil's death, it was voted "that Messrs. Jeffries, Hancock & Cooke be a Committee to provide a Frame for the Picture of Peter Faneuil Esq. Deced in the best manner they can."[23]

The following December they wrote to Christopher Kilby in London:

Boston, Decr. 7, 1743.

Sir,

The Inhabitants of the Town of Boston at a meeting in September, 1742. Voted, That the Select men of this Town be desired to procure the picture of Peter Faneuil Esqr. to be put in Faneuil Hall at the Expence of the Town. which Picture being now furnished by Mr. Smibert We find upon Enquiry that a Frame for said Picture can be got in London Cheaper & better than with Us. We therefore beg the favour of You Sir to procure & Send a Neat Gold Carved Frame of Eight feet in length & Five Feet in Wedth by the first Ship in as small a box as may be, as it will reduce the Freight. Your Expence for the same shall be remitted as soon as known, which Frame we hope may be bought for about Eight Guineas.

We are Sir
Your most humble Servants,
J. J. &c. Select men.[24]

On January 13, 1761, the interior of the Hall was gutted by fire, though the exterior walls were uninjured. It was rebuilt in 1763, the cost of restoration being defrayed from a lottery granted by the General Court. The town records were saved from the fire, as apparently was the portrait of Faneuil, though too badly injured to be rehung. Forty-four years later, on February 4, 1807, the selectmen voted "to appropriate 350 Dollars for the purpose of procuring an elegant picture with frame complete of Peter Faneuil, Esq., to be placed in a suitable position in Faneuil Hall, Mr. Wright was desired to employ Mr. Henry Sargeant [Sargent] to paint the same in the best manner & to complete it as soon as possible."[25]

[22] I have listed this portrait as Peter Faneuil No. 1 in Section B of the Descriptive Catalogue. Probably about the same time Smibert painted the portrait of Peter Faneuil now owned by the Massachusetts Historical Society and its replica, which I have listed in Section A as Peter Faneuil No. 1 and No. 2.
[23] *Report of the Record Commissioners of the City of Boston: Selectmen's Minutes from 1742/3 to 1753*, p. 11.
[24] *Ibid.*, p. 41.
[25] *Records Relating to the Early History of Boston, Containing Minutes of the Selectmen's Meetings, 1799, to, and including, 1810* (1904), p. 325.

Henry Sargent was a portrait painter then working in Boston and his picture of Faneuil, now hanging in the hall, in its general appearance, though not in its technique, seems to be a fairly close copy of Smibert's original, of which enough may have survived the fire to serve Sargent as a guide.

This commission to Sargent followed the enlargement of Faneuil Hall which had been made a year or two earlier. As originally planned by Smibert it was only two stories high, of the same length as the present building but less than half as wide, the market on the ground floor having a single aisle flanked by a row of stalls on either side. As the population of the town grew the hall on the second floor became too small for public meetings which often were obliged to adjourn to the Old South Meeting House, and the market accommodations no doubt also became inadequate. In 1805 the selectmen accepted a plan for the enlargement of the building proposed by their chairman, the famous architect Charles Bulfinch, who was authorized to carry it into effect.

In accordance with this plan the building was more than doubled in width by an addition on the north side which provided a second aisle with rows of stalls in the market and a central entrance, and likewise doubled the seating capacity of the hall for meetings on the second floor, while a third story was added with further accommodations. As Bulfinch noted in his memorandum, "on the outside it has been the object of the architect to conform to the original stile of the building, that with the additions it should appear a uniform and consistent pile." [26] The original brick walls were retained (except on the north side) and the joints where the extensions began can still be traced in the brickwork on the southeast and southwest corners.[27] We may well be grateful that Bulfinch carefully conformed to the "stile" of the original structure, so that the exterior of the building still represents what Smibert projected, though on a larger scale. And although no picture of the original interior survives, it was probably not very different from that which the modern visitor sees.

[26] The memorandum, though unsigned and undated and written in the third person, is unquestionably in Bulfinch's handwriting. It is attached to his drawings of elevations of the enlarged hall, owned by the City of Boston.
[27] A cut of Faneuil Hall with a line showing where the new brickwork joins the old is in The Re-dedication of the Old State House (6th ed., Boston, 1893), opp. p. 151.

CHAPTER VI

The "Colour Shop"

FIVE OF SMIBERT'S LETTERS SURVIVE, AND THEY THROW SOME LIGHT on his business activities in his "colour shop," and on his relations with the friends whom he had left behind in London. On September 22, 1735, he wrote to Sueton Grant of Newport,[1] referring to a shipment sent to him which included the frames for Grant's painted coat of arms and for Rev. James McSparran's portrait, which Smibert had apparently brought to Boston, as well as a number of prints.

Sir: I suppose your patience is quite tired in expecting your arms, etc. —but it was impossible to send them sooner. the frame makers having so much work bespoke before, and being also not disposed to work any more than necessity forced, occasioned me to call upon them at least twenty times, before Mr. McSparran's frame and yours could be got from them. Last week I put them on board a Connecticut Sloop bound for your Port, Capt. Thorp. they are carefully packed up and the case is directed for you which I hope will arive safe and be to your satisfaction. Mr. McSparran's Picture is in the case which I desire you to inform him of and the reason for its not being sent sooner. give my service to him and my respects to Mrs. Grant. I am Sir your most obedient Humble Servt,

John Smibert.

In the case is

A Naval fight, Mantuanes[2]	0–16–6
Scipio's Victory, C. Cort[3]	0–11–0
the Virgin, C. Moratt[4]	0–16–0
frames for ye above	0– 6–0
the Harlots Progres—Hogarth	1– 5–0
the coat of arms	3– 0–0
a gold frame for ditto	3–10–0
a glass for ditto	0–10–0
your half of the case cost	0– 4–0
	£11– 6–6
Received	10– 0–0

The footnotes for this page appear on the following page.

The other four surviving letters written by Smibert were addressed to his London agent, Arthur Pond, and they are supplemented by two more letters which John Moffatt wrote to Pond and to his executors after Smibert's death.[5] Arthur Pond (c.1705–1758) was an etcher, painter, dealer, and art connoisseur who as a young man had traveled to Rome with Roubiliac, the sculptor. Pond was elected a Fellow of the Royal Society in 1752. Vertue, in a moment of bad temper, made a sarcastic entry about him in his notebooks: "Mr. Pond is the greatest or top virtuoso in London, followed, esteemed and cried up—Mr. Pond all in all."[6] When Smibert sailed for America he left part of his collection of pictures in Pond's care, either for sale or to be stored until he sent for them, and it was natural that he should turn to him when ordering supplies for the "colour shop" when he opened it in 1734. His earliest surviving letter to Pond is dated "Boston, Jully 1st, 1743," but it clearly indicates considerable previous correspondence between them. It is as follows:

Dear Sir:—I wrote you the 6th of May by Capt. Bonner & then troubled you with 2 Bills one on Messr; Tryons for £30 and the other on Messr: Walter Hayter & Sons for £11—the 2d Sett of which Bills are now inclosed as also a Bill of Lading for eight Guineas and twenty-five oz and a half of silver plate. I have for a long time intended to send for y[e] pictures etc which my Nephew left with you, but delayed on act. of the war, which as there is no apearance of being over think, it now best to have them over here again, for as you long ago wrote me you had sold none of them, nor thought it likely you should. I am in hopes I shal make something of them here so desires you will order them to be carefully packed up in a good case & sent by the first opportunity for this Port & insure on the Virtu[7] cargo for £150. I must further trouble

---

[1] M.H.S. Proc., XLIX, 26–28 (October 1915). Sueton Grant came to America in 1725 and settled at Newport, R.I., as a merchant. He was a member of the Philosophical Society. He was killed by an explosion of gunpowder in 1744.
[2] Giovanni Battista Britano, called Mantuano (c. 1500). This plate is described as a "large naval Combat, from his own design, 1538."
[3] Cornelius Cort (1536–1578). The plate is better known as the "Battle of the Elephants," and was made from a picture by Raphael.
[4] Carlo Maratti (1625–1713). He made a set of plates of the life of the Virgin, from his own composition.
[5] Part of Smibert's letter of March 15, 1744/45 is reproduced with our illustrations. All four letters were printed, with a good many minor errors in transcription, in The Smibert-Moffatt Letters, by Worthington C. Ford (M.H.S. Proc., XLIX, 28–30). The original of the first letter was formerly owned by Charles Henry Hart of Philadelphia, from whom it was purchased by the late Thomas B. Clarke of New York. The originals of the other letters are in the British Museum. Two of them are also printed in Whitley's Artists and their Friends in England, 1700–1800, I, 64–66.
[6] Whitley, I, 18.
[7] Virtu-art.

you to buy me 3 doz ¾ Cloaths strained, & two whole Length Cloaths which pray order to be good and carefully rolled up & put in a Case. Fann Paper ten Reams this is an article which we shal probably want considerable of so would desire you to write ye mans name you buy it of & where he lives that we may send to him directly without troubling you again. there are many women that paints Fanns for the country use and as they buy the Collours of us the paper has of late come naturally in to be an article in the Shop let it be of the sort commonly used for cheap Fanns & should be glad ye man would Send a Sheet or 2 of the different sorts of paper with ye prices. Lake of the common midling sort about two Guineas and of good Lake about two Guineas more. Prussian Blew 50 l[8] @ 2 shillings per pound. Do 6 l @ 20 shill or a Guinea per pound. Do 6 l @ 18 shill. per pound. that may be had cheapest of ye maker M Mitchell at Hoxton who you may send to by a peny post letter or a Porter. the old Cups and spoons are a commission from my Wiffe who desires you will be so good as to get her a Silver tea pott of the midle size but rather inclining to ye Large and weighty ye fashion she leaves intirely to you only would not have the top with hinges, but to take of. I have sent a Sketch of ye Arms which I know you wil take care to get done by a good engraver with proper Ornaments. I do not expect the old silver wil pay for the tea pott which I would have a pretty one. what remains of ye money after paying for those articles and al charges on Board please to lay out in gold leaf.

I am sorry the State of the Virtu is at so low an ebb. if the arts are about to leave Great Britain I wish they may take their flight into our new world that they may, at least remain in some part of the British dominions.[9] remember me to al my old friends among the Painters. I would willingly have acknowledged your favours by something from this Country but can think of nothing worth sending that is our own produce. amongst ye Pictures with you my Nephew tells me he thinks you used to like ye Venus Nymphs etc. by Poolenburgh. be so good as to accept of that picture to remember me by or any other of the Pictures you like except ye Scipio [10] & if there be any of ye drawings that you fancy pray take them. when you write me let me know the State of Painting, who makes a figure, & what eminent ones are gone of ye stage. as for my self I have as much as keeps me employed, has my health better than I could have expected, having near 3 years ago recovered from a dangerous ilnes, but thank God has had no return of it. I am happy in 4 clever Boys & lives as easily as my friend could wish me. ye affairs of the shop with my Nephew goes on well he Joins me in respects to

[8] Here, and elsewhere l = lb. = pound weight.
[9] This sounds like an echo of Berkeley's verses, quoted in Chapter II. By "the State of the Virtu" he means what we should call "the level of art."
[10] This was evidently the copy by Smibert of Nicholas Poussin's painting, the "Continence of Scipio."

your Father & to Messr. Knaptons.[11] I shal not make any further ap-
pollgys for the trouble now given you only assures you I wil not try
your patience every year but only now and then. I am Sir your most
obliged humble ser^t.

John Smibert.

P.S. please to insure besides ye £150 on the Pictures, etc. at your house,
£50 more for the money you lay out in al £200 I wish you could send
2 copies of a Pamphlet Published by A Millar entitled as I remember ye
Apostles no Enthusiasts by—Campbell of St. Andrews.[12]

Nearly nine months later Smibert wrote again to Pond.

Boston, March 24, 1743/4.

Dear Sir: I had the favour of yours by Capt. Anstill with the Virtu
Cargo and bill. the other things in good order. for your care of which
and present of the prints I am much your debtor. You know I was always fond of Landskips so that you could not have sent anything more
to my taste and I assure you I esteem them as the finest Collection of
Prints in that way I ever saw. the smal sett I have sold and desire you
will send 5 setts of the 7 numbers on the smal paper which with the
sett already received wil amount to eight guineas allowing the 20 per
cent for those who sell them again. its probable more will sell but we
wil try them first, you may send one of every Print you do perhaps some
of them may hit the General taste of this place.

All the things you sent are good and bought well. The season for
Fann painting is not yet come so there has been no opportunity to try
the papers and mounts but no doubt they will answer. I now trouble
you for some small matters to come with the Prints as by invoice
anexed. to pay for these things inclosed are a Bill for £12.12.0 on Fredk
Frankland Esq and a Bill of Lading for some gold and silver as is speci-
fied in the Bill. We are very sorry for the loss of Mr. Charles Knapton
who was a worthy man. Your act. of the state of painting and the Painters
with you shows a very fickle temper and is no recommendation of your
great Town. as you do not mention the Lady's head after Titian to be
amongst the Pictures stolen by the frame maker I hope you forgot to
put it up with the others and that its stil at your house. if it is, be so good
as to send it with the things now wrote for. the tea pot is a mighty
pretty one and so much liked that you [will] be troubled with my nephew's request for a friend. He joins with me in our Respects to your
Father and al friends I am, Dear Sir your most obliged Humble Sert

John Smibert.

---

[11] George Knapton (1698–1778) was a portrait painter. His brother Charles (1700–
1744) was associated with Pond in the publication of a volume of imitations of
original drawings by the old masters, published in 1735.
[12] Archibald Campbell (1691–1756), professor of church history in St. Andrews. The

At this point Moffatt inserted his request:

Sir:—I hope youl excuse the trouble I now give you, occasioned by the Tea Pott you sent which is admired by all the Ladies and so much that in behalf of one of them (who I assure you has great merit) I must beg the favour of you to send such another one of the same fashion and size only the top to have a neat hinge, for the payment of it the silver is appropriated. If it should not be enough to pay it and engraving the arms according to the Sketch and Insurance do not let that prevent its being done in the same manner as the last desiring you wil forgive this freedom I am Sir Your most obliged humble sert.

John Moffatt.

Smibert then continued with his list of goods desired:

half length Cloats primed 1 doz.

kit kat do 1 doz ½ to be rolled up as the last

Pallet knives 1 doz. black led pencils of different sizes about ½ a guineas' worth.

Black a more street pencils pointed about ½ a guineas' worth, but no fitches [13]

Silver leaf six thousand it cost about 10 shil per thousand

Prints 5 setts of the 7 numbers smal paper

A set of ships published by Lempriere and sold by H. Toms in Union court Holburn.

These ships I want sometimes for to be in a distant view in Portraits of Merchts etc who chuse such, so if there be any better done since send them. but they must be in the modern construction. the last edition of Perspective commonly calld Pricks,[14] the rest of the money after paying for insurance (for tho of small value yet its best to be insured) and charges please to lay out in Post paper [15] and a writting paper, called Pott paper [16] the article of paper will be easy to you as you have occasion for much, tho of another kind.

You will please to send the above out by Capt. Jones on one of the first ship.

| Coined silver sent | 13 d 10 dwt. | Gold 4 Pistol piece | 17–8 gram |
| Old Plat | 14   2 | Coined gold | £4, 13, 0. |

---

tract, printed in 1730, was entitled: *Discourse proving that the Apostles were no Enthusiasts.*

[13] A brush made of the hair of a fitchew or polecat.

[14] Robert Pricke (fl. 1669–1698), engraver. The book wanted was *Perspective Practical*, translated from the French of the Jesuit, J. Dubreuil, of which an edition was published by Pricke in 1698.

[15] A size of writing paper, the half-sheet of which when folded forms the ordinary quarto letter paper.

[16] So called from its original watermark of a pot, and suited for printing or writing paper.

Smibert's request for the prints of ships by Lempriere throws an interesting light upon the practice of artists in drawing upon prints for illustrative materials in their portraits. It was customary to show vessels at anchor or under way in portraits of merchants or naval officers, and such persons naturally wished their ships to be correctly represented. Vessels of various types appear in Smibert's portraits of Richard Bill, Charles Chambers, Peter Faneuil, Sir Richard Spry, John Turner, Sir Peter Warren, and others. Nor was the use of prints limited to the copying of such minor accessories. London prints of recent portraits of both men and women provided colonial artists with examples of pose and costume which they did not hesitate to copy rather closely. Thus Copley's portrait of Mrs. Bowers, now at the Metropolitan Museum in New York, is a copy in every detail, except the face, of Reynolds' portrait of Lady Caroline Russell, engraved by Marcadello.[17]

In July and August, 1744, Smibert was twice visited by Dr. Alexander Hamilton,[18] a Scottish physician resident in Annapolis, Maryland. Hamilton's first call was on July 24, on which occasion he was so taken with the "Scipio," the picture which Smibert a year earlier had asked Arthur Pond to send out, that he unfortunately recorded little else that he saw.

I went this night to visit Mr. Smibert, the limner, where I saw a collection of fine pictures, among the rest that part of Scipio's history in Spain where he delivers the lady to the prince to whom she had been betrothed. The passions are all well touched in the severall faces. Scipio's face expresses a majestic generosity, that of the young prince gratitude, the young lady's gratitude and modest love, and some Roman souldiers, standing under a row of pillars apart in seeming discourse, have admiration delineated on their faces. But what I admired most of the painter's fancy in this piece is an image or phantome of chastity behind the solium upon which Scipio sits, standing on tiptoe to crown him and yet appears as if she could not reach his head, which expresses a good emblem of the virtue of this action. I saw here likewise a collec-

[17] *Connoisseur* (June 1930), p. 392. The two portraits are also reproduced in J. T. Flexner's *American Art: First Flowers of Our Wilderness*, pp. 218–219.
[18] Alexander Hamilton, probably born in Edinburgh, wrote an account of his tour of the colonies undertaken in the year 1744. It was privately printed under the title of *Itinerarium* in St. Louis, 1907, edited by Albert Bushnell Hart. When Hamilton reached Newport he was taken about the town by Dr. Thomas Moffatt, "an old acquaintance and school fellow of mine." Moffatt took him to the studio of Robert Feke, the painter, of whom Hamilton left an interesting account. Moffatt may reasonably be supposed to have given Hamilton an introduction to his brother John and his uncle Smibert in Boston. The *Itinerarium*, newly edited by Carl Bridenbaugh, has been reprinted under the title of *Gentleman's Progress* by the University of North Carolina Press, 1948. The quotations from it here cited are from this later edition.

tion of good busts and statues, most of them antiques, done in clay and paste, among the rest Homer's head and a modell of the Venus of Medicis.[19]

A few days later, on August 9, Hamilton noted briefly: "I visited Mr. Smibert in the afternoon and entertained myself an hour or two with his paintings." [20]

The "Scipio" which Hamilton so much admired, and which he apparently supposed to be an original work of Smibert's rather than a copy from Poussin, is now at Bowdoin College. It caught the eye of other visitors as well, for it had a strong appeal to the moral sentiment of the times.[21] Copley was, of course, acquainted with it [22] and Stuart later called it "a first rate copy." Trumbull copied it in 1779.

The spring following Hamilton's visit we find Smibert writing again to Arthur Pond:

Boston, N.E., March 15, 1744/5

Dear Sir,–I had the favour of yours by Capt. Carrey with ye cargo in good order, for your care of which & present of ye Prints I am much obliged, ye View from Greenwich & Antiquities by P. Panini[23] please more here than ye others and I hope some number of them wil sell. last August I wrote you & inclosed a Bill for £8.8.0 on Mr. Elliakim Palmer to be laid out chiefly in Fann mounts, but I hear ye Vessel was taken & caried into France. I now enclose you ye 2d of that Bill with one for £18 on messrs. Samuell & Wm. Baker, which I must trouble you to lay out by ye invoice anexed to be sent by the first opportunity & insured.

at present here is litle talked or thought of but war, our forces are imbarking for Cape Bretton, four Vessels of force are sailed to ly off Lewisbourg harbour to prevent any succours or provisions going in. this Expedition is a great undertaking for this Country if it succeeds wil be of great importance & be a terrible blow to France as it wil effectually destroy their fishery & make ye navigation to Canada very dangerous. but if it dos not succeed we shall be almost undone here, for our best men, the flower of ye country are going & ye expence wil be a prodigious sum of money, which if we are not assisted in ye charges

[19] Gentleman's Progress, p. 114.
[20] Ibid., p. 134.
[21] That its sentimental appeal was not limited to colonials is indicated by the fact that in 1741, when the original picture was at Houghton, the Norfolk seat of the Walpole family, it was engraved by Claude Dubosc, whose portrait Smibert had painted in London. The original was later purchased, with many other pictures from the Houghton Collection, by Catherine the Great and was hung in the Hermitage in St. Petersburg.
[22] Copley-Pelham Letters (Boston, 1914), pp. 245–249.
[23] Giovanni Paolo Pannini, 1691–1764.

Smibert's Letter of March 15, 1744/45, Showing Signature

of it from home must ruin this Province. but I hope we shal not be
deserted by our Mother Country. my Nephew thanks you for the care
of his Commission which pleases much. our respects to your Father.
I am Sir your most obliged humble sert.

John Smibert.

This comes by the *Eltham* man of war, who convoys ye mast Ships.
there has been an Embargo here for more than 6 weeks & still continues.
Gold leaf 3000
Views of Greenwich and antiquities P. Panini a doz of each
¾ Cloaths 1 doz Dark Prussn: Blew 3 l about 18 or 20 Shill per l
Fann mounts 1 doz @ 8 shill. 3 doz Do @ ⅚ 20 doz do @ ⅙
40 doz @ 1 shill. and about 10 or 15 Shill. worth of coloured prints
slight and cheap for Japanning. please to advise of ye Price of Franck-
fort black by the hundred, and send a specimen of fann mounts printed
but not coloured of ye cheapest sorts.

To Mr. Arthur Pond Painter in great Queen Street Lincolns inn fields
London.

That Smibert occasionally had opportunity to pick up supplies
from other sources is suggested by the purchase of gold leaf by a
person of his name at a "vendue sale" on May 31, 1745, of articles
captured on a prize brigantine sent in to Newport by Captain John
Dennis.[24] Smibert is not known to have been in Newport at that time,
and no one else of his family name is known to have come to the
colonies, but if word of the gold leaf had reached him he might easily
have arranged to have Thomas Moffatt make the purchase for him.

The siege of Louisburg, to the preparations for which Smibert
refers in the last quoted letter, turned out happily for New England.
Louisburg was taken on June 17, 1745, and when the conquering
heroes returned, nearly a year later, there were great celebrations.
Sir William Pepperell, who had been commander in chief of the colonial troops coöperating with the British naval forces, and Sir Peter
Warren, the naval commander who had been promoted rear-admiral
for his services, arrived in Boston from Louisburg on the ship *Chester*,
on June 1, 1746, and were met with an ovation. With them, probably,
came Sir Richard Spry of the navy, who had been promoted fleet-
captain and who left Boston soon after, and General Samuel Waldo
of the American forces, who was certainly in Boston the next year.

Peter Pelham seized the opportunity to produce an engraving of
the plan of Louisburg, which was advertised in the *Boston News-
Letter* of September 4, 1746, and in the *Boston Gazette* of September
16 as follows:

[24] George H. Richardson, *Scrap-Book*, p. 140.

PLAN OF LOUISBOURG. This day is published (Price Twenty Shillings, Old Tenor.) A Plan of the City and fortress of Louisbourg: with a small plan of the Harbour. Done in Metzotinto on Royal Paper, by Mr. Pelham, from the original Drawing of *Richard* Gridley Esq: Commander of the Train of Artillery at the Siege of *Louisbourg*. Sold by J. Smibert in Queen-Street, Boston.

More important for Smibert was the demand that the leaders should have their portraits painted. It fell to him to do full lengths of Pepperell, Warren, and Waldo, a three-quarter length of Spry, and a portrait which was either full or three-quarter length of Governor William Shirley, who had taken part in the expedition. His portrait of Sir William Pepperell is one of Smibert's most pretentious and least satisfactory pictures. He was never good at standing figures, and Pepperell's body and arms are far too long in proportion to the legs, which seem to have little connection with the rest of the figure. The background shows the besieged Louisburg upon which two huge cannon balls are falling, their trajectory clearly indicated. Pepperell's self-complacency and pomposity verge on the ridiculous, and seem to suggest that Smibert may have mixed a little malicious Scottish humor with his paint. The portrait is so bad that Professor Hagen writes, "were it not for the legend on Pelham's engraving I should never believe that Smibert had anything to do with the monstrous painting in which the obese, red-coated victor of Louisburg appears to have been pasted upon a landscape back-drop . . . The execution is by some very inferior assistant." [25] The same suggestion, that Smibert had an unskilful assistant, has been advanced by Mr. Alan Burroughs as an explanation of the very inferior quality of the portrait of Mrs. William Browne. The only known person who could have assisted him from about 1740 on, and who may have done so, was his nephew John Moffatt; he may have been responsible for some of the deficiencies noted. The portrait of Pepperell, however, had a popular appeal and was promptly reproduced in a half-length mezzotint by Pelham with the inscription:

Sir William Pepperell Bar^t. Colonel of one of his Majesty's Regiments of Foot, who was Lieutenant General and Commander in Chief of the American Forces employ'd in the Expedition against the Island of Cape Breton which was happily Reduced to the Obedience of his Britannick Majesty, June the 17, 1745.
J: Smibert Pinx   *J. Pelham fecit et ex: 1747*

The portrait of Warren must have been painted in 1746, since the Admiral left Boston before the end of June in that year. In 1751

[25] *Ibid.,* pp. 58–59.

Warren wrote to Pepperell from England, "Smybert has not sent me your and Captain Spry's portraits, which I admire." [26] This would imply that he had seen both portraits before leaving for England, and is another bit of evidence that Smibert often held on to finished portraits before delivering them. Warren went on to say that he "hoped" to send his own portrait to Pepperell as a token of personal regard.[27] Unfortunately he did not mention the artist's name; there is no direct evidence that his "hope" was fulfilled, or that Smibert's picture actually made the voyage to England and return. A portrait of Warren, to which a label reading "painted in London, 1751," obviously based on Warren's letter, was later attached, did, however hang for many years in the Pepperell Mansion at Kittery, Maine, whence it eventually passed to the Portsmouth, N. H., Athenaeum. It is in all probability the one Smibert painted and which Warren did take to England. It shows Sir Peter at full length and has many of the faults which mark that of Pepperell, the pose being similarly pompous and awkward, while the legs appear on a plane nearer to the spectator than the head and body and the feet are unduly prominent. It should be said, however, that what appear to us to be the false proportions of the figures in these full-length portraits is due in part to the costume. The great length of the waistcoats tends to make the legs seem too short for the torso, while the conspicuous white and black of the stockings and shoes tends to throw them into another plane than the rest of the figure. Copley's full-length portraits of Nathaniel Sparhawk (1764) and of Jeremiah Lee (1769) have these defects in some measure, though not so glaringly as in Smibert's full-length portraits. The portrait of Sir Richard Spry at three-quarter length is a more satisfactory picture, though the right hand is clumsily painted. The Portsmouth Athenaeum also owns a portrait of Sir Charles Knowles, another naval officer at Louisburg, which has been attributed to Smibert, but it is painted in a different style and can hardly be his workmanship.

The portrait of Governor William Shirley has not been located,[28] but that one was painted by Smibert is proved by Pelham's reproduction of it in a mezzotint similar to that of Pepperell. In the mezzotint Shirley is represented at three-quarter length, but, since it would not

[26] Possibly Warren was referring to the smaller portrait of Pepperell, listed in The Descriptive Catalogue as No. 2., which was more nearly the same size as that of Spry, rather than to the portrait listed as Pepperell No. 1.
[27] Parsons, *Life of Pepperell* (3rd ed., Boston, 1856), p. 237.
[28] A portrait said to represent Shirley and signed with Smibert's name, followed by a date which appears to be 1748, was acquired by the late Thomas B. Clarke of New York and passed with his collection to the A. W. Mellon Educational and Charitable Trust, Washington, but it is certainly not the original from which Pelham made his mezzotint, since it shows a man with different features, costume, pose, and accessories.

have been politic to raise any question of distinction between the Governor and Pepperell, it is probable that the portrait was a full-length one of proportions similar to those of Pepperell and Warren. Shirley is shown standing, his head turned right nearly full front, dressed in a handsome costume with white wig, ruffles, long coat, and waistcoat with large frogs and buttons. At his side stands a table holding a plan of fortifications. His right arm, held across his body, points to a fleet of ships putting to sea from a bay with islands and a lighthouse, presumably Boston Harbor. The effusive legend reads:

His Excellency William Shirley Esqr Captain General & Governour in Chief &c of the Province of the Massachusetts Bay in New England, & Collonel of one of his Majesty's Regiments of foot. To whom this Plate (done from the original, painted by Mr. J. Smibert at the request of several Merchants & Gentlemen in Boston, as a *Memorial* of their Grateful Acknowledgments to his Excellency for his Signal Services in the Preservation of Nova Scotia from falling into the enemies hands in 1744, and the Reduction of the Island of Cape Breton to the Obedience of his Majesty in 1745) is Humbly Dedicated by his Excellency's Obedient ser^t

P. Pelham, 1747

It is impossible to pass judgment upon the unseen original, but the mezzotint seems to indicate that it was of the same general character as the portraits of Pepperell and Warren.

Not least among the conquering heroes of Louisburg whom Smibert painted was General Samuel Waldo. The record that such a portrait was executed was found in 1914 by Miss Virginia Robie in the diary of the general's first cousin, Edward Waldo of Windham, Connecticut. At this time the diary was in the hands of a descendant, Edward Waldo Pendleton, of Bloomfield Hills, near Detroit, at which time it was examined by Miss Robie, who was Mr. Pendleton's niece. She then copied from it a single entry, in which, under date of 1747, Edward Waldo described a visit to Smibert's studio, as follows:

Spent the morning with my illustrious cousin Samuel who is having his Likeness made by the renowned Mr. Smybert. It promises to reflect great Honour on Both though prodigious deare at the Price. I was favorably impressed by Mr. S. whose Ingenuity is equalled by his Industry and surpassed by his Deportment.

Lack of time and an expectation of future opportunities withheld Miss Robie from copying verbatim other passages, of which there were several, relating to Smibert, although she made some notes of their tenor. The diary was later entrusted to an "expert" for "restoration," but the result was its complete disintegration soon after it left his hands. No exact copy of any part of it, other than the entry just quoted, is in existence, and Miss Robie's brief notes about other passages which she planned to examine at her leisure, reinforced by her recollections of the contents of the diary, are now the sole surviving source of information about it.[29] Miss Robie writes:

An important part of the diary relates to Smibert's comments on his Waldo patrons, including the youthful Joseph, the gracious Anne Tyng, sister of the General, and the great Samuel himself who proved a difficult subject. Being painted, to this man of action, was evidently a greater strain than battle and siege, and all his real estate trials in Maine and elsewhere. From time to time he would lose the pose and pace the floor to the great perplexity of the artist.

It is lamentable that this diary should have been irretrievably lost, for it evidently contained accounts of the artist at work such as have come down to us from no other source. Its evidence that Smibert painted *a* portrait of Samuel Waldo is irrefutable, and Waldo family tradition has maintained that the portrait of the General which was given to Bowdoin College in 1855 is *the* portrait painted by Smibert. In my book on Robert Feke,[30] however, I attributed the portrait at Bowdoin to Feke, and a number of critics familiar with colonial art have concurred in that attribution. Professor Hagen, indeed, is inclined to reject the attribution to either Smibert or Feke, on the ground that it is too good to have been done by either, and suggests that at least the head was repainted by Copley.[31] This last suggestion is ruled out by the X-ray examination of the picture which discloses no repainting.

The case for attributing the portrait at Bowdoin to Smibert rests on the above-quoted entry in Edward Waldo's diary; upon family tradition; and upon the fact that no second portrait of Waldo is known to exist. Waldo's reported impatience as a sitter suggests that he would have been reluctant to submit to the ordeal a second time within a few months, and, if he had, the fact would presumably have been recorded.

[29] Ordinarily such notes and recollections of a document read some thirty-five years ago, and not now verifiable, might seem open to question as to their reliability. It should, however, be pointed out that Miss Robie is an exceptionally well-qualified witness. She was a mature woman when she examined the diary, which she then expected to inherit, and she was keenly interested both in colonial art and in the Waldo family traditions. At the time she was editor of *House Beautiful;* later she was for seventeen years professor of art at Rollins College, Winter Park, Florida; and she is the author of three books on antiques. There is, therefore, no ground for questioning the reliability of her statement.
[30] Foote, *Robert Feke,* pp. 73-74, 198-199.
[31] Hagen, pp. 76-77, note.

Finally, what has become of Smibert's portrait of him if it be not the one now at Bowdoin College? On the basis of evidence and probabilities the case for Smibert is a strong one.

On the other hand the portrait is not at all in Smibert's manner and is strongly characteristic of Feke at his best. We know that Feke was at work in Boston in 1748 and the fact that Smibert had painted Waldo the previous year would not in itself have prevented Feke from accepting a commission to do so also. Comparison with Smibert's portraits of Sir William Pepperell and Sir Peter Warren, and his earlier full-length of William Browne, clearly disclose Smibert's inability to master the correct proportions of a full-length, or to give it the grace, strength, and dignity which the portrait of Waldo shows. It is hardly credible that the same man who did the first three pictures could also, at the same period of his career, have achieved so different and so successful a portrait as that of Waldo. Furthermore, many of the details are very similar to those in other portraits by Feke. The head so closely resembles that of Tench Francis, in Feke's signed and dated (1746) portrait now at the Metropolitan Museum in New York, and the pose of the figure and the painting of the gold braid are so nearly identical with those items in Feke's portraits of James and William Bowdoin, which are also signed and dated, that it is very difficult not to accept all these portraits as from the same hand. No other painter than Smibert or Feke is known who could possibly have painted the portrait of Waldo, unless one supposes it to be the work of the youthful Copley executed shortly before Waldo's death in 1759, an attribution which no one has ventured to make except for Professor Hagen's unsupported suggestion that Copley repainted the head. Unless Smibert's painting of Waldo turns up elsewhere, or good documentary evidence is found that Feke did paint Waldo, opinions as to the attribution of the portrait at Bowdoin are likely to remain divided, but, as the case now stands, I feel that the portrait is so strongly characteristic of Feke's brush, and so far beyond Smibert's capacity, that it should be assigned to Feke in spite of the evidence cited above.

Miss Robie's notes on the contents of Edward Waldo's diary also contain references to portraits by Smibert of other members of the Waldo family. "The youthful Joseph," who graduated from Harvard in 1741, was the son of Edward Waldo's first cousin, Cornelius Waldo III. He later went to England, apparently taking his portrait with him, and died there at a great age. His portrait may still be extant in England, but, if so, its location is unknown.

"The gracious Anne Tyng" was Edward Waldo's cousin, Anne Waldo, wife of Edward Tyng. A portrait of her, with one representing her husband, is now in the Yale Gallery of Fine Arts. That of Mrs. Tyng appears to be a fine example of Smibert's painting, characteristic of his defects, as in the foreshortening of the left arm and the subject's uneasy posture in a chair too small for her, as in its excellencies. The portrait of Captain Edward Tyng is a handsome one, and its attribution to Smibert is questioned on the ground that he was hardly capable of executing so fine a picture. Certainly, if it be his, it is one of his best. Some critics, including the late Mr. Edward Morehouse, an English scholar especially interested in Joseph Blackburn's work, have attributed both pictures to Blackburn. They could not, however, have been painted after Blackburn's arrival in Boston because, in the first place, the subjects are shown too young and, secondly, Mrs. Tyng died in January 1754, and her husband in September 1755, about the time of Blackburn's arrival. Mr. Morehouse met these objections by supposing that Mr. and Mrs. Tyng visited England in the seventeen-forties and were painted by Blackburn there. It is, of course, possible that the Tyngs made such a visit, but no record of it exists. Furthermore the accessories shown in Captain Tyng's portrait suggest another interpretation. He holds a telescope in his left hand, and with his right points to a frigate under sail and flying a red ensign. Now Captain Tyng attained great prestige in Boston by his capture of a French privateer off Cape Cod in 1744, and in 1745 commanded the frigate *Massachusetts* in the expedition against Louisburg. The picture would appear to have been painted to commemorate these naval services, and the age at which both he and his wife are represented fits either the summer or fall of 1744 or the date of the return of the Louisburg expedition in 1746. At the Yale University Art Gallery, while the portrait of Mrs. Tyng is accepted as Smibert's work, that of her husband is labeled "Artist Unknown," because of its lack of conformity to Smibert's characteristic style, although, if it was painted in Boston on either date suggested above, it is difficult to say who else could have painted it.[32]

The quotation from Edward Waldo's diary reporting his visit to Smibert's studio while the artist was painting his "illustrious Cousin" suggests in its comment on Smibert's "deportment," that he had not previously met him. The acquaintance thus begun was, however continued, for Miss Robie reports that there were entries in Edward Waldo's diary recording a visit which Smibert made at the homestead, still standing, which Waldo had built in 1714 at Windham, Connecti-

[32] Another portrait by Smibert, now in the Museum of Fine Arts, Boston, was also formerly supposed to represent Mrs. Tyng, but the identification is very uncertain and it probably depicts some other woman of the Tyng family connection.

cut, where Smibert was a guest while painting portraits of both Mr. and Mrs. Waldo. Miss Robie thinks that this visit took place about two years later, in 1749. It seems hardly likely that it was postponed to so late a date, since in his letter to Arthur Pond, of London, dated April 6, 1749, and quoted in full below, Smibert wrote, "I grow old, my eyes has been for some time failing me . . . but . . . hath been diverting myself with somethings in the Landskip way." This seems to indicate that he had ceased to paint portraits. If so, the visit to Windham must have taken place somewhat earlier. It is the only record to indicate that Smibert ever slept so much as a single night out of Boston after he settled there. Unfortunately his portrait of Mrs. Edward Waldo was destroyed by fire early in the nineteenth century, and that of her husband is now lost, although, as its descent to a grandson of Edward Waldo's is recorded, it may still be in the hands of descendants. There is also a family tradition, although not recorded in the diary, that during this visit to Windham Smibert also painted Waldo's son, Edward Waldo, Jr., and his wife. If he did so, the present location of these pictures is not known.

There are but few other portraits by Smibert which can be assigned to the last five years of his activity as a painter, but among them are two delightful little pictures of the children of Gershom and Hannah Flagg. That of James Flagg, four or five years old, is perhaps his most attractive portrait of a child. That of James' little sister, so-called "Polly Flagg," must represent Hannah, since Polly was not born until 1750.[33] The parents were painted by Feke in 1748,[34] and Mr. Alan Burroughs, on grounds of technique, attributes the portraits of the children to that painter also. Aside, however, from a strong family tradition attributing them to Smibert, the ages at which the children are represented indicate that they were painted about 1743–1744. At the time of Feke's visit to Boston in 1741, James was less than two years old and Hannah was not yet born, and both children are shown too young to have been painted in 1748 when Feke again came to Boston. At the date to which the portraits must be assigned Feke was in Newport and was not available, whereas Smibert lived just around the corner from the Flaggs.

[33] Both portraits are reproduced in *Mary Wilder White*, ed. Mary W. Tileston, fol. pp. 5 and 11, where the portrait of "Polly" is attributed to Blackburn, 1753.
[34] Foote, *Robert Feke*, pp. 82, 145–147.

CHAPTER VII

Closing Years

THE LAST THREE YEARS OF SMIBERT'S LIFE WERE MARKED BY DECLINING health and failing eyesight. The business of the "colour shop" went on as usual, however, though no doubt increasingly in the hands of the devoted John Moffatt. Its character is further illustrated in Smibert's fourth surviving letter to Arthur Pond, dated "Boston, April 6th, 1749."

Dear Sir,—The first of last moneth I wrote you & inclosed two Bills of Exchange one for £15 on Mr. Bethel yᵉ other for £33 on Mr. Partridge & now inclose you the 2d of each of those Bills & yᵉ first of another for £15 on Mr. Bethel making in al £63.00 which I must trouble you to lay out in the underwritten articles & to get the Cargoe insured. I hope you have received yᵉ first letter where in yᵉ Prussian Blew was desired to be got ready, but in case you have not and can not soon get the sorts wrote for, desires you wil take what sorts there is ready that you like best your self, for as several of yᵉ articles are much wanted would be glad to have them sent by the first vessel, the last things you sent came safe but received no Letter.

I'm ashamed to give you so much trouble, but you have encouraged me & there is none of my friends so well acquainted with the people who deal in those articles, as for myself I need not tell you that I grow old, my eyes has been some time failling me, but is [I'm] stil heart whole & hath been diverting my self with somethings in the Landskip way which you know I always liked. I had lately a present of a Cast of yᵉ modell for Shakespears Monument from my friend Mr. Schymaker [1] which pleases me much. when you see him please to make my Compli-

---

[1] Peter Scheemakers, a Flemish sculptor born in Antwerp, 1691. As a young man he was so eager to visit Italy that he walked all the way to Rome and return. He came to London in 1716 and departed again for Rome in 1728, about the time that Berkeley's party sailed for America. He was back in England by 1735 and remained there till 1769, when he retired to Antwerp where he died soon afterwards. He was one of the foremost sculptors in the London of his day, sharing the patronage of the court with Roubiliac and Rysbrack. There are several busts by him in Westminster Abbey, besides the statue of Shakespeare which he carved from Kent's design.

ments to him, and to Mr. Gibson [2] of whose welfare I should be glad to know. if you have got the little Picture of Mischan & ye Lady after Titian back again (for I think you wrote you had lent them) should be glad you sent them with this Cargoe. my Nephew sends his service to you, with our services to your Father I am Sir your most obliged humble sert.

John Smibert.[3]

Prussian Blew 4 l @ 18 or 20 Shill
Do 6 l   @ 12 or 15 Shill
Do 10 l   @ 8/ or 9 Shill
Do 20 l   @ 4/ or 5 Shill
Pallet and Stone Knives 1 doz of each
Brown Pink ½ l.
Carmine 1 oz.
gold leaf three thousand ⎫ Please to direct that the gold and silver leaf
silver Do 4000   ⎭ be carefully done up in a box by it self.
¾ Primed Cloaths 3 doz.
Kit Kats 1 doz.
½ Lengths 2 doz
2 gold frames for 2 Pictures 20 inches by 14 inches and a half. the pictures are not extraordinary, so would not go higher than 12 or 15 Shill. apiece. a French Bible a good Edition and neatly bound. this is for my second Son a present from my Nephew whose favorite he is.
Red chalk 1 l.
Pencils (blackamore Street) in Sorts 20 Shil. value
Fann Brushes or tools for Portraits 20 Shil. value
200 doz black and white mounts @ 8 d per doz
50 doz colloured mounts at one shil. per doz
50 doz Do @ one Shill & six pence per Doz
10 doz Do @ 2 or 3 Shill. per Doz
10 doz Do @ 4 or 5 Shil. per doz
2 doz Do @ 6 or 8 Shill. per Doz
1 doz Do @ 10 Shil. per Doz
Black and white mounts 20 Doz @ one Shil per doz
Do 10 doz @ one shill & six pence per doz
Silver paper 1 Doz @ 3 Shill
Do 1 Doz @ 4 Shill
Black mounts for mourning smal paper 20 doz and 20 doz larger paper
Do we know not ye Price of ye black mounts but suppose the smal paper may be a Shilling a dozen and the larger eighteen pence a doz.

The repeated greetings to his old associates in London which Smibert sends in these letters imply that messages came to him in return, but still better evidence of the regard in which they held him was the

2 Thomas Gibson (1680?–1751), portrait painter; a member of the Rosa-Coronian Club.   3 British Museum, Add. Mss. 23, 725, fol. 5.

present he refers to from Peter Scheemakers, a cast of the model for the monument to Shakespeare upon which Scheemakers was working. It was more than twenty years since they had parted, Scheemakers to go to Rome, Smibert to come to America. No wonder that Smibert was pleased that his friend, who had become the foremost sculptor then in London, should thus remember him. If Smibert had lived only a few years longer than he did he would have had the gratification of seeing a monument by Scheemakers erected in Boston, the stately memorial to Frances, wife of Governor William Shirley, which her husband placed in King's Chapel. It is probably the only work by Scheemakers in America.

Smibert, as this last letter to Pond indicates, was feeling the weight of increasing years, though he was but sixty-one, and his health was not good during his last two or three years. Perhaps he had never been very vigorous, for Vertue says that he suffered from "hip or Vapours" in London, and that the mild climate of Bermuda was one of the attractions which led him to accept Berkeley's invitation to go to America. And in the second letter to Pond, quoted above, he speaks of his recovery from "a dangerous ilnes." Furthermore, his eyesight was failing, so that about 1748 he gave up portrait painting, although he still did "landskips" for his own amusement. He had always been fond of "landskips" and had a number in his studio, including some which he had brought from Italy, though these last may have been copies of Italian pictures. It is much to be regretted that all of these landscapes, and particularly those painted in the vicinity of Boston, have disappeared.

Death overtook him on April 2, 1751. The *Boston News-Letter* of April 4 reports the event as follows:

JOHN SMIBERT. On Tuesday last died here, much lamented, Mr. John Smibert, well known for many fine Pictures he has done here, and celebrated in Italy, as well as Britain, for a good Painter, by the best judges. As a Member of Society, he was a valuable Gentleman of a happy Temper, great Humanity and Friendship, a Kind Husband, tender Father, and steady Friend: But what is above all, an exemplary Christian, eminently so in Practice and constant Resignation to the Will of God. We hear his Funeral will be Tomorrow Evening.[4]

He was buried in the Granary Burying Ground, in the tomb of his father-in-law, Dr. Nathaniel Williams. It is the third tomb to the

[4] The *Boston Gazette* of April 9 reprinted this notice verbatim, except for the last sentence, which reads "and on Friday was decently inter'd." The *Boston Post-Boy* for April 8 only states that "Last Tuesday died here Mr. *John Smibert*, an ingenious and celebrated Painter in this Town."

right of the entrance gate, but the stone is now marked "Thomas and John Bradlee Tomb 1816." [5]

Making due allowance for the exaggeration of virtue to be expected in obituaries and eulogies, it seems probable that the notice in the *Boston News-Letter*, quoted above, does fairly report the general opinion of his character. It fits in well with Vertue's account of his modesty and his unwillingness to push himself forward by intrigue and chicanery.

It was several months before the news of his death reached London, but in June, 1752, Vertue made the following entry in his notebook (apropos of nothing before):

having lately heard from an acquaintance & familiar Country man of Mr. John Smibert painter, who went to settle in Boston in New England above two [or] three & twenty years ago. their he met with good encouragement in business & employments, being a sedate man. he marryd a woman of some considerable fortune soon after. by her he had several children, broght forward a nephew of his Mr Moffet in his business, who still follows the same. but Mr John Smibert I was told dyd, about March was twelve month—that is March 1751—& left a widow and two children—in very good circumstances. in the art of painting he was a skilfull painter, had made great improvements by study in England and at Rome, were [*sic*] he staid a considerable time, at his return to England he was well esteemed by the Curious and the Judges of Art. but he was not contented here, to be on a level with some of the best painters. but desird to be were [*sic*] he might at the present, be lookt on as at the top. his profession then, & here after. in which no doubt, he there succeeded in. and Smibert's name in after Times. by his works will be there remembered in a superior degree.[6]

Six months later still John Moffatt wrote the news to Arthur Pond.

Boston, New England, Dec'r 28th, 1752.

To
    Mr Arthur Pond
       Painter in great Queen Street
          Lincoln inn fields
            London

Sir,—No doubt you have long ago heard of the Death of Mr. Smibert, and which I ought to have acquainted you of before now, as I know the regard you had for him & ye obligations we are under to you. He had been for many years in a Declining State of health, and for some

[5] Boston Record Commissioners Report, XIII, 185.
[6] Vertue, III, 161.

years unable to paint at al, but to yᵉ last preserved his cheerfulness & serenity of temper, free from al uneasiness & happy in his family. He has Left a Widow and three sons, yᵉ eldest is apprentice to a Merchant, yᵉ second inclines to Painting & seems to me of a Promising Genius, yᵉ youngest is at yᵉ Gramar School. my Honest Uncle never was rich, but Lived always handsomely & with great reputation. He hath left enough I hope with prudent management to put his Children in yᵉ way of doing well in yᵉ world & which you may easily think I am not unconcerned about.

a friend here who valued Mr. Smibert much, has wrote a Character or Epita[p]h to be put on the Tomb. I have sent you a Copy of it for your opinion & your friends, it wil apear too long and perhaps might be shortned to advantage. I shal be glad of your opinion of it & would acquaint you that ever since Mr. Smibert died I have intended something should be erected to his memory. yᵉ tomb Joins to a wall which will admit of but a smal monument, yᵉ measure of which will now be sent. Mr. Scheemaker was Mr. Smibert's friend & therefore yᵉ properest person to apply to, what I would desire to be done, is yᵉ Inscription on Marble with some little ornament as you & Mr. Scheemaker shal think best, if it can be done for about twenty Guineas and should be glad of two or three diferent drawings that we might choose from, what pleases best here. I am a stranger to yᵉ expence of marble monuments but as this is only yᵉ marble and yᵉ writting & some litle ornament, perhaps it may be done for near that money. however I am forced to take the freedom to trouble you in this affair for there are none of Mr. Smiberts friends who can so well direct me in this affair as you & I suppose you are no stranger to Mr. Sheemaker but must be acquainted with him.

I am ashamed further to trouble you with yᵉ inclosed Bills of Exchange one for fifty and yᵉ other for twenty Pounds, to lay out in sundry articles as per Invoice anexed, the remittance is made yᵉ larger that we may not soon give you the like trouble. my Aunt & I Jointly cary on the Collour business & every thing goes on as in my Uncles life time. Gratitude obliges me to do al I can for yᵉ interest of so worthy a Persons familly as wel as yᵉ nearnes of my Relation. if this Commission could be made easier to you for yᵉ future by applying to yᵉ Fann man & some of yᵉ other people directly, you wil please to direct me, yᵉ Bill for fifty pounds is drawn by so good a man as that its certain wil be duly honoured, nor do I doubt yᵉ other Bill being so too, but in case that should be protested must desire you to get yᵉ whole of yᵉ Fann Mounts sent & the remainder in Prussian Blew, for as we are near out of Fann mounts it would be of great advantage could you favour us with them by the first ship after you receive the money, and let the whole value be insured. I wish yᵉ taste here was good eneough for yᵉ Prints of your Landskips, etc. but there are few virtuosi here, yᵉ Roman Ruins pleases & now & then there are a customer for them. Mrs. Smibert with her Sons Joins me in their Respects to you. I shal be obliged for your ordering the cargo particularly the Fan mounts as soon as possible. I am with the greatest respect Sir, your most obliged Humble ser't,

John Moffatt.

one Bill of Exch. drawn by Peter Bulkeley on Christopher Kilby
Esqr. for 20.0.0
one Do. drawn by John Erving Esqr. on Mr. William Hodshon
for 50.0.0

Sterling $£$70.0.0

Invoice of the particulars, y^e above Bills are desired to be laid out in & marked S. M.
no.

Ordinary white Fan mounts 5 groce .... @ 5/^{6}
Plain printed mounts 16 groce .... @ 8/
Colloured mounts 8 groce .... @ 12/
    Do   8 groce .... @ 18/
Colloured mounts & guilt 1 groce .... @ 30/
    Do   1 groce .... @ 36/
    Do   6 doz .... @ 6/
    Do.   2 doz .... @ 10/
    Do.   2 doz .... @ 12/
Black & white mounts   1 groce .... @ 12/
    Do   2 groce .... @ 18/
    Do   1 groce .... @ 24/
Black mounts 3 groce @ 12/ .... @ 12/
    Do   1 groce .... @ 18
Childrens mounts Collored 3 groce about 8/ or 9/
the 4 Prints of ye Roman Buildings & Ruins by Panini twelve of each print.
Prussian Blew 6 l. about 18/ or 20/ per pound
Carmine 1 oz
Stone knives 1 doz.
Pallet Do 1 doz.
Black Lead pencils 6 doz chiefly large sort
¾ Primed Cloaths 3 doz.
Kitkat Do. 1 doz
½ Length Do 1 doz.
Gold leaf 2000 & some gold Beatters skin
Crayons to the value of a Guinea
Black chalk & some French Chalk about 5/ or 6/ worth.

    If there should not be Fan mounts exactly of y^e above prices, please to do what you think best, only that they be near y^e above prices, what is now wrote for wil I imagine, with the Insurance, Cases & shipping Charges etc. be near about the $£$70.0.0 now remitted, if there be any Left it may be laid out in gold leaf, Pruss. Blew or y^e plain printed mounts, either of them as wil be y^e least trouble.

The Tomb Joins to the Brick wal of y^e Burying ground & wil admit a monument of a little more than 5 foot wide, but as the wal is but Low I believe 5 foot wide wil be sufficient to alow for a proper heighth. the Inscription wil require a large piece of Marble & that is what I principaly regard. as for any show I would avoid it & desire what little ornaments can be afforded to be in ye plain & good taste, which you wil please to direct Mr. Scheemaker, and to favour us with 2 or 3 sketches with ye Estimate of ye charge, that so we may choose what wil please best here. Mr. Smibert had a great friendship for Mr. Scheemaker to whom please to give my service. I doubt not but He wil readily do what is in his power to ye memory of ye deceased.[7]

The epitaph is written in a careful copper-plate hand, such as engravers used, with *Deum. O.M.* and the dates heavily capitalized. We know that Peter Pelham wrote such a hand and it may well be that before his own death in December 1752, he paid a last tribute to his friend and fellow worker by making fair copies of his epitaph which some latinist, perhaps Smibert's pastor, had prepared. The Latin original is translated as follows:

EPITAPH

Why should there be shame or limits to the longing for one so dear?
Hor. *Carmina* 1, xxiv

In the adjacent tomb are buried the frail and mortal remains of the excellent man, John Smibert, a famous painter, to whose art, even Italy, dear nurturing mother of painting, once recognized that praises were due. In Britain too, you will surely not find his superior, very few who are his equal. It is therefore not strange if in America, which he preferred for health's sake to his native soil, he neither found nor left a rival. Because of their great art and skill, numerous pictures, painted with elegance by his hand, will offer, in the estimate of the best judges, enduring proof of these facts.

But however great this praise of him, it is little compared to his excellent character. Particularly in the cultivation of his character, he combined in felicitous manner zeal and effort, and in all circumstances of life, was an exemplar of true and unadorned virtue. He was a singularly worthy member of the community by reason of his unstained integrity of life, a calm, kindly, and humane nature, together with an affability in behavior, and a pleasing and ingenuous simplicity. He was an affectionate husband and parent, mindful of his duties to each member of his family, friendly, sincerely helpful, loyal, and stable; in sum, his whole life was a sermon. His soul was deeply imbued with reverence and love of God in his greatness and goodness. In his worship he was steadfast

[7] From the Chamberlain Collection (F. 4, 7) Boston Public Library. This letter, and the epitaph which follows, were in the collection of Dawson Turner, in 1859, and were priced at 10s.6d. in the sale catalogue.

and very devoted, with true faith and a living hope in Christ Jesus. Supported by these, happy and at peace, on the second day of April in the year 1751 of our Christian era, his pious spirit was returned to God who had given it.

He was born of honest parents at Edinburgh in Northern Britain on the twenty-fourth day of March in the year 1688. He married his wife, Mary, whom he ever cherished, truly a dutiful woman, worthy of his love, and now, alas, his grief-stricken widow, on the thirtieth day of July in the year 1730. She was the eldest daughter of a reverend and learned man, formerly departed this life, Nathaniel Williams of Boston. Of this union were born seven sons and two daughters, of whom four sons and two daughters rest in the same tomb with their father; the others survive.

Reader, if you can cherish a man such as this and seek to be like him, you will be ever blessed.[8]

For some reason which, in the absence of further letters on the subject we do not know, the proposed tablet was never erected and Smibert's place of burial is unmarked.

Smibert left what was for the time and place a comfortable estate. His earnings from painting and from his shop, when added to the income of his wife's modest fortune, had enabled him, as Moffatt wrote to Pond, to live "handsomely and with great reputation"—by the standards of eighteenth-century Boston—and to leave enough to provide for his widow and surviving children. The inventory of his estate bears out Moffatt's statement and provides an interesting list of the contents of what was evidently a very well-furnished house, with "5 carpets," a substantial amount of silver plate, and something of a library. The "foyles and flutes," and the "horse chaise and runners" give a hint as to Smibert's pastimes. The inventory is of sufficient interest to be worth printing in full.

Inventory of the Estate of Mr. John Smibert, Painter, taken by the subscribers, in February, 1752.

The easterly half of the House and land in Queen St.	£446.13.4
Fourteen acres of land in Roxbury	186.13.4
A House lott of land in the Westerly part of Boston	10. 0.0
Plate, 109 oz. & 15 pᵗ	36. 6.4.
Silver watch and seal & 2 rings	8. 2.8.
Wearing apparel 12.12, Library 11.18.5	24.10.5
Fire arms & silver hilted sword	3.17.4
Colours & oyls 307.16.5 35 portraits 60.5.4	368. 1.9.
41 History pieces & pictures in that taste	16. 0.0.
13 Landskips 2.13. 2 Conversation Pictures 23.6.8	25.19.8

[8] See Latin in Appendix 1. A copy is in the British Museum, Add. Mss. 23, 725, fol. 49–50. Another copy is in the Chamberlain Collection, Boston Public Library.

Bustoes & figures in Paris plaister & models 4. 5.8
Prints and books of prints 11.12.8 Drawings 4.16 .... 16. 8.8
Pillows, prospect glass & magnifying glass, foyles and flutes .. 1.11.4
An eight day clock 9.6.8 Desk and book case 8 .... 17. 6.8
Escrutore 2. Table linnen 9.18.8 Sheeting do 16.9.11 .... 28. 8.7.
two pieces of brown linnen 5.15.8
4 feather beds Bolsters & pillows Bedsteads & Curtains 21. 6.8
3   do   do   do   8. 0.0
12 pr. of blankets & 3 rugs 3.12.0
two silk quilts & a coverlid 4.13.4 five looking glasses 6.17 11.10.8
China and earthen ware 3.17.4
Three chests⁹ of drawers & 1 table 5.13 4 Easy chairs &
couch 1.17.4 .... 7.10.8
Three dozen & 10 chairs 12.3.4. Ten tables 4.6 5 carpets 2.4 18.13.4
Pewter 8.9.2. Iron and tin ware 11.2.11 .... 19.12.1
Brass and copper ware 13.19.2
Bell metal skillits 49/2 oz 2.12.9
Gross of glass bottles 1.2 Lumber in the garrett 2.1.4 ..... 3.13.4
Negro girl Phillis 26.13.4. Horse chaise & runners 24.5.4 ... 50.18.8
Cloathes press, chest, boxes, brushes, baskets, bellows etc. ... 1.16.8

£1387. 4.9

David Cutter
Joseph Gale
John Greenwood

22 Sept. 1752

Mary Smibert ⎱ admʳˢ ¹⁰
John Moffatt ⎰

John Greenwood,¹¹ the young Boston painter and engraver, was
no doubt employed as one of the appraisers because of the one unusual
feature of the estate, namely, the large number of paintings and prints

⁹ The Worcester (Mass.) Historical Society owns two fine old leather-bound trunks,
beautifully studded with brass nails, and lined with stenciled papers, which were
given to it in the last century as having been the property of John Smibert. Unfortunately the evidence for his ownership is very uncertain. One of them is marked,
in brass nails:

M
· ·
G M 1679

The M might stand for Moffatt, but the other initials cannot be identified as any
known members of the Moffatt family of that date. If it was made for one of the
earlier members of the Moffatt family it might have been brought to this country by
John Moffatt. The nailing in the other and smaller trunk gives no clue as to its
origin. The inventory of John Smibert's estate, which could hardly have overlooked
such fine pieces if they had been his property, does not list them. Therefore the
tradition that they came from his house must be regarded as very doubtful.
¹⁰ Suffolk Wills, XLVI, 277, printed in M.H.S. Proc., L (May 1866).
¹¹ John Greenwood, born in Boston on December 7, 1727, died at Margate, England,

which it included. Some of these items invite further comments or raise questions. The "2 Conversation pieces" were no doubt the "Bermuda Group" and the "Ancient Philosophers" which Smibert had left unfinished. The low-priced "13 Landskips" may have been the small paintings which Smibert had done for his amusement in his last years. The "41 History pieces & pictures in that taste" no doubt included Smibert's copies of the "Scipio," the "Hector and Andromache," the "Danaë and the Golden Shower," and perhaps the Madonna and Child by Raphael. The "35 Portraits" presumably included the heads of Bentivoglio, Cornaro, Montfort, and Charles and James Stuart. Some of the others may have been copies of European pictures, or portraits painted by Smibert and still in his studio. It is regrettable that so little is recorded of the contents of what was undoubtedly the largest collection in America at that time, and one which must have crowded the house and the large painting room which Smibert had built.

John Moffatt carried on the business of the "colour shop" for many years, at first with the aid of his aunt, Mary Smibert, the date of whose death is not recorded. He also continued to correspond with Arthur Pond. A copy of a letter to him from Pond is in the British Museum. It is addressed:

> To Mr. John Moffatt Boston, New England
> By ye Devonshire, Capt. Jacocks.
>
> London, may 10, 1757.
> Sir,—Your letter of the 15th Decr. came to my hands ye latter end of february, and I have this day sent the two boxes to be shiped in two different Ships being the last which go this Spring. you have only one sort of Prussian Blew of a fine deep Sort and I could now [not] get any other I liked ready made; I could not under a fortnight get any flake white, without going to the Collour Shops, who sell it dear, but have sent one pound for the present. many things are so dear on account of ye war and ye Insurance so high Your money is all laid out, if you want more of any of ye articles I shal get them on your Order. not knowing where directly to get any Indian Ink at a good hand, have put up one Stick of my own which desire you to accept of.
> I am Sir your most humble Sert.
>
> > Art. Pond

September 15, 1792. In 1742 he was apprenticed to Thomas Johnston, a Boston engraver. About that time he began to paint portraits; Burroughs (*John Greenwood in America*, Andover, 1943) attributes some fifty portraits to him before he left for Surinam in 1752, some time after the appraisal of Smibert's estate. From Surinam he went to Holland and in 1763 he established himself in London as a painter and engraver of mezzotints, but ten years later he abandoned art and became an auctioneer with a high reputation.

Some of the things I divided by Gues Consequently not exactly equal. Porter & Shipping last cargo Six shillings remained in my

hands	0–14–9
A Bill now Sent	60– 0–0

£60–14–9

the word Painter is not necessary in my direction, and I may leave [it] off.

Fann Mounts	38–15–0
Carmine one oz very fine	1– 1
two doz stone knives	1– 4–0
one doz pallet knives	0– 6–0
four pounds fine Prussn. Blew 18/	3–12–0
two pounds English Safron 1–14–0	3– 8–
one pound flake white 0–1–4	0– 1–4
one pound French Sap Green	0–13
one pound Distiled Verdigres	0–15
Boxes, Porter & packing	0–14–6
Insurance on two pollicys	9–18–0

60– 7–10

Ballance   6–11

60–14–9

part of the Insurance to be returned if with Convoy
Shipping charges to be paid

This letter is endorsed "24th August, 1759 reced [payment?] from Mr. James Urwin [Erving] Merchant at New England Coffee House."

Pond died in September 1758, but the news did not reach Moffatt until 1759, leading him to write to Pond's executors:

Boston New England, Jully 2ᵈ 1759
Gentlemen,–I latley Saw an advertisement in a London news paper of ye Sale of Mr. Ponds Collection by Order of His Executors. Mr. Ponds death gives me much concern as I am under great obligations and have received many favours from him. but I should not have troubled you with a Letter were it not on account of Some goods He was to Ship for me. ye state of ye affair is Just this. Decr. 15th 1756 I wrote Mr. Pond & inclosed a Bill of Exch. for £60.0–0 Sterling and febr. 10th 1757 I again wrote him with a Copy of ye articles wrote for & the 2nd. of ye Bill and no doubt you wil find those Letters amongst his papers. Mr. Pond favoured me with an answer dated may 10th 1757 a Copy of which is here unto anexed [12] by which you wil see he did not mention in what Ship the other half of ye goods were to be sent and as I never heard further from him, concludes ye Ship must either have

[12] This letter is the one printed just above.

been taken or Lost. now as you have the Pollicy it wil be easy to know by what Ship and if either taken or Lost there can be no difficulty in getting ye Insurance paid. this is the reason of writing you Gentn desiring you wil be so kind as to receive the Insurance for me as you have the Pollicy, ye Bearer Mr. James Erving of this place wil be very ready to Assist in ye affair and when you have received the money, please to pay it to Mr. Erving who wil pay the charges arissing and give you ye proper discharge. I must desire another favour more and that is to let Mr. Erving know of whom Mr. Pond used to buy the Fann mounts for I have given Mr. Erving a Commission to get me a parcel of ye same person if you can direct him to ye man. I hope you will excuse this trouble & if ever it is in my Power to do any Service for any of Mr. Ponds friends in this part of ye World it would give me a Singular Satisfaction to Gentlemen your most obedient Humble Sert.

                                                        John Moffatt.

P.S. The goods by Capt. Jacocks came Safe.
To the Executtors of the Will
    of the Late Mr. Arthur Pond
        in London.

With this letter the extant correspondence about Smibert's "Colour Shop" comes to an end.

Smibert's Place and Influence as an Artist

IT IS NOT DIFFICULT TO MAKE A FAIR ESTIMATE OF JOHN SMIBERT'S standing as a painter. Only in the unsophisticated eyes of the young enthusiast in the Boston of 1730 and his fellow provincials has Smibert ever appeared to be a "great Master" and "wondrous Artist." Yet Rev. Ebenezer Turell did not exaggerate the esteem in which Smibert was held when he wrote, concerning the portrait of Rev. Benjamin Colman, "his picture drawn in the year 1734 by the greatest Master our Country has seen, Mr. John Smibert, shows both his Face and Air to Perfection." Smibert at that period unquestionably was the best-trained and most skilful painter who had ever come to the Colonies, and in his most successful portraits he pictured his subjects realistically and attractively.

Among the London artists with whom he had worked he was, indeed, rated by Vertue as belonging in the second rank, although it may be observed that the three "old masters" whom Vertue places in the first group (Jervas, Richardson, and Dahl) are today all but forgotten, and that Joseph Highmore and the more celebrated Hogarth are among those bracketed with Smibert in the second group. Highmore was a respectable painter, whose style was not very different from Smibert's. Hogarth later far surpassed Smibert in originality and technique, although, incidentally, he must have been a much less comfortable person to get along with. But in the seventeen-twenties he was just beginning his career as a painter of small figures, and all his portraits were painted later. He really belongs with the great English painters of the second half of the eighteenth century, Gainsborough, Reynolds, Romney, and others who made that period illustrious but who at the time of Smibert's death were still young men whose star had not yet risen above the horizon.

Rev. Ebenezer Turell

It is important to remember that Smibert's career as an artist fell entirely within the first half of the century, and that throughout the period of his sojourn in New England there was so little promise of the coming renaissance of British art that Pond in 1743 had written despondingly to him of the "low State of Virtu" in England. It was a dull period and Smibert, though industrious and ambitious, had no extraordinary talents wherewith to illuminate it. If he had remained in London there is no reason to suppose that he would have acquired a much greater reputation than he already had there, or would have developed into a much better painter than he shows himself to be in the Ferne portraits and the 1728 portrait of Berkeley, which, with those executed soon after his arrival here, indicate the level of his accomplishment by the time he was forty years old. As has been noted, he had few persons of much distinction among his English patrons, and he abhorred the insinuating ways and the ingratiating approach which too often enable a second-rate painter to attain a popular reputation. If he had returned to Scotland when Aikman quitted the scene in 1723 he might perhaps have been remembered as the best Scottish painter of his day. As it is, he has been all but forgotten in his native land and in England, in spite of the not inconsiderable number of portraits by him which must still be extant in Great Britain.[1]

That, however, has been the fate of other British artists who came to the American colonies seeking better opportunities for work than they could find at home. Charles Bridges, Joseph Blackburn, and John Wollaston all followed Smibert hither between 1735 and 1755, and remained for several years, Blackburn in New England, the other two in the middle and southern colonies, but all three eventually returned to England, where they are almost unknown and their work is generally unidentified. In the history of British art so much attention has been paid to the outstanding figures that the lesser men, such as they, have been almost completely overlooked. In this unexplored field there must be a great number of portraits of minor personages, hidden in the smaller country houses, by forgotten provincial artists whose work would be well worth investigation and study.

Although not a great artist Smibert was, when he came to Boston, a competent painter who could produce a satisfactory portrait, especially when the subject was a man seated or shown at not more than

---

[1] Anderson's *Scottish Nation* (1863) III, 478, col. 1, gives a brief account of him, based on Horace Walpole's *Anecdotes of Painting* and Dunlap's *History of . . . the Arts . . . in the United States;* the *Encyclopaedia Britannica* has a short article under "Smybert," and the *Dictionary of National Biography* has a good account of him by Lionel Cust.

three-quarter length. Lawrence Park made a fair estimate of him when he wrote:

His work was of an uneven quality and it is somewhat difficult to limit the period of his best production. Broadly speaking, however, it may be said to ante-date 1740 . . . In his methods of painting he followed closely those in vogue in the first quarter of the eighteenth century in England, and at its best his work compares favorably with that of Michael Dahl, Charles Jervas and Joseph Highmore. It has, however, sufficient individuality to prevent its being confused with the work of others. His most glaring faults are discovered when he painted his subjects full length, for he habitually made the head too small, the arms too long, and the distance from the waist to the feet too short. In his portraits of women of bust or half-length size he occasionally exaggerated the relation between the size of the head and the torso. During his active life here he had no serious rival in his profession, if we except Robert Feke who at his best surpassed him as an artist.[2]

Full-length standing figures, as has often been pointed out, he could never manage well, for the legs are too short for the bodies, to which they seem to give little support, and the feet are too large and are awkwardly placed. These defects are common to all his full-length portraits of men. In his one full-length of a woman, that of Mrs. William Browne, the ample skirts saved him, but the picture is so poorly done in other respects that some critics have questioned whether it is his work. But his portraits of seated men, or half-lengths, especially when the subjects are elderly, are often vigorous and strongly characterized. With women he was usually less successful because more conventional, but that is equally true of all the other colonial portrait painters before Copley, and even of the famous Kneller in England.

As Lawrence Park indicates, in the passage just quoted, Smibert's best work in this country is usually to be found among the portraits painted in the earlier part of his sojourn here. His identified portraits painted in Great Britain are too few and too inaccessible to enable us to form a really just estimate as to what effect his transplantation to the colonies may have had on him, but his 1728 portrait of Berkeley, now in the National Portrait Gallery in London, is clearly inferior to many of his portraits of men painted after his arrival here.

No doubt for a time he found his new environment stimulating and soon felt himself at home in its middle-class mercantile society. That society did not, of course, lack social distinctions and gradations in economic status, but it was not dominated by a titled and often

[2] Cleveland Museum of Art, *Bulletin* (January 1921).

corrupt aristocracy who expected obsequious deference; it did not show the vast discrepancy between the very rich and the very poor which he had known in London; and it presented no insuperable obstacles to prevent an enterprising youth of the humblest origin from rising to its top levels if he had the requisite intelligence and character. Here the finesse practiced by London artists to secure fashionable patrons was unnecessary, and he must have found the change of atmosphere agreeable. The Bostonians expected great things of him and he responded with his best efforts, the more readily because his new public wanted frank, realistic portraits of his subjects as they really looked, in the clothes they actually wore, with familiar accessories about them. They neither knew nor desired the pomposities and artifices which the Kneller school passed off on Londoners in the name of art.

Copley, a generation later, accurately interpreted the wishes of his clients when he wrote in 1765 to the English engraver who was to make a mezzotint of one of his portraits: "I shall likewise depend on Your perticular care in the preservation of the likeness that being a main part of the exellency of a portrait in the opinnion of our New England Conoseurs." [3] Smibert's clients, as he doubtless quickly discovered, held the same opinion that "the exellency of a portrait" consisted in its being a good likeness of the subject, and that opinion harmonized well with his own inclination to sincerity and straightforward dealing. Here he could paint Sewall's grim countenance and Byfield's pudgy, toothless face as they really looked. The ladies who came to him for sittings are more conventionalized, with the inevitable curl on the shoulder, but they demanded less artifice than the women of fashion in London. But with no rivals in his first decade here, with the lack of any higher standards to which his work could be compared, with lessening physical vigor and the premature approach of old age, and perhaps with increasing attention to the business of his color shop, he felt no urge to improve his workmanship, and his later pictures are usually less interesting. The very worst picture he ever painted is his full-length of Sir William Pepperell. That portrait, like the one of Sir Peter Warren and, in lesser degree, that of Spry, is painted according to the formula for pompous official portraits in the worst tradition of the Kneller school.

Smibert should not be judged by such productions but by his more domestic pictures of the men and women who were his neighbors and acquaintances, and whose "Face and Air" he realistically portrayed. Alan Burroughs writes:

[3] *Copley-Pelham Letters*, p. 31.

To claim that he was a second rate follower of the English tradition
. . . is to evade the evidence that he was a consistent and independent
portraitist, who brought "foreign" training to bear on the local taste for
face painting. His bold work inspired the most realistic work of Feke
and gave John Greenwood the background for a thoroughly non-English
manner. Whereas Feke in his later years adopted British elegance, Smibert late in life adopted the forceful mode of the self-taught artisan.
He was American, not by accident but by assimilation and choice.[4]

Professor Sizer intimates the same point of view when he writes:

In spite of his European training he must be regarded as a provincial
painter. He is often awkward, but there is a sincerity, honesty and vi-
tality about his work which many regard as peculiarly characteristic of
early American work. The Revolutionary painter, Col. John Trumbull,
was near the truth when he entered in his notebook (1818) that "some
of his [Smibert's] pictures were very respectable."[5]

Though these opinions as to the "Americanization" which Smibert
underwent find some justification in the portraits painted during the
earlier part of his sojourn in Boston, he must nevertheless, I think, be
viewed as a transplanted British painter who, in the main, carried on
here the traditions in which he had been bred, as Bridges, Blackburn,
and Wollaston did a little later. It could hardly have been otherwise
in a man who was past forty before he ever set eyes on this continent.
Oskar Hagen in his *Birth of the American Tradition in Art* has made
an interesting comparison between Smibert and Robert Feke in which
he points out this fact as regards Smibert, whereas he believes that
Feke represents the effort of the native American to express himself
in fresher and less traditional ways.[6]

Smibert's relations with other colonial portrait painters, whether
his contemporaries or successors, are of importance in estimating his
influence in the rise of American art. Although the story of his sojourn
in Italy and his associations with artists in London gave him an un-
questioned prestige in the eyes of younger practitioners of art, there
is no evidence that he was the "master" of any of them in the sense
that he gave them regular instruction, with the possible exception of
his own son Nathaniel, who was but little over sixteen years of age
when Smibert died. It was too early in American history for him, or

---

[4] *Art in America*, XXX, 121.
[5] *DAB*.
[6] Chaps. II and III. Unfortunately Professor Hagen cites as typical works by Smibert
several portraits which appear to be mistakenly attributed to him, and which are so
listed in the present volume, e.g., the portraits of Benjamin Pratt, of Joseph Crawford, of Mr. and Mrs. Johannes Schuyler, and of Lady Warren.

any other man, to have gathered a group of disciples who could be described as a "school," yet as he passed off the stage there were three young men in Boston who had set their hearts on becoming professional painters—his son Nathaniel, John Greenwood, and John Singleton Copley—for each of whom his career was unquestionably a stimulating example.

Older than these three and not so close at hand was Robert Feke, whose relations with Smibert require close scrutiny and careful elucidation because of the highly speculative theories about Feke's career which have been advanced by Professor Hagen and by Mr. J. T. Flexner. Referring to the former Mr. Flexner says, "In this book, the Feke legend loses all contact with reality, and floats off into a stratosphere of unrestrained theory." [7] But the same criticism applies with equal force to Mr. Flexner's own imaginative reconstruction of Feke's development, and his dating of some of Feke's portraits, on theoretical grounds, runs counter to all the evidence. To cover all his points would take us far afield, and it is unnecessary to go into details except in so far as the question of Smibert's influence on the younger, American-born artist is concerned.

Mr. Flexner pictures Feke as a seafaring man who made Smibert's acquaintance in Boston in 1741, came under his influence, saw the "Bermuda Group" in the painter's studio, and somehow secured a commission to paint the Royall Family, a work directly based on the "Bermuda Group." That Feke knew Smibert's greatest painting and paraphrased it with the Royall Family is beyond question, but Mr. Flexner goes further and points out that Feke's Early Self-Portrait so closely resembles the portrait of himself which Smibert included in the "Bermuda Group" as to prove that it must also have been painted during Feke's 1741 visit to Boston. He explains the immaturity, flatness, and lack of three-dimensional quality which the Early Self-Portrait shows, as compared with Feke's fully developed style in other portraits of about the same period, by asserting that an unskilful restorer has "skinned" the picture, destroying "the shadows and highlights with which it was originally modeled." [8]

It must be remembered that Feke is an elusive figure and that we have very few recorded facts about his life. The first full-length biography of him was not published until 1930,[9] and was largely con-

[7] Flexner, *American Painting: First Flowers of Our Wilderness*, p. 334, of Hagen's *Birth of the American Tradition in Art.*
[8] Flexner, pp. 131, 305–306, where other writers are cited as supporting the date 1741 or thereabouts for the picture. See also pp. 119, 120, and 134 for reproductions of both Smibert's and Feke's portraits.
[9] Foote, *Robert Feke.*

jectural, based on the few known facts and on a study of the pictures attributed to him. Since that date, in spite of a greatly increased interest in American colonial art, only three or four pictures, not listed in that book, have come to light which can with assurance be attributed to him; no fresh facts about his career as a painter have been discovered; and the only new information bearing on his origin and background is contained in Mr. Belknap's scholarly study of the records of the Feke family and of the close business and social connections between the settlers in the neighborhood of Oyster Bay, Long Island, and those in Newport.[10] His article effectively answers Mr. Flexner's far-fetched speculations as to Robert Feke's origin. There is no question that one of Feke's aunts had married in Newport while he was still a youth; that he himself was married there in 1742, and was then described as "of Newport"; and that he lived in that city until his disappearance in 1750 or a little later. Mr. Belknap has shown, however, that 1705, the year previously assumed to have been that of his birth, is too early. He may have been born between 1706 and 1710.

These facts have a definite bearing on the question of the date of his Early Self-Portrait and on his relations with Smibert. It is quite true that that portrait does strikingly resemble Smibert's portrait of himself,[11] yet the pose is one naturally taken by any painter who attempts a self-portrait. It is clearly the picture of a very young man, twenty to twenty-five years of age, at most, whereas by 1741 Feke was a man in his thirties, no longer the youth of the Early Self-Portrait. Mr. Flexner's theory that its flatness and "primitive" quality is due to overcleaning is pure speculation to support his thesis that it must have been painted in 1741 after Feke had seen Smibert's "Bermuda Group" in Boston. The hypothetical overcleaning (of which there is no record) does not explain its obvious immaturity in contrast to the portraits of Gershom Flagg IV and Hannah Flagg with which Mr. Flexner compares it, and which he mistakenly assumes were painted shortly afterward. Many years ago, before I knew anything about Feke and his works except the family tradition that all three pictures in question were painted by a man named Feke, I showed them to Mr. Charles Hopkinson and asked whether he, as a professional portrait painter, judged all three to be the work of the same artist. His reply was that if they were the work of the same man

[10] W. Phoenix Belknap, "The Identity of Robert Feke," *Art Bulletin*, vol. XXIX, no. 3, pp. 201–207 (September 1947).
[11] This resemblance was pointed out more than sixty-five years ago in correspondence now in my possession.

the portraits of Mr. and Mrs. Flagg must have been painted many years later than the Early Self-Portrait.

The critics who postpone the date of Feke's Early Self-Portrait until 1741 entirely overlook the possibility, or probability, that Feke might have seen Smibert's masterpiece in Newport in 1729, soon after it was painted and before it was brought to Boston. If the resemblance of Feke's figure of himself to Smibert's is anything more than a purely coincidental one of pose the most reasonable explanation is that Feke, when a youth of twenty or a little more, was visiting relatives in Newport, formed acquaintance with Smibert, and was inspired by Smibert's picture to try a portrait of himself. His picture, though immature, is far from being the first attempt of a novice, and if Feke had already set his heart on painting he would have eagerly turned to Smibert if such an opportunity offered.

A final consideration for dating this Early Self-Portrait 1729 rather than 1741, which all the proponents of the later date appear to have overlooked, is revealed by comparing it with his Late Self-Portrait. This later picture, now in the Rhode Island Historical Society, is certainly one of his latest works, about 1750, because it was left unfinished, though the head was completed and the figure outlined. The pose is almost identical in the two pictures, and they indubitably represent the same man, but the later one shows a person at least twenty years older than he was when the earlier one was painted.[12]

The simplest interpretation of all these considerations is that Feke, at the beginning of his career, met Smibert in Newport, and painted his Early Self-Portrait at that time. It also makes more understandable his sudden appearance in Boston a dozen years later as the painter of the Royall Family. We have no indubitable evidence as to what he was doing in this interval, only the uncertain tradition that he had been a "mariner," a prisoner in Spain, and had done some painting. His earliest Philadelphia portraits, which have been tentatively dated 1740, and the Royall Family, certainly show a great advance in skill over his Early Self-Portrait, though far short of his later accomplishments. Obviously he must have acquired some reputation as a painter to secure the commission from Isaac Royall, for the latter certainly would not have employed an unknown "seafaring man" who casually turned up. But if Feke, on reaching Boston, had presented himself to Smibert as the aspiring young artist whom Smibert had encouraged in Newport twelve years earlier, and who could now report one or more visits to Europe and some opportunities to develop

12 Both pictures are reproduced in Foote, *Robert Feke*, frontispiece and opp. p. 96.

his skill, Smibert might well have recommended him to Royall and have permitted him to use the "Bermuda Group" as the basis for his own most ambitious painting. Smibert was, at the time, recovering from a "dangerous ilness," and may have, for that reason, declined the commission which he passed on to Feke. The latter was some twenty years his junior and still inferior to Smibert, and, although his figure of young Isaac Royall has much charm, the group as a whole is a rather naïve imitation of Smibert's work. He followed the latter's pattern of a figure standing at the spectator's right, at the end of a table covered with a Turkey cloth, about which are seated three young women, one of whom is a direct copy of one of Smibert's figures. Although when Feke returned to Boston for his long visit in 1748 he had acquired a skill of characterization and a charm of presentation which equaled or surpassed anything which Smibert could achieve, in 1741 the latter was still the greatly respected elder artist whose work he sought to emulate.

Smibert's masterpiece was, indeed, his one picture which had a marked influence on the younger painters in America. Besides Feke's Isaac Royall and Family no less than five other conversation pieces were painted before the end of the eighteenth century by artists who must have been acquainted with Smibert's picture. About 1750 young John Greenwood painted the Lee Family, including himself in the group because he was then engaged to one of the Lee girls, even as Smibert had included himself in the "Bermuda Group." A little later Blackburn painted the Winslow Family; about 1765 Copley painted his own family, including his father-in-law, Dr. Clarke; in 1773 (or possibly a little earlier) C. W. Peale did a group of his own family; and near the end of the century John Trumbull painted a group picture of Governor Jonathan Trumbull of Connecticut and Family.

Of these painters Feke and Greenwood clearly derived their inspiration from Smibert. Blackburn, acquainted with painting in England for a score of years after Smibert's emigration, may well have felt that the latter had nothing to teach him, but he can hardly have avoided seeing Smibert's group in the course of his sojourn in Boston, and his patron presumably knew it also and may well have asked for something of the same sort. Copley, Peale, and Trumbull had developed their own style before painting their family groups, but Smibert's painting was indubitably the earliest example of a conversation piece, except in engravings, which any of them had previously seen.

Aside from the "Bermuda Group," Smibert's portraits do not appear to have had any great influence on later painters,[13] and are of more value as colonial documents in our cultural history than for any high intrinsic merit as works of art. Smibert came too late to influence the little-known Boston painter Nathaniel Emmons. Peter Pelham, already an accomplished engraver of mezzotints on his arrival in Boston in 1727, painted a few portraits here, but all which can with assurance be attributed to him were apparently executed to serve as the basis for mezzotints, and in the close collaboration which must have existed between Pelham and Smibert there is no evidence that the former thought of himself as either a disciple or a rival of the latter. The local house painter, Joseph Badger, perhaps tried to imitate Smibert, and Nathaniel Smibert undoubtedly felt strongly his father's influence; but for John Greenwood, and Copley a little later, Smibert was beginning to be out of date.

So far as the example of his own undistinguished technical skill was concerned Smibert's influence on American art was slight, but it was very considerable through the presence in Boston of the art collection which he brought with him from Europe, chiefly his own copies of Italian paintings; and through the higher regard for the artist's career which his reputation for travel in Italy and his association with Berkeley brought about. He was the first professional artist with any such reputation to settle in the colonies, where the painting of pictures, though occasionally indulged in, had hitherto been regarded rather as a pastime, or as an adjunct to house and sign painting, than as a serious occupation. Even Copley complained in 1765 that his fellow townsmen thought of it as no more than a trade.

In his exhibition in 1730, and in the display of his collection in his painting room, Smibert gave the provincial Bostonians, and occasional visitors from other colonies, their earliest introduction, even though at second hand, to the great paintings of the Old World. His house for nearly half a century remained the most notable art center in the colonies, as has already been noted, and its contents stimulated the imagination of the budding painters who visited it. Copley from his youth was familiar with its contents. His early sketchbook has a

[13] Flexner (p. 135) thinks that Feke's portrait of Hannah Flagg was directly inspired by Smibert's portrait of his own wife, saying that the pictures are "practically identical in composition." They are, and it cannot be doubted that Feke was acquainted with the portrait of Mrs. Smibert as well as with the lady herself. Perhaps, however, the similarity is due less to conscious imitation on the part of the younger painter than to the use by both artists of a well-established conventional formula for the presentation of likenesses of young women. Thus Smibert's portrait of Mary Hall bears an even closer resemblance to that of Mary Smibert than does Feke's portrait of Hannah Flagg.

drawing of the Medici Venus and Oskar Hagen infers from other drawings in it that Smibert also had a cast of the Laocoön.[14]

Still more significant is the story reported of young Copley's portrait of a "Boy with a Turban," which Copley sent to London to be exhibited in the Royal Academy. Sir Joshua Reynolds is said to have remarked to Benjamin West, to whom Copley had consigned the portrait, that the painter had studied Van Dyck. West replied that he could assure him that Copley had never seen a painting by Van Dyck. West's statement was correct, but he did not know that Copley had seen and studied Smibert's copy of Van Dyck's portrait of Cardinal Bentivoglio, and had been clearly influenced by it, as other young Americans were to be. When Copley went abroad he wrote letters home to his beloved half brother Henry Pelham. In an undated one from London, probably written in July 1774, he gives advice about the play of light on the face, "as in Bentivoglio's portrait," "colours . . . rich and warm like Bentivoglio's." And in letters written from Italy a little earlier he refers twice to Smibert's collection. Writing from Rome on March 14, he says:

I wish I could convey to you a just Idea of Raphael's Painting, but I am at a loss how to do it unless I could recollect some one Picture that I could refer you to; but I cannot think of one. I will refer you than [then] [to] the Coppy at Smibert's of the Holy Family, which although a Coppy from Raphael, is notwithstanding very diferent from his Painting. I will explain to you in what it differs; the Original, which is at Florence, I have seen, and find that it has nothing of the olive tint you see in the Copy, the read not so bricky in the faces, the whole Picture finished in a more rich and correct manner. you remem[ber] the hands of the Virgin & of the St. John, they are very incorrect in the one you have seen, but in the original they are correctly finished and the whole Picture has the Softness and general hew of Crayons, with a Perlly tint throughout.

And in a letter from Parma, dated June 25, he says that "the Picture of the Naked Venus and Cupid at Smibert's is Copy'd from one of Titiano's in the possession of the Great Duke of Tuskany." [15]

In November 1767, Pierre Du Simitière, whose mention of Smibert's drawing of the pictographs on Dighton Rock has already been cited, reached Boston, where he stayed several weeks and, as was his wont, made notes on the pictures which he saw in private houses as well as at "the town House," Faneuil Hall, and Harvard College. He visited Smibert's residence and wrote:

[14] Hagen, p. 46, note.
[15] Copley-Pelham Letters, pp. 240, 304, 340.

at Dr. William Smibert is a large collection of original Drawings of the best masters Prints mostly italian, Pictures, several of them originals & some done by his father John Smibert a good painter chiefly portraits & a good collection of casts in plaister of Paris from the best antiques, besides basso relievos seals & other curiosities.[16]

The next recorded visit was that of Charles Willson Peale. In a letter written many years later to his son Rembrandt Peale, then in England, and dated "Bellafield, October 28, 1812," he wrote:

In 1768-9 I visited Boston in the commencement of my painting and hunting for colours I found a colour-shop which had some figures with ornamental signs about it, these I suspect was painted by a Mr. Smibert. Becoming a little acquainted with the owner of the shop he told me that a relation of his had been a painter, and he said he would give me a feast. Leading me upstairs he introduced me into a painter's room, an appropriate apartment lined with green cloth or baise, where there were a number of pictures unfinished. He had begun a picture, several heads painted, of the ancient philosophers, and some groups of figures, these were the last works of Smibert. He had been in Italy and spent a fortune in travelling to gain knowledge in the art. Mr. Copley very probably can give a full account of him. It was at this shop I heard of Mr. Copley [17] and taking directions I went out and introduced myself to him as a person just beginning to paint portraits. He received me very politely. I found in his room a considerable number of portraits, many of them highly finished. He lent me a head done by and representing candle-light, which I copied.[18]

The next visitor was John Trumbull. After resigning his commission in the Revolutionary Army, in 1777, he went, in the early autumn of 1779,

[16] Ms., Library Company of Philadelphia. While this memorandum does not specifically identify any of the objects in Smibert's studio it does give some additional information as to its contents. No other visitor mentioned "a large collection of original Drawings by the best masters," or the "basso relievos seals and other curiosities," or plaster casts other than the head of Homer and the statue of Venus de Medici. All these objects must have been sold after Williams Smibert and John Moffatt died, for all trace of them has been lost.

[17] This implies that Copley's name was previously unknown to Peale. If that is a correct interpretation it indicates how local Copley's reputation still was in the colonies. Perhaps the head done by candlelight was Copley's candlelit portrait of his half brother Henry Pelham, painted about 1764, reproduced in Parker & Wheeler's *John Singleton Copley* (Cambridge, Mass., 1938, plate 51; see also p. 150).

[18] Quoted by John Sartain, *Reminiscences of a Very Old Man*, p. 145. Sartain says that C. W. Peale's letter had been found among Rembrandt Peale's papers after his death and had been given to Sartain by Caleb Cope, president of the Pennsylvania Academy of Fine Arts.

to Boston, where I thought I could pursue my studies to more advantage. There I hired the room which had been built by Mr. Smibert,[19] the patriarch of painting in America, and found in it several copies by him from celebrated pictures in Europe, which were very useful to me, especially a copy from Vandyck's celebrated head of *Cardinal Bentivoglio,*—one from the *Continence of Scipio,* by Nicolo Poussin, and one which I afterwards learned to be from the *Madonna della Sedia* by Raphael.[20] Mr. Copley was gone to Europe, and there remained in Boston no artist from whom I could gain oral instructions, but these copies supplied the place, and I made some progress.[21]

Trumbull gives a list of the pictures which he painted before his first voyage to Europe and before he received any instruction. The following items are noted:

37. Head of Cardinal Bentivoglio; copied from Smibert's copy of Vandyck's celebrated portrait in the Florence gallery.
38. Heads of two boys (Charles and James 2ᵈ), copied from Smibert's copy of Vandyck's beautiful picture.
45. The Continence of Scipio; copied, with essential variations, from Mr. Smibert's copy of N. Poussin; at Mr. Wadsworth's, Hartford, in perfect preservation.[22]

All these copies must have been made during Trumbull's visit in the fall of 1779. This last picture was shown at an exhibition of art at Yale in 1858, in the catalogue of which it was listed as "J. Trumbull, 1775" (*sic*), with the note: "from Smybert's copy after N. Poussin, one of the earliest productions of the Artist. Scipio is restoring to her husband the captive wife of a Spanish general."

The head copied from Van Dyck's Cardinal Bentivoglio was given by Trumbull to Harvard College, with the expressed hope that it might serve for purposes of instruction in art, but there has been some uncertainty whether the painting is Smibert's own copy, or Trumbull's copy of Smibert's copy. The Harvard Corporation evidently believed at the time that the College was getting Smibert's own copy, for they "Voted: That the thanks of this Corporation be given to Col. John Trumbull for his polite and generous attention to

[19] In the Executor's Account of the estate of John Moffatt, filed by Belcher Noyes September 22, 1785, among the receipts is the item: "Of John Trumbull for the Chamber to Nov. 16, 1779, In Old Emission Currency, £61.6"
[20] Oskar Hagen (p. 45), identifies it as the Madonna dell' Impannata, the "holy family by Raphael" which Copley saw in the Medici collection at Florence and which reminded him of Smibert's copy. Quite possibly Smibert had copies of both pictures.
[21] *Autobiography, Reminiscences and Letters of John Trumbull from 1756–1841* (New Haven, 1841), p. 7.
[22] *Ibid.,* p. 61.

Mrs. Stephen Sewall

this University in his present of a copy by the late Mr. Smibert of Boston from a painting by Vandyck of Cardinal Bentivoglio, a portrait highly celebrated. At the same time they join Col. Trumbull in hoping that this copy will be highly useful to beginners." On the other hand there is an entry in Trumbull's manuscript catalogue of his works in the Yale Library reading: "Copied from a copy by Mr. Smibert of Van Dyck's wonderful picture at Florence. Given to Harvard College, 1789." This would indicate that the picture given was Trumbull's copy, and not Smibert's. In *Harvard Portraits* it is noted, "The smooth, tight style is that of the youthful Trumbull," and the picture is now attributed to him.[23]

Trumbull's pious wish that the picture might be "useful to beginners" was fulfilled when, a score of years later, the youthful Washington Allston, as a student, found inspiration in it. Writing of his early attempts at art he said:

The leisure hours at college were chiefly devoted to the pencil, to the composition equally of figures and landscapes . . . But I had a higher master in the head of Cardinal Bentivoglio, from Vandyke, in the college library, which I obtained permission to copy one winter vacation. This copy of Vandyke was by Smybert, an English painter, who came to this country with Dean, afterwards Bishop, Berkeley. At that time it seemed to me perfection, but when I saw the original, some years afterward, I found I had to alter my notions of perfection. However, I am grateful to Smybert for the instruction he gave me—his work rather. Deliver me from kicking down even the weakest step of an early ladder.[24]

Other painters beside Trumbull rented rooms in Smibert's former residence. Among them was Mather Brown, who paid £8.14 for "the Upper Chamber" to Feb. 16, 1780. He was followed by Samuel King, painter; and in 1785 by John Mason Furnass (1763–1804), a nephew of Nathaniel Hurd the engraver, who later produced a few vigorous portraits. In *The Chronicle* of April 28, 1785, Furnass invited the patronage of the public in an advertisement the last sentence of which defies the rules of syntax but is intended to convey the hope that a native artist may receive as much "encouragement" as "foreigners" received.

[23] Alan Burroughs, ed., 1936. That the Bentivoglio frequently attracted the notice of others is indicated by an entry in the journal of Nathaniel Cutting, who on September 5, 1792, visited the Harvard College Library and noted: "There are several paintings and engravings at the end of the room that attract attention, particularly a portrait of the Cardinal Bentivolio [sic], executed by Smybert from the original by Raphael [sic]. It is certainly an excellent painting, and does much honor to the copyist" (M.H.S. Proc., XII, 61).
[24] Jared B. Flagg, *The Life and Letters of Washington Allston* (1892), p. 13.

John M. Furnass Begs leave to inform his Friends and the Public. That he has taken a large and commodious Chamber at Mrs. Sheaffe's (nearly opposite Mr. Carter's Writing-School) formerly improved by Mr. Smibert, and lately by Mr. King, limners, where he executes Portrait-Painting in Oil and Water Colours, also Hair-Work done in the neatest manner. As a native of Boston he hopes for as much encouragement as foreigners and invites them to call at his Painting-Chamber.

The last recorded occupant of the studio was John Johnston (1752–1818) who had, presumably, rented it for a considerable period previous to 1808, when he was still in residence there and in possession of the picture of the "Bermuda Group," which he sold in that year to Isaac Lothrop. Before that time the rest of Smibert's collection had been dispersed, but it is interesting to note that painters gravitated to Smibert's house for more than half a century after his death. Professor Hagen is correct in saying that "in everything but name, Smibert's house was the first British academy in New England" [25] or, for that matter, anywhere in the colonies.

Smibert's name and reputation were not forgotten in Boston, even in the nineteenth century when the names of most of the colonial painters had passed into oblivion and their works were often relegated to the attic. At that time almost all the surviving pre-revolutionary portraits were indiscriminately attributed to either Smibert or Copley, who alone were well remembered. In our day Copley's fame is secure. Smibert's place as an artist is on a lower plane, but he left behind an honorable record as a man, and a series of portraits of value as historical documents. And he had an influence such as no other man of his period in the colonies exerted in awakening the provincial Americans to a faint realization of the part which great paintings had played in the European civilization which the wide Atlantic had for four generations made so remote. We may well be grateful that Providence led him to establish himself in Boston.

[25] Hagen, p. 62; but he makes a number of unfounded statements in the preceding sentences, saying: "Before 1740, when Smibert took it over, it had been the home of Nathaniel Emmons. After 1751, Smibert's pupils, John Furnass and Samuel Minot, moved in. Charles Wilson [sic] Peale visited there in 1768. A frequent caller was John Copley, who lived only a short distance away. Eventually John Trumbull rented the place as did, still later, John Johnston and Washington Allston." I know of no evidence that Emmons ever lived in the house, and by the time Allston set up as an artist it had become the New England Museum. Furnass and Minot (a goldsmith) were not "Smibert's pupils"; the former had not been born, and the latter was but nineteen years old when Smibert died. Alan Burroughs in *Limners and Likenesses*, p. 39, mistakenly records the same tradition, speaking of "Furnass, a Servant of Smibert who occupied his studio after 1751, and Samuel Minot, who did the same."

Descriptive Catalogue
of Portraits

SECTION A

EXTANT PORTRAITS BY JOHN SMIBERT

Portraits which can be attributed to Smibert with reasonable certainty or with a high degree of probability that they are his work.

DEAN GEORGE BERKELEY, NO. I

Subject: George Berkeley, born at Thomaston, Kilkenny, Ireland, March 12, 1685; Trinity College, Dublin, B.A. 1704, M.A. 1707, Fellow of Trinity College 1707. He took Anglican orders; traveled on the Continent between 1713 and 1720; was appointed Dean of Derry in 1721; lived at Newport, R. I. 1729–1732; was appointed Bishop of Cloyne 1734; died at Oxford January 18, 1753. Philosopher, author, and prelate.

Size: H. *c.* 30 in.; W. *c.* 25 in.

Date: 1718? On the back is an inscription in nineteenth-century handwriting which reads, "George Berkeley, Bishop of Cloyne, painted at Rome before he had taken orders." Berkeley had been ordained deacon before going to Rome, but is shown in secular dress. Presumably he did not wear clerical attire while in Italy. He was in Rome from January to March 1717, and from April to November 1718. Perhaps this picture was painted during his second visit there, at the close of which he wrote to Lord Percival of his "friend . . . who having an excellent genius for painting designs to continue a year longer in Rome" (see Chapter I). There is no certain indication that this friend was Smibert, but the latter was painting portraits in Rome about that time, and it was probably there that he met Berkeley. Their later friendship gives some ground for thinking that this early portrait of Berkeley may be the first fruit of that friendship.

Description: The bust of Berkeley is shown in profile, the right shoulder towards the spectator, the head turned right, three-quarters front. It is a pleasing picture of a young man with blue eyes and ruddy complexion, wearing a full gray wig, white neckcloth, and a peacock-blue robe. The background is olive green.

Owner: George F. A. Berkeley, Esq., of Hanwell Castle, Banbury, England. Fraser, *Life and Letters of George Berkeley*, p. 348, note, said that a "portrait of Berkeley, now in Dublin, is possessed by his descendant, Mr. Robert Berkeley, Q. C., Upper Mount Street. It seems to have been the earliest one done of all, for I am told it was painted when he was in

Italy. It came to its present possessor from Mrs. Sackville Hamilton, daughter of Dr. Robert Berkeley."
Reproduced: F.A.R.L. photo.

DEAN GEORGE BERKELEY, NO. 2

Size: H. 36¾ in.; W. 29½ in.
Date: Signed: *John Smibert p*
1728.

Description: This half-length portrait shows Dean Berkeley against a greenish-brown background, seated in an oak armchair stuffed with green plush, half front, his right shoulder towards the spectator, his face turned slightly to the right. He is dressed in a black cassock with clerical bands at his neck. A black cap covers his closely cropped head. His left hand holds a book upright in his lap; his right elbow rests on the arm of the chair with the hand across his body, the index finger rather awkwardly pointing to a vista of water and trees which appears through an opening in the background on the right.

Owner: National Portrait Gallery, London. In Fraser's *Life and Letters of George Berkeley,* p. 132, note, it is stated that Smibert "made a portrait of Berkeley in 1725 [*sic*], now in possession of the Rev. Dr. Irons of Brompton," to whom it had been bequeathed by his friend Rev. Thomas W. Bowdler (1782–1856). Bowdler had acquired it at a sale about 1840, as indicated by a letter written to him by I. Winter from Maidstone, May 21, 1840, saying: "The picture was sold at auction at the death of Rev. Mr. Kennedy, late Vicar of Teston, whose widow, distantly related to me, assured me that he had been curate to Dr. Berkeley the Bishop's son for many years, and that at the death of the Dr. both his own and his father's portraits were left to him. This is the whole history of the picture as far as I know it." In spite of the discrepancy in the date of the picture as given by Fraser, which might easily have arisen from reading "8" as "5," there seems no doubt that the portrait above described is the same one that was presented in February 1882, by Rev. Prebendary William Josiah Irons, D.D., to the National Portrait Gallery in London.

Reproduced: Updike, *History of the Episcopal Church in Narragansett, R. I., New England Magazine,* new series, vol. XXVI, no. 1 (March 1902). N.E.H.G.S., *Register,* XXIX, 241 (July 1875). George Sampson, ed., *Works of George Berkeley* (1898), frontispiece, vol. I. Rand, *Berkeley's American Sojourn.*

DEAN GEORGE BERKELEY, NO. 3

Size: H. 30 in.; W. 25 in.
Date: Unsigned and undated, but probably painted in Newport, 1729.
Description: The subject is shown half front, his right shoulder towards the spectator, his head turned right, three-quarters front, against a dark background. He wears a short gray wig, black cassock and gown, and white bands.

Owner: Massachusetts Historical Society, Boston. In the Society's *Catalogue of Portraits* it is recorded as follows: "Painted by Smibert, on his passage to Newport, R. I., in 1728. Restored by Darius Chase, 1845. Given by Thomas Wetmore, Esq." In the Society's *Proceedings, II,* 65 (1801), is the following vote: "The thanks of the Society were voted to Thomas Wetmore for his donations of sundry pamphlets, etc., the property of his late father, Judge Wetmore, deceased." The portrait in question must be included in the "etc." of this vote, because there is no mention of any other gift from Thomas Wetmore. There is no record of the portrait previous to the date of gift, and both the attribution to Smibert and the statement that it was painted in 1728, "on his passage to Newport," appear to be a tradition which cannot be traced to a date earlier than one more than seventy years after the supposed event. Henry Collins, the Newport merchant, is supposed to have commissioned Smibert to paint a portrait of Berkeley for him. If that tradition is well founded this portrait may be the one painted for Collins. The face strongly resembles that of Berkeley in the "Bermuda Group," and the portrait, though now in poor condition from overcleaning and repainting, appears to be Smibert's work.

Exhibited: Yale University Art Gallery, "The Smibert Tradition," exhibition, October–November 1949.

Reproduced: Bayley, p. 349.

THE BERMUDA GROUP, NO. 1
(DEAN GEORGE BERKELEY AND HIS ENTOURAGE)

Subjects: Dean Berkeley, Mrs. Berkeley and son Henry, Miss Handcock, Messrs. John James, Thomas Moffatt, Richard Dalton, and John Smibert.

Size: H. 70¾ in.; W. 94½ in.

Date: Signed *Jo. Smibert fecit 1729* on the edge of the book which lies flat on the table and serves as a rest for the open book in which Dalton is writing. Faint traces of what was probably the word *Newport* appear below the signature.

Description: A conversation picture depicting a group of individuals against a background which shows three large columns and a distant vista of water, shore, and trees, possibly intended to represent Narragansett Bay. For detailed description see Chapter III.

Owner: Yale University. The picture remained in Smibert's studio until 1808, before which time it had become the property of John Johnston, a painter who had occupied the premises for several years and who presumably had purchased it when the other contents of the studio had been dispersed. In 1808 it was purchased by Isaac Lothrop of Plymouth, Mass., and was sent by him to President Dwight of Yale, as a present to Yale College.

Exhibited: Chicago Art Institute, April–June 1949. Yale University Art Gallery, "The Smibert Tradition," exhibition, October–November 1949.

Reproduced: A small replica in the National Gallery of Ireland, Dublin (see Berkeley Group, No. 2). Berkeley's head and shoulders, as shown in the large picture, were reproduced in a steel engraving which forms the frontispiece to Fraser's *Life and Letters of George Berkeley,* and have been copied in oil on canvases at the Redwood Library, Newport, R. I. (by Hart); at Brown University, Providence (by Pratt); and at the University of California, Berkeley.

In recent years the picture has been many times reproduced in part or in whole. The following is a chronological list of the more important and accessible reproductions in books. I have not included those appearing in newspapers and in other ephemeral articles. (Full citations only of books not cited before in this volume.)

Catalogue, U. S. Centennial Commission's International Exhibition (Philadelphia, 1876), p. 55, no. 5 (as Bishop George Berkeley).

Kingsley, *Yale College* (1879), p. 58.

Benjamin, S. G. W., *Art in America* (1880), p. 16.

Green, J. R., *Short History of the English People* (1885), IV, 1612.

Porter, *Discourse on Berkeley* (1885).

Cook, Clarence C., *Art and Artists of our Time* (1888), vol. III, opp. p. 150.

Sampson, George, ed., *Works of George Berkeley* (1898), II, frontispiece.

Wilson, Rufus R., "America's First Painters," *New England Magazine,* new series, vol. XXVI, no. 1 (March 1902).

Updike, *History of the Episcopal Church in Narragansett, R. I.,* vol. II, opp. p. 171.

The Pageant of America, The American Spirit in Art, (1927), XII, 9.

Mather, F. S., *The American Spirit in Art* (1927), p. 9.

Sizer, Theodore, "New Gallery of the Fine Arts at Yale," *Parnassus,* vol. I, no. 2 (February 1929), cover.

Bayley, F. W., *Five Colonial Artists of New England* (1929), p. 353.

Bolton, T., and H. L. Binsse, *The Antiquarian,* vol. XV, no. 4, p. 36 (October 1930).

Handbook of the Gallery of Fine Arts, Yale University (1931), p. 46.

Rand, *Berkeley's American Sojourn,* frontispiece.

Sherman, F. F., *Early American Painting* (1932), opp. p. 43.

Isham, Samuel, and Royal Cortissoz, *History of American Painting,* p. 12.

The Yale University Library Gazette, vol. VIII, no. 1 (July 1933).

The American Magazine of Art, vol. XXVII, no. 2 (February 1934), frontispiece.

Sizer, Theodore, "The Berkeley Portrait," *Bulletin of the Associates in Fine Arts,* Yale University, vol. VII, no. 2 (June 1936).

Burroughs, *Limners and Likenesses,* frontispiece.

Art Association of Newport, *Retrospective Exhibition* (1936), frontispiece.

Art Digest, vol. XIII, no. 15, p. 6 (May 1, 1939).

Catalogue, Life in America, Special Loan Exhibition of Paintings, Metropolitan Museum of Art (New York, 1939), p. 7.
Catalogue, Exhibition Survey of American Painting, Carnegie Institute (Pittsburgh, 1940).
Hagen, *Birth of the American Tradition in Art,* plate III, opp. p. 56.
St. Gaudens, Homer, *The American Artist* (1941), opp. p. 20.
Shoolman, R., and C. Slatkin, *The Enjoyment of Art in America* (1942), plate 619.
Walker, John, and Magill James, *Great American Paintings from Smibert to Bellows* (1943), plate 1.
Flexner, J. T., *American Painting: First Flowers of our Wilderness,* pp. 120–121.

References:

Tuckerman, H. T., *Book of the Artists* (1867), pp. 42–43.
Dunlap, *History of the . . . Arts . . . in America,* pp. 17, 25, 27.
Perkins, A. T., M.H.S. *Proc.,* vols. XVII (December 1878) and XVIII (May 1879).
Dexter, F. B., *Catalogue, with Descriptive Notices of the Portraits, Busts, etc., belonging to Yale University* (1892), pp. 9–12.
Rand, *Berkeley and Percival,* pp. 36–37, 39, 257.
Coburn, F. W., "John Smibert," *Art in America,* vol. XVII, no. 4, p. 185 (June 1929).
Literary Digest, vol. XVI, no. 3 (July 19, 1930), p. 17.
Lee, Cuthbert, "John Smibert," *Antiques,* vol. XVIII, no. 2, pp. 118–119 (August 1930).
Bolton, T., "John Smibert: Notes and a Catalogue," *Fine Arts,* vol. XX, no. 4, pp. 4, 15, 41 (August 1933).
Sizer, Theodore, "The College Portrait," *Bulletin of the Associates in Fine Arts of Yale University* (June 1934).
Burroughs, Alan, "Notes on Smibert's Development," *Art in America,* vol. XXX, no. 2, pp. 110, 113 (April 1942).

THE BERMUDA GROUP, NO. 2

In the National Gallery of Ireland, in Dublin, there is a small copy of, or study for, the large painting of the Bermuda Group owned by Yale University. Size: H. 24 inches; W. 29 inches. In the Dublin catalogue it is described as "Oil painting by John Smibert. Portrait group of Bishop Berkeley, wife and friends." It was purchased in 1897.

Aside from slight differences of position, the picture is practically a much reduced replica of the one at Yale, but there is a little more space at each edge of the picture and the legs of Dalton and of Berkeley are shown to the floor.

In all probability this is the picture which Thomas Moffatt bequeathed to George Chalmers in his will dated London, August 5, 1786, as "The Bermuda Group" (see p. 47). Presumably it was painted in Newport in

1729 and given by Smibert to his nephew. Its history after its acquisition by George Chalmers until its purchase by the Dublin Gallery is unknown.
Reproduced: There is a modern copy in Berkeley College, Yale University.

RICHARD BILL

Subject: Richard, son of Samuel and Elizabeth Bill, of Boston; born March 25, 1685; married (1) on June 30, 1709, Sarah Davis (1683–1727), (2) on October 1, 1733, Mehitabel (1692–1741), daughter of Col. Stephen and Mercy (Clark) Minot, of Boston. Member of the Ancient and Honorable Artillery Company 1707, ensign 1716, lieutenant 1720; merchant; member of Provincial Council 1737–1741. Died insolvent in 1757. In his inventory his portrait is valued at £15.

Size: H. 50 in.; W. 40¼ in.

Date: Probably before 1740, since soon after that date the sitter became involved in financial difficulties.

Description: This fine portrait shows the subject nearly three-quarter length, half front, his right shoulder towards the spectator, his fine and attractive face turned slightly to the right nearly full front. He stands beside a table covered with a green cloth, upon which is a pewter inkstand with pen, and a letter addressed "To Richard Bill, Esq. in Boston." Behind him is a walnut chair upholstered in dark-blue velvet, set against a plain brown wall. A window shows a ship at anchor, with sea and clouds. The subject has blue eyes and heavy eyebrows. He wears a rather long wig; shirt with ruffles at neck and wrists; and a brownish red velvet coat and waistcoat.

Owner: Art Institute, Chicago. In the inventory of Richard Bill's estate (Suffolk Probate Records, LII, 769), is listed "the Decd. Picture—15" (pounds). His daughter Elizabeth married Joshua Henshaw. In 1861 the portrait was owned by Andrew Henshaw Ward and in 1866 by his granddaughter Mrs. Miles Washburn, whose daughter, Mrs. Warren P. B. Weeks of Boston, owned it in 1934. In 1944 it was acquired through Knoedler by the Art Institute of Chicago.

Exhibited: Copley Society Loan Exhibition, Boston, 1922. Yale University Art Gallery, "The Smibert Tradition," exhibition, October-November 1949.

Reproduced: A copy was painted about 1865 by E. H. Emmons of Norwich, Connecticut, for Ledyard Bill of New York, and is reproduced in *The Bill Genealogy*, by Ledyard Bill (New York, 1867), attributed to Copley.

Another copy by Henry E. Kinney, 1898, hangs in the Executive Department, Massachusetts State House, Boston.

J. Avery, *History of the Town of Ledyard* (1901), p. 105. Bayley, p. 355. F.A.R.L. photo.

References: New York Historical Society Quarterly Bulletin, XVIII, 33 (July 1934). *P. F. Mass.* 206.

MRS. LOUIS BOUCHER

Subject: Sarah, daughter of Richard and Sarah (Winslow) Middle-cott, granddaughter of John and Mary (Chilton) Winslow. Born June 2, 1678. Married Louis Boucher, of Paris and Boston. Neither the date of her death nor that of her husband is recorded.

Size: H. 50 in.; W. 40 in.

Date: c. 1740.

Description: The subject is a large, erect, elderly woman, apparently in her sixties or perhaps seventy years of age. She is shown against a shaded background, three-quarter length, half front, her right shoulder towards the spectator, her head turned to her right, nearly full front. Her right arm rests on the arm of the chair in which she is seated; her left hand holds a book in her lap. She wears a black scarf, lined with gray, over her dark hair, and a black dress with white muslin trim at the neck and sleeves. The costume suggests that she was a widow. The portrait has been relined and is in excellent condition.

It is attributed to Joseph Blackburn in "An Extension of Lawrence Park's Descriptive List of the Work of Joseph Blackburn," by John Hill Morgan and Henry Wilder Foote, *Proceedings of the American Antiquarian Society* (April 1936), and in *P. F. Mass.* 229, but I now believe this attribution is mistaken and consider the portrait to be an excellent example of Smibert's work.

Owner: Mrs. Alexander Breese Porter, Boston, to whose father-in-law, the late Alexander S. Porter, the portrait passed by descent.

JAMES BOWDOIN II (AS A BOY)

Subject: James, son of James Bowdoin I by his second wife, born in Boston August 8, 1727; graduated from Harvard 1745; married Elizabeth Erving, September 15, 1748; died November 6, 1790. Delegate to the First Continental Congress; governor of Massachusetts; first president of The American Academy of Arts and Sciences; Fellow of the Royal Society of London.

Size: H. 33⅝ in.; W. 25⅜ in.

Date: c. 1739–1740.

Description: The subject is a slender boy, perhaps as much as twelve years of age, standing against a delicately painted background showing a meadow with a winding stream, woods, hills and clouds; half front, his right shoulder towards the spectator, his head turned right nearly full front. He has light-brown curling hair hanging to his shoulders, and a pleasant boyish face with a dimpled chin. He wears a green silk coat and waistcoat, white neckband, shirt ruffles, and wristbands. His left hand grasps a strung bow at his side, while his upraised right hand holds an arrow.

The portrait is an exceptionally pleasing eighteenth-century picture of a youth, and in *Robert Feke* (1930), pp. 46–47, 126–128, I attributed it to Feke as having been painted during his first visit to Boston in 1741. Most authorities on colonial portraiture, however, attribute it to Smibert, both on the ground of style and because in 1741 James Bowdoin would have been fourteen years old, whereas in the picture he appears to be at least two and perhaps as much as four years younger, so that the portrait must be dated earlier than Feke's visit. In point of style the portrait seems to me to be a borderline case, and that it might reasonably be attributed to either painter. The argument from the apparent age of the subject is much more cogent, and upon reëxamination of the portrait I now find it difficult to date it as late as 1741 and therefore think that it is probably the work of Smibert.

Owner: Bowdoin College, Brunswick, Maine. In 1811 the portrait was bequeathed, with other family pictures, to Bowdoin College, by James Bowdoin III, and hangs in the Walker Art Building, Brunswick, Maine.

Reproduced: Foote, *Robert Feke,* opp. p. 46. F.A.R.L. 21407.

FRANCIS BRINLEY

Subject: Francis Brinley, born in London 1690. Married Deborah Lyde 1718. Died at Roxbury, Mass., 1765.

Size: H. 50 in.; W. 39¾ in.

Date: 1731 or 1732.

Description: Col. Brinley, a short, rather corpulent man, is shown seated in an armchair, against a background which shows, on the spectator's right, a vista of meadows with haystacks, water, and a distant town. This represents the view from Brinley's mansion in Roxbury, and is one of the earliest views of Boston. Beacon Hill is clearly discernible at the edge of the vista. The figure of Brinley is shown half front, his right shoulder towards the spectator, his head turned slightly, nearly full front. His elbows rest on the arms of his chair, his hands clasped in front of his waistcoat. He wears a full white wig; a steenkirk scarf twisted and with the ends thrust through a waistcoat buttonhole; a reddish-brown coat and waistcoat.

Owner: Mrs. Henry Wharton, Philadelphia. This portrait and its companion piece descended to Edward L. Brinley of Philadelphia, thence (1920) to his daughter, Mrs. Henry Wharton. It hangs in the house of Mrs. Bispham McKean, "Byfield," Ithan, Pa., a descendant of the subject.

Exhibited: Hudson-Fulton Celebration, exhibition held in the Metropolitan Museum of Art, New York, 1909. Yale University Art Gallery, "The Smibert Tradition," exhibition, October–November 1949.

Reproduced: Hudson-Fulton Exhibition, II (Catalogue, Exhibition of American Paintings, Metropolitan Museum of Art, 1909), 19: Francis Brinley, no. 35. Theodore Bolton, article "John Smibert," in *Fine Arts,* vol. XX, no. 4, p. 14 (August 1933). F.A.R.L. photo.

MRS. FRANCIS BRINLEY AND SON HENRY

Subject: Deborah Lyde of Boston; born 1698; married Francis Brinley in 1718; died 1761; and her infant son Henry Brinley (1729–1816). She was a granddaughter of Judge Byfield (*q.v.*).

Size: H. 50 in.; W. 39¾ in.

Date: 1731 or 1732.

Description: Mrs. Brinley is shown three-quarter length, nearly full front, seated in an armchair, against a curtain. To her right is a large potted plant on a table, beside a window. She wears a blue silk dress, with white muslin guimpe and undersleeves. In her lap she holds her young son with her left arm about him. He is unclothed save for a piece of loose white linen wrapped about his middle. Her right hand holds a spray of orange blossoms, towards which the child holds out his right hand.

Owner: Mrs. Henry Wharton, Philadelphia. With the companion portrait of Col. Brinley this picture passed by descent to Edward L. Brinley of Philadelphia, thence to his daughter, Mrs. Henry Wharton. It hangs in the house of Mrs. Bispham McKean, "Byfield," Ithan, Pa., a descendant of the subject.

Exhibited: Hudson-Fulton Celebration, exhibition held in the Metropolitan Museum of Art, New York, 1909. Yale University Art Gallery, "The Smibert Tradition," exhibition, October–November 1949.

Reproduced: Hudson-Fulton Exhibition, II (Catalogue, Exhibition of American Paintings, Metropolitan Museum of Art, 1909), 19: Mrs. Francis Brinley, No. 36. F.A.R.L. photo.

MRS. BENJAMIN BROWNE (MRS. NATHANIEL BALSTON)

Subject: Eunice, daughter of John and Mary (Kitchen) Turner of Salem, born April 17, 1713; married (1) Benjamin Browne of Salem June 19, 1729; (2) in 1751, Nathaniel Balston; died March 1783. (Sister-in-law of Mr. and Mrs. William Browne and sister of John Turner, all of whom Smibert also painted.)

Size: H. 49½ in.; W. 30¼ in.

Date: Presumably painted in the seventeen-thirties.

Description: Mrs. Browne is shown as a large, robust woman, standing nearly full front beside a table upon which her right hand rests while her left holds an old-rose scarf across her body. She has dark-brown hair and eyes, and a fresh complexion, and wears a soft brown dress with the usual trim at bodice and sleeves. The figure is set against a plain brown background.

Owner: Mrs. Arthur W. Bell, Boston.

Reproduced: Bayley, p. 345, listed as Mrs. Joseph Balston (Eunice Turner). A copy was owned by the late Edward N. Fenno; another copy is in the House of Seven Gables, Salem. F.A.R.L. 8006.

Reference: P. F. Mass. 122, as Mrs. Balston.

SAMUEL BROWNE

Subject: "Colonel the Honorable" Samuel Browne, of Salem, born in 1669; died 1731. He was the leading merchant, richest man, and most prominent citizen of Salem in his day, and held various public offices, being town treasurer, councilor, judge of the Court of Common Pleas, and colonel of the regiment. He made handsome donations to Harvard College and to the Salem school. Benjamin Pickman (1741–1819) wrote, "The family of the Brownes has been the most remarkable family that has ever lived in the Town of Salem, holding places of the highest trust in the Town, County and State, and possessing great riches. Their donations to the schools have been considerable, and their mercantile engagements have very much contributed to the growth of the Town." [1] Samuel Browne married Abigail Keach and was brother-in-law to Judge Benjamin Lynde (*q.v.*), and father of William Browne (*q.v.*).

Size: H. 29½ in.; W. 24½ in.

Date: 1730.

Description: The head and bust of the subject are shown against a dark, shaded background with spandrels in the four corners, half front, his right shoulder towards the spectator, his head turned slightly right, nearly full front. He wears a full gray wig, long steenkirk tie, gray coat and waistcoat. His full, rather florid face, with long nose and brown eyes, is strong and vigorous, with much character.

Owner: Mrs. Stanard Funsten, Pasadena, California. The portrait passed by descent to Mrs. James T. Wallis, of Germantown, Pa., and is now (1949) owned by her daughter, Mrs. Funsten.

WILLIAM BROWNE

Subject: William, son of Samuel (*q.v.*) and Abigail Browne, born in Salem May 7, 1709; died April 27, 1763. He was graduated at Harvard in 1727, his social status being indicated by his being placed first in his class, above Thomas Hutchinson and Jonathan Trumbull. He married (1) in 1737, Mary, daughter of Governor Burnet, who died in 1745; (2) Mary French of New Brunswick, N. J. About 1740 he built, on what the neighbors called "Folly Hill," in Danvers, a few miles out of Salem, the mansion which he named "Browne Hall" after the Lancashire seat of his ancestors.

William Browne represented the fourth generation of wealthy merchants in his family in Salem. He possessed "an extraordinary library of books by the best ancient and modern authors," and is described as "a great virtuoso."

Size: H. 96 in.; W. 58⅔ in.

Date: c. 1744. On July 1, 1743, Smibert ordered from Arthur Pond "two whole length cloths," presumably to be used for the full-length portraits of William Browne and his wife.

[1] *Essex Institute Hist. Coll.*, XXXI, 214.

Description: The subject is shown at full length, half front, his right shoulder towards the spectator, his head turned right, full front, against a background which shows a column on the spectator's left, and to the right a wide, open landscape showing a stream, hills, woods, and sky. He is handsomely dressed in a white wig, a long, brown velvet coat, waistcoat, and knee breeches, white ruffles at neck and wrists, white stockings, black shoes with gold buckles. His left arm holds his cocked hat against his side, his left hand holds a pair of white gloves. The right hand points across his body to the distant view. The picture is a handsome one, but, as usual with Smibert's standing figures, the pose is uneasy, and the legs from the knees down are badly drawn, the feet being toed out at an impossible angle.

Owner: Johns Hopkins University, Baltimore, Md. The picture was bequeathed to his son, William Burnet Browne, who moved to Virginia in 1769; it passed from him by descent to J. L. Deans of "Rosewell," Gloucester County, Virginia, who, about 1880, gave it to his cousin Junius Browne, from whom it was later purchased by Dr. W. L. Halstead, who bequeathed it to Johns Hopkins University.

Exhibited: Baltimore Museum of Art, 1923. Yale University Art Gallery, "The Smibert Tradition," exhibition, October–November 1949.

Reproduced: Bayley, p. 357. Engraving by George Elmer Browne in *Essex Institute Collections,* vol. XXXII, nos. 7–12, p. 237 (July–December 1896). F.A.R.L. 3293.

MRS. WILLIAM BROWNE

Subject: Mary, daughter of William Burnet, who had been Governor of New York, Massachusetts, and New Hampshire, and granddaughter of Gilbert Burnet, Bishop of Salisbury; born 1722. In 1737, when not yet fifteen, she married William Browne, of Salem. She was the mother of six children before her death on August 1, 1745, at the age of twenty-three.

Size: H. 96 in.; W. 58 in.

Date: 1744. Browne Hall, shown in the background, was in process of building between 1740 and 1745, and the subject died in the latter year.

Description: Mrs. Browne is shown full length, standing against a background which shows a column on the right, and on the left a view of stream, meadow, and woodland, including Browne Hall, built by her husband near Salem. She has brown hair and eyes, and wears a velvet dress of soft blue with white muslin trim at the bodice, and muslin undersleeves. A rose-colored mantle about her waist is held with her left hand, while the right points to Browne Hall in the distance. Although she is a fine-looking woman this portrait is so poorly executed that some critics have assigned it to another painter than Smibert, or have thought that it might be in large part the work of an assistant. There appears to be no reason for doubting that the companion portrait of William Browne is by

Smibert; it is extremely unlikely that he would have turned over so important a commission to a rival, if he had had one; and he is not known to have had any assistant. The portrait must, therefore, I believe, be accepted as an unsatisfactory example of Smibert's work in his declining years.

Owner: Johns Hopkins University, Baltimore, Maryland, by the same line of descent as the portrait of the subject's husband (*q.v.*).

Exhibited: Baltimore Museum of Art. Yale University Art Gallery, "The Smibert Tradition," exhibition, October–November 1949.

Reproduced: Cleveland Museum of Art, *Bulletin,* eighth year, no. 1 *Historical Collections,* vol. XXXII, nos. 7–12, p. 237 (July–December 1896). Bayley, p. 359. F.A.R.L. 3292.

MRS. THOMAS BULFINCH

Subject: Judith, daughter of John and Judith (Hobby) Colman, born in Boston May 1, 1707; married, June 1724, Dr. Thomas Bulfinch (1694–1757), a physician educated in Paris, whose portrait was painted by Blackburn. Charles Bulfinch, the distinguished architect, was their son. Mrs. Bulfinch died in Boston July 20, 1765.

Size: H. 29 in.; W. 24¼ in.

Date: c. 1733.

Description: The head and bust of Mrs. Bulfinch are shown in a painted oval against a shaded background, nearly full front. She is shown as a rather large, deep-bosomed woman between twenty and thirty years of age, with a pleasing and intelligent countenance, brown eyes, and light brown hair, a long curl of which hangs over her left shoulder. She wears a blue dress, trimmed with white muslin ruffles. A fine example of Smibert's work.

Owner: Purchased November 1920 by the Cleveland Museum of Art from Miss Emily Hallowell, West Medford, Mass.

Reproduced: Cleveland Museum of Art, *Bulletin,* eighth year, no. 1 (January 1921). Bayley, p. 361. F.A.R.L. photo.

JUDGE NATHANIEL BYFIELD, NO. I

Subject: Nathaniel, twenty-first child of Rev. Richard Byfield of Long Ditton, Surrey, England, born 1653; arrived in Boston 1674; married (1) Deborah, daughter of Capt. Thomas Clarke, 1675; invested in Rhode Island lands and lived for a time at Bristol; joined the Ancient and Honorable Artillery Company, Boston, 1679; member of the General Court, 1696 and 1697; judge of probate; the first judge of the Court of Vice-Admiralty; married (2) Sarah, daughter of Gov. Leverett, 1718; died at Boston June 6, 1733. As his portrait indicates, he was aggressive, dictatorial and ambitious, but he was also sound in judgment, generous in charity, and sufficiently independent in opinion to oppose the witchcraft delusion.

Size: H. 30 in.; W. 25 in.

Date: In the lower left-hand corner: *Ætatis 78, 1730.*

Description: The head and bust of the subject are shown in a painted oval, against a shaded background, three-quarters front, his right shoulder towards the spectator. Byfield is shown as a pudgy old gentleman with a broken nose, small mouth, and thick lips. He wears a very long, flowing gray wig, golden-brown coat and waistcoat, and a white steenkirk tie. This portrait is referred to in the poem addressed "to Mr. Smibert, on the Sight of his Pictures," in which the author writes, "Fixt strong in thought there Byfield's Lines appear." It must therefore have been painted not later than early March, 1730.

Owner: Metropolitan Museum, New York. This portrait was owned in 1919 by Mrs. R. W. King of Montclair, N. J., a descendant of Sir William Pepperell through the Sparhawk-Jarvis-Cutts line. She sold it in that year to Charles A. Munn as a portrait of Governor Belcher which he had given to Pepperell, such being the family tradition. Upon being cleaned it was discovered to represent Byfield rather than Belcher (see Bolton, III, 741). Mr. Munn in 1924 bequeathed it to the Metropolitan Museum.

Exhibited: Yale University Art Gallery, "The Smibert Tradition," exhibition, October–November 1949.

Reproduced: Bolton, II, 359–360; also III, 741, 934. *Bulletin of the Metropolitan Museum of Art,* vol. XX, no. 1 (January 1925). *Catalogue of Paintings, Metropolitan Museum* (8th ed., 1926). Bayley, p. 363. F.A.R.L. photo.

JUDGE NATHANIEL BYFIELD, NO. 2

What appears to be a contemporary replica of No. 1 is now (1949) on loan at the Essex Institute, Salem, Mass., from the owner, the First Parish of Byfield, Mass. It is labeled on the back, "Portrait of Hon. Nathaniel Byfield given to Byfield Parish June 1, 1825, by one of his descendants, George Lyde of New York." *P. F. Mass.* 345.

JUDGE NATHANIEL BYFIELD, NO. 3

This portrait is nearly identical with that listed as *Nathaniel Byfield,* No. 1. It is discussed in Bolton's *Portraits of the Founders,* pp. 359–361, where it is said: "The portrait was owned, in 1880, by the Honorable Francis Brinley, of Newport, a descendant. At Mrs. Brinley's death the picture was bought by George Tucker Bispham, Esq., of Philadelphia." It is now owned by his sister, Mrs. Bispham McKean, Ithan, Pa.

Exhibited: Yale University Art Gallery, "The Smibert Tradition," exhibition, October–November 1949. A copy of one of these three portraits, by Jane Stuart, is at the Byfield School, Bristol, Conn.

SAMUEL CARY

Subject: Captain Samuel Cary of Charlestown, Mass., born 1683, died February 1739/40. Married (1) Mary Foster, December 9, 1712; (2) Mary

Martyn, February 21, 1722/23. He was a prosperous ship chandler and merchant, with large holdings of real estate, and his property at his death was valued at £1969.

Size: H. 35½ in.; W. 28 in.

Date: 1730 or soon after.

Description: The subject is shown against a dark background with a window on the right through which a ship is seen; half front, his right shoulder towards the spectator, his head turned to his right nearly full front. He is a fine-looking man who appears to be at least forty years of age. He wears a full white wig, one bob end of which hangs on his right shoulder, a steenkirk tie with fringed ends, and a tobacco-brown coat and waistcoat. His right forearm and hand, the large sleeve cuff turned far back, rest on a table beside him. The picture appears to be the work of Smibert.

Owner: Miss Katrina Kipper, Boston. The year after Cary's death his eldest son purchased the Bellingham house in Charlestown. This house was visited by Pierre Eugène Du Simitière when he came to Boston in 1767/68, and he noted that it contained "Several curious pictures" including "a Ceres head, an Italian piece by Batista . . . some little battle pieces . . . Still life of game, etc." No mention is made of the portrait of Capt. Cary, presumably because before that date his other sons Edward and Nathaniel had moved to Nantucket and had taken the portrait with them. The portrait is said to have passed down the line of descendants from Nathaniel into the Folger and then the Vincent family, and to have been purchased, about 1930, in Nantucket by Mr. Frank Sylvia from a Vincent who had moved to California. Mr. Sylvia sold it to Mr. Herbert Lawton of Boston who owned it in 1937, and afterwards sold it to Miss Katrina Kipper.

Reference: P. F. Mass. 374, listed as belonging to Herbert Lawton.

JUDGE CHARLES CHAMBERS

Subject: Charles, son of Edward and Elizabeth (Palmer) Chambers, of Torksey, Lincolnshire, England, born 1660; sea captain; merchant in Boston; justice of the peace; judge of court of common pleas; married (1) January 30, 1687, Rebecca (1657–1735), daughter of John and Mary Patefield, (2) February 10, 1735/36, Margaret, daughter of William and Mary Vaughan, and widow of Captain Foye; died at Charlestown, Mass., April 27, 1743.

Size: H. 47¾ in.; W. 37¾ in.

Date: Probably soon after 1730, judging by his apparent age and his costume.

Description: Judge Chambers is shown seated, half front, his right shoulder towards the spectator, his head turned nearly full front. He wears a long white wig, steenkirk tie, ruffles at his wrists, a brown velvet coat and waistcoat. His left hand rests upon his knee. His right arm rests upon the table at his side, the hand holding a quill pen. The table is covered with a green cloth, upon which rests a pewter inkstand, quill pen, and letter. A ship is seen through a window at the left.

Owner: Mr. Charles R. Codman, Boston, by inheritance from his father, Russell S. Codman, 1941. The portrait now hangs in the house of Dorothy S. F. Codman, Lincoln, Mass., who also has a life interest in it.

Exhibited: Loan Exhibition of One Hundred Colonial Portraits, Museum of Fine Arts, Boston, 1930.

Reproduced: Bolton, II, 536c. Bayley, p. 365. *Catalogue, Loan Exhibition of One Hundred Colonial Portraits,* Museum of Fine Arts (Boston, 1930), p. 18. F.A.R.L. photo.

References: Bolton, II, 536a, b. M.H.S. *Proc.* vol. XVII (1879–1880). *P. F. Mass.* 379.

REV. JOHN CHECKLEY

Subject: John Checkley, born at Boston *c.* 1680, died at Providence, R. I., February 15, 1754. Educated at Boston Latin School and by private tutors at Oxford, England. Being a young man of some means he traveled in Europe and collected works of art. Returned to Boston about 1710 and set up as a merchant and bookseller. Married May 28, 1713, Rebecca, daughter of Samuel Miller of Milton, Mass., a sister of Ebenezer Miller (*q.v.*). He was an ardent controversialist on behalf of the Church of England and returned to England, where he was ordained in 1738, returning to serve as rector of King's Church, now St. John's, in Providence, from 1739 until his death.

Size: H. *c.* 27 in.; W. *c.* 21 in.

Date: Before 1739, when he left Boston.

Description: The head and bust of the subject are shown nearly full front, his right shoulder slightly advanced. He wears a gray wig, black gown, and clerical white bands. The portrait is in the original frame. There is a long family tradition that the subject was Rev. John Checkley and the painter Smibert, a tradition supported by the anecdote on pp. 73–74, but the countenance shown in the portrait does not indicate any grounds for the satirical remarks there reported, and looks younger than Checkley would have been when Smibert reached Boston, or at the time he himself had taken orders. The portrait, however, is reported to have been in bad condition until its recent (1948) restoration by Horace G. Bentley of London, and a photograph of it (I have not seen the original) seems to indicate that a substantial amount of repainting was necessary.

Owner: Mrs. Edmund Gosling, "Bloomfield Cottage," Paget, Bermuda. The portrait was inherited by Checkley's only surviving child, Deborah, who married Henry Paget, a merchant of Providence and Boston, and passed to their daughter Anne, who married Capt. Joseph Olney, Jr.; to their daughter Rebecca, who married Dr. Henry Malcolm; to their daughter Angelica, who married Joseph Gibbons Malcolm; to their daughter Esther, who married John Lloyd; to their daughter Mary, who married Norman Harriott Jones; to their daughter Ethel, now Mrs. Gosling.

DAVID CHESEBRO

Subject: David Chesebro (or Cheseborough), a wealthy merchant of Newport, R. I., born February 2, 1702; married, (1) June 1729, Abigail Rogers, (2) Margaret Sylvester; removed about the time of the Revolution to Stonington, Conn., where he died February 27, 1782. His portrait and those of his second wife and daughter Abigail were also painted by Blackburn in 1754.

Size: H. 30 in.; W. 25 in.

Date: Probably painted in Newport in 1729.

Description: The subject is shown as a young man in his later twenties, half front, with his right shoulder towards the spectator, his face turned right nearly full front, against a dark brown background. There are spandrels in the lower corners. He wears a gray wig and brown coat and waistcoat, with white ruffles. The well-colored face has dark, bushy eyebrows, brown eyes, and a prominent nose. The portrait is unsigned but looks like Smibert's work, and from the age of the subject, who was first married in 1729, the picture fits in well with the period of Smibert's stay in Newport in that year.

Ownership: Stonington Historical Society, Stonington, Conn. The portrait descended to his daughter Abigail, wife of Alexander Grant; to her daughter Elizabeth (Grant) Smith; to her son David Cheseborough Smith; to his daughter Betsy (Smith) Williams; and to her daughter Bessie S. (Williams) Sherman of Chicago, who gave it, about 1916, to the Stonington Historical Society.

Reproduced: Bayley, p. 367. F.A.R.L. 3957.

MISS JANE CLARK

Subject: The subject is said to be Jane, daughter of Jonathan Clark; she was born in England in 1723 and married John Lewis. A label on the back of the frame reads: "Portrait of Miss Jane Clark at the age of 17 years, painted in England about 1739. Artist unknown, possibly Blackburn." The portrait is said to have been brought to Groton, Mass., by Jonathan Clark Lewis, son of the subject.

Size: H. 50 in.; W. 40 in.

Date: 1739?

Description: The subject is a pleasing young girl of about seventeen years, seated outdoors against a background with a dark cliff on the spectator's left and a landscape to the right; three-quarters front, her right shoulder towards the spectator, her head turned nearly full front. She wears a rose-colored dress with white muslin trim. In her lap she holds a round basket of fruit with her left hand, while her right hand holds up a peach.

The statement on the label reports what appears to be an unreliable family tradition and the attribution to Blackburn or to Hogarth (as in *P. F. Mass.* 425) may be dismissed. William Sawitzky thought the portrait characteristic of Smibert, and it is attributed to him in Flexner's *First Flowers of Our Wilderness*. From the point of view of style that attribution appears reasonable. The identification of the subject as Jane Clark may be correct. If so, she must have come to this country in early girlhood, before her marriage.

Owner: Massachusetts Historical Society, Boston. The portrait has a label on the back reading, "Presented to the Trustees of the Museum of Fine Arts by Mrs. Henry Edwards." The Trustees evidently declined the gift, because in 1916 the portrait was given to the Massachusetts Historical Society by Miss Susan Minns of Boston.

Reproduced: Flexner, p. 129. F.A.R.L. photo. *P. F. Mass.* 425, attributed to Hogarth.

HENRY COLLINS

Subject: Henry Collins, of Newport, Rhode Island; born March 25, 1699, son of Arnold and Ammi (Almy) Collins; died at Newport, April 29, 1765. He was educated in England for a mercantile career, and was long the most public-spirited and richest merchant in Newport, though late in life he lost his property. He was also a student and a lover of art and literature. He gave the land for the Redwood Library in Newport. Dr. Benjamin Waterhouse called him "the Lorenzo de Medici of Rhode Island."

Size: H. 49 in.; W. 39 in.

Date: 1729.

Description: Collins is shown standing against a dark-brown background, three-quarter length, half front, his right shoulder towards the spectator, his head turned slightly right, nearly full front. He wears a gray wig, reddish-brown velvet coat and waistcoat, white stock with ruffle, plain wristbands. His right hand rests upon a table covered with a bluish-green cloth, upon which lie a book, inkstand, and letter addressed "To Mr. Henry Collins, Newport." His left hand holds an open letter. The portrait is a fine specimen of Smibert's work.

Owner: Countess Lâzlo Széchényi, New York. Henry Collins died unmarried. His portrait descended in the family of his half brother, Governor Richard Ward, to W. J. Flagg, and thence by inheritance to the present owner.

Reproduced: Engraving, *The Seventh Day Baptist Memorial* (*c.* 1750), in reverse; reproduced in the extra-illustrated ed. of G. C. Mason's *Reminiscences of Newport* (1884), VI, 12. Engraving, *Newport Historical Magazine*, about 1880. This engraving is reproduced in Bridenbaugh, *Cities in the Wilderness* (1938), frontispiece. *Rhode Island Historical Magazine*, vol. V, no. 2 (October 1884), frontispiece. F.A.R.L. 10370.

BENJAMIN COLMAN, 2ND

Subject: Benjamin, son of John and Judith (Hobby) Colman (nephew of Rev. Benjamin Colman); born in Boston 1710; graduated from Harvard

1727; married in 1739 to Hannah Pemberton (*q.v.*); died 1765. A Boston merchant.

Size: H. 49 in.; W. 39 in.

Date: About 1740.

Description: The subject is shown standing against a plain, dark background, three-quarter length, half front, his right shoulder towards the spectator, his head turned nearly full front. He wears a gray wig, ruffles at neck and wrists, and a dark-red coat and waistcoat. His right hand rests upon a table by his side, while his left holds a letter addressed

> *To*
> *Mr Benjn Colman*
> *Merch^t*

He appears to be not above thirty years old.

Owner: Art Museum of the New Britain Institute, New Britain, Conn. The portrait passed by descent to Dr. Colman W. Cutler, New York, and was sold by his heirs through the Macbeth Gallery to the Art Museum of the New Britain Institute, in 1947.

Exhibited: Museum of Fine Arts, Boston, 1878. A Benefit Exhibition, Bundles for Britain, New York, March 26 to April 25, 1941.

Reproduced: F.A.R.L. 32289.

References: Bolton, III, 1025. *Colonial Society of Massachusetts Publications,* vol. VI (February 1899).

REV. WILLIAM COOPER

Subject: William, son of Thomas and Mehitabel (Minot) Cooper of Boston, born in Boston March 20, 1694. He was graduated from Harvard College in 1712, and from 1716 until his death in Boston on December 12, 1743, he was a colleague of Rev. Benjamin Colman at the Brattle Square Church. He was elected president of Harvard College in 1737, but declined the position. He married (1) Judith Sewall, (2) Mary Foye.

Size: H. 29⅛ in.; W. 24⅛ in.

Date: 1743.

Description: The subject is shown nearly full front, his right shoulder slightly advanced, within a painted oval. He wears a white wig, bands, and a black coat, and carries a drape over his right arm.

Smibert is known to have painted a portrait of Rev. William Cooper because Peter Pelham made a mezzotint inscribed:

> *I. Smibert Pinx − − − − P. Pelham fecit*
> *The Rev^d Mr. William Cooper*
> *of Boston in New England Æ^t 50, 1743*
> *Printed for and Sold by Step^n Whiting at*
> *ye Rose & Crown in Union Street Boston.*

This portrait must have been painted in the earlier part of 1743, because Cooper died on December 12, 1743, in his fiftieth year.

On February 12, 1880, what was supposed to be the portrait of Cooper painted by Smibert was given to the Massachusetts Historical Society by William Perkins. The late Lawrence Park, however, in his Descriptive List of paintings attributed to Joseph Badger, lists this portrait as Badger's rather than Smibert's, but adds that "Smibert painted a portrait of Cooper which was engraved in mezzotint by Peter Pelham," indicating his belief that there were two different portraits of Cooper. The difficulty in accepting this theory is that no second portrait of William Cooper is known to exist and that Pelham's mezzotint is clearly a close reproduction of the portrait now at the Massachusetts Historical Society. It is true that in its present condition that portrait does not look like Smibert's work, but the face has been so heavily repainted that it looks like a mask, though still somewhat resembling the face shown in Pelham's mezzotint. It is my opinion that it was this repainting which misled Lawrence Park into attributing the portrait to Badger and that Smibert's work lies beneath the repainting.

Owner: Massachusetts Historical Society, Boston.

Reproduced: Mezzotint by Peter Pelham as noted above. Winsor, II, 212. *The Manifesto Church: Records of the Church in Brattle Square* (1902), p. 24. F.A.R.L. photo of Pelham's engraving.

References: M.H.S. *Proc.*, XVII, 328. *P. F. Mass.* 496, attributed to Badger.

REV. JOHN COTTON (SO-CALLED; JOSIAH COTTON?)

Subject: This portrait was purchased about 1850 by John E. Thayer from a Boston dealer who sold it as a likeness of the Rev. John Cotton (1585–1652) who was rector of St. Botolph's Church, Boston, Lincolnshire, and who emigrated to Boston, Massachusetts, in 1633 and became the minister of the First Church and one of the leading figures of the colony. The person represented, however, does not in any way answer to the description of John Cotton given in Mather's *Magnalia;* he wears a wig and costume of a century later than the period of the emigrant John Cotton; and the picture appears to be the work of Smibert. Mr. Charles K. Bolton, discussing this portrait (as a representation of the first Rev. John Cotton) in *Portraits of the Founders*, p. 651, says, "The origin of the Cotton tradition is unknown, but the face has a surprising resemblance to Pelham's engraved portrait of Cotton Mather."

The "Cotton tradition" is probably due to the fact that there were no less than six men in the colonial period named John Cotton, one of whom was a second Rev. John Cotton, son of Rev. Rowland Cotton, and great-grandson of the emigrant. He was born in 1693; was graduated from Harvard in 1710; was ordained as minister of the church at Newton, Mass., November 3, 1714; married Mary, daughter of Robert Gibbs of Boston, February 19, 1719; and died May 17, 1757, after a ministry at Newton lasting forty-two years and six months. The dealer who sold the portrait had secured it at a sale in Newton, as representing "Rev. John Cotton." If the sale was one of goods which had descended from this second Rev. John Cotton it is easy to see how the name "Rev. John Cotton" should have been attached to it, and both the dealer and the purchaser were probably aware of the existence of only the earlier and more famous bearer of that name. Recognizing the impossibility of this identification, the late F. W. Bayley suggested that the subject might be the second Rev. John Cotton. This possibility, however, also appears to be ruled out, first because the subject appears to be an older man than Cotton would have been until the very end of Smibert's career as a painter and, second, because of the costume, which is that of a layman and not of a minister, and which includes a long, white steenkirk tie such as elderly gentlemen still wore in the seventeen-thirties, but which later passed out of use.

Inasmuch as the face is of the Mather-Cotton type it is probable that the portrait represents a member of that family connection. The late Lawrence Park pointed out that Josiah Cotton (1680–1756), who studied theology and preached occasionally but was never ordained, who taught school in Marblehead and Plymouth, and was Justice of the Peace, Clerk of the County Court and Registrar of Probate for Plymouth County, might be the subject. No other plausible identification has been advanced.

Size: H. 30 in.; W. 27 ¾ in.

Date: About 1740, judging from the costume.

Description: The head and bust of the subject are shown against a dark background, with spandrels in the lower corners, nearly full front. He wears a short gray wig, long white steenkirk tie, and golden-brown coat. He has a long nose, rather wide mouth with a full lower lip, dark brown eyes with straight brown bushy eyebrows, and ruddy complexion. The face, while not handsome, is strong, vigorous, and intelligent. It appears to be that of a man approaching or in his sixties.

Owner: John E. Thayer, Milton, Mass. It was inherited by Mr. John E. Thayer's daughter, Miss Adele G. Thayer, and was bequeathed by her to the late John E. Thayer (the younger). It is now owned by the present John E. Thayer.

Reproduced: The portrait was reproduced as a picture of the first John Cotton (1585–1652) in Drake, *History and Antiquities of Boston* (1856), p. 156, and in Thompson, *History of Boston, England* (1856), in both of which the engravers changed the costume by substituting clerical bands for the steenkirk tie shown in the portrait. The engraving in Drake was copied in a woodcut in Winsor, I, 157. The picture has also been reproduced as the first Rev. John Cotton in: A. B. Ellis, *History of the First Church in Boston* (1881), p. 35. *The New England Magazine* (1887, 1896, 1899). Fiske, *Beginnings of New England* (1898). *Harper's Magazine* (1901). Wilson, *History of the American People* (1902). A. M. Earle, *Two Centuries of Costume* (1903), I, 42. Bolton, II, 563. C. K. Shipton, Sibley's *Harvard Graduates* (1937), V, 517 (as the younger John Cotton, with clerical bands). F.A.R.L. photo.

The portrait was used as the model for the head of the modern recumbent figure commemorating the first John Cotton in the present building of the First Church in Boston.

References: Bolton, II, 561–563. *P. F. Mass.* 511, as the younger John Cotton.

LORD CULLEN AND HIS FAMILY

Subject: Sir Francis Grant, Bart. (*q.v.*), Lord Cullen, of Monymusk, Aberdeenshire, Scotland, and eleven other members of his family.

Date: 1720.

Description: James Lewis Caw, in *Scottish Painting Past and Present* (1908), p. 26, says, "At Monymusk there is a cabinet-sized oval of Lady Grant, dated 1717, and a large group of twelve life-size figures, 'Lord Cullen and his Family,' painted three years later [by Smibert]. These I have not seen, but J. M. Gray noted that the group was hard in execution and smooth in handling, and had little colour in the shadows, but was carefully drawn, with much character in the faces." I have not seen this picture, but assume from the foregoing description that it must be signed and dated.

Owner: Sir Arthur Grant, Bart., Monymusk, Aberdeenshire, Scotland.

MRS. NATHANIEL CUNNINGHAM

Subject: Ann, daughter of Louis and Sarah (Middlecott) Boucher, of Boston; born 1703; married, in 1722, Nathaniel Cunningham, a Boston merchant. Her mother was painted by Smibert; her husband by Joseph Badger.

Size: H. 49½ in.; W. 40 in.

Date: About 1733.

Description: The subject is shown seated out-of-doors at the foot of a rocky cliff, full front, with her head turned slightly to her left. She has brown eyes and dark brown hair, a curl of which rests on her left shoulder. She appears to be a rather large woman, not more than thirty years of age. She wears a low-cut gown of bluish-green silk, with white muslin ruffles at bodice and sleeves. Across her lap lies a plum-colored silk scarf. Her left hand is raised to her bodice; her right hand rests upon her scarf at her side, beside a small brown and white spaniel.

Owner: Toledo Museum of Art, Toledo, Ohio. The portrait descended to Mrs. Charles F. Russell of Boston, who owned it in 1922; at her death it passed to Miss Mary Otis Porter, and from her to Miss Frances R. Porter and Mrs. William Stanley Parker, in 1942. Sold in 1947 to the Toledo Museum of Art.

Reproduced: Bayley, p. 375 (but her maiden name is erroneously given as Sarah Kilby, and her dates as 1732–1779). F.A.R.L. 1426.

Exhibited: Copley Society Loan Exhibition, Boston Art Club, 1922. Museum of Fine Arts, Boston, on loan 1916–1947.

REV. CALEB CUSHING

Subject: Rev. Caleb Cushing, born 1672; graduated from Harvard College 1692; minister at Salisbury, Mass., 1698–1752; died 1752.

Size: H. 28¾ in.; W. 24 in.

Date: About 1740, or later.

Description: The subject is shown nearly full front against a dark background, with spandrels in the lower corners. He is shown as an old man, with long white hair, parted in the middle and falling to his shoulders, brown eyes, a long, hooked nose, and heavy chin. He is dressed in ministerial gown, stock, and bands.

From the apparent age of the subject it would seem that the portrait must have been painted between about 1740 and the date of his death, and it is difficult to surmise who the artist could have been if not Smibert, although it is not particularly characteristic of Smibert's work.

Owner: Miss Margaret W. Cushing, Newburyport, Mass. The portrait has come down in the family, and was formerly owned by Mr. Caleb Cushing, an uncle of the present owner.

WILLIAM DUDLEY

Subject: William, son of Governor Joseph and Rebecca (Tyng) Dudley, of Roxbury, born October 20, 1686; married March 10, 1720/21, Elizabeth, daughter of Addington and Elizabeth (Wainwright) Davenport; Speaker of the House; died 1743.

Size: H. 35⅛ in.; W. 27½ in.

Date: c. 1730? The subject appears to be not much more than forty years of age, which would indicate that the picture was painted soon after Smibert reached Boston.

Description: The subject is shown standing, half length, half front, his right shoulder towards the spectator, his head turned nearly full front, against a dark background, which to the right shows a glimpse of distant trees and sky. He wears a full, gray wig, white neckcloth, and long twisted steenkirk tie, the ends of which are thrust through a waistcoat buttonhole, red coat and waistcoat, ruffles at wrists. His right hand rests on his hip. The original carved and gilded frame matches that on the portrait of his wife.

Owner: Mrs. Arthur W. Bell, Boston.

Reproduced: Art in America, vol. XVII, no. 4 (June, 1929), opp. p. 176 (as Paul Dudley). Bayley, p. 377, as Paul Dudley. F.A.R.L. 9008.

References: M.H.S. *Proc.* (January 1886), p. 197. *P. F. Mass.* 654.

MRS. WILLIAM DUDLEY (ELIZABETH DAVENPORT)?

Subject: This painting was formerly supposed to represent Mrs. Paul Dudley, and to have been painted by Blackburn. It is clearly not by Blackburn, and the subject does not at all resemble other portraits of Mrs. Paul Dudley. The late Lawrence Park attributed the picture to

Smibert and thought that it probably represented Elizabeth, daughter of Addington and Elizabeth (Wainwright) Davenport of Boston, who was born December 20, 1704; married William Dudley March 10, 1720/21; and died in 1756.

Size: H. 35¼ in.; W. 27⅛ in.

Date: c. 1730?

Description: The subject is shown full front, half length against a dark background faintly showing landscape and sky at upper right. She is a rather plump woman in her late twenties or early thirties, with dark brown hair and eyes, and a fresh complexion. She is dressed in a bluish-green gown, with white guimpe and sleeve ruffles. An old-rose scarf is thrown over her right shoulder and is held in place by her left hand. The original carved and gilded frame matches that on her husband's portrait.

Owner: Mrs. Arthur W. Bell, Boston.

Reproduced: F.A.R.L. 9009, as Rebecca Dudley.

Exhibited: Copley Society, Loan Exhibition, Boston, 1922.

References: M.H.S. *Proc.* (January 1886), p. 197. *P. F. Mass.* 645.

MRS. JOHN ERVING

Subject: Abigail, daughter of John and Mary (Grosse) Phillips, born in Boston 1702; married John Erving 1725; died in Boston 1759.

Size: H. 39¾ in.; W. 30¾ in.

Date: About 1732.

Description: Mrs. Erving is shown standing against a plain dark background, half front, nearly three-quarter length, her left shoulder towards the spectator, her head turned slightly, nearly full front. Her left hand rests upon an old-rose scarf which lies upon a table at her side. The scarf is carried round behind her and over her right shoulder and arm. She wears a plain blue-green silk dress, with muslin trim at the bodice and elbows. She is shown as a rather large woman, with dark eyes and hair, a curl of which hangs over her right shoulder. She appears to be about thirty years of age. A fine example of Smibert's portraits of women.

Owner: Mrs. James Gore King, New York. The picture has passed by descent to the present owner, a great-great-great-granddaughter of the subject.

Reproduced: F.A.R.L. 20057.

PETER FANEUIL, NO. 2

Subject: Peter Faneuil.

Size: H. 50 in.; W. 40½ in.

Date: 1742?

Description: Faneuil is shown three-quarter length, half front, his right shoulder towards the spectator, his head turned slightly right, nearly full front, against a dark background with a sea view to the right, showing a ship at anchor. He is a large man with a full, round face, gray wig, white neckcloth and ruffles, light brown velvet coat and waistcoat.

Owner: Massachusetts Historical Society, Boston. In the Society's *Proceedings,* II, 19, it is recorded that "Donations were presented from Mr. Charles Faneuil Jones and Miss Eliza Jones, heirs of the late Edward Jones, embracing many books and pamphlets, and a portrait of the late Mr. Faneuil."

Exhibited: Yale University Art Gallery, "The Smibert Tradition," October–November 1949.

Reproduced: Winsor, II, 260. *Magazine of American History,* vol. VIII, pt. 2 (1882), p. 251. Foote, H. W., *Annals of King's Chapel,* II, 81. Bayley, p. 383. F.A.R.L. Photo.

References: M.H.S. *Proc.* XVI, 395. Coburn, *Art in America* (June 1929), p. 387.

PETER FANEUIL, NO. 3

This portrait appears to be a replica of Peter Faneuil, No. 2, although the owner calls it the original and No. 2 the replica. It shows the subject in the same pose and costume except that the coat and waistcoat are of a dark brown broadcloth. The costume, especially the right sleeve, is less carefully executed. Perhaps John Moffatt executed this part of the work. It is impossible to say definitely which of these portraits is the original and which the replica, and both appear to be unmistakably the work of Smibert, but I am inclined to give priority to the portrait designated as No. 2.

Owner: Miss Frances Jones, Cocoa, Florida. It has descended from Mary Ann Faneuil, sister of Peter Faneuil and wife of John Jones of Boston (see portrait of Mrs. John Jones), to their son Edward Jones, to his son Charles, to his son Peter Faneuil Jones, to his daughter Miss Frances Jones; it has recently hung in the house of her nephew, Philip Faneuil Robinson, Scituate.

MRS. FERNE

Subject: Elizabeth Langton, of Langton Hall, near Spilby, Lincolnshire, born 1654; married ——— Ferne; died after 1726, in which year she made her will, describing herself as Elizabeth Ferne of Hammersmith, widow.

Size: H. 49 in.; W. 39½ in.

Date: Signed and dated, lower right, above the dress:

> *Eliz^{th} Fern.*
> *Aged 70*
> *Jo. Smibert*
> *ft. 1724*

Description: Mrs. Ferne is shown as a well-preserved elderly woman seated in a high-backed chair, three-quarters front, her left shoulder towards the spectator, her face turned left, full front, against a dark wall in which a window frame shows dimly at the left. She wears a full black dress, with white lawn undersleeves, and a head covering of black, lined with white, from which white lappets fall to her bosom. Her right hand rests on a white lawn scarf in her hand. At her side is a table covered with a red cloth, on which lies a brown velvet cushion. An open Bible lies on the cushion, held open by Mrs. Ferne's left arm and hand. There is a black mourning ring on the middle finger of the left hand.

Owner: Bennet Langton, Esq., Langton Hall, Spilsby, Lincs., England.

Mrs. Ferne's will mentions only a daughter, though she is believed to have had other children. Presumably her descendants died without issue, and the portrait, with that of Henry Ferne (*q.v.*), went back to the Langton family from which she sprang. It has long hung at Langton Hall, where I saw it in 1931.

HENRY FERNE

Subject: Henry Ferne of London. The letter upon which his hand rests in the picture is addressed

To
    Henry Ferne, Esq.,
      Receiver General of her
      Majesty's Customes,
        London.

Inasmuch as the portrait is dated 1727, several years after George I had come to the throne, it is possible that the phrase *"her* Majesty" refers to a former appointment held by Ferne as Receiver-General of Customs under Queen Anne.

Henry Ferne was presumably related to Mrs. Elizabeth Ferne (*q.v.*), but it is not known whether he was her son or a connection by marriage.

Size: H. 49 in.; W. 39 in.

Date: signed *Jo. Smibert ft. 1727.* (on lower edge of table).

Description: Ferne is shown seated in a high-backed chair which is covered with green cloth, half front, with his right shoulder towards the spectator, his face turned right nearly full front, against a dark background. He wears a crimson velvet cap on his close-cropped head, a dove-colored dressing gown, a shirt open at the neck and ruffled at the wrists. He appears about forty years old, has a round, full face, full lips, and brown eyes. His right arm rests on the arm of his chair, the hand holding a quill pen. A table of brown wood stands at his left side, holding a pewter pen box, and papers, including the letter addressed to him, upon which his left hand rests.

The portrait has been slightly injured in a few places, but remains an excellent example of Smibert's work. It has been relined with paper.

Owner: Bennet Langton, Esq., Langton Hall, Spilsby, Lincs., England. The portrait apparently came into possession of the Langton family with that of Mrs. Elizabeth Ferne, and has hung for many years at Langton Hall, where I saw it in 1931.

FLAGG CHILDREN

Subjects: James (?) and Hannah (?; so-called "Polly") Flagg

These portraits of two small children are companion pieces of the same size (H. 17½ in.; W. 13¾ in.), the subjects shown against a shaded background, with spandrels in the lower corners, their faces turned towards each other. One represents a boy, perhaps three and a half to four years old, with large brown eyes and dark-brown hair parted in the middle, full front, his head turned slightly to his left. He wears a low-cut white dress. The other represents a girl, perhaps one and a half years old, three-quarters front, her left shoulder towards the spectator, her head turned slightly left. She wears a white cap, a dress similar to her brother's, and a white scarf about her left side. In her right hand she holds a ball to her bosom.

There is no question that the subjects are a son and a daughter of Gershom Flagg IV of Boston and his wife Hannah Pitson, who were married July 4, 1735, and had seven children, as follows.

(1) Ebenezer, "died young," no dates.
(2) James, b. Oct. 28, 1739, d. unmarried, 1775.
(3) Hannah, b. Nov. 27, 1741, married Joseph North.
(4) Gershom, b. Sept. 1, 1743, married, left descendants.
(5) Elizabeth, b. Aug. 13, 1745, married Jacob Bigelow.
(6) Mary ("Polly") b. Oct. 25, 1750, married Josiah Wilder.
(7) Grizzel Apthorp, b. May 1753, married Benjamin Gould.[1]

Of the above children the first, Ebenezer, and the last two, Mary and Grizzel, cannot be the subjects of the portraits in question, the first because of early death (presumably in infancy), the last two because born too late to have been painted by either Robert Feke or John Smibert, the only painters to whom the portraits can reasonably be attributed. If the ages of the two children represented here have been correctly estimated, the pictures may show either James and Hannah as they would have appeared in the spring and early summer of 1743, or Gershom and Elizabeth, early in the year 1747.

Psychologically it seems more probable that the parents, having lost their first child, would have had their next two painted before the arrival of later offspring, instead of waiting several years and then having their fourth and fifth children done. The portrait of the boy bears a label reading, "James Flagg, a son of Gershom Flagg, painted by John Smibert, an artist who died in 1751." It is in the handwriting of Benjamin Apthorp Gould, a descendant of Grizzel Apthorp (7), wife of Benjamin Gould, and grandfather of the present (1948) owner. A second label, also in his

[1] Genealogical data from James W. North's *History of Augusta* (Maine; 1870). North was a reliable historian and was descended from Hannah (3), who married Joseph North. The data in the *Flagg Family Records* (1907), are incomplete and inaccurate for the children of Gershom and Hannah Flagg, except for descendants of (6) Mary, wife of Josiah Wilder.

handwriting, reads, "The property of Benjamin A. Gould and his heirs." These labels are at least seventy-five years old.

The lack of a label on the companion portrait may indicate uncertainty as to which of the daughters of Gershom and Hannah Flagg the portrait represents, but in the nineteenth century she was supposed to be Mary, commonly called "Polly." This identification is clearly impossible, and it is curious that the mistake should have been made, since the portrait, like that of the subject's brother, has come down in the Gould line and not in that of the descendants of "Polly." In view of this mistake in the case of one picture it is unsafe to place too much reliance on the accuracy of the label on the back of the other, either as to the identity of the subject or the attribution to the artist. I believe, however, that it is probable that the portraits represent James and Hannah, rather than Gershom and Elizabeth.

The attribution to Smibert has recently been questioned by critics, especially by Mr. Alan Burroughs, on the ground that the technique of the painter is that of Feke rather than of Smibert, as illustrated by comparison of these portraits with certain later ones by Feke. It might be argued, however, that in 1741 and perhaps for some time thereafter, Feke was more or less under Smibert's influence, and that, if Smibert painted these portraits, they indicate that at times he used a technique which Feke may have picked up from him and may later have adapted to his own use. To me these two portraits appear to be borderline cases which, on grounds of style, might be attributed to either artist.

There is no question that the parents of the children were acquainted with both painters. Smibert lived within a stone's throw of their residence. The portraits of the two children, whether painted in the spring or early summer of 1743 or early in 1747, fall within the period of Smibert's activity. On the other hand, Feke painted the portraits of their parents, presumably during his Boston visit of 1748; he left his Early Self-Portrait with them; and he may have met them as early as his Boston visit of 1741, for Gershom Flagg IV had both cousins and connections by marriage in Newport. But there is no evidence whatever that Feke was in Boston between the end of September 1741 and 1748 or, at the earliest, very late in 1747. In September 1741 James Flagg was still under two years old and Hannah had not yet been born. In 1748 they would have been much older than the children shown in the portraits, and even their younger brother and sister, Gershom and Elizabeth, would have been older than the portraits indicate.

For these reasons, in the absence of conclusive evidence to the contrary, I believe that the portraits represent James and Hannah Flagg, about 1743–1744, and are correctly attributed to Smibert.

Owner: (1948) Miss Rosanna D. Thorndike, 133 Marlborough St., Boston, by descent from Benjamin Gould, Benjamin Apthorp Gould I and II, to Mary Quincy Gould, wife of Albert Thorndike, parents of the present owner.

Reproduced: Oil copies of the portrait of the little girl were made about 1880 under the impression that it represented "Polly," now owned by her descendants, Rev. Henry Wilder Foote, Cambridge, Mass., and Dr. Wilder Tileston, New Haven, Conn.

Both portraits reproduced by photogravure in *Memorials of Mary Wilder White*, ed. Mary Wilder Tileston, Boston, 1903.

REV. JOSHUA GEE, NO 1

Subject: Joshua, son of Joshua and Elizabeth (Thacher) Gee, born in Boston June 29, 1698; graduated from Harvard 1717; died in Boston May 22, 1748. Colleague of Cotton Mather as pastor of the Second Church, Boston, 1723–1748. Married (1) Sarah Rogers; (2) Anna, daughter of Captain John Gerrish and widow of Samuel Appleton; (3) Sarah Gardiner. In 1721 he was appointed librarian of Harvard College on a salary of £8, which post he held for a year, during which he compiled a catalogue of the library.

Size: H. 30 in.; W. 25 in.

Date: Inscribed *Aetat: 33.* (1731), but this inscription was presumably added later, and since the portrait appears to be a companion piece to that of Gee's second wife Anna (Gerrish) Appleton, whom he married in 1734 and who died in 1736, it is probable that both portraits were painted during that period.

Description: The subject is shown nearly full front against a dark background, with spandrels in the lower corners. He wears a long dark wig or, perhaps more probably, his natural hair; has a round, full face, with dark eyes and a small Cupid's-bow mouth. Dressed in a black gown with white bands.

The portrait does not look like Smibert's work, but has been so heavily repainted that the face is only a mask. Since the only other painters then in Boston were Peter Pelham or Nathaniel Emmons, and it does not appear to be the work of either, and since the companion portrait of Mrs. Gee seems to be by Smibert, it is probable that the attribution to that painter is correct. The inventory of Gee's estate mentions portraits of Cotton Mather and of Gee.

Owner: Massachusetts Historical Society, Boston, gift from Rev. Chandler Robbins, July 26, 1849.

Reproduced: Bayley, p. 387. Sibley's *Harvard Graduates*, Vol. VI, opp. p. 176.

References: M.H.S. *Proc.* II, 430. Tuckerman, *Book of the Artists* (1867), p. 42. Champlin & Perkins, IV, 192. Bolton, III, 1032. *P. F. Mass.* 850.

REV. JOSHUA GEE, NO. 2

A portrait of Joshua Gee, of the same dimensions, which appears to be a contemporary replica of No. 1, is owned by Miss Neilson of Boston, but is hung on loan (1949) in the Widener Library, Harvard University.

It is in fairly good condition and gives a better impression of the subject than does No. 1 because it has been repainted but little, if at all.

MRS. JOSHUA GEE

Subject: Anna, daughter of Captain John Gerrish, born in 1700, in Boston. She married (1) Samuel Appleton, (2) Joshua Gee, April 27, 1734. She died September 4, 1736.

Size: H. 30 in.; W. 25 in.

Date: Between 1734 and 1736.

Description: The head and bust of Mrs. Gee are shown above spandrels in the lower corners against a dark background, nearly full front, the head turned slightly to the left. She has large, dark eyes and dark hair, a curl of which falls over the left shoulder. She is dressed in a pearl-gray silk gown, with white guimpe at the bosom. The portrait has been somewhat repainted, but not with such damaging effect as in the case of the portrait of her husband.

Owner: Massachusetts Historical Society, Boston.

Reproduced: Bayley, p. 389. F.A.R.L. photo.

References: Bolton, III, 1032. Tuckerman, *Book of the Artists* (1867), p. 42. Champlin & Perkins, IV, 192. *P. F. Mass.* 849.

MRS. BENJAMIN GERRISH?

Subject: This portrait, formerly supposed to represent Mrs. Paul Dudley, shows a much younger woman, probably Rebecca, daughter of William and Elizabeth (Davenport) Dudley, born November 28, 1726; married (1) April 19, 1744, Benjamin, son of John and Sarah Gerrish of Boston; (2) October 14, 1775, in Halifax, John Burbridge; died January 30, 1809.

Size: H. 35¼ in.; W. 27⅛ in.

Date: 1746.

Description: The subject is a young woman seated against a dark background with what appears to be a cliff on the right; nearly full front, her left shoulder slightly advanced, her head turned slightly to her left. She has dark hair, a curl of which lies on her shoulder, and gray-blue eyes. She wears a blue dress with white muslin trim at bodice and sleeves. Her left elbow rests on what appears to be a stone pedestal or ledge at her side.

Owner: Mrs. Arthur W. Bell, Boston.

Reproduced: Bayley, p. 379, as Mrs. Paul Dudley, Lucy Wainwright. F.A.R.L. 9010.

Reference: P. F. Mass. 655.

CAPTAIN JOHN GERRISH

Subject: John, son of Judge John Gerrish, of New Hampshire; born 1668, died 1737/38, Boston.

Size: H. 30⅛ in.; W. 24⅞ in.

Date: c. 1735?

Description: The subject is shown against a dark background, with spandrels in the lower corners, half front, his left shoulder towards the spectator, his head turned left, nearly full front. He has a full, strong face with ample double chin. He wears a full bob wig, a brown, collarless velvet coat and waistcoat, and a long steenkirk tie.

Owner: Barrett Wendell, Chicago, Ill. The subject's daughter Sarah married John Barrett of Boston, through whom the portrait descended to Sarah Dow Barrett of Boston (1909) and from her passed to the late Professor Barrett Wendell and to his son, Barrett Wendell, Jr., the present owner.

Reproduced: L. V. Briggs, *The Cabot Genealogy* (1927), I, 42. Bayley, p. 391. F.A.R.L. 598.

References: M.H.S. *Proc.*, XLIII, 200. Champlin & Perkins, IV, 192, as "Judge I. Gerrish." *P. F. Mass.* 853.

JAMES GOOCH, JR.

Subject: James Gooch (the third of the name, but known as James Gooch, Jr.) was born in Boston, October 12, 1693, and died, probably at Marshfield, Mass., January 9, 1786. He owned considerable land in the "West End" of Boston, a house on Green Lane, and an estate in Hopkinton, Mass. He married (1) September 30, 1715, Elizabeth, born *c.* 1695, daughter of Sir Charles Hobby (Hobbie). She died before 1729, in which year he married (2) Hester, widow of Francis Plaisted. She died after 1749. He married (3) Elizabeth Craister, March 8, 1761.

Size: H. 36 in.; W. 28 in.

Date: Probably about 1740.

Description: The subject is shown seated in a chair upholstered in blue, half front against a plain background, the right shoulder towards the spectator, his head turned right, three-quarters front. He wears a full white wig, brown coat and waistcoat, and long steenkirk cravat. His right hand rests on a letter lying on a table covered with a green cloth by his side. He has brown eyes and a rather full face, with an animated, somewhat jovial expression. He appears to be about fifty years of age.

Owner: Brooklyn Museum, Brooklyn, N. Y. The portrait descended to the late Otis Barker, of La Mesa, California, who sold it about 1927 to André Rueff of Brooklyn, from whom it was purchased in that year by the Brooklyn Museum (see *Brooklyn Museum Quarterly*, vol. XIV, no. 3, July 1927).

Exhibited: Yale University Art Gallery, "The Smibert Tradition," exhibition, October–November 1949.

Reproduced: F. A. Gooch, *The History of a Surname; the Line of John Gooch in New England* (New Haven, 1906), opp. p. 100. *Antiques* (November 1939), p. 223. F.A.R.L. photo.

MRS. JAMES GOOCH

Subject: Hester Stanton, widow of Francis Plaisted, married James Gooch, Jr., of Boston in 1729.

Size: H. 31 in.; W. 28 in.

Date: Probably about 1740.

Description: The subject is shown seated nearly full front, against a faintly painted landscape background, showing sky, trees, and distant hills to the left. She is dressed in an orange-colored gown, with the usual white guimpe and undersleeves. A greenish-blue scarf over her right arm is carried behind her to her left side. A curl of her dark hair falls over her right shoulder. Her left arm rests on a table by her side and with her left hand she holds a pink moss-rose bud to her bosom. The picture has been so largely repainted that in its present condition it does not look like Smibert's work. There appears to be no doubt, however, that the portrait of the subject's husband was painted by Smibert and it is probable that he executed this picture also.

Owner: The portrait descended, with that of her husband, to the late Otis Barker, who sold it to André Rueff, from whom it was purchased by the Brooklyn Museum in 1927.

Reproduced: F. A. Gooch, *The History of a Surname; the Line of John Gooch in New England* (New Haven, 1926), opp. p. 100. *Antiques* (November 1939), p. 225. F.A.R.L. photo.

SIR FRANCIS GRANT, BART., LORD CULLEN

Subject: Francis Grant, born 1658; married (1) Jean Meldrum, 1694, (2) Sarah Fordyce, (3) Agnes Hay; lawyer and philanthropist; created a baronet of Nova Scotia in 1705; appointed a senator of the College of Justice of Scotland in 1709 by the title of Lord Cullen; died 1726.

Size: H. 30 in.; W. 25 in.

Date: Before 1726; probably during Smibert's visit to Edinburgh before he went to the continent in 1717, or in 1720 after his return.

Description: The head and bust of Lord Cullen are shown within a painted oval, nearly full front, his head turned slightly to the right. He wears a long, full gray wig, the ends of which hang to his breast; a red velvet judicial robe with red ribbons, and a long steenkirk tie with fringed ends. He has a fresh complexion and blue eyes. A later inscription at top left reads, "Sir Francis Grant / of Cullen Bar.ᵗ" (The above description supplied by The Scottish National Portrait Gallery.)

Owner: The Scottish National Portrait Gallery, Edinburgh. This portrait was formerly in the hands of Sir Arthur Grant of Monymusk, Aberdeenshire, Scotland, to whom it had passed by inheritance. It was recently acquired by the Scottish National Portrait Gallery from a Glasgow dealer who had bought it at a wartime sale in Edinburgh.

Reproduced: In 1744, as a mark of filial devotion, Lord Cullen's son had the portrait engraved in mezzotint by Samuel Taylor. The engraving, which is 11⅞ × 9¾ inches, displays the arms of Monymusk, and has a long Latin inscription, ending with the date of the engraving and the words *Jo. Smibert pinxit, Samˡ Taylor Fecit.* The engraving is listed in the British Museum *Catalogue of Engraved British Portraits*, II, 369.

LADY GRANT

Subject: The wife of Sir Francis Grant, Bart., Lord Cullen, of Monymusk, Aberdeenshire, Scotland.

Date: 1717 (probably signed).

Description: James Lewis Caw, in *Scottish Painting Past and Present* (1908), p. 26, says: "At Monymusk there is a cabinet-sized oval of Lady Grant, dated 1717, and a large group of twelve life-size figures, 'Lord Cullen and his Family,' painted three years later [by Smibert]. These I have not seen, but J. M. Gray noted that the group was hard in execution and smooth in handling, and had little colour in the shadows, but was carefully drawn, with much character in the faces."

Owner: Sir Arthur Grant, Bart., Monymusk, Aberdeenshire, Scotland.

MRS. HUGH HALL

Subject: Family tradition has called the subject either Elizabeth or Mary, daughters of Hugh Hall III, of Boston, and Elizabeth (Pitts) Hall, and has attributed the portrait to Copley. The portrait is, however, clearly the work of John Smibert, and both daughters of Hugh and Elizabeth (Pitts) Hall were born too late to have been painted by him at the age at which the subject is represented. In all probability the portrait represents their mother, Elizabeth Pitts, who married Hugh Hall III in 1722. John Smibert also painted her parents, Mr. and Mrs. John Pitts (*q.v.*), and her husband's half sisters, Sarah and Mary Hall (*q.v.*); and Nathaniel Smibert painted her daughters, Mary Hall II and Sarah Hall II.

Size: H. 50⅛ in.; W. 40⅛ in.

Date: Early seventeen-thirties.

Description: The subject is a rather large woman, apparently about thirty years of age, seated very upright in a green stuffed armchair, half front, her left shoulder towards the spectator, her head turned left three-quarters front, against a background which is dark on the right, with a landscape vista showing a brook and trees on the left. She has a rather long nose, brown eyes and hair, a curl of the latter hanging over her right shoulder. She wears a low-cut golden-brown dress with white guimpe and undersleeves. Her left hand rests upon one arm of the chair, her right arm on the other, and the forefinger of her right hand points across the picture.

Owner: Mrs. Marcus Morton, Cambridge, Mass. The portrait passed to the subject's daughter Elizabeth, who married John Welch, from whom it has passed by descent to the present owner.

Exhibited: Museum of Fine Arts, Boston, on loan 1928–1940. Yale University Art Gallery, "The Smibert Tradition," exhibition, October–November 1949.

Reproduced: F.A.R.L. 31186, as "Mary Hall."

Reference: P. F. Mass. 961.

MARY HALL I

Subject: Mary, daughter of Hugh Hall, of Barbados, later of Boston; born 1713 (probably in Barbados); died 1795 at Portsmouth, N. H. Married (1) Adam Winthrop, (2) Captain William Wentworth (1705–1767), son of Lieutenant Governor John Wentworth of New Hampshire.

Size: H. 32 in.; W. 25 in.

Date: c. 1732.

Description: The head and bust of the subject are shown nearly full front against a shaded background with spandrels in the lower corners. She is a pleasing young woman about twenty years of age, with a rather long neck, round face, brown eyes and brown hair, a curl of which hangs over her left shoulder. She wears a golden-yellow gown, with white muslin trim at her bosom. The portrait closely resembles that of the painter's wife, Mary Smibert, in the way the subject is posed for presentation according to a conventional formula.

Owner: Mrs. E. W. Taylor, Cambridge, Mass. With the portrait is a label reading,

> This is Grandmother's
> Great Aunt Mary Hall,
> daughter of Hon. ——— Hall
> of Barbadoes, wife of
> Capt. William Wentworth
> Son of Lieut. Governor
> John Wentworth
> Born 1713 Died 1790 [*sic*]
> at Portsmouth, N. H.

As Mary Hall had no children her portrait, as this label indicates, passed to one of her great-nieces and descended to the late E. W. Taylor, husband of the present owner, Mrs. E. W. Taylor.

REVEREND JOHN HANCOCK

Subject: Rev. John Hancock, born 1671; graduated from Harvard 1689; died 1752. Pastor in Lexington for fifty years. Father of Thomas Hancock, merchant, and grandfather of John Hancock, Governor of Massachusetts.

Size: H. 28 in.; W. 23 in.

Date: c. 1740.

Description: The subject is shown as a vigorous old man, facing nearly full front within a painted oval. He wears a short white wig, white bands, and a black gown.

Owner: Lexington (Mass.) Historical Society.

Reproduced: F.A.R.L. photo.

Reference: P. F. *Mass.* 974.

MRS. JOHN HANCOCK

Subject: Elizabeth Clark, born 1687; married Rev. John Hancock, 1700; died 1760.

Size: H. 28 in.; W. 23 in.

Date: c. 1740.

Description: The subject is a large woman with brown eyes and hair, a curl of which falls over her left shoulder. She is shown nearly full front, her head turned slightly to her left, against a plain background, with spandrels in the four corners. She wears a low-cut plum-colored taffeta gown with white bodice.

Owner: Lexington (Mass.) Historical Society.

Reproduced: F.A.R.L. photo.

Reference: P. F. Mass. 973.

THOMAS HANCOCK

Subject: Thomas, son of Rev. John and Elizabeth (Clark) Hancock of Lexington, Mass., born in Lexington 1702; died in Boston August 1, 1764. As a youth he was apprenticed to Daniel Henchman of Boston, whose daughter he married, November 5, 1730. He became a prosperous merchant, and was a member of the Council. In 1737 he built the Hancock House on Beacon Street, afterwards occupied by his nephew and heir John Hancock. He bequeathed £1000 to Harvard College to found a professorship; £1000 to propagate the Gospel among the Indians; and £600 to the Town of Boston to establish a hospital for the insane.

Size: H. 28½ in.; W. 23¾ in.

Date: About 1730.

Description: The subject is shown within a painted oval, against a plain, dark background, half front, his right shoulder towards the spectator, his head turned right, nearly full front. The face is the attractive one of a young man with dark complexion, brown eyes, and heavy, dark eyebrows. He wears a gray wig, white stock and ruffles, and a tobacco-brown coat and waistcoat, the latter partly unbuttoned.

Owner: Miss Ellyn L. Edwards, Boston. The portrait was owned in recent times by Mrs. Lydia Taft, of Milton, from whom it passed to her nephew, Ray Baker Taft, of Hingham, Mass., and from him to Miss Ellyn L. Edwards of Boston, and is now (1949) on loan at the Museum of Fine Arts, Boston.

Reproduced: F.A.R.L. 1428.

Reference: P. F. Mass. 987.

MRS. THOMAS HANCOCK, NO. 1

Subject: Lydia, daughter of Daniel and Elizabeth (Gerrish) Henchman of Boston, born October 4, 1714. Her father was a noted and prosperous bookseller, and on November 5, 1730, she married his apprentice and assistant, Thomas Hancock (1703–1764). At the beginning of the siege of Boston in 1775 she retired to Fairfield, Connecticut, where she died April 15, 1776.

Size: H. 30¾ in.; W. 25 in.

Date: 1730 or soon after.

Description: The head and bust of the subject are shown within a painted oval nearly full front, against a plain, dark background. She is a rather large woman with fair hair, a curl of which hangs over her left shoulder, and a fair complexion. She wears a low-cut greenish blue silk gown, with white muslin insert at the bosom.

Owner: Mrs. William E. Faulkner, Keene, N. H. Formerly owned by Mrs. Lydia B. Taft, Milton, Mass., who transferred it to Roy Baker Taft in 1935, who in turn transferred it in 1938 to Mrs. Faulkner. On loan at Museum of Fine Arts, Boston (1948).

Reproduced: F.A.R.L. 1429.

Reference: P. F. Mass. 983.

MRS. THOMAS HANCOCK, NO. 2 (?)

Subject: If this is a second portrait of Mrs. Hancock it must have been painted a good many years later than No. 1. One would say that there was a difference of at least twenty years in their ages. If No. 1 was painted in 1730 at the time of her marriage, No. 2 must be dated in the late seventeen-forties, just before the close of Smibert's career.

Size: H. 29¼ in.; W. 24¼ in.

Date: ?

Description: The head and bust of the subject are shown above spandrels in the lower corners, nearly full front, her head turned slightly left against a plain, grayish-green background. She is shown with light brown hair, and brown eyes. She wears a greenish-blue gown, with white muslin guimpe.

Owner: Mrs. Lydia B. Taft, Milton, Mass.

REV. SAMUEL JOHNSON

Subject: Samuel, son of Samuel and Mary (Sage) Johnson, born October 14, 1696, at Guilford, Conn.; died at Stratford, Conn., January 6, 1772. He studied at the Collegiate School, Saybrook, Conn., which soon after was removed to New Haven and named Yale College. In 1720 he was ordained minister of the Congregational Church at West Haven. Two years later he joined the Episcopal Church and sailed for England. There he was ordained in the Church of England and appointed by the Society for the Propagation of the Gospel a missionary at Stratford, Connecticut, to which place he returned in 1723. The next year he opened the first Episcopal church in Connecticut, of which he remained rector until his appointment in 1754 as first president of King's College, New York (founded 1753, now Columbia University). He served as president until 1763, when he returned to Stratford and again served the church as rector.

He was a friend and correspondent of Dean Berkeley's, whose philosophy he adopted. As a philosopher and writer in the colonies he ranks second only to Jonathan Edwards in intellectual power, though far less influential.

Size: H. *c.* 30 in., W. *c.* 25 in.

Date: 1729.

Description: The head and bust of the subject are shown against a dark background, within spandrels, half front, the right shoulder towards the spectator, the head turned slightly right. He wears a short wig, gown, and bands. The pleasing face is that of a man in his early thirties.

Owner: Columbia University, New York. The following item appears in *Samuel Johnson, President of King's College; His Career and Writings*[1] (IV, 262), in an undated "List of the Benefactors to King's College": "Mr. Kilbourn painter gave the President Dr. Johnson's portrait." This "List of Benefactors" is said in one place to belong to the year 1757, in another place to 1770, after Myles Cooper had succeeded Johnson. Since the list is in Johnson's handwriting the earlier date is probably correct. The reference to himself in the third person seems curious, but his autobiography, printed in vol. I of the above-named work, is written entirely in the third person.

"Mr. Kilbourn" was Lawrance Kilbourn (Kilburn, Killbrunn), a painter who arrived in New York from London in 1754, and who died in New York in 1775. Because he made the gift it has sometimes been assumed that he painted the portrait. He cannot, however, have done so, because Johnson is shown as a rather slender man in his early thirties, whereas in 1754, the earliest possible date at which Kilbourn could have executed a portrait of him, he was 58 years old and had grown very portly. Another (unidentified) painter portrayed Johnson in 1762, and a comparison of the two portraits suggests an interval of at least thirty years between them.

The portrait was also attributed to Smibert at an early date. Under date of April 15, 1842, William Dunlap wrote, "See G. C. Verplank at City Library — Smybert is noticed by him in his Historical discourse. One of his pictures in Columbia College," and, later, "We [Verplank and himself] go to Columbia College to see a Smibert."[2] Since Columbia University owns no other portrait attributable to Smibert it would seem certain that these entries refer to the picture of Samuel Johnson.

The attribution to Smibert can hardly be questioned. It is characteristic of his style, and we know that Johnson visited Newport while Dean Berkeley was there. In his autobiography, written 1768–1770, he says that he took an early opportunity to go to Newport where Mr. Honyman introduced him to Berkeley; that he made several visits to Berkeley during the latter's stay there; and that he himself suggested to Berkeley that he might make a donation to Yale, although the magnitude of Berkeley's gift

[1] Ed. by Herbert and Carol Schneider (New York, 1929).
[2] *Diary of William Dunlap*, III, 675, 722.

far surpassed his expectations. Smibert would have had opportunity to paint Johnson's portrait during one of the latter's earlier visits to Newport, and the picture can be dated as having been executed between April and October, 1729.

The only unsolved question is how Kilbourn acquired the portrait before presenting it to King's College. Perhaps the most plausible explanation is that the portrait may never have belonged to Johnson but may have remained in Newport in other hands until Kilbourn picked it up.

Exhibited: Century Association, New York, March 1908.

Reproduced: Samuel Johnson, President of King's College (New York, 1929), frontispiece to vol. IV. F.A.R.L. photo.

MRS. JOHN JONES

Subject: Mary Ann, a daughter of Benjamin and Ann Faneuil, born at New Rochelle, N. Y., 1715; sister of Peter Faneuil, with whom she lived in Boston until his death in 1742, shortly after which she married John Jones of Roxbury; died October 19, 1790.

Size: H. 50 in.; W. 40 in.

Date: 1740–1742?

Description: The subject has a tall, meager figure and plain face, and is shown standing nearly full front, her face turned slightly to her left, out-of-doors against a landscape background with a stream, hills, and clouds. She is dressed in brown silk, with a pink bow at her bosom and another in her hair, and white muslin trim at the bodice and sleeves. The right hand rests on a table at her side; her left hand holds a small white flower.

Owner: Massachusetts Historical Society. In the Society's *Proceedings,* XL, 409 (June 1906), it is recorded that Miss Mary Ann Jones presented the portrait of her great-grandmother, Mrs. Mary Ann (Faneuil) Jones, sister of Peter Faneuil, painted by Smibert. Miss Mary Ann Jones was the daughter of Charles Faneuil Jones who gave the Society the companion portrait of Peter Faneuil in 1835.

Exhibited: Yale University Art Gallery, "The Smibert Tradition," exhibition, October–November 1949.

Reproduced: Bayley, p. 397. F.A.R.L. photo.

Reference: P. F. Mass. 1198.

WILLIAM LAMBERT

Subject: William Lambert, born in England in 1681; emigrated to Boston before 1731; Comptroller of Customs for Massachusetts Bay. Died 1749.

Size: H. 35⅛ in.; W. 27 in.

Date: c. 1735?

Description: The subject is shown against a dark background, half front, his right shoulder towards the spectator, his head turned right nearly full front. He has a full face and brown eyes. He wears a full, white wig, a steenkirk tie with a fringed end, and a black velvet jacket. He is seated beside a table, on which lies a thick book held open by his right hand.

Owner: William Lambert Barnard, Brookline, Mass. The subject died childless. In his will, probated December 5, 1749, appears: "I give to my nephew William Lambert my Picture & my Wife's Picture which was drawn by Mr. Smibert." From the younger William Lambert both portraits have passed by descent to the present owner.

Exhibited: Yale University Art Gallery, "The Smibert Tradition," exhibition, October–November 1949.

Reference: P. F. Mass. 1252.

MRS. WILLIAM LAMBERT

Subject: Harriet ——, married William Lambert in England before emigration to Massachusetts. She probably died before her husband.

Size: H. 35¼ in.; W. 27½ in.

Date: c. 1735?

Description: The subject is shown seated in a high-backed chair, against a dark background, nearly full front, her head turned slightly to her left. She is a young woman, possibly thirty years of age, with dark eyes and dark hair, a curl of which hangs over her left shoulder. She wears a low-cut garnet dress with white muslin trim. Her left hand lies in her lap. The pose is graceful and easy, and the portrait is less conventionalized than most of Smibert's portraits of women, of which this is one of the best.

Owner: William Lambert Barnard, Brookline, Mass., to whom it has come by the same line of descent as the portrait of the subject's husband (*q.v.*).

Exhibited: Yale University Art Gallery, "The Smibert Tradition," exhibition, October–November 1949.

Reference: P. F. Mass. 1253.

MRS. JAMES LINDALL

Subject: Susannah, wife of James Lindall, born 1660, died 1733. Their daughter Elizabeth married John Pitts (*q.v.*).

Size: H. *c.* 36 in.; W. *c.* 28 in.

Date: 1730 or soon after.

Description: The subject is a rather large, well-preserved woman of about seventy years of age, shown seated against a dark background, half front, her right shoulder towards the spectator, her head turned right nearly full front. She has brown hair, a curl of which hangs over her left shoulder, and a face which, while not particularly agreeable, is much more vigorously characterized than is the case with most of Smibert's portraits of women. She wears a gown of gray-blue silk with white muslin trim at the bosom and sleeves. Her right arm rests on the arm of her chair.

Owner: Mrs. Lendall Pitts, Norfolk, Va. The portrait passed by descent to the late Lendall Pitts, of Paris, and now belongs to Mrs. Lendall Pitts, but it has hung for many years in the home of Mr. Pitts' sister, Mrs. Arthur Maxwell Parker, Grosse Pointe Farms, Michigan.

Reproduced: Photogravure, in reverse, in Daniel Goodwin, Jr.'s *The Dearborns: a discourse commemorative of the 80th anniversary of the occupation of Fort Dearborn, Chicago, 1884.*

BENJAMIN LYNDE, SR., NO. 1

Subject: Benjamin, son of Simon and Hannah (Newgate) Lynde, born in Salem, September 22, 1666; was graduated from Harvard 1686; studied law at the Middle Temple, London; returned to New England 1697; married, April 27, 1699, Mary, daughter of William and Hannah (Curwen) Browne of Salem. Justice of Superior Court of Judicature, 1712–1728. Chief Justice 1729–1745. Died in Salem January 28, 1745.

Size: H. *c.* 30 in.; W. *c.* 25 in.

Date: 1737. The portrait bears an inscription, *Ætat* 72, probably a later addition.

Description: The head and bust of Justice Lynde are shown in a painted oval against a brown background, half front, the right shoulder towards the spectator, the fine and intelligent face turned right nearly full front. He wears a full, long wig, a steenkirk tie, and a greenish velvet coat and waistcoat with gold buttons. One of the finest examples of Smibert's work. Augustus T. Perkins called it a "quite remarkable picture, and one in which the artist seems to have excelled himself." [1]

Owner: Mrs. F. S. Moseley, Boston. The portrait was owned in 1878 by Mrs. William B. Richards of Boston, to whom it had passed by descent. It was later acquired by the late Mr. F. S. Moseley of Boston, who was also descended from Judge Lynde, and is now owned by Mrs. Moseley.

Exhibited: Harvard Tercentenary, 1936. The Addison Gallery, Andover, Mass., November 1942.

Reproduced: The Diaries of Benjamin Lynde (Boston, 1880), frontispiece. In this book a copy of the portrait is said to be in possession of Samuel H. Russell, of Boston. Winsor, II, 558. C. W. Bowen, *The History of Woodstock, Connecticut* (1926), p. 66. Bayley, p. 401. F.A.R.L. photo. A copy by an unknown artist is in the Social Law Library, Boston.

References: M.H.S. *Proc.* (1878). *The Diaries of Benjamin Lynde* (Boston, 1880). *P. F. Mass.* 1358. Alan Burroughs, "Notes on Smibert's Development." *Art in America*, XXX, 115–117 (April 1942).

GENERAL JEAN PAUL MASCARENE

Subject: Jean Paul, son of Jean and Margaret de Salavy Mascarene, born at Castras, France, in 1684. His father left France on the revocation of the Edict of Nantes, and he himself was sent to Geneva at the age of

[1] M.H.S. *Proc.*, XVI, 396.

twelve. He later went to England where he was naturalized in 1706; officer in the British army; arrived in Boston in 1709; was employed by the governors of Massachusetts and New Hampshire in negotiations with the Indians; was Lieutenant-Governor and Acting Governor of Nova Scotia 1740–1749; rose to rank of Major-General; returned to New England, settled in Boston, where he died January 22, 1760. He married Elizabeth Perry of Boston.

Size: H. 40½ in.; W. 31½ in.

Date: 1729–1730.

Description: Mascarene is shown standing against a wall, half front, his right shoulder towards the spectator, his handsome face turned right, three-quarters front. To the right an aperture shows a bay bordered with hills, and a fortified town in the distance, intended to represent Annapolis Royal. The fingers of his left hand rest upon a map; his right hand points to the distant view. He is dressed in a formal suit of steel armor, without helmet or gauntlets, with linen neckband and wristbands showing. On his head is a full white wig. The picture is mentioned in the poem, "To Mr. Smibert, on viewing his pictures" and must therefore have been painted between the arrival of Smibert in Boston in November 1729 and March 1730.

Owner: Mrs. Paul Mascarene Hamlen, Wayland, Mass. The portrait is reported to have remained in Halifax in the hands of descendants, the last of whom was a Mr. Sterling. About 1871 a photograph of it was secured by one of Mascarene's Boston descendants, and when, many years later, Mr. Sterling died in England and his goods were sold, it was identified from the photograph and purchased by the late Paul Mascarene Hamlen of Boston, a descendant of the subject.

Exhibited: Loan Exhibition of One Hundred Colonial Portraits, Museum of Fine Arts, Boston, 1930. Yale University Art Gallery, "The Smibert Tradition," exhibition, October–November 1949.

Reproduced: Copy by Miss Fraser of Boston, in the Museum at Annapolis Royal, N. S.

There is a replica or copy of the portrait in Halifax, N. S., which was copied by William H. Whitmore in February, 1871, size 17 × 14 in. On March 9, 1871, Mr. Whitmore presented his copy to the Massachusetts Historical Society, Boston.

Massachusetts Society Colonial Dames Register (1927), p. 368. Bayley, p. 403. *Catalogue, Loan Exhibition of One Hundred Colonial Portraits,* Museum of Fine Arts (Boston, 1930), p. 55. *Art in America,* vol. XXX, no. 2, p. 111. F.A.R.L. photo.

Reference: P. F. Mass. 1393.

REV. JAMES MCSPARRAN

Subject: James McSparran, born in Ireland about 1680; married, 1722, Hannah Gardiner, of Boston Neck, Narragansett, R. I.; died at Narragansett 1757. Received the degree of Doctor of Divinity from Oxford; rector of St. Paul's Church, Narragansett, for thirty-seven years. McSparran baptized Gilbert Stuart, who may well, when a boy, have seen this portrait and that of Mrs. McSparran.

Size: H. 29¾ in.; W. 24⅞ in.

Date: Painted in May 1729, when Smibert visited Dr. McSparran in Narragansett.

Description: The head and bust of Dr. McSparran are shown against a dark background, with small spandrels in the lower corners, three-quarters front, the right shoulder towards the spectator, the head turned nearly full front. He wears a gray wig, black gown, and white neckcloth and bands. The face, though full, shows exceptional refinement, strength, and nobility of character.

Ownership: Bowdoin College, Brunswick, Maine. Dr. and Mrs. McSparran left no children and their portraits passed to her brother, Dr. Silvester Gardiner. That of Dr. McSparran was inherited by Dr. Gardiner's daughter, Mrs. Oliver Whipple, then by her daughter, Mrs. Frederic Allen, whose son, Charles E. Allen, bequeathed it to Bowdoin College in 1835. At some point in this line of descent the portraits were separated, that of Mrs. McSparran passing to Mrs. M. A. Elton, who bequeathed it to the Museum of Fine Arts, Boston.

Exhibited: Exhibition of Colonial Portraits, Metropolitan Museum of Art, New York, 1911.

Reproduced: Poor copy in oils by Mary Updike, daughter of Wilkins Updike, in the Rhode Island Historical Society, Providence, painted "many years ago," i.e., mid-nineteenth century. Bayley, p. 405. *Antiques,* vol. XVIII, no. 3 (August 1930). Updike, *History of the Episcopal Church in Narragansett,* I, 405. *Descriptive Catalogue of the Art Collections of Bowdoin College* (1930). F.A.R.L. photo.

MRS. JAMES MCSPARRAN

Subject: Hannah, daughter of William Gardiner, of Boston Neck, Narragansett, R. I., born December 7, 1704; married Rev. James McSparran, May 22, 1722; died in London, June 24, 1755, while on a visit to England with her husband; buried in Broadway Chapel Burying Ground, Westminster.

Size: H. 30¼ in.; W. 25¼ in.

Date: Painted in May 1729, when Smibert visited Dr. McSparran in Narragansett.

Description: The head and bust of Mrs. McSparran are shown in a painted oval against a dark background, nearly full front, with her head turned a little to her right. She has large dark eyes, a small mouth, and dark hair, a heavy curl of which falls over her right shoulder. She wears a blue silk dress, cut low, with muslin insert in the bodice.

Owner: Museum of Fine Arts, Boston, Mass., bequest of Mrs. M. A. Elton, 1888.

Exhibited: Yale University Art Gallery, "The Smibert Tradition," exhibition, October–November 1949.

Reproduced: Poor copy in oils by Mary Updike in the Rhode Island Historical Society, Providence, painted "many years ago," i.e., mid-nineteenth century. Updike, vol. I, opp. p. 70. Bayley, p. 407 (dates of birth and death incorrect, and name misspelled "Gardner"). *Antiques,* vol. XVIII, no. 3 (August 1930). F.A.R.L. photo.

Reference: P. F. Mass. 1373.

REV. EBENEZER MILLER

Subject: Ebenezer, son of Samuel and Rebecca (Belcher) Miller of Milton, Mass., born June 20, 1703; graduated from Harvard 1722; became an Anglican under the influence of his brother-in-law John Checkley (*q.v.*), and was ordained in England in 1727. Married Martha Mottram of London, 1726. Minister of Christ Church, Braintree, Mass., 1727–1763. Died February 11, 1763.

Size: H. 30 in.; W. 24¼ in.

Date: Judging from the apparent age of the subject and the style of wig, the portrait was probably painted in the seventeen-forties.

Description: The head and bust of the subject are shown half front, the right shoulder towards the spectator, within a painted oval against a shaded background. He wears a full short white curled wig, bands, and black Geneva gown. The face is intelligent and pleasing, and represents the subject as about forty years of age.

Owner: Alexander F. Wadsworth, Dedham, Mass., who inherited the portrait from his aunt, Miss Caroline Amory of Boston, to whom it had descended from her Miller grandmother. There is a photograph of the portrait in the Frick Art Reference Library, New York, with identification of the subject and attribution to Smibert, but with no information as to the owner or location of the portrait.

Reproduced: Sibley's *Harvard Graduates,* vol. VII, opp. p. 94. F.A.R.L. photo.

TIMOTHY MINOT

Subject: Timothy Minot was born at Concord, Mass., June 18, 1692. In 1712 he was engaged by the town authorities to teach the grammar school in the town. He continued to do so during vacation periods while a student at Harvard, from which he graduated in 1718, and remained the town schoolmaster for forty years thereafter, having a high reputation and being widely known as "Master Minot." He studied theology at Harvard and was licensed to preach but was never ordained. He did, however, often preach as a supply at Concord and elsewhere, and his epitaph says that "as a preacher of the Gospel his praise was in all the churches." He married (1) Mary Brooks (*q.v.*), and, after her death in 1760, (2) Mrs. Beulah Brown of Sudbury. He died November 30, 1776.

Size: H. 27½ in.; W. 23½ in.

Date: About 1730.

Description: The head and bust of subject are shown set against a dark background, half front, the left shoulder toward the spectator, the head turned left, three-quarters front. There are small spandrels in the lower corners of the picture. Minot wears a short gray wig, black coat, and white ministerial bands, and a brown robe is thrown over his left shoulder and arm. He has a rather full face, pointed nose, brown eyes, and a Cupid's-bow mouth. The face appears to be that of a man about forty years old and is intelligent and attractive.

The family tradition is that Smibert painted this picture and that of Mrs. Minot at the time of their marriage. That marriage took place, however, in December 1724, five years before Smibert came to Boston. The portraits of Timothy Minot and his wife are characteristic of Smibert, and there is no reason to doubt that they are his work, but, if so, they cannot be dated earlier than December 1729, and are likely to be a little later. The only difficulty with dating them as late as 1730 is that both persons portrayed appear rather younger than they would have been at that date, but perhaps the artist was flattering them.

Owner: Mrs. Stedman Buttrick, Concord, Mass. The portrait of Timothy Minot, like that of his wife, passed by direct descent from the Minot family into the Brooks family, to the present owner, Mrs. Stedman (Mary Brooks) Buttrick, Sr.

Exhibited: Loan Exhibition, Concord Art Association, Concord, Mass., 1932.

Reproduced: Sibley's *Harvard Graduates,* vol VI, opp. p. 258. F.A.R.L. 17889.

Reference: P. F. Mass. 1457.

MRS. TIMOTHY MINOT

Subject: Mary, daughter of Noah and Dorothy (Wright) Brooks, was born at Concord, July 24, 1699. Married Timothy Minot, December 1724. Died February 15, 1760.

Size: H. 27½ in.; W. 24 in.

Date: About 1730.

Description: The subject, an attractive young woman, is shown nearly full front against a shaded background, with small spandrels in the lower corners. Her head is turned slightly to her left. She has brown hair, a curl of which hangs over her left shoulder, brown eyes, a pretty complexion and attractive features. She wears a blue-green dress, cut low, with white guimpe.

Owner: Mrs. Stedman Buttrick, Concord, Mass. This portrait, like that of Mrs. Minot's husband, has been transmitted by direct descent from the Minot family back into the Brooks family, to the present owner, Mrs. Stedman (Mary Brooks) Buttrick, Sr.

172   DESCRIPTIVE CATALOGUE

Exhibited: Loan Exhibition, Concord Art Association, Concord, Mass., 1932.

Reproduced: F.A.R.L. 17888.

Reference: P. F. *Mass.* 1451.

JOHN NELSON

Subject: John, son of Robert Nelson, of Gray's Inn, and Mary, daughter of Sir John Temple of Stantonbury, was born in or near London in 1657; emigrated to Boston in 1680; about 1686 married Elizabeth Tailer, sister of William Tailer (*q.v.*); was captured by the French in Nova Scotia, imprisoned in France for several years; returned to Boston 1698; died in Boston, November 15, 1734.

Size: H. 44½ in.; W. 36 in.

Date: Inscribed *Aet. 78 1732,* lower left.

Description: The picture shows a large, vigorous man of advanced years, seated, half front, his right shoulder towards the spectator, his head turned nearly full front. He has a prominent nose, and a well modeled, intelligent countenance. He wears a gray wig, knotted at the ends; long, hanging scarf; brown velvet coat buttoned up in front, white linen sleeves showing. His left hand holds his robe in his lap; his right hand rests on two books placed on the table at his side. The background behind the figure shows a plain dark wall, opening on the right to a distant vista of hills enclosing an arm of the sea. In the upper left corner is a coat of arms, said to be that of the Temple family. In pose and costume the portrait closely resembles that of James Gooch, Jr. (*q.v.*).

Owner: Roger Alden Derby, Jr., New York. John Nelson's daughter married Henry Lloyd of Lloyd's Neck, Long Island, and on the back of the frame is a paper reading, "H. Lloyd, Lloyd's Dock." The portrait was purchased about 1890 from a Mrs. Higbee, a descendant from Henry Lloyd, by other descendants and from them was inherited by James Lloyd Derby, who gave it to his brother, Roger Alden Derby, from whom it has passed to his son.

Reproduced: Melancthon Lloyd Woolsey, *The Lloyd Manor of Queen's Village* (Baltimore, 1925), p. 17. Bolton, III, 795. F.A.R.L. 33200. A copy by Frothingham (?) is owned by John Nelson Borland, New York. Another copy was made by O. L. Lay of New York in 1869.

References: Constance Borland, *The Borland Family.* Samuel Adams Drake, *John Nelson: a Romance of Colonial Days.*

MRS. ANDREW OLIVER AND SON ANDREW, JR.

Subject: Mary, daughter of Col. Thomas Fitch, born October 28, 1706, married Andrew Oliver, Lieutenant Governor of Massachusetts; died November 26, 1732. Her son, Andrew Oliver, Jr., was born 1731, died 1799.

Size: H. 50½ in.; W. 40½ in.

Date: 1732.

Description: Mrs. Oliver is shown rather awkwardly seated in a fiddle-back mahogany chair, half front, her left shoulder towards the spectator, her head turned left nearly full front, against a plain greenish-brown background. She wears a dull-yellow gown, with white muslin guimpe and undersleeves. In her lap she holds her son, shown as a child of about two years; he is unclothed save for a white linen cloth about his middle, and is looking at some cherries which he holds in his right hand.

Owner: W. H. P. Oliver, Morristown, N. J. The picture passed by descent to Dr. Fitch E. Oliver, of Boston, then to his son Edward Oliver. It is now owned by W. H. P. Oliver.

Reproduced: F.A.R.L. photo.

Reference: M.H.S. Proc., XVI (1878), 397.

Probably this portrait is the one erroneously listed as "Mrs. Andrews" under "Smibert" in Champlin & Perkins *Cyclopedia of Painters and Paintings,* vol. IV.

MRS. ANDREW OLIVER, NO. 2

Description: Half length, showing the head and bust of the subject.

Ownership: Peter Oliver, Mt. Kisco, N. Y. Presumably this is the portrait referred to in her husband's will, under the item reading, "I give and bequeath unto my beloved Son Andrew my Gold Watch and the painting done by Smibert of my two Brothers and myself [see Three Oliver Brothers] having already given him a half Length Picture of his Mother done by the same hand." It passed by descent to W. H. P. Oliver of Morristown, N. J., and was given by him to his son Peter Oliver.

DANIEL OLIVER, NO. 1

Subject: Daniel, son of Peter and Sarah Oliver, of Boston, born February 28, 1664; married, April 23, 1696, Elizabeth Belcher (died 1735), sister of Gov. Jonathan Belcher; died April 23, 1732.

Size: H. 50 in.; W. 39⅝ in.

Date: About 1731.

Description: The subject is shown as an old man, seated in an armchair beside a table, three-quarters length, half front, his right shoulder towards the spectator. The background is dark, with a window through which a ship is faintly seen in the distance. He wears a short gray wig, a long steenkirk tie, the ends of which are thrust through a waistcoat buttonhole; plain wristbands; and brown coat and waistcoat left unbuttoned. His right arm rests upon the arm of the chair, the hand holding a quill pen. His left hand lies upon papers on the table, among which is a letter addressed to "Daniel Oliver, Merchant, Boston." He has a long nose and brown eyes. The figure is unusually well posed, and has dignity. Lawrence Park called the picture "one of the best Smiberts, particularly the characterization of the face."

Owner: W. H. P. Oliver, Morristown, N. J. The picture was inherited by the subject's son, Governor Andrew Oliver, who, dying in

1774, bequeathed it to his son Daniel in the following words: "I give to my beloved son Daniel a half length Picture of his Grandfather whose name he bears, and another of his Grandmother, both done by Smibert." It descended to Dr. Fitch E. Oliver of Boston, and is now owned by the latter's nephew, W. H. P. Oliver.

Reproduced: F.A.R.L. 5438.

DANIEL OLIVER, NO. 2

Size: H. *c.* 30 in.; W. *c.* 25 in.

Date: 1731 or later.

Description: This picture is a replica of the head and bust shown in the portrait of Daniel Oliver, No. 1, and might have been painted at any time between 1731 and Smibert's death in 1751.

Owner: Seabury Oliver, Morristown, N. J. This portrait, with the companion picture of Mrs. Daniel Oliver (No. 2), was inherited by their son Peter, Chief Justice of Massachusetts, who, being a Loyalist, took both to England at the time of the Revolution. They descended to Thomas Hutchinson Oliver, who, dying at a great age, unmarried, left them to his Hutchinson kinsfolk, from one of whom, Mrs. Walsham How, they were purchased about 1938 by W. H. P. Oliver, of Morristown, N. J. The present owner is his son.

MRS. DANIEL OLIVER, NO. 1

Subject: Elizabeth, daughter of Hon. Andrew Belcher, and sister of Gov. Jonathan Belcher; married, April 23, 1696, Daniel Oliver; died 1735. On the back of the picture is an inscription, "Madam Elizabeth Oliver, daughter of the Hon. Andrew Belcher."

Size: H. 50 in.; W. 39½ in.

Date: Before 1732, in which year she became a widow.

Description: The subject is a very plain elderly woman shown seated full front at a table, upon which her right elbow rests, against a background which shows a vista of woods and a stream to the right. She has dark eyes and hair and is plainly dressed in a deep-rose gown, with white guimpe and ruffles. Her left hand rests in her lap. The portrait is not so good a one as her husband's.

Owner: W. H. P. Oliver, Morristown, N. J. This portrait, like the companion piece representing her husband (*q.v.*), was bequeathed by her son, Governor Andrew Oliver, to his son Daniel, from whom it descended to Dr. Fitch E. Oliver of Boston, an uncle of the present owner.

Reproduced: A copy in oils, by Mrs. W. H. P. Oliver. F.A.R.L. 5440.

MRS. DANIEL OLIVER, NO. 2

Size: H. *c.* 30 in.; W. *c.* 25 in.

Date: 1731 or later.

Description: A replica of the head and bust of Mrs. Oliver No. 1, with slight variations in the pose and dress.

Owner: Miss Alice Oliver, Morristown, N. J. The line of descent is the same as for the companion portrait of Daniel Oliver No. 2.

MRS. DANIEL OLIVER, NO. 3

Date: After 1732, in which year she became a widow, but not later than 1735, in which year she died.
Size: H. 30 in.; W. 25 in.
Description: The head and bust of the subject are shown against a plain background, with spandrels in the corners, three-quarters front, her left shoulder towards the spectator, her head turned slightly left, nearly full front. She wears widow's weeds, a dark dress with white muslin guimpe, and a black hood with white linen lining gathered into a "widow's peak" above her forehead.
Owner: W. H. P. Oliver, Morristown, N. J. Owned in 1867 by Dr. Fitch E. Oliver of Boston, an uncle of the present owner.
Reproduced: F.A.R.L. 5441.

PETER OLIVER

Subject: Peter, son of Daniel and Elizabeth (Belcher) Oliver, born Boston, March 26, 1713, graduated from Harvard 1730, married Mary, daughter of William and Hannah (Appleton) Clark, July 5, 1733. Chief Justice of Massachusetts, 1771. He lived in Boston until the outbreak of the Revolution, when, being a Loyalist, he went to England where he lived in Birmingham until his death in October 1791.
Size: H. 29½ in.; W. 24½ in.
Date: Perhaps about the time of his marriage, 1733.
Description: The head and bust of the subject are shown against a dark background, within a painted oval, half front, his right shoulder advanced, his head turned right three-quarters front. He is easily identified as the same youth whom Smibert painted two or three years earlier as the youngest of the Three Oliver Brothers. He wears a full brown wig, a brown coat, and silver-embroidered waistcoat, white neckband and ruffles. He has brown eyes, a rather large nose, and full lips.
Owner: Peter Oliver, Mt. Kisco, N. Y. The portrait, with its companion piece, representing Mrs. Peter Oliver, was taken to England when Peter Oliver retired to that country, and descended to Thomas Hutchinson Oliver, who, dying unmarried at a great age, left them to his Hutchinson kinsfolk, from one of whom, Mrs. Walsham How, both pictures were purchased about 1938, by W. H. P. Oliver, of Morristown, N. J. Now owned by the latter's son.

MRS. PETER OLIVER

Subject: Mary, daughter of William and Hannah (Appleton) Clark, married Peter Oliver of Boston, July 5, 1733.
Size: H. 29¼ in.; W. 24½ in.
Date: Perhaps about the time of her marriage, 1733.

Description: The subject is a rather large young woman whose head and bust are shown against a dark shaded background within a painted oval, full front, her head turned slightly to the left. She wears a gray silk dress with white muslin trim at her bosom. She has abundant light-brown hair, a curl of which hangs over her left shoulder; brown eyes and a rather large nose. While not handsome, the face is pleasing and intelligent, and is more strongly characterized than is the case in most of Smibert's portraits of women.

Owner: Andrew Oliver, New York, to whom it has come by the same line of descent as that by which the portrait of the subject's husband has passed to the present Peter Oliver.

THREE OLIVER BROTHERS (DANIEL, ANDREW, AND PETER)

Subject: Three sons of Daniel and Elizabeth (Belcher) Oliver, Daniel, Andrew, and Peter. Daniel, Jr., was born in Boston, January 14, 1703/04, was graduated from Harvard in 1722, and died in London of smallpox, July 5, 1727. Andrew was born March 28, 1706; was graduated from Harvard in 1726; became Lieutenant-Governor of Massachusetts, and died in 1774. Peter was born March 26, 1713, was graduated from Harvard in 1730, and became Chief Justice of the Superior Court in Massachusetts, being the last to hold that office before the Revolution. He died in 1791.

Size: H. 39⅝ in.; W. 57½ in.

Date: 1730.

Description: The three brothers are shown seated about a round table, covered with a green cloth, on which lies a large, closed book. Daniel is at the spectator's left, half front, his right shoulder towards the spectator, his head turned right nearly full front. He wears a gray wig, a plum-colored coat, a twisted cravat, the end of which is thrust through a buttonhole, and ruffles at his wrists. His left hand rests on the table, his right hand on his knee. Andrew sits in the middle, nearly full front. He wears a light-brown wig (or perhaps his natural hair parted in the middle and falling to his shoulders), a blue coat, and ruffles at neck and wrists. His right hand is thrust into his coat, his left arm is thrown over the back of his chair. Peter is seated at the right, half front, his left shoulder towards the spectator. His right elbow rests upon the book, the hand at his face; his left hand rests on the table. He wears a gray wig, a golden-brown coat, with ruffles at neck and wrists. (In showing the elder brother with a long twisted cravat and the two younger ones in shirt ruffles the portrait illustrates the transition in style.)

The portrait was attributed to Smibert by Augustus Perkins in his list in M.H.S. *Proc.* (1878), p. 397, but Charles Henry Hart assigned it to Nathaniel Emmons, who had painted a portrait of the boys' mother, on the ground that Daniel, Jr., had died in London nearly three years before Smibert reached Boston and that therefore Smibert could not have painted it. The surmise seemed well-founded, but Hart neglected to observe that the three young men are shown at an age considerably greater than they would have attained if the portrait had been painted by Emmons before Daniel, Jr., went to London, and his theory is decisively refuted by the statement in the will of Andrew, who bequeathed to his son Andrew the "painting done by Smibert of my two Brothers and myself." The problem of how Smibert could have painted the deceased Daniel is solved by the existence of a miniature which Daniel, Jr., had had painted in London before his death and sent to his parents. In the portrait Smibert reproduced this miniature in enlarged form, merely giving the wig the style of a slightly later date.

Owner: The portrait descended to Dr. Fitch Edward Oliver of Boston and is now owned by his children, Messrs. Andrew, Edward, and Lawrence Oliver, and Miss Susie Oliver. On loan at the Museum of Fine Arts, Boston.

Exhibited: Loan Exhibition of One Hundred Colonial Portraits, Museum of Fine Arts, Boston, 1930.

Yale University Art Gallery, "The Smibert Tradition," exhibition, October–November 1949.

Reproduced: Bayley, p. 409. *Catalogue, Loan Exhibition of One Hundred Colonial Portraits*, Museum of Fine Arts (Boston, 1930), p. 59. Copy, 1949, by George Smith for W. H. P. Oliver, Morristown, N. J. F.A.R.L. photo.

Reference: P. F. Mass. 1539.

LIEUTENANT GENERAL CHARLES OTWAY

Subject: Lieutenant General Charles Otway, born 1690, died 1753.

Size: H. 48 in.; W. 40 in.

Date: Signed: *J. Smibert* (in black, lower left corner).

    1724

A tablet on the frame says the portrait was painted 1727, an evident misreading of the date painted with the signature.

Description: The subject is shown three-quarter length, in armor, wearing a large gray wig and a brown sash, against a background which shows on the right a battle scene with cannon blazing.

Owner: Captain Otway Ruthven, Penns, Genghill, Guildford, England.

Note: I have not seen this picture, information about which has been given by Mr. C. K. Adams, National Portrait Gallery, London.

HANNAH PEMBERTON

Subject: Hannah, daughter of James and Hannah (Penhallow) Pemberton, born *c.* 1715; married Benjamin Colman II (*q.v.*) in 1739. Sister of Mary and Samuel Pemberton (*q.v.*).

Size: H. 29½ in.; W. 24½ in.

Date: About 1734 or 1735.

Description: The head and bust of the subject are shown within a painted oval, nearly full front, the head turned slightly to the left, against a plain background. She is a rather plump young woman, with a fresh complexion, dark eyes, and level eyebrows, and dark hair, a curl of which falls on her left shoulder. She is dressed in the usual low-necked gown of plum-colored silk, with white guimpe. Since the portrait is not a companion piece to that of her husband and shows the subject as about eighteen years old, it was probably painted before her marriage, about the same time as that of her younger sister Mary Pemberton (q.v.).

Owner: Metropolitan Museum, New York. On the back of the portrait is a label of the Museum of Fine Arts, Boston, stating that "Henry Davenport probably was the owner Oct. 1, 1878." It was later owned by Mrs. Clayton Colman Hall of Ruxton, Maryland; then by Dr. Colman W. Cutler of New York; then by Paul C. Cutler of Rocky River, Ohio, who sent it in 1938 on consignment to the Macbeth Gallery, New York. It was purchased in 1943 by the present owner.

Reproduced: F.A.R.L. 32291.

MARY PEMBERTON

Subject: Mary, daughter of James and Hannah (Penhallow) Pemberton (sister of Samuel Pemberton, q.v., and Hannah Pemberton, q.v.), born 1717, died 1763.

Size: H. 30½ in.; W. 25½ in.

Date: About 1734 or 1735.

Description: The head and bust of Mary Pemberton are shown in a painted oval, full front, her head turned slightly to the right, against a plain dark background. She is a very young woman, just emerging from girlhood, with brown hair, curls of which fall over either shoulder, large hazel eyes, and a fresh complexion. Her greenish-blue gown is cut very low, with white muslin ruffles showing above its edge. A narrow pink ribbon hangs untied from the opening of her gown. One of the most pleasing colonial portraits of a very young woman.

Owner: Mrs. William T. Aldrich, Brookline, Mass. Owned by Miss Julia Ward of Boston, who died about 1900; then by her cousin, George H. Davenport of Boston, who died in 1932. Now owned by his daughter, Mrs. William T. Aldrich.

Exhibited: Loan Exhibition of One Hundred Colonial Portraits, Museum of Fine Arts, Boston, 1930.

Yale University Art Gallery, "The Smibert Tradition," exhibition, October–November, 1949.

Reproduced: Bayley, p. 411. Catalogue, Loan Exhibition of One Hundred Colonial Portraits, Museum of Fine Arts (Boston, 1930). F.A.R.L.

Reference: P. F. Mass. 1646.

SAMUEL PEMBERTON

Subject: Samuel, son of James and Hannah Pemberton; born 1723, brother of Mary and Hannah Pemberton (q.v.); graduated from Harvard 1742; selectman of Boston 1769–1772; died 1779.

Size: H. 30¼ in.; W. 24½ in.

Date: About 1735.

Description: The head and bust of the youthful subject are shown within a painted oval nearly full front, against a shaded gray-green background. The boy, who appears to be about twelve years old, wears a short curled wig, stock with ruffled shirt front, grayish-brown coat and waistcoat, with embossed silver buttons.

Owner: Mrs. William T. Aldrich, Brookline, Mass. Formerly owned by Miss Julia Ward of Boston, who died about 1900; then by her cousin George H. Davenport, Boston, who died in 1932. Now owned by his daughter.

Exhibited: Loan Exhibition of One Hundred Colonial Portraits, Museum of Fine Arts, Boston, 1930.

Yale University Art Gallery, "The Smibert Tradition," exhibition, October–November, 1949.

Reproduced: Bayley, p. 413. *Catalogue, Loan Exhibition of One Hundred Colonial Portraits,* Museum of Fine Arts (Boston, 1930), p. 68. F.A.R.L. photo.

Reference: P. F. Mass. 1647.

SIR WILLIAM PEPPERELL, BART., NO. 1

Subject: William, son of William and Margaret (Bray) Pepperell, born 1696 at Kittery Point, Maine; married 1722–1723 Mary, daughter of Grover and Elizabeth (Sewall) Hirst; died 1759. Merchant and soldier; captured Louisburg 1745; created baronet in 1745.

Size: H. 96 in.; W. 56 in.

Date: 1747.

Description: Sir William Pepperell is shown full length, nearly full front, standing on a hill from which is seen a distant view of besieged Louisburg, upon which two huge cannon balls are falling with the trajectory of their flight clearly shown! He is in full-dress uniform, with a white wig, ruffles at neck and wrists, a long scarlet coat decorated with many large buttons, a long scarlet waistcoat with heavy gold braid, breeches, white stockings, and black shoes with buckles. The corner of his gold-edged cocked hat shows against his left side. His right hand awkwardly grasps a baton; the forefinger of his left hand points down the hill. The face is full and self-complacent. The pose is awkward and illustrates Smibert's inability to do well a full-length figure.

Owner: The Essex Institute, Salem, Mass. The portrait hung during the eighteenth century in the Pepperell Mansion at Kittery, and descended to his daughter, Mrs. Sparhawk. In 1821 it was given to George A. Ward of Salem, a connection of the family, and was transported on top of a stagecoach to Salem, where Ward presented it to the Essex Institute.

Reproduced: A full-sized copy signed "U. D. Tenney, after Smybert, 1747," is in the Portsmouth Athenaeum, Portsmouth, N. H. Tenney was a nineteenth-century painter.

Another copy in oils is owned by Mrs. George L. Montague of Chelsea, Mass., a descendant of Sir William's sister, Dorothy Pepperell.

Because Pepperell was a popular hero this picture was promptly reproduced in mezzotint by Peter Pelham, but the figure is shown only half length. The engraving bears the following inscription:

> *Sir William Pepperell Bar*^t*. Colonel of one of his Majesty's Regiments of Foot, who was Lieutenant General and Commander in Chief of the American Forces Employ'd in the Expedition against the Island of Cape Breton which was happily Reduced to the Obedience of his Britannic Majesty, June the 17, 1745.*
>
> *J: Smibert Pinx*   *P: Pelham fecit et ex: 1747*

Winsor, II, 115. *Essex Institute Historical Collections*, XXXVII, 273. Dunlap, III, 334. Bayley, p. 415. Rogers, *Glimpses of an Old Social Capital* (1923), p. 4. *Antiques*, vol. XVIII, no. 3 (August 1930). *Catalogue, Portraits in the Essex Institute* (1936), p. 152. F.A.R.L. 14151–14152.

References: Essex Institute Historical Collections, XXI (1884), 161; XXXI (1894), 59; XXXVII (1901), 287–289. P. F. *Mass.* 1653.

SIR WILLIAM PEPPERELL, BART., NO. 2

Date: c. 1747.

Size: H. 49¾ in.; W. 39¾ in.

Description: The second portrait of Pepperell shows him standing against a background faintly showing a column at the right and a harbor with vessels at the left; half length, three-quarters front, his left shoulder to the spectator, his face turned left, nearly full front. He wears a white wig, the usual ruffles, a blue coat heavily brocaded with gold, held back by the left hand posed upon his hip, and a red waistcoat, also heavily braided in gold. His right hand grasps a baton. His gold-braided cocked hat is held against his side by his left arm. In the lower left corner is a map inscribed, "Plan of ye City and Fortress of Louisburg." The face is better painted than in No. 1, and the picture, while much less pretentious, gives the impression of being a far better portrait.

Owner: Mrs. Kenneth P. Budd, New York. The portrait remained in the possession of Pepperell's descendants until 1815, when it was given to a member of the Sheafe family and was by him loaned to the Portsmouth Athenaeum. Given in 1864 to Mrs. Hampden Cutts (Mary Pepperell Sparhawk Jarvis), a great-great-granddaughter of the subject, passing to her daughter, Mrs. Underhill A. Budd, and to the late Kenneth P. Budd, of New York.

Reproduced: Catalogue, Exhibition of Colonial Portraits, Metropolitan Museum of Art (New York, 1911), p. 62. N.E.H.G.S., *Register,* vol. XX. Engraving by unknown artist in Appleton's *Encyclopedia of American Biography* (1894), IV, 721. Copy, owned by Mrs. Everett Pepperell Wheeler, 340 E. 72nd St., New York. F.A.R.L. photo.

MRS. WILLIAM PEPPERELL (LADY PEPPERELL)

Subject: This portrait has been passed down through several generations of descendants of Sir William Pepperell as representing Lady Pepperell. The tradition is presumably correct. If so, it represents Mary, daughter of Grover and Elizabeth (Sewall) Hirst, born 1703, married William Pepperell 1722/23, died 1759. Since she appears to be a woman still in her late twenties it must have been painted soon after Smibert's arrival in Boston, and some fifteen years before her husband was created a baronet, entitling her to be called "Lady Pepperell."

Size: H. 31 in.; W. 25¼ in.

Date: c. 1730.

Description: The subject is shown against a shaded brown background, full front, her head turned slightly to her right. She has dark brown eyes, and dark hair, a curl of which hangs over either shoulder. She wears a gray-blue dress with white lawn guimpe and undersleeves. The picture is in Smibert's characteristic manner, but the head appears to have been considerably repainted.

Owner: Mrs. Arthur Shipman, Jr., 120 Scarborough St., Hartford, Conn.; in 1948 the portrait was hanging in the apartment of her mother, Mrs. R. H. Dana, New York.

Reproduced: F.A.R.L. 20526, as Lady Pepperell, attributed to Smibert.

REV. GEORGE PHILLIPS

Subject: George, son of Rev. Samuel and Sarah (Appleton) Phillips of Rowley, Mass., born at Rowley June 3, 1664; died at Brookhaven, Long Island, N. Y., April 3, 1739. Graduated from Harvard, 1686. Preached at Suffield, Conn., 1690–1692; at Jamaica, Long Island, 1693–1697; settled at Setauket in the town of Brookhaven, 1697. Married, about 1697, Sarah, daughter of William Hallett, Jr.

Size: H. 30 in.; W. 25¼ in.

Date: Not later than 1736, since it is mentioned in the subject's will dated January 18, 1736/37. A memorandum by a former owner stated that the portrait was painted "by John Smybert about 1730" (see below), and this attribution was followed in the listing by the Historical Records Survey (*P. F. Mass.* 1674). This memorandum, however, cannot be regarded as authoritative. There is nothing to indicate that it repeats a continuous tradition, and it may merely represent an early nineteenth-century attribution. The portrait is not a clear-cut example of Smibert's work, but it was executed during the period of Smibert's activity in Boston, in the neighborhood of which the subject had numerous relatives, including his youngest son, John, who entered Harvard in 1732, so that he might well have had occasion to come to Boston. Although the portrait does not conform to the pattern of the more conventional pictures of ministers by Smibert, the difference may be due to the absence of a wig and to the marked individuality of the subject, and the style of painting is sufficiently close to Smibert's to make the attribution to him at least a plausible conjecture.

Description: The subject is shown full front, his head turned slightly to the left, within an oval formed by spandrels ornamented with a flat molding, against a brown background, the light coming from the upper left. He appears as a vigorous man who might be as old as sixty-five or seventy years. He wears a black coat, white neckcloth and ministerial bands, and a black cloak thrown over his right shoulder. His natural gray hair falls to his shoulders; he has heavy dark eyebrows, brown eyes, a long straight nose, and a straight mouth. While not handsome, the face shows strength and dignity. It is recorded that he was "distinguished for a peculiar vein of natural wit," a comment which his face does not belie. The portrait is in the original frame.

Owner: Estate of W. Phoenix Belknap, Jr., Boston. The subject in his will, noted above, bequeathed to his son, George Phillips (1698–1771) of Smithtown, Long Island, "my picture . . . and my portmanteau." The younger George Phillips passed it to his son Samuel (1728–1806) of Smithtown, who left "family portraits" to his son Samuel, and he in turn to his son George Smith Phillips (died 1881) of Smithtown. Benjamin F. Thompson, *History of Long Island* (2nd ed., New York, 1843), I, 423, says: "A portrait of him [Rev. George Phillips] taken from life, is in possession of . . . George S. Phillips of Smithtown." In his will George S. Phillips left to Elbert Brush, the son of his cousin Isaac Brush, "The portraits of his and my ancestors, Rev. George Phillips and Samuel Phillips dec'd, now in my possession." It is possible that the portrait owned in 1843 by G. S. Phillips was the one described above, but that the portrait bequeathed by him to Elbert Brush was the one listed below as Copy No. 1, because the original portrait was acquired about 1856 by William Roe of Newburgh, N. Y., a descendant of the subject's daughter Elizabeth, from whom it passed by inheritance to his great-grandson William J. Roe, of Newburgh, the owner in 1942. In a note written at that time Mr. Roe quoted a memorandum left by his father stating that the portrait was acquired by his grandfather, William Roe, "in about the year 1856 and was painted by John Smybert about 1730," and that he understood the consideration to have been two copies in new frames. The portrait is recorded in the Historical Records Survey as in the hands of the Goodman-Walker Gallery, Boston, 1937, in whose keeping it was temporarily at that time (*P. F. Mass.* 1674). In 1942 it was acquired by Mr. Belknap, a descendant of the subject's great-granddaughter, Anna Lewis Phillips, who married Major Daniel Phoenix of Morristown, N. J. Mr. Belknap supplied the foregoing information as well as that relating to copies of the portrait (see below).

Reproduced: Copy No. 1. Similar to the original, but the spandrels form a simple flat plane with oval opening; the light is cast from above; the hair appears less gray, and the folds of the cloak are less defined. It appears to be an old copy, and may be the portrait owned by George

S. Phillips at the time of his death, and bequeathed to Elbert Brush, since it is now in the possession of an owner of the same surname, Charles Francis Brush of Woodbridge, Conn. From present information it is impossible to judge whether it is one of the copies alleged to have been made about 1856, or a still earlier copy perhaps of the eighteenth century. It is said to be in a frame resembling that of the original portrait.

Copy No. 2. In the memorandum quoted by William J. Roe (see above) two copies are said to have been exchanged for the original portrait when it was acquired by William Roe in 1856. Copy No. 2, painted by Miss Katherine Janeway for the late E. Hicks Herrick, is known only from a photograph of it owned by Mr. Morton Penny-packer, the Long Island historian, and another photograph at the New York Historical Society. The portrait which Miss Janeway copied may have been the original, or one of the copies said to have been painted about 1856, but the fact that in her copy a star appears in each of the upper spandrels, a Bible in the lower left spandrel, and a manuscript and quill pen in the lower right spandrel suggests that she may have copied a copy, since these accessories do not appear in the original.

Other copies. If Mr. Roe's memorandum is accurate in respect to the two copies said to have been painted about 1856, there are either one or two copies yet unlocated, depending upon whether Copy No. 1 should be identified as one of them. If so, the other may be the portrait said to have been in bad condition and perhaps now destroyed, from which Copy No. 2 was painted.

JOHN PITTS

Subject: John Pitts of Boston, born in England 1668, settled in Boston 1694, died 1731.

Size: H. 35¼ in.; W. 27 in.

Date: c. 1730.

Description: The subject is shown half length against a dark background, half front, with his right shoulder towards the spectator, his full, round face turned nearly full front. He wears a white wig, brown coat, and waistcoat, ruffled shirt and sleeves. His right hand rests upon his hip holding back his coat, his left hand is thrust into his waistcoat. The figure is rather wooden, and the face somewhat lacking in expression.

Owner: Mrs. Lendall Pitts, Norfolk, Va. The portrait passed by descent to the late Lendall Pitts, of Paris, and now belongs to Mrs. Lendall Pitts, but it has hung for many years in the house of Mr. Pitts' sister, Mrs. Arthur Maxwell Parker, Grosse Pointe Farms, Michigan.

Exhibited: Detroit Museum of Art, between 1920 and 1927.

Reproduced: Photogravure, in reverse, in Daniel Goodwin, Jr., *The Dearborns: a discourse commemorative of the 80th anniversary of the occupation of Fort Dearborn* (Chicago, 1884).

MRS. JOHN PITTS

Subject: Elizabeth, daughter of James and Susannah Lindall (*q.v.*); born 1699, died 1763; wife of John Pitts of Boston.

Size: H. 35⅜ in.; W. 27¼ in.

Date: c. 1730.

Description: Mrs. Pitts is shown half length against a plain background, full front, with her face turned slightly to the left. She is a robust, rather heavy woman, with fresh complexion, dark eyes, and dark hair, a curl of which hangs over her right shoulder. She wears a blue-green dress, with white lawn guimpe and undersleeves, and a dark-brown scarf lined with old rose is thrown about her and is held by her right hand, while her left hand hangs concealed at her side.

Owner: Mrs. Lendall Pitts, Norfolk, Va. The portrait passed by descent to the late Lendall Pitts, of Paris, and now belongs to Mrs. Lendall Pitts, but it has hung for many years in the home of Mr. Pitts' sister, Mrs. Arthur Maxwell Parker, Grosse Pointe Farms, Michigan.

Exhibited: Detroit Museum of Art, between 1920 and 1927.

Reproduced: Photogravure, in reverse, in Daniel Goodwin, Jr., *The Dearborns: a discourse commemorative of the 80th anniversary of the occupation of Fort Dearborn* (Chicago, 1884).

JUDGE EDMUND QUINCY, NO. I

Subject: Edmund, son of Edmund and Elizabeth (Gookin) Quincy, born in Braintree, Mass., October 4, 1681. He was graduated from Harvard College in 1699. Married Dorothy Flynt of Dorchester, 1701. Judge of the Supreme Court. In 1737 he was sent to London to represent Massachusetts in a boundary dispute with New Hampshire, and died there of smallpox February 23, 1738. His granddaughter married John Hancock.

Size: H. 30¼ in.; W. 24½ in.

Date: About 1733, according to family tradition, corroborated by the apparent age of the subject.

Description: The head and bust of Judge Quincy are shown within four spandrels against a dark background, half front, his right shoulder to the spectator, his fine and intelligent face turned right nearly full front. He has hazel eyes and a rather fair complexion. He wears a full white wig, reddish-brown coat, stock, and steenkirk tie. Mr. Alan Burroughs in *Limners and Likenesses,* p. 37, is inclined to assign this portrait to Peter Pelham, saying that it "might on the basis of comparison with the best of the Cotton Mather portraits be called a Pelham; at least it is delicately, thinly painted, without Smibert's natural vigor." Pelham, however, is not known to have painted any portraits besides those which served as a basis for his mezzotints, of which this is not one. Furthermore, there was a strong tradition in the Quincy family that Smibert painted two portraits of Edmund Quincy. While this picture, as regards style, may be regarded as a borderline case between Pelham and Smibert, the weight of evidence is decidedly in favor of the latter.

Owner: Museum of Fine Arts, Boston, given in 1876 by the children of President Josiah Quincy of Harvard.

Exhibited: Harvard Tercentenary Exhibition, Cambridge, 1936.

Reproduced: D. M. Wilson, *Where American Independence Began* (1904), p. 160. *Massachusetts Law Quarterly,* vol. IV (November 1920). *Antiques,* vol. XVIII, no. 3 (August 1930). Sibley's *Harvard Graduates,* vol. IV, opp. p. 492. Alan Burroughs, *Limners and Likenesses,* fig. 27. F.A.R.L. photo.

References: Mentioned, *Encyclopaedia Britannica,* 11th ed., under "Smybert." *New England Magazine,* new series, vol. XXVI (March 1902). N.E.H.G.S. *Register,* XXXVIII (1884), 156. *P. F. Mass.* 1764.

JUDGE EDMUND QUINCY, NO. 2

Augustus T. Perkins in his paper on the portraits by Blackburn and Smibert (M.H.S. *Proc.,* XVI, 398–399, 1878) quotes from a memorandum by Miss Eliza Susan Quincy as follows: "John Smibert painted two portraits of Judge E. Quincy; the date is not precisely known, but it must have been 1737, and probably earlier. The portrait inherited by the late Josiah Quincy (1772–1864) was presented by his children, in 1876, to the Art Museum in Boston [No. 1]. The other portrait was for many years in the possession of the late Edmund Quincy, of Dedham (1808–1877), by whom it was bequeathed to his eldest son, Edmund Quincy, in 1878, its present owner."

This statement is corroborated in an article in *The New England Historical and Genealogical Register* (XXXVIII, 156), which says: "Smibert painted two portraits of Edmund Quincy in his official dress [*sic*]. The one inherited by President Quincy has been placed for safe keeping in the Art Museum in Boston [No. 1]; the other became the property of his daughter Dorothy, and was given by her son Jonathan Jackson, in 1810, to Edmund Quincy, the youngest son of President Quincy. It was much injured by the British."

Owner: Mrs. Henry (Margaret D.) Ross, Delray Beach, Florida. I have not seen this portrait but believe it to be the one recorded above. It was recently in the possession of the late Frederick R. Nourse, Jr., of Dedham, Mass., and passed to his widow, now Mrs. Ross.

ALLAN RAMSAY, NO. 1

Subject: Allan, son of Robert Ramsay, born in Lanarkshire, Scotland, October 15, 1686; died at Edinburgh, January 8, 1758. Wigmaker, bookseller, and poet in Edinburgh. In 1720 Thomas Ruddiman published Ramsay's *Poems* in octavo. The next year they appeared in a quarto edition, and frequently thereafter. In 1725 he published *The Gentle Shepherd,* his best-known work. Both the portraits which Smibert painted of Ramsay were reproduced in engravings to serve as the frontispiece for several of the numerous editions of his works (see Allan Ramsay, No. 2, in Section B).

Size: H. 30½ in.; W. 25½ in.

Date: Painted in 1717, when Smibert visited Edinburgh before going to Italy.

Description: Ramsay is shown to his waist, nearly full front but with his head turned to the left nearly profile, in a painted masonry oval. He wears a thick black cap over his short hair, and a dark brown coat and shirt, unbuttoned at the neck, down to the fifth button of the coat (description courtesy Scottish National Portrait Gallery). The pose is an unfortunate one as it emphasizes Ramsay's heavy jowl, small eyes, and upturned snub nose. It is of this picture that Caw wrote, "it must have taken a good deal of friendship on the poet's part to stand the strain of that record of his appearance" (*Scottish Painting Past and Present*).

Owner: The Scottish National Portrait Gallery, Edinburgh. The portrait remained in Ramsay's possession, and in that of his last surviving daughter, Miss Jane Ramsay, until her death in 1804, and then was transferred to Newhall House, where it was hung in "Pennicuik's Parlour." In 1925 Newhall House was sold and its contents dispersed. The portrait was then purchased by Sir Hew Dalrymple of Edinburgh, and in 1945 was presented by him to the Scottish National Portrait Gallery.

Reproduced: A sepia drawing by Alexander Carse, a Scottish painter who worked in Edinburgh early in the nineteenth century, showing Ramsay half length within an oval, surrounded by conventional ornaments lightly sketched. The size of this drawing is H. 6 in., W. 4¾ in. It is now in the Scottish National Portrait Gallery, Edinburgh, where it is marked as having been drawn from the portrait by Smibert.

From this drawing A. Wilson made the line engraving used as the frontispiece to the edition of *The Gentle Shepherd* published in 1808 by Abernathy and Walker, in which it is labeled, "Drawn by A. Carse from the Original Family Picture in New Hall House & eng^d by A. Wilson." In this engraving Ramsay is shown turned to the right, within an oval frame about which is draped a tartan surmounted by a mask of Pan, and four pipes. The same engraving appears in the 1814 edition of *The Gentle Shepherd*.

GEORGE ROGERS

Subject: George, son of Rev. Nathaniel and Sarah (Purkiss) Rogers, of Portsmouth, N. H. He entered Harvard but left without taking his degree. Merchant in Boston. Married (1) Rebekah Parr, (2) Lydia, daughter of Hon. Thomas Hutchinson. His sister married Rev. John Gee (*q.v.*). He died previous to February 20, 1748.

Size: H. 36 in.; W. 30 in.

Date: 1735 (at head of letter on the table, partly hidden by the frame).

Description: The subject is a middle-aged man with a strong, vigorous countenance, shown seated in a high-backed stuffed chair at a table, against a dark background, with a window and ship at anchor showing dimly on the right, his body nearly in profile, the right shoulder towards the spectator, his head turned to his right, three-quarters front. He has a round, full face, a dimpled chin, and a pleasing, half-humorous expression. He wears a full, white wig, white neckcloth and ruffles, and a golden-brown coat and waistcoat. The table at which he is seated is covered with a blue-green cloth, upon which is a square silver (or pewter) inkstand with quill pen, similar to the one which appears in the portraits of Jacob Wendell and Henry Collins. A letter leaning against the inkstand is addressed "To the . . . Joshua Gee, Boston." The subject's right hand rests upon an open letter lying on the table which begins: "Dear Br . . . 1735 . . . To . . . Rogers, Esq.," and is signed "Joshua Gee." The two letters appear to commemorate some correspondence between the brothers-in-law. The portrait is an unusually fine and characteristic example of Smibert's work.

Owner: The portrait was in the possession of Miss Helen Keeling Mills, Kent, Conn., at the time of her death in 1939. Now owned by Mrs. Robert Brumbacher, Salt Lake City, Utah.

Reproduced: F.A.R.L. photo. *Art in America,* XXX, opp. p. 113 (April 1942). Sibley's *Harvard Graduates,* vol. VII, opp. p. 252.

REV. JOHN ROGERS, NO. 1

Subject: John, son of Rev. John and Elizabeth (Denison) Rogers. His father was fifth president of Harvard College; his mother a granddaughter of Gov. Thomas Dudley. He was born July 7, 1666; Harvard College 1684; married Martha Whittingham, March 4, 1690/91; minister at Ipswich, Mass., from a time soon after his graduation, but not ordained until October 1692; died December 28, 1745, after fifty-four years' service at Ipswich.

Size: H. 30¼ in.; W. 25 in.

Date: 1732.

Description: The portrait shows the head and bust of an old clergyman against a gray-green background with spandrels in the corners, three-quarters front, the left shoulder towards the spectator, the head turned left nearly full front. He wears a full white wig, stock and bands, black Geneva gown, over which is a cloak. The portrait is in the original frame. On the back, in very faint letters, is painted *AE 66.*

Owner: Derby Rogers, New Canaan, Conn., who inherited it from an aunt who had inherited it from her father, John Rogers of Boston, who in turn had inherited it from his father, Daniel Denison Rogers.

Exhibited: Yale University Art Gallery, "The Smibert Tradition," exhibition, October–November 1949.

Reproduced: See under Rev. John Rogers No. 2.

REV. JOHN ROGERS, NO. 2

The Essex Institute, Salem, Mass., owns a portrait of Rev. John Rogers which is either a contemporary replica or a very early copy of the portrait by Smibert. It shows slight differences from No. 1.

In the *Catalogue of Portraits in the Essex Institute* it is stated that the portrait is lettered *Smibert fecit. Aetas suae 66.* This inscription does not appear on the face of the portrait. Presumably it was a later addition painted on the back, but as the portrait has been relined it is not now visible.

An undated engraving was published, no doubt soon after the death of Mr. Rogers, with the following inscription:

Engraved from a copy of the original by Smibert—T. Kelley.
Rev. John Rogers
of Ipswich, Mass., AE66
Died Dec. 28ᵗʰ 1745, in his 80ᵗʰ year.

The "copy of the original" from which this engraving was made must have been either No. 1 or No. 2, depending on which was held to be the original. Regarding No. 2, Mr. Alan Burroughs in *Limners and Likenesses*, p. 38, wrote that "the softly outlined portrait [at the Essex Institute] . . . is too tame in modelling and feeble in brushwork to compare with the bulk of Smibert's work." If his opinion is accepted this portrait may be the contemporary copy of Smibert's original from which the engraving was made, perhaps from the hand of John Moffatt. In my opinion, however, it is a replica by Smibert.

Reproductions (in addition to the engraving noted above): Engraved for N.E.H.G.S. *Register*, vol. V, no. 2 (April 1851). Bayley, p. 421. *Antiques*, vol. XVIII, no. 3 (August 1930). *Catalogue of Portraits in Essex Institute* (Salem, 1936), opp. p. 184. F.A.R.L. photo.

References: P. F. *Mass.* 1830. Holyoke Diary, p. xiii.

REV. JOSEPH SEWALL, D.D.

Subject: Joseph, son of Chief Justice Samuel and Hannah (Hull) Sewall, born in Boston August 26, 1688; died Boston, June 27, 1769. He was graduated from Harvard in 1707, and was ordained copastor of the Old South Church, Boston, 1713. In 1724 he was elected president of Harvard College, but declined. He made large gifts to the college library, and his general benevolence won him the title of "The Good." At his death he had been associated with the ministerial work of the Old South Church for fifty-six years.

Size: H. 30 in.; W. 25 in.

Date: After 1731.

Description: The portrait shows a large, robust man in middle life, against a light background, within a painted oval. He wears a black gown, and bands. He is without a wig, and his dark hair, parted in the middle, falls to his shoulders, curling at the ends. The face is kindly, but is that of a vigorous and determined man, with a large nose, firm mouth, and heavy chin.

Owner: Mrs. Theodore S. Woolsey, New Haven, Conn. The portrait descended in the Salisbury family to Miss Salisbury; inherited by her cousin, Prof. Theodore S. Woolsey, Jr., of New Haven.

Exhibited: Yale University Art Gallery, "The Smibert Tradition," exhibition, October–November 1949.

Reproduced: Mezzotint by Peter Pelham, with the inscription:

> *The Reverend Joseph Sewall, D.D.*
> *J. Smibert, Pinx.–P. Pelham Fc.*

Catalogue, Exhibition of Colonial Portraits, Metropolitan Museum (New York, 1911). *American Art Annual,* X, 145 (1913). Winsor, Ill, 241 (wood engraving after Pelham). There is a poor copy in the New Old South Church, Boston. F.A.R.L. photo.

References: P. F. Mass. 1946. Listed, British Museum, *Catalogue of Engraved Portraits.*

CHIEF JUSTICE SAMUEL SEWALL, NO. I

Subject: Samuel, son of Henry and Jane (Dummer) Sewall, born at Bishopstoke, Hants, England, March 28, 1652. His parents had previously been settled at Newbury, Mass., and returned thither in 1661. Samuel Sewall was graduated from Harvard in 1671; was first a printer, then a merchant, then Judge of Probate (1717), and Chief Justice of the Supreme Court of Judicature from 1718 to 1728. He married (1) Hannah ———, by whom he had fourteen children, (2) Abigail Melyen, (3) Mary Shrimpton. Author of the famous *Diary*, and of a broadside in opposition to Negro slavery entitled *The Selling of Joseph.* He died in Boston January 1, 1729/30.

Size: H. 30 in.; W. 25 in.

Date: November or December 1729.

Description: The aged Judge Sewall is shown nearly full front, within spandrels, against a dark background, his right shoulder slightly advanced. He wears a black cap on his own hair, which falls in rather abundant white curls to his collar; a black coat, pleated shirt, and steenkirk tie. The face is clearly that of the same man shown in the portrait of Sewall painted by Nathaniel Emmons the previous year, now owned by the Massachusetts Historical Society. The portrait is in the original frame and is in poor condition, though the head is uninjured. It is to this picture which Mather Byles referred when he wrote, "In hoary majesty, see Sewall here."

Owner: Benjamin Flayderman, Boston, Mass. The portrait was inherited by Judge Sewall's son, Rev. Joseph Sewall (1688–1769) from whom it passed to Samuel (1715–1776), Judge Samuel (1757–1814), Rev. Samuel (1785–1866), Samuel (1819–?) Samuel B. (1846–?), and Nellie L.

(Sewall) Bennett, who, about 1943, sold the portrait to the present owner.

Exhibited: Yale University Art Gallery, "The Smibert Tradition," exhibition, October–November 1949.

Reproduced: Ye Olde Meeting House, addresses and verses relating to the Meeting House, Burlington, Mass. (Boston, 1909), ed. Martha E. Sewall Curtis, see opp. p. 54 a picture of the "Best Room" in the Sewall House, Burlington, which shows the portrait hanging on the wall.

CHIEF JUSTICE SEWALL, NO. 2

Owner: The Essex Institute, Salem, Mass.

This portrait is a contemporary replica, or, possibly, a very early copy of the portrait listed as *Samuel Sewall, No. 1.* It was bequeathed to The Essex Institute by George Rea Curwen in 1900, as a portrait of Samuel Sewall's younger brother, Stephen Sewall, and was so listed in the *Catalogue of Portraits in the Essex Institute* (Salem, 1936). It was formerly attributed to Smibert, but in the *Catalogue* is labeled "artist unknown."

William Bentley, in his *Diary*, II, 223, referring to transfer of several portraits of Salem worthies, under date of May 21, 1797, noted that "Judge [Stephen] Sewall and his wife have been given by the late Mrs. Higginson, a daughter, deceased last month in Beverly, to his daughter Lee, in Beverly." This identification of the subject followed the then accepted family tradition but is clearly mistaken, since the portrait duplicates in every detail Smibert's portrait, *Samuel Sewall, No. 1,* which, in turn, unquestionably shows the same person as the man portrayed in Nathaniel Emmons' portrait of Samuel Sewall, painted in 1728 and now owned by the Massachusetts Historical Society. The mistake is easily explained. Stephen Sewall, who died in 1725, was a prominent figure in Salem, where he left numerous descendants. One of his sons was named Samuel, after his distinguished uncle, the replica of whose portrait he may have inherited or acquired. But with the passing generations the belief arose that the picture represented Stephen Sewall, a mistake the more easily made because Smibert did paint Sewall's widow, Margaret Mitchell Sewall (*q.v.*), whose portrait was also bequeathed to the Essex Institute by George Rea Curwen.

Reproduced: Bolton, II, 473, as Stephen Sewall.

MRS. STEPHEN SEWALL

Subject: Margaret Mitchell, born 1664, married, in 1682, Major Stephen Sewall, brother of Samuel Sewall the Chief Justice. She was the mother of ten children; died 1736.

Size: H. 36 in.; W. 30 in.

Date: Before 1736.

Description: In this fine portrait Mrs. Sewall is shown as an old woman seated against a dark background, half front, her right shoulder towards the spectator, her face turned right nearly full front. She is dressed in black, with white ruffles at her elbows, a white wimple and black hood over her head. In her lap she holds a Bible from which she has just looked up. The figure is one of much dignity, and the face, with its long nose, while not handsome, shows strength and serenity.

Owner: Essex Institute, Salem, Mass. *Diary of William Bentley,* II (1907), 223: [The portraits of] "Judge [Stephen] Sewall [1] and his wife have been given by the late Mrs. Higginson, a daughter, deceased last March [March 1797] at Beverly, to his daughter Lee, in Beverly—" In the 19th century both portraits were owned by George Rea Curwen of Salem, and were bequeathed by him in 1890 to the Essex Institute, Salem, Mass.

Exhibited: World's Columbian Exposition, Chicago, 1893.

Reproduced: Antiques, vol. XVIII, no. 3 (August 1930). *Essex Institute Hist. Coll.,* vol. LXXII, opp. p. 238 (July 1936). *Catalogue of Portraits in Essex Institute* (1936), p. 202, no. 285. There is a copy by an unknown artist in the Essex Institute. F.A.R.L. photo.

Reference: P. F. Mass. 1948.

MRS. JOHN SMIBERT

Subject: Mary, daughter of Dr. Nathaniel Williams, born in Boston, *c.* 1707–1708, married John Smibert, July 30, 1730; date of death unrecorded, but later than 1753.

Size: H. 30 in.; W. 25 in.

Date: Presumably painted about the time of her marriage in 1730.

Description: The head and bust of Mrs. Smibert are shown within a painted oval against a plain dark background. She is seated in a chair, nearly full front, her head turned slightly to the spectator's left. Her head is small, set on a rather long neck, and she has dark hair, one curl of which falls over her left shoulder, dark eyes, a small mouth, and a good complexion. She wears a green silk dress, lined with mauve, held together at the bodice by a button, above which shows her white linen guimpe. A dark-red scarf is thrown over her left arm and carried round behind to her right shoulder. The portrait has been somewhat repainted.

Owner: Massachusetts Historical Society, Boston. Presented by Samuel Parker, November 27, 1848.

Reproduced: Bayley, p. 427. F.A.R.L. photo.

References: M.H.S. *Proc.,* II, 418. *P. F. Mass.* 1989.

SIR RICHARD SPRY

Subject: Sir Richard Spry, K.C.B. Spry was a naval officer who was promoted to be fleet captain for service before Louisburg, 1745; later rear admiral; died in Cornwall, 1775.

Size: H. 49½ in.; W. 39½ in.

---

[1] This portrait does not represent Stephen Sewall, but his older and more famous brother, Chief Justice Samuel Sewall (*q.v.*).

Date: The picture, which is probably by Smibert, was no doubt painted soon after the return of the expedition from Louisburg in 1746, at the time when a number of the leaders of that triumphant adventure were painted.

Description: The subject is shown three-quarter length, half front, his right shoulder towards the spectator, his face turned right, nearly full front. He wears a dark brown wig, a blue coat with gold braid, a red waistcoat trimmed with gold braid, and white shirt ruffles. His right hand, with extended forefinger, points across his body to ships of war lying on the calm waters of a harbor. His left hand rests on the gilded hilt of his sword. His pose is easy and dignified but his right hand is awkwardly painted. He has light brown, level eyebrows, a fair complexion, and a full face with a long nose and wide mouth. The picture is in poor condition.

Owner: Portsmouth Athenaeum, Portsmouth, N. H.

Reproduced: F.A.R.L. 1189.

REV. SETH STORER

Subject: Seth, son of Col. Joseph and Hannah Storer, of Wells, Maine; said to have been born at Saco on May 27, 1702, or at Wells on May 6 or 26 or November 27; died at Watertown, Mass., November 27, 1774. Graduated from Harvard in 1720, and studied theology there in 1723. Minister at Watertown, Mass., 1724 to 1774. Married Mary Coney of Boston, May 9, 1734.

Size: 29½ in.; W. 24¾ in.

Date: c. 1735?

Description: The subject is shown above spandrels in the lower corners, against a dark background, three-quarters front, his right shoulder towards the spectator, his head turned right nearly full front. He wears a small white wig; neckcloth and bands, and a black coat nearly covered by a dark-brown robe. He has gray eyes and a fresh complexion, and appears to be in his early thirties. The face is thoughtful and serious, but gentle, and the portrait is one of Smibert's most pleasing pictures of Puritan ministers.

Owner: The First Parish of Watertown, Mass. It passed by descent to the maternal grandparents of Langdon Warner, Cambridge, Mass., who owned it in 1930. Soon afterwards he gave it to the First Parish of Watertown.

Reproduced: G. F. Robinson, *Great Little Watertown* (1930).

Reference: Malcolm Storer, *Annals of the Storer Family* (Boston, 1927), p. 50.

REV. EBENEZER TURELL

Subject: Ebenezer, son of Samuel and Lydia (Stoddard) Turell, born at Boston February 5, 1701/02; graduated from Harvard, 1721; minister of the First Parish in Medford, Mass., 1724–1778; died 1778. Married (1)

Jane, daughter of Rev. Benjamin Colman (*q.v.*, Section B); (2) Lucy, daughter of Addington Davenport; (3) Jane Pepperell. Author of *The Life and Character of the Rev. Benjamin Colman* (Boston, 1749).

Size: H. 28⅞ in.; W. 24 in.

Date: c. 1735.

Description: The subject is shown within painted spandrels, against a dark background, half front, his right shoulder towards the spectator, his head turned right, three-quarters front. He is shown as a rather handsome man of not more than thirty-five, with a fresh complexion, brown eyes, level eyebrows, long straight nose, and rather small mouth. He wears a short gray wig, white stock and bands, and black Geneva gown over a black coat.

Owner: First Parish in Medford, Mass. Turell, dying childless, bequeathed his portrait to his nephew, Turell Tufts, that "his shadow might remain in Medford." It has for many years been in the possession of the First Parish in Medford.

Reproduced: An engraving, in reverse, in Charles Brooks' *History of the Town of Medford* (1855).

References: Sibley's Harvard Graduates, vol. VI, opp. p. 574. *P. F. Mass.* 2210.

JOHN TURNER

Subject: John, son of John and Mary (Kitchen) Turner of Salem, and brother of Mrs. Benjamin Browne (*q.v.*), born in Salem May 20, 1709; died in Salem December 19, 1786. He was a naval officer; Collector of the Port of Salem; Deputy 1757–1758.

Size: H. 35¼ in.; W. 27¾ in.

Date: From the apparent age of the subject this picture must have been painted in the late seventeen-forties.

Description: John Turner is shown standing, half length, half front, his right shoulder turned towards the spectator, his head turned right nearly full front, against a wall. An aperture to the spectator's right discloses a sea view, showing a sloop and part of a ship, which appears to be hove to. Perhaps the sloop is intended to represent a pilot boat, or the boat used by the Collector of the Port to board incoming vessels. Turner is handsomely dressed in a short white wig, ruffled shirt, and olive-green coat and waistcoat, the former ornamented with rather elaborate buttons and frogs. He has a ruddy complexion, blue eyes, large nose, an expression indicating humor, and a conspicuous dimple in his chin. His right hand, held across his body, points to the distant ships.

Owner: Museum of Fine Arts, Boston. The picture passed by descent to Winthrop Sargent, who left it to his sister-in-law, Mrs. Horatio Appleton Lamb, who in 1918 gave it to the Museum.

Exhibited: Yale University Art Gallery, "The Smibert Tradition," exhibition, October–November 1949.

Reproduced: Bayley, p. 431. A modern copy is in The House of the Seven Gables, Salem. F.A.R.L. photo.

MRS. EDWARD TYNG

Subject: Anne, daughter of Jonathan and Hannah (Mason) Waldo of Boston; born April 13, 1708; married January 27, 1731 (as his second wife), Edward Tyng (1683–1755) of Boston; died before January 14, 1754.

Size: H. 50 in.; W. 40 in.

Date: 1744–1745.

Description: Mrs. Tyng is shown as a large plump woman in her thirties, seated in an armchair upholstered in red, three-quarters front, her right shoulder towards the spectator, head turned right. She has a fair complexion, full lips, and brown hair, a curl of which hangs over her right shoulder. She wears a blue-green dress with white trim at bodice and sleeves. Her right elbow rests on the arm of her chair, the hand holding a pink rosebud to her bosom. Her left hand holds three roses in her lap. The background shows a plain brown wall behind her figure, with a vista of stream, woods, and hills on the right.

Owner: Yale University, New Haven, Conn. In 1902 this portrait, then attributed to Blackburn, was owned by "the heirs of Rev. Timothy Hilliard" whose wife was the adopted daughter of William Tyng, a son of the subject. It descended through their son, William Tyng Hilliard, to the latter's granddaughter, Miss Mabel Harlow, and passed at her death, about 1940, to Miss Elsie P. Lord, from whom it was acquired in 1944 by the Yale University Art Gallery.

Exhibited: Yale University Art Gallery, "The Smibert Tradition," exhibition, October–November 1949.

Reproduced: William Goold, *Portland of the Past* (1886), opp. p. 251 (attributed to Blackburn). Waldo Lincoln, *Genealogy of the Waldo Family* (1902), I, 110 (attributed to Blackburn). F.A.R.L. photo.

UNIDENTIFIED MAN

Subject: A man whose name is unknown.

Size: H. 29½ in.; W. 24½ in.

Description: The subject is a heavily built man in later middle life, with a full, round face, shown in three-quarters front, his right shoulder advanced, his head turned slightly to his right, nearly full front. He wears a full white wig, neckband, and long steenkirk tie with fringed ends, and a plain coat with cloth buttons.

Owner: Dr. Fiske Kimball, Lemon Hill, Fairmount Park, Philadelphia; purchased in 1926 from Joe Kindig, Jr., York, Pa., who had found the portrait in New England but knew nothing of its pedigree or provenance.

Attribution: Attributed to John Smibert by the owner and by William Sawitzky. I have seen only a photograph of this picture, but am in agreement with the attribution to Smibert.

Reproduced: Photograph.

UNIDENTIFIED WOMAN (MRS. EDWARD TYNG, so-called)

Subject: The subject of this portrait has been called Mrs. Edward Tyng (*q.v.*), but she bears no resemblance to the person shown in the portrait of Mrs. Tyng (see above), which has a better pedigree and is more likely to be the authentic likeness of that lady. The person here shown is probably another member of the Tyng family connection, whom it is not now possible to identify.

Size: H. 35¾ in.; W. 28½ in.

Date: ?

Description: The subject is shown half length, nearly full front, standing against a dark background. She has rather large, dark eyes, and dark hair, a curl of which falls over her left shoulder. She wears a bluish-green dress with the usual white muslin trim at bodice and elbows. Her left elbow rests upon a shelf beside her, the hand holding the end of a brownish-red (or old rose) scarf thrown over her right shoulder and covering her right arm and hand.

Owner: Museum of Fine Arts, Boston, Mass., bequeathed by George Nixon Black, 1929, who bought it from the collection of W. B. T. Smith, who was descended from the Tyngs but who had no assured identification of the subject.

Reproduced: Bayley, p. 433, as Mrs. Edward Tyng. *Bulletin,* Museum of Fine Arts, Boston, XXVII, 34 (April 1929). F.A.R.L. photo, as Mrs. Edward Tyng.

RICHARD WALDRON III

Subject: Richard, son of Richard and Eleanor (Vaughan) Waldron, born in Portsmouth, N. H., 1694, died in Portsmouth in 1753. Married Elizabeth Westbrook in 1718. He was a Judge and Councillor, and for many years Secretary of the Province after his appointment in 1737.

Size: H. 49 in.; W. 39 in.

Date: c. 1745?

Description: The subject is shown against a background with an olive-brown curtain to the left and a shelf of large books to the right, standing nearly full front beside a table on the corner of which his right hand rests, holding down a parchment with an ornamental scroll reading *Salus Populi Suprema Lex.* He wears a short wig, greenish-gray coat and waistcoat, white neckcloth, and long steenkirk tie, the ends of which are thrust through a buttonhole in his coat. His left hand is open in gesture.

Owner: Miss Catherine Dimick Parry, Kittery Point, Maine. From the subject the portrait passed to his son, Thomas Westbrook Waldron, to his son, Daniel Waldron, to his daughter, Mrs. C. Waldron Dimick, to her daughter, Frances Dimick Parry, to her daughter, the present owner.

Reproduced: A poor copy belongs to the Society for the Preservation of New England Antiquities and is now loaned to the Wentworth Gardner House, Portsmouth, N. H.

JOSEPH WANTON (so-called)

Subject: This picture is reputed to represent Joseph, son of William and Ruth (Bryant) Wanton, born at Newport, R. I., August 15, 1705, died at New York, July 19, 1780. His father was Governor of Rhode Island 1732–1734; his brother John was Governor 1734–1741; and his cousin Gideon Wanton was Governor 1745–1746 and 1747–1748. Joseph Wanton was graduated from Harvard, married Mary, daughter of John Winthrop; was Deputy Collector of Customs 1738–1748, and Governor 1769–1775, when the Assembly deprived him of power on account of his Tory sympathies. When the British troops evacuated Newport he went with them to New York, where he died. Most of his large estate had melted away by the end of the Revolution.

Size: H. *c.* 50 in.; W. *c.* 40 in.

Date: 1729?

Description: The subject is shown standing against a landscape background, three-quarter length, three-quarters front, his right shoulder towards the spectator, his face turned slightly right, nearly full front. He wears a full white wig, white neckband, and ruffles at neck and wrists; light green coat heavily ornamented with embroidered gold frogs; light green waistcoat with gold buttons. His right hand is extended in gesture; his left is thrust into his waistcoat. He is shown as a large and corpulent young man, of fair complexion. The portrait, with that of Mrs. Wanton, was purchased in 1891 by Edward Perry Warren from a Mrs. Destailleur of New Forest, Hampshire, England, to whom it was alleged to have passed by descent from Governor Wanton. Both portraits were then attributed to Thomas Hudson but could not have been by him unless Mr. and Mrs. Wanton were in England about 1730. The late Lawrence Park attributed them to Smibert and, in the case of the portrait supposed to represent Mrs. Wanton, that attribution is supported by its resemblance to other portraits of women by Smibert, notably that of Mrs. Samuel Browne (Mrs. Epes Sargent, *q.v.*). If by him they must have been painted in the summer of 1729, when Smibert was in Newport. It is difficult, however, to reconcile the appearance of the corpulent youthful Joseph Wanton in this picture with that of the very different-looking individual, also supposed to be Joseph Wanton, shown in a portrait by an unknown artist in the Redwood Library, Newport. I, therefore, question the identification of the subject of the portrait.

Owner: Rhode Island Historical Society, Providence, R. I.

Reproduced: Bayley, p. 453. *Art in America*, vol. XVII, no. 4 (June 1929), second plate following p. 176. F.A.R.L. photo.

References: Updike, II, 281, note 615. Lawrence Park, *Joseph Blackburn*, p. 9.

MRS. JOSEPH WANTON (so-called)

Subject: This picture is reputed to represent Mary, daughter of John Winthrop, born September 18, 1708; married Joseph Wanton; died at

Newport, February 1767. If this portrait does represent her and was painted by Smibert, it must have been painted in 1729, in her twenty-first year, but the identity of the subject is open to question, since the woman represented in this picture bears so little resemblance to the charming likeness of Mrs. Wanton painted by Robert Feke that it is difficult to believe that it represents the same woman (see H. W. Foote, *Robert Feke*, pp. 200, 201).

The portrait, with that supposed to represent Joseph Wanton (*q.v.*), is reputed to have passsed by descent to a Mrs. Destailleur of New Forest, Hampshire, England, from whom they were purchased in 1891 by Edward Perry Warren, who gave them to the Rhode Island Historical Society, Providence. They were formerly attributed to Hudson, but the late Lawrence Park considered them to be the work of Smibert.

Size: H. *c.* 50 in.; W. *c.* 40 in.

Date: 1729?

Description: The subject is shown seated, full front, against a cliff, with a vista to the left showing a stream, meadow, and trees. She wears a low-necked dress of blue silk, with the usual white guimpe and undersleeves. An old-rose scarf is thrown about her left arm and carried round her body. Her right hand lies in her lap, holding some loose flowers. Her right elbow rests upon a shelf of the rock, the hand holding a couple of flowers. The picture is in poor condition, the face being badly marred. The figure, arms, hands, and costume resemble those in other portraits of women by Smibert, so that the attribution to him seems reasonable, but, in my opinion, the picture probably represents some other person than Mrs. Wanton.

Owner: Rhode Island Historical Society, Providence, R. I.

Reproduced: F.A.R.L. photo.

References: Updike, II, 281, note 615. Lawrence Park, *Joseph Blackburn*, p. 9.

SIR PETER WARREN

Subject: Born in Ireland, 1703 or earlier; entered the British Navy, 1727; commodore 1745; promoted rear-admiral for his services at Louisburg; married, in 1731, Susan (Susannah), daughter of Stephen De Lancey of New York; died in Ireland, 1752.

Size: H. 7 ft. 8 in.; W. 4 ft. 10 in.

Date: The label on the portrait reads, "painted in London, 1751." This is the date of the letter from Warren to Pepperell saying that he hoped to send his portrait to the latter, without mentioning the artist's name. But if the portrait is by Smibert, to whom the late Lawrence Park attributed it, and whose style it resembles, it must have been painted sometime in the later half of 1746, or in 1747, since Pepperell and Warren arrived in Boston from Louisburg on June 1, 1746.

Description: Sir Peter Warren is shown at full length, half front, his right shoulder towards the spectator, his head turned slightly to the right, standing against a curtained wall and balustrade. His right hand holds a large telescope the end of which rests upon a table at his side which is covered with a green cloth having a gold fringe. His left hand points to the vista beyond the balustrade showing the sea and three frigates under sail. He wears a gray wig, blue coat with heavy gold frogs, white neckband and ruffles, red waistcoat embroidered with gold braid, red breeches, white stockings, and black shoes with gold buckles. His face is full, florid, and self-complacent. His pose, the left foot advanced, is awkward, the feet being unduly prominent and on a plane nearer the spectator than the upper part of the body and head.

Owner: The Portsmouth Athenaeum, Portsmouth, N. H. Given by Sir Peter Warren to Sir William Pepperell, of Kittery, Maine, as a mark of friendship; bequeathed to his daughter, Mrs. Sparhawk; sold to John Fisher of Portsmouth, N. H., who presented it to the Portsmouth Athenaeum.

Reproduced: Bayley, p. 437. F.A.R.L. 1186.

References: Parsons, *Life of Pepperell*, pp. 237, 329, 345. Cutts, *Essex Institute Collection*, no. 31 (1894–1895), pp. 56–58. Bolton, "John Smibert, Notes and a Catalogue," *The Fine Arts*, XX, 42.

COL. JACOB WENDELL

Subject: Jacob, son of Johannes Wendel, was baptized August 5, 1691. He moved to Boston in his youth, and became a wealthy merchant. Commander of Ancient and Honorable Artillery, 1735–1745; member of Council 1737–1760; married August 12, 1714, Sarah, daughter of Dr. James and Mercy (Bradstreet) Oliver, of Cambridge. Both Oliver Wendell Holmes and Wendell Phillips were descended from this marriage.

Size: H. 48½ in.; W. 38½ in.

Date: The subject appears to be not above forty years old, and the picture must therefore date from 1730 or soon after.

Description: Jacob Wendell is shown seated in a mahogany armchair against a dark wall, with a window to the spectator's right through which a snow-rigged vessel is seen, hove to, with a second vessel in the distance. The figure is half front, right shoulder towards the spectator, the head turned nearly full front. The subject has dark eyes and eyebrows, and a ruddy complexion. He wears a full, long wig; a stock, with ruffles at neck and wrists; and a mulberry-colored coat, waistcoast, and breeches. In his right hand he holds a quill pen, while his left hand rests upon papers lying on a table beside him, upon which is also a pewter inkstand and quill pen.

Owner: Arthur H. Phillips, Cambridge, Mass. The picture passed by inheritance to Wendell Phillips; then to John C. Phillips, and to his son, the present owner.

Exhibited: Yale University Art Gallery, "The Smibert Tradition," exhibition, October–November 1949.

Reproduced: F.A.R.L. 17157.

EXTANT PORTRAITS BY SMIBERT 199

References: *P. F. Mass.* 2402. N.E.H.G.S. *Register*, XXXVI (1882), 246, note LIV (1900), 419, note.

EDWARD WINSLOW III

Subject: Edward, son of Edward Winslow II, and grandson of the governor of Plymouth Colony; born in Boston November 1669; died in Boston 1753. His mother was Elizabeth Hutchinson, daughter of Mistress Anne Hutchinson. Edward Winslow III became a silversmith in Boston; overseer of the poor, 1711–1712; selectman, 1714; High Sheriff of Suffolk County, 1728–1743; Captain in the Ancient and Honorable Artillery Company; Judge of the Court of Common Pleas, 1743. Married (1) in 1692, Hannah Moody (1672–1711); (2) in 1712, Elizabeth Dixie, widow of Benjamin Pemberton; (3) in 1744, Susanna Farnum, widow of Caleb Lyman.

Size: H. 30 in.; W. 25 in.

Date: 1730 or soon after.

Description: The subject is shown half front against a dark background, his right shoulder towards the spectator, his head turned slightly right, three-quarters front. He wears a full, brown wig; a dark red coat with broad cuffs buttoned back to the elbow with large ornamented metal buttons; and a white neckcloth with ruffles. His left hand is tucked into his coat; his right hand holds two documents tied with green ribbon. "While there is no signature or inscription upon the canvas, the draftsmanship, colors, brushwork and small mannerisms, when compared with such a key picture as *Bishop Berkeley and his Entourage*, painted in 1729 and presented to Yale in 1808, substantiate the family tradition that it is one of the early works of Smibert" (*Bulletin of The Associates in Fine Arts at Yale University*. June, 1935, pp. 45–46).

Owner: Yale University, New Haven, Conn. In the second inventory of the estate of the subject's son, Joshua Winslow, 1778, presumably after the death of the latter's widow, are listed:

2 Family Pictures Mr. Winslow & Wife £4.3.0
1 Gilt Picture Olde Mr. Winslow £2.0.0
In the back parlor.

The second item refers to this portrait of Edward Winslow III. It passed to Joshua's son Isaac, to Isaac's only daughter Elizabeth (Winslow) Pickering, from whose granddaughter, Miss Susan Pickering of Boston, it was purchased in 1935 by Francis Garvan and given to the Yale University Art Gallery.

Reproduced: There are four oil copies of this portrait: (1) Painted by Blackburn and signed *J. Blackburn pinx 1757*. Similar to the original except that the right forearm and hand are not shown. This picture was owned about 1937 by Miss Julia Winslow of New York, now (1949) owned by Mrs. Ernest Newsome but loaned to the Yale Art Gallery. See Morgan and Foote, *Joseph Blackburn* (1937), p. 46. F.A.R.L. 20707.

(2) A replica, or an eighteenth-century copy of Blackburn's copy, owned by Willard Winslow of Scarsdale, N. Y. (3) A nineteenth-century copy of Blackburn's copy, formerly owned by Arthur Winslow, owned (1949) by Mrs. Robert Lowell of Boston. *P. F. Mass.* 2499. (4) A copy of the original portrait, about 1870, owned (1949) by Charles Parker, Boston. *New York Herald-Tribune*, June 23, 1935 (rotogravure section). *Art Digest*, IX, 11 (August 1, 1935). F.A.R.L. photo.

SECTION B

PORTRAITS DESTROYED OR NOT LOCATED

Portraits recorded as having been painted by Smibert but known to have been destroyed, or, if extant, not located.

In the past two centuries a considerable number of portraits which Smibert undoubtedly painted have been destroyed, generally by fire, or have disappeared, in the sense that their present location, if they are still extant, has not been discovered. In some cases the name of the subject of a portrait known to have been destroyed has been preserved, e.g., Mrs. Edward Waldo. In other cases there is no record of the identity of the subject, e.g. (M.H.S. *Proc.* XVII, 233), it is recorded that a number of unnamed portraits by Smibert, Emmons, and Copley were destroyed by fire in 1872. It is impossible to make any exact estimate of the number of portraits thus destroyed.

The portraits which have not been located, but which we know formerly existed, may also, in some cases, have been destroyed, but it is probable that the majority of them are still extant in the hands of descendants or private collectors. It may be expected that some of them will sooner or later come to light.

GOV. JONATHAN BELCHER

Subject: Jonathan, son of Andrew and Sarah (Gilbert) Belcher, born in Cambridge, January 8, 1681/82, died August 31, 1757. He was graduated from Harvard in 1699; traveled in Europe; returned to Boston and made a fortune as a merchant. Member of the Council for several years between 1717 and 1729. He was in London representing the colony, in 1729, and on the death of Governor Burnet, was appointed governor of Massachusetts and New Hampshire. He was dismissed from office in 1741. He was appointed governor of New Jersey in 1746, where he had a more tranquil administration until his death.

Size: Full length.

Date: Before March 1730/31.

Description: The only account of this hitherto unrecorded portrait is found in a letter written by John Boydell of Boston to Hon. John Yeamans. In this letter, dated March 1, 1730 (1730/31), Boydell writes: "His [Governor Belcher's] Picture is a Drawing at full length to answer the King and Queen's it's Supposed he intended it as a present to the General Court if they had fixed his Salary. Mr. Smibert the Painter has £80 for drawing it."

Owner: Belcher evidently retained possession of the portrait and had it with him in New Jersey. While governor there he took an active interest in the establishment of the College of New Jersey, now Princeton University, and in the records of the Board of Trustees of that institution for May 1755 there is an entry stating that Governor Belcher had given the College his "Picture at full Length." The name of the painter is not given and the portrait was destroyed in the Revolution, so that absolute proof is lacking that the picture presented to the college was the one which Smibert had painted twenty-five years earlier, but the probability is very high that such was the case.

The portrait of Belcher now at Princeton is a copy of a contemporary portrait of him by Franz Lippold (or Liopoldt), owned by the Massachusetts Historical Society.

REV. HENRY CANER

Subject: Henry, son of Henry and Abigail Caner of Fairfield, Conn., was probably born in England about 1700. He was graduated from Yale in 1724, and afterwards studied theology under Rev. Samuel Johnson of Stratford, Conn. (*q.v.*). He went to England in 1727, took orders in the Church of England and was appointed missionary for the church at Fairfield by the Society for the Propagation of the Gospel, where he labored from 1727 until called to King's Chapel, Boston, in December 1746. He received the degree of Master of Arts in 1736, and of Doctor of Divinity in 1766, from Oxford University. He continued as rector of King's Chapel until General Gage evacuated the city in 1776, when he went with the British troops first to Halifax and thence to England, whence he never returned. He took with him the church silver and records of King's Chapel, but most of his personal effects were left behind. His death took place either in London about the end of 1792, or at Long-Ashton, England, early in 1793.

Size: Probably H. *c.* 30 in.; W. *c.* 25 in.

Date: Peter Pelham's mezzotint engraving of this portrait is dated 1750 (*vide infra*). Probably the portrait was painted soon after Caner's arrival in Boston in March, 1747.

Description: Pelham's mezzotint shows Caner's head and bust set against a plain background in an oval frame, half front, right shoulder towards the spectator, the face turned right nearly full front. He wears a white wig and clerical costume, cassock, girdle, black silk gown, and bands. The face is rather full and well modeled with heavy dark eyebrows.

Owner: The portrait no doubt remained in Caner's possession until he left Boston, but is supposed to have been left behind with his other effects. Its later history is unknown, nor whether it is still extant.

Reproduced: Pelham's mezzotint shows the figure in an oval set in a paneled rectangle, 11.12 × 9.13 inches, inscribed:

The Reverend Henry Caner, A:M.
Minister of King's Chapel, Boston
J: Smibert pinx:—P: Pelham, fecit 1750
Sold by P. Pelham in Boston.

This engraving is listed in Stauffer, *American Engravers on Copper and Steel*, II, 407, and was reproduced in 1901 by the Pelham Club of Boston. A print of this reproduction is in the Frick Art Reference Library, New York. H. W. Foote, *Annals of King's Chapel* (1896), II, 23.
Reference: H. W. Foote, *Annals of King's Chapel*, II, 23.

LORD CARPENTER

Subject: George, son of Warncombe and Eleanor (Taylor) Carpenter, born February 10, 1657; married, in 1693, Alice, daughter of Viscount Charlemont; a soldier in the British army serving in Flanders and Spain; lieutenant-general in 1709; governor of Minorca in 1716; created Baron Carpenter of Killaghy, Kilkenny County, Ireland, in 1719; member of Parliament for Westminster, 1722–1729; died February 10, 1731/2. His grandson was created Viscount Carlingford and Earl Tyrconnel, but all these titles became extinct at the death without issue in 1853 of the sixth Baron Carpenter and fourth Viscount and Earl.
Size: Half length.
Date: Painted in London, about 1724.
Description: George Vertue in his notes, about 1724, records seeing several portraits in Smibert's studio, among them one of "the Lord Carpenter in Armo ½ length very well" (see p. 20).
Owner: The portrait presumably passed down the line of descent of holders of the title Baron Carpenter until that title became extinct. The present owner and the location of the portrait are unknown.

ROBERT CAY

Subject: Robert Cay was a merchant of Newcastle-on-Tyne, England, who died in 1754.
Size: H. 29 in.; W. 24½ in.
Date: Before 1728.
Description: This portrait, said to represent Robert Cay of Newcastle, shows the subject wearing a large, gray wig, white stock, and yellow gown (description from sale catalogue).
Owner: In 1910 this picture was owned by Salto Montgomery Cay. It was offered for sale on July 8, 1910, by Christie, Manson and Woods of London, and is reported by them to have been "bought in at the sum of £189." Its present location has not been traced.

REV. BENJAMIN COLMAN

Subject: Benjamin, son of William and Elizabeth Colman, born in Boston October 19, 1673; graduated from Harvard in 1692. He was the first minister of the Brattle Square Church in Boston, 1699–1747, and was treasurer of Harvard College 1717–1728. He was offered the presidency of the College in 1724, but declined. In 1731 he received from Glasgow University the honorary degree of S.T.D. He died August 29, 1747.

Size: H. *c.* 30 in.; W. *c.* 25 in.

Date: 1734.

Description: In Peter Pelham's mezzotint (see below), Colman is shown within a painted oval, half front, his left shoulder towards the spectator, his head turned left nearly full front. He wears a rather large wig, white neckcloth with long bands, and a black coat over which a robe is thrown on his left shoulder. He has a fine face, with a long nose, and appears rather younger than his age. The mezzotint is perhaps the most attractive of all those made by Pelham in Boston. Rev. Ebenezer Turell of Medford (*q.v.*, Section A) in his biography of his father-in-law, *The Life and Character of the Reverend Benjamin Colman* (Boston, 1749, p. 231), says: "His picture drawn in the year 1734 by the greatest Master our Country has seen, Mr. John Smibert, shows both his Face and Air to Perfection; And a very considerable Resemblance is given us in the Metsotinto done from it by Mr. P. Pelham, which is in many of our Houses."

Another portrait formerly supposed to represent Rev. Benjamin Colman is now owned by Harvard University, but it does not at all resemble the person shown in the mezzotint, and X-ray examination of the portrait reveals that the subject was originally shown in a red coat over which the clerical costume was later painted. This portrait undoubtedly dates from very early in the eighteenth century but cannot be accepted as by Smibert or as representing Benjamin Colman (see *Harvard Portraits*, pp. 42–43).

Owner: The inventory of the estate of Rev. Ebenezer Turell of Medford, Rev. Benjamin Colman's son-in-law, lists several portraits, including one of Colman. It would seem probable that this was Smibert's portrait of Colman, referred to in Turell's *Life,* but its present location is unknown.

Reproduced: In mezzotint by Peter Pelham, with the inscription:

> *The Reverend Benjamin Colman, D.D.*
> *I. Smibert, Pinx—P. Pelham, Fecit, 1735*

Reference: Winsor, II, 212.

CLAUDE DU BOSC

Subject: Claude Du Bosc, a second-rate French engraver, born about 1682. He came to London about 1712 to assist N. Dorigny in a series of engravings of Raphael's cartoons at Hampton Court. He soon broke with Dorigny, but apparently remained in London until his death, about 1745, producing many engravings, though coarsely and inaccurately. Among them was a plate done in 1741 showing the "Continence of Scipio," by Poussin, from the original painting then at Houghton (see Section D, pictures copied by Smibert).

Date: Vertue noted, *c.* 1723, "of many pictures of Mr Smybert's doing a head done of C. Dubosc Engraver. on a Kit-Cat. well disposed. strongly painted tho clear. the action mightily well disposed & like him" (III, 28).

Owner: The location of this portrait, if it is extant, is unknown.

PETER FANEUIL NO. 1 (AS REPRODUCED BY HENRY SARGENT)

Subject: Peter, son of Benjamin and Anne (Bureau) Faneuil. His father was a French Huguenot from Rochelle, France, who emigrated to New Rochelle, N. Y., where Peter was born in 1700. As a young man Peter Faneuil came to Boston, where his uncle Andrew Faneuil had settled as early as 1709, became a merchant and prospered greatly. He subscribed £200 towards the building of the present King's Chapel; gave £100 to Trinity Church towards the purchase of an organ; and in 1740 offered to build a market house for Boston, later known as Faneuil Hall. He died, unmarried, in Boston March 3, 1742/43.

Size: H. 108 in.; W. 72 in.

Date: 1742.

Description: A full-length portrait of Faneuil was painted by Smibert at the expense of the Town, to be placed in Faneuil Hall (pp. 81–82). When the interior of the Hall was gutted by fire in 1761 the picture was too badly injured to be rehung, but in 1807 the selectmen commissioned Henry Sargent to paint a new portrait of Faneuil and apparently enough of the original survived to serve Sargent as a basis for his picture, which now hangs in the Hall. It shows Faneuil standing, nearly full front, his head turned slightly to the right, with his left arm on the back of a wing chair, upholstered in golden-brown brocade, over which his black cloak is thrown. He holds in both hands a plan of Faneuil Hall showing the cupola and weathervane. He wears a dull-red coat with gold buttons, waistcoat and breeches of the same material, white stock and ruffles, ruffles at sleeves, a white wig, white stockings, and black shoes with silver buckles. Behind him is a dark curtain, with a sunset sky and clouds on the right. The face resembles that shown in Peter Faneuil (Section A), but appears older. The general appearance of the pictures suggests that Sargent had at least Smibert's general outline before him, but the manner of painting is quite different from Smibert's.

Owner: City of Boston.

Exhibited: Faneuil Hall.

References: Dunlap, II, 196, note. *P. F. Mass.* 736.

SARAH HALL I

Subject: Sarah, daughter of Hugh Hall II, of Barbados, by his second wife; born *c.* 1712, married John, son of Lieutenant Governor John Wentworth of New Hampshire, 1732. She died at Portsmouth, N. H., March 26, 1790. Her sister, Mary Hall (*q.v.*, Section A), married John Wentworth's brother William.

Size: H. *c.* 32 in.; W. *c.* 25 in.

Date: c. 1732.

Description: The subject is a young woman, about twenty years of age, whose head and bust are shown full front, her head turned slightly to her left. She has dark hair and eyes, and wears a low-cut dress with white muslin trim. I have seen only a photograph of this portrait, but there appears to be no doubt as to either the identification of the subject or the attribution to Smibert, or that the portrait is a companion piece to that representing the subject's sister, Mary Hall.

Owner: The present location of this portrait is not known to me.

Reproduced: N.E.G.H.S. *Register* (July 1888). Wentworth Genealogy, I, 308.

NEGRO

W. Updike, in his *History of the Episcopal Church in Narragansett* (1907), I, 523, speaking of Smibert, says: "His first essay in colours is said to have been the portrait of a young Negro, brought from Martinique to Scotland."

This is the only known record of such a portrait, but it presumably reports an oral tradition founded on a statement made by Smibert himself. If correct, this "portrait of a young Negro" must have been painted in Edinburgh at the time of Smibert's first visit home in 1717, when, according to Vertue, he first attempted to paint portraits.

REV. EDWARD PAYSON

Subject: Edward, son of Edward and Mary (Eliot) Payson (his mother was a sister of Rev. John Eliot); born Roxbury, Mass., June 20, 1657, died Rowley(?), Mass., August 22, 1732. Graduated from Harvard in 1677 and ordained in 1682 as colleague of Rev. Samuel Phillips of Rowley, whose daughter Elizabeth he married in 1683; by her he had eight sons and nine daughters. She died 1724, and two years later he married Elizabeth, widow of Samuel Appleton of Ipswich and daughter of William Whittingham of Boston.

Size: H. *c.* 30 in.; W. *c.* 25 in.

Date: Between 1730 and 1732.

Description: The head and bust of the subject are shown nearly full front against a shaded background, within spandrels. He wears a black gown and white shirt, neckcloth, and rather large ministerial bands. He has no wig and his hair is rather short and thin on top of his head, but falls abundantly over his ears and to his collar. The face, with heavy eyebrows, is not handsome, but is that of an old man who is at once shrewd and kindly, a strongly characterized likeness of a type similar to that of Rev. George Phillips (*q.v.*, Section A).

Owner: Said to have been inherited by a nephew(?), Rev. Phillips Payson, by his son Phillips Payson, and by his son Samuel Payson, who died in 1860. Purchased from his estate by Harold Fletcher, and passed to his sister, Eliza Fletcher, from whom it was purchased in 1926 by Mr. M. L. Walker of Brighton, Mass., whom I have not been able to locate.

Reproduced: F.A.R.L. photo.

Note: I have seen only the photograph in the Frick Art Reference Library, and have taken the foregoing information from the memoranda accompanying it. The portrait appears to be the work of Smibert, but as its present location is unknown to me I reserve judgment on it.

ALLAN RAMSAY, NO. 2

Date: 1720, when Smibert visited Edinburgh after his return from Italy.

Size: Probably H. *c.* 30 in.; W. *c.* 25 in.

Description: In the engravings of this portrait Ramsay's bust is shown in profile, the head turned to his left nearly full front. He is dressed in a shirt, open at the neck, a coat with a slashed sleeve, and a tartan over his shoulder. On his close-cropped head is a tam-o'-shanter cap with a bow of ribbon and a pin or medal showing a St. Andrew's cross. The picture represents him a good deal more attractively than does portrait No. 1 (Section A), for, though no one could call him handsome, the face shows keen intelligence and humor.

Owner: In his will dated August 5, 1786, Thomas Moffatt, then in London, bequeathed to "George Chalmers of Berkeley Square," among other pictures, one of "Allen [*sic*] Ramsay by Smibert." Since Moffatt had lived in Newport, R. I., until 1765, and later in New London, Conn., until the outbreak of the American Revolution, this would seem to indicate that Smibert had brought the portrait to America, or had it sent after him, and that Moffatt had acquired it by gift (with several other pictures) from his uncle, or by purchase after Smibert's death. Moffatt died in 1787, and the portrait presumably passed into George Chalmers' hands, but I have found no further information regarding it, and do not know its present location, if it is extant.

Reproduced: (1) An engraving used as the frontispiece for the quarto edition of Ramsay's *Poems*, published by Thomas Ruddiman (Edinburgh, 1721). It is inscribed *I.S.P./T. Vercruysse S.* Size, H. 6½ in.; W. 4¼ in. Reproduced in Oskar Hagen's *Birth of the American Tradition in Art*, opp. p. 42.

(2) An engraved frontispiece in *Poems*, Vol. II (Edinburgh, 1728). The head and bust are shown within an oval set in a masonry wall identical with the setting of (1), on the base of which is inscribed:

Allan Ramsay

I. Smibert P.   *G. Vertue S.*

Size: H. 6⅝ in.; W. 4¼ in. A copy of this engraving is on file at the Frick Art Reference Library.

(3) An engraved frontispiece for the London edition of Ramsay's *Poems* (1731). In this engraving the position of the subject is reversed, the right shoulder being advanced. It is inscribed: *I. Smibert, P./I Basire, Scupl.* Size: H. 4½ in.; W. 2¾ in. This engraving was used again in the edition of 1761.

(4) An engraved frontispiece in the Dublin edition of Ramsay's *Poems* (1733). The position is the same as in (1), but the engraving is inscribed: *P. S. Sculpt.* Size, H. 5⅝ in., W. 3¾ in.

Vertue's engraving is the best of the series. Vercruysse is mentioned in note 17, Chapter I. Basire is probably Isaac (died 1768), first of four generations of Basire engravers.

ROSA-CORONIANS

Subject: A group of twelve men, the virtuosi who called themselves the Rosa-Coronian Club.

Size: Vertue calls it "a large picture."

Date: 1723–1724.

Description: For a detailed account of this picture see pp. 20–24. Nothing further is known of the picture or whether it is still extant.

ENOCH SEEMAN

In Vertue, III, 12, in his list of "Names of Living Painters of Note in London and their pictures by whom painted," he includes: "Mʳ Enoch Seeman . . . Mʳ. Smybert." Seeman, or Zeeman, was one of two brothers living in London in 1723, when the portrait was painted. The present location of the portrait is unknown.

A portrait of Elihu Yale painted by Seeman in 1717 is owned by Yale University.

GOVERNOR WILLIAM SHIRLEY

Subject: William Shirley, born Preston, Sussex, England, 1693 or 1694; died Roxbury, Mass., 1771. Governor of Massachusetts 1741–1745, and again in 1753.

Size: Full or three-quarter length.

Date: 1747.

Description: The original of this portrait appears to have been lost, but it was reproduced in mezzotint by Peter Pelham in 1747, probably immediately after it was painted. In the engraving Shirley is shown standing, three-quarter length, half front, his right shoulder towards the spectator, his head turned right nearly full front. He wears a white wig, tied behind with a bow, ruffles at neck and wrists, and a long coat and waistcoat with large buttons and frogs. His left arm holds his cocked hat against his side, while his left hand rests on his sword hilt. His right arm crosses his body as his forefinger points to a fleet of ships putting out to sea from a bay with islands and a lighthouse, presumably intended to represent Boston Harbor. At Shirley's right is a table with plans of fortifications, and behind him is a masonry wall and looped curtain. The inscription beneath the mezzotint reads:

His Excellency William Shirley Esq' Captain General & Governour in Chief &c of the Province of the Massuchusetts Bay in New England, & Collonel of one of his Majesty's Regiments of Foot. To whom this Plate (done from the Original, painted by Mr. J. Smibert at the request of several Merchants & Gentlemen in Boston, as a *Memorial* of their Grateful Acknowledgments to his Excellency for his Signal Services in the Preservation of Nova Scotia from falling into the enemies hands in 1744, and the Reduction of the Island of Cape Breton to the Obedience of his Majesty in 1745) is Humbly Dedicated by his Excellency's Obedient ser^t

P. Pelham 1747

Owner: The present location of this portrait is unknown. It is clearly not the same picture as the portrait alleged to represent William Shirley and attributed to Smibert in the Thomas B. Clarke Collection which was purchased by the Mellon Educational Trust (see Section E).

Reproduced: A reproduction of the mezzotint by Peter Pelham, issued July 27, 1747, was made for the Pelham Club, Boston, 1901. A print is on file at the Frick Art Reference Library, New York.

EDWARD WALDO, SR.

Subject: Edward, grandson of Cornelius Waldo I, the founder of the family in New England. In 1714 he built a house still standing in Windham, Conn. Married Thankful Dimmock.

Date: Between 1740 and 1747?

Owner: Smibert is said to have made a trip to Windham, Conn., to paint several members of Edward Waldo's family, whose guest he was during his visit (see pp. 98–99). His portrait of Edward Waldo, Sr., passed to the subject's eldest son and is said to have descended from him in the male line for several generations. Its present whereabouts, if it still exists, are unknown, and there is no description of it.

MRS. EDWARD WALDO, SR.

Subject: Thankful Dimmock, wife of Edward Waldo.

Date: Between 1740 and 1747.

Description: The subject was shown wearing a cap and kerchief and holding a spaniel. According to Edward Waldo's diary (now destroyed), Smibert journeyed to the family residence at Windham, Conn., to paint the portrait.

Owner: The portrait descended to her granddaughter, Abigail Waldo, Mrs. Jacob Johnson, and to the latter's granddaughter, Susan Johnson,

Mrs. George Pendleton, and while in her possession was destroyed by fire, in the early part of the nineteenth century.

EDWARD WALDO, JR., AND WIFE

Subject: Edward, son of Edward and Thankful (Dimmock) Waldo, of Windham, Conn., and his wife, the former Abigail Elderkin of Norwich, Conn.

Note: Family tradition says that Smibert, on his visit to Windham, painted Edward Waldo, Jr., and his wife. If so, the present whereabouts of the paintings are unknown.

JOSEPH WALDO

Subject: Joseph, son of Cornelius Waldo, III, born *c.* 1726, graduated from Harvard 1741; married, 1762, Martha Jones of Boston. The *Post* of March 15, 1762, described her as "a young Lady with a Fortune and endowed with the amiable Accomplishments which conspire to render the Marriage State agreeable and with those noble Virtues of a Social Nature that may conduce to a Life of Peace and uninterrupted Happiness." She died a few years later and Joseph Waldo went to England, where he first lived in Bristol and later in Cheltenham, dying in the latter place in 1816, more than ninety years of age. (See Waldo Lincoln, *Genealogy of the Waldo Family*, Worcester, Mass., 1902.)

Date: Miss Virginia Robie states that "Smibert painted the youthful Joseph soon after his graduation from Harvard."

Owner: Miss Virginia Robie reports the following family tradition, which appears to be well founded. Jacob Johnson, who had married Abigail Waldo, was in England in 1780 and visited Bristol, where he noted a building with the sign, "Joseph Waldo, Merchant." Guessing that the proprietor might be related to his wife, he entered, learned that the proprietor and his wife were second cousins, and became a guest at Joseph Waldo's home, where he saw Smibert's portrait of his host. It is not known whether the portrait is still extant, or, if so, where it is located.

SAMUEL WALDO

Subject: Samuel Waldo, born in Boston 1695, died 1759. Married (1) Grizzell Apthorp, (2) Sarah Erving. A wealthy merchant and proprietor of a large grant of land on the Penobscot in Maine. He commanded a regiment at the siege of Louisburg, 1745, and was rewarded for his services by promotion to the rank of brigadier general.

Size: Full length?

Date: 1747.

Note: That Smibert painted a portrait of General Samuel Waldo is substantiated by the reported entry in the diary of Edward Waldo (1747): "Spent the morning with my illustrious cousin Samuel who is having his Likeness made by the renowned Mr. Smybert." See p. 95.

Family tradition maintains that the portrait of Samuel Waldo now at Bowdoin College, to which it was given in 1857, is the picture which Smibert painted. That portrait, however, is not at all characteristic of Smibert and appears to be the work of Robert Feke, to whom it was attributed in my book on that painter.[1] Most students of colonial portraiture agree with that attribution. It may also be pointed out that in 1748 Feke painted the portraits of Waldo's brother- and sister-in-law, Mr. and Mrs. James Bowdoin II. If the attribution of the portrait at Bowdoin College to Feke is accepted, the question arises as to what has become of Smibert's portrait, of which no other record exists. It is possible that Smibert, though he started to paint a portrait of Waldo, was unable to complete it owing to ill health and poor eyesight, and that the commission was turned over the following year (1748) to Feke when the latter reappeared in Boston. Or Smibert's picture may have been destroyed. The problem is a puzzling one, but I am still of the opinion that the portrait of Waldo at Bowdoin College is by Feke and not by Smibert.

Reproduced: There is in the Frick Art Reference Library, New York, a small woodcut reproduction of the Bowdoin College portrait, probably made about the year 1880, in which the figure is shown half length with the background altered to show a paneled room.

The same portrait, in some cases attributed to Smibert, in others to Feke, is reproduced in: Earle, *Two Centuries of Costume in America* (1902), II, 204; *Art in America*, VII, 218; Catalogue, *Loan Collection of Portraits by American Painters before the Revolution, Copley Society* (March 1922); *International Studio*, LXXVII, 432; Bayley, p. 333.

GIDEON WANTON

Subject: Gideon Wanton, Governor of Rhode Island, 1745–1746 and 1747–1748.

Note: There appears to be no doubt as to the existence of a portrait of Gideon Wanton, since Mr. Alan Burroughs had an old photograph of it on loan for a brief period, and the pedigree for it seems fairly well established, but I have been unable to obtain a description of it or to learn its present location.

Family tradition attributed the portrait to Copley, but inspection of the above-mentioned photograph indicated that it must have been painted by either Smibert or Feke. If by the former, it must date from 1729; if by the latter it presumably was painted in the seventeen-forties.

The portrait is said to have come down through the Gould family to Mrs. Charles C. van Zandt of Newport, R. I., and was inherited by her daughter, Mrs. Charles Potter. At her death it was inherited by her daughter, Mrs. Roscoe Bonsal of Lenox, Mass., and in 1943 was said to be in the possession of Mrs. Roscoe Bonsal, Jr. Recent inquiries about it have brought no response.

[1] *Robert Feke* (1930), pp. 72–74, 104, 198–200.

REV. ELISHA WILLIAMS

Subject: Elisha Williams, born 1694; Rector of Yale College 1726–1739; died 1755.

Size: H. *c.* 30 in.; W. *c.* 25 in.

Date: c. 1736.

Description: The original of this portrait has not been located, but a copy of it (see below) is in the possession of Yale University. The copy shows the head and bust of Williams within a painted oval, against a dark background, half front, his right shoulder towards the spectator, his head turned right, full front. He has brown eyes and a medium complexion, and wears a short gray wig, clerical bands, and a black Geneva gown over a black coat.

Reproduced: The copy at Yale University was painted in 1795 by Reuben Moulthrop (1763–1814). It is signed, lower right corner, *R. Moulthrop, pinxit,* and inscribed in the lower left corner, *Rev. et Hon. Elisaus Williams, Rector Coll. Yale, ob. July 25, 1755, Æt 61.*

In *The Literary Diary of Ezra Stiles, D.D., LL.D., President of Yale College,* edited by Franklin Bowditch Dexter, M.A., III, 558, is the entry: "Jan. 20 (1795) . . . Received Rector Williams's Picture by Smibert, taken about 1736 while he was Rector of Yale Coll. He died 1755, aet. 61 cir." To this entry is appended the following footnote: "The picture now belonging to the College is a copy by Moulthrop; the original, which still remains in the family, was sent for the purpose of having this copy made." F.A.R.L. photo. of Moulthrop's copy.

This portrait may still be extant, in the hands of some of Elisha Williams' numerous descendants, but I have been unable to locate it.

SECTION C

PORTRAITS OF QUESTIONABLE ATTRIBUTION

*Portraits of which the attribution to Smibert is open to
question, or which have been mistakenly assigned to him.*

In this section I have listed a number of portraits attributed to Smibert,
either by tradition or by recent opinion, which may be his work, although
sufficient evidence is lacking to prove that such is the case, and also portraits which in the past have, in my opinion, been mistakenly assigned to
him. Throughout the nineteenth century Smibert and Copley were the
only pre-Revolutionary painters in New England whose names were well
remembered, with the result that many pictures now attributed to Feke,
Badger, Greenwood, Blackburn, and the anonymous painters of the last
quarter of the seventeenth and the first quarter of the eighteenth century
were, in ignorance, assigned to either Smibert or Copley. I have included
only those portraits thus attributed to Smibert to which some publicity
has been given as his work, omitting others which have had little or no
publicity and with which the name of Smibert is associated only by a
dubious family tradition or by a plausible guess springing from the desire
to assign them to a known artist.

LORD BALTIMORE

A miniature, said to represent George Calvert, first Lord Baltimore
(1580–1632), but more probably depicting his son, Cecil, the second
baron, founder of Maryland, was shown at the exhibition of early American paintings, National Gallery (Smithsonian Institution), Washington,
D. C., 1925, and in the catalogue was attributed to John Smibert. The attribution is certainly mistaken, because even the second Lord Baltimore
flourished nearly a century too early to have been painted by Smibert,
who, in any case, is not known to have painted any miniatures.

MRS. SAMUEL BROWNE, JR. (MRS. EPES SARGENT)

Subject: Katherine, daughter of John and Anne (Dudley) Winthrop,
born March 9, 1711, married (1) Samuel Browne, Jr., of Salem 1732. He
died November 26, 1742, and she married (2) Col. Epes Sargent, II, of
Gloucester 1744. She had two children by her first husband, one of whom,
Abigail, married Joseph Blaney and was painted by Blackburn. She died
January 11, 1781.

Size: H. 50½ in.; W. 40¾ in.
Date: In the seventeen-thirties.
Description: The subject is shown seated, full front, out-of-doors beside rocks which rise to a cliff above her. To the left a stream meanders through a meadow set with trees. She has light-brown eyes and auburn hair, curls of which hang over either shoulder. She wears a low-cut blue silk gown with white muslin trim, and an old-rose drape is thrown over her left shoulder and drawn across her lap. The left elbow rests upon a rock, the hand holding a rose to her bodice. Her right hand rests in her lap, holding more flowers.

This portrait is wholly characteristic of Smibert in the pose of the figure, the background, and general pattern, but the painting of the head, bust, arms, and hands does not appear to be his brushwork. This suggests the possibility that the existing picture may be an eighteenth-century copy of a lost original by Smibert, although family tradition has attributed it to that painter.

Owner: Bequeathed in 1929 to the Museum of Fine Arts, Boston, by George Nixon Black, who acquired it from the subject's great-grand-nephew, J. D. Sargent.

Reproduced: Bayley, p. 423, as Mrs. Epes Sargent II. *Antiques,* vol. XVII, no. 3 (August 1930), as "Aunt Blaney." There is a modern copy of the portrait in the Sargent-Murray-Gilman-Hough House at Gloucester, Mass. F.A.R.L. photo.

References: Attributed to Copley in F. W. Bayley's *John Singleton Copley* (1915), p. 215. *P. F. Mass.* 1899.

JOHN CHANDLER?

Subject: This portrait is supposed to represent John Chandler, of Worcester, Mass., born 1693, died 1762. Judge, colonel of militia, and member of the Governor's Council of Massachusetts.
Size: H. 29 in.; W. 24 in.
Date: ?
Description: Single-breasted gray coat, with black cuffs and buttons, powdered wig, white muslin neckcloth. A book in his left hand.
Owner: Not located. The above description is that given in *P. F. Mass.* 382, where it is taken almost verbatim from Augustus T. Perkins (M.H.S. *Proc.,* XVII, 394), who recorded that the portrait, and that of Mrs. Chandler, was then in the possession of Mrs. Franklin Dexter of Beverly, Mass. Since the description of the portrait is in Mr. Perkins' characteristic style and is obviously based on direct observation, and since a later communication from him to the Massachusetts Historical Society on the subject of Smibert's portraits contains no correction, his statement as to the owner of the pictures at that time must be accepted. The Mrs. Franklin Dexter in question was the mother of Franklin Gordon Dexter of Boston. In the *Historical Records Survey, American Portraits Found in Massachusetts,* the name of Mrs. Gordon Dexter, 55 Beacon St., Boston, is given as

the owner in 1937. This Mrs. Dexter, now of Lenox, Mass., is the widow of the son of the above F. G. Dexter by his second wife. Mrs. Gordon Dexter, however, declares that she does not own, and never has owned the portraits, and knows nothing of them, and the present Franklin Dexter, a great-grandson of the Mrs. Franklin Dexter named by Mr. Perkins, knows nothing of them. Their present location is unknown, and it is a mystery how they came to be listed among *American Portraits Found in Massachusetts*, unless the compilers took the items from Mr. Perkins' list and assumed that the pictures had passed to Mrs. Gordon Dexter.

There is a further question as to the identity of the subjects, concerning which Mr. Perkins may not have been correctly informed. Mr. Herbert H. Hosmer, Jr., The Fessenden School, West Newton, Mass., in answer to an inquiry from the Frick Art Reference Library, stated (1946) that he owns two copies of the Chandler family genealogy, in which the pictures are recorded on p. 121. These copies he inherited from members of the Chandler family of two generations ago. In one copy the record of the portraits is marked "incorrect"; in the other copy it is noted, "This is a mistake, they are Dexter ancestors."

References: M.H.S. *Proc.* XVI, 394. N.E.H.G.S. *Register*, XLIX, 141. *P. F. Mass.* 382.

MRS. JOHN CHANDLER?

Subject: This portrait is supposed to represent Hannah Chandler, born 1699, died 1738, Worcester, Mass. Married John Chandler, 1716.

Size: c. 29 × 24 in.

Date: ?

Description: Green overdress trimmed with lace, dress fastened with gold clasps, black scarf over head, lace cap, fan in right hand.

Owner: See under John Chandler.

Reference: P. F. Mass. 381.

RICHARD CHECKLEY

Richard Checkley of Boston, b. 1694, d. 1742. Listed in the *Catalogue of the Essex Institute*, Salem, Mass., as by Smibert. A pleasing portrait, but the attribution to Smibert is, in my opinion, a mistaken one. It is probably by an earlier colonial limner, as yet unidentified.

CLARK CHILDREN (WILLIAM AND SAMUEL?)

Subject: The portrait is reputed to represent William (born February 23, 1738/39) and Samuel (born October 16, 1744), sons of William and Sybil (Adams) Clark of Boston, and came from a house which had been built by William Clark.

Size: H. 36½ in.; W. 49¼ in.

Date: The younger child appears to be about a year and a half to two years of age, which would give the date 1746 for the painting.

Description: The elder boy is shown on the left, full length, standing; the younger one on the right, seated on a red cushion, against a plain background with a circular seat in the center, a reddish-brown curtain on the right, a vista of trees on the left. The elder boy has brown hair and eyes, and a fresh complexion. He is half front, his right shoulder towards the spectator, his head turned right nearly full front. His shirt is unbuttoned at the neck, he wears a black coat with gold embroidery, long stockings, laced buskins, and has an old-rose scarf over his right arm. In his left hand is an apple, with leaves attached, held out towards his little brother. The younger boy is dressed in a white gown, with a blue scarf partly covering his bare legs. A brown-and-white spaniel is shown between the two children.

The picture has much charm and looks a good deal like an early work of Copley's, to whom it was formerly attributed. If the identification of the subjects is correct, however, it must have been painted about 1746, as the apparent ages of the children would indicate, and in that case is presumably the work of Smibert. If his, it is an unusually attractive and decorative specimen of his work.

Owner: Rhode Island School of Design, Providence, Rhode Island; purchased in 1923 from Henry Warren.

Exhibited: Rhode Island School of Design, Providence.

Reproduced: Bayley, p. 369. F.A.R.L. photo.

MRS. JETHRO COFFIN

Subject: Mary Gardner, wife of Jethro Coffin of Nantucket, born 1670, died 1767.

Size: H. 30 in.; W. 24 in.

Date: The subject is said by family tradition to have taken one or more trips to Boston, to have her portrait painted, which is quite possible since her husband was a sea captain with business interests there. The portrait is variously stated to have been painted when she was forty years old, which would be in 1710, and in 1717, when she was 47. Either date is too early for Smibert to have painted the portrait, and if either is accepted the picture must be by an unknown limner, but neither seems to have any more reliable source than a guess at her apparent age.

Description: The subject is shown half length, in a brown dress, with lace at the neck and sleeves. She holds a flower in her right hand.

Owner: Nantucket Historical Society, Nantucket, Mass.

Reference: P. F. Mass. 462, attributed to John Smibert.

Note: I have not seen this picture and reserve my opinion of it.

JOSEPH CRAWFORD

Subject: Supposed to represent Joseph Crawford, born 1705, died 1770.

Size: H. 30 in.; W. 25½ in.

Description: The subject is shown against a dark background, half front, right shoulder turned out; face turned right, nearly full front. He wears a full, long wig, tobacco-brown coat and waistcoat, and steenkirk tie. The portrait has no recorded pedigree previous to its purchase by the Wadsworth Athenaeum; the identification of the subject is unverified; and the painting, in my opinion, does not appear to be the work of Smibert.

Owner: Wadsworth Athenaeum, Hartford, Conn.; acquired in 1930.

Reproduced: Bulletin, Wadsworth Athenaeum, Hartford, Conn., vol. VIII, no. 4 (October 1930). *Art News Annual,* May 27, 1927.

NATHANIEL CUNNINGHAM

This portrait was included among the reproductions of Smibert's portraits in Bayley's *Five Colonial Artists of New England,* p. 373. It is not, however, painted in Smibert's manner, but is very stiff and awkward. It appears to be a very early work of Joseph Badger's, the apparent age of the subject and the costume indicating that it was painted about 1740.

ANNE ENGS

Subject: Anne, daughter of William and Anne (Adams) Engs, born in Boston, October 20, 1715; married Capt. John Phillips, September 29, 1734; buried from Trinity Church, Boston, November 17, 1794.

Size: H. 35½ in.; W. 28 in.

Date: 1734? Probably shortly before or after her marriage.

Description: I have not seen the original of this portrait, which is reputed to be extant "somewhere in Connecticut." A copy, which appears to date from the early nineteenth century, shows an attractive young woman with brown hair and eyes, nearly full front against a dark background, her left shoulder slightly advanced. She wears a pink silk gown, cut low, with white trim, with four white stripes and tassels across her corsage. A dark scarf is thrown over her right arm and carried around behind her. Her left hand holds what appears to be a silver-headed cane.

The picture appears to be a copy of an original by Smibert, as is affirmed by family tradition, but, not having seen the original, I reserve judgment as to the attribution.

Owner: The copy descended through the Phillips and Rowe families to the late Caleb Loring Cunningham of Milton, Mass. Now owned by Mrs. Cunningham.

CATHERINE HUTCHINSON?

Subject: A woman called Catherine Hutchinson.

Size: H. 30½ in.; W. 25½ in.

Date: ?

Description: The head and bust of the subject are shown within painted spandrels nearly full front against a dark background, the head turned slightly left. She has brown eyes and hair, a curl of which falls over either shoulder. She wears an ivory-white satin dress. I have been unable to locate this portrait, but a photograph of it, with the information noted above, is in the Frick Art Reference Library. William Sawitzky, from the photograph, attributed the portrait to Smibert, but the picture appears to have been considerably repainted, and in the absence of further information about the subject, and not having seen the picture, I reserve my opinion.

Owner: (1938) Miss Katherine F. Adams, Boston, according to information on file at the Frick Art Reference Library, but I have not been able to locate the portrait.

Reproduced: F.A.R.L. 31228.

SIR CHARLES KNOWLES, BART.

Reproduced in Bayley, *Five Colonial Artists of New England*, p. 399, as Smibert's, from the original in the Portsmouth Athenaeum, Portsmouth, N. H. The identification of the subject, a British naval officer who was at the siege of Louisburg, is presumably correct, but the attribution to Smibert must be rejected as the painting is in a style quite different from his.

BENJAMIN LYNDE, SR. NO. 2.

Size: H. *c.* 30 in.; W. *c.* 25 in.

Owner: Essex Institute, Salem, Mass.

Description: This portrait is either a replica of No. 1, by Smibert, or a later copy by another hand.

Attribution: In *The Diaries of Benjamin Lynde* (Boston, 1880), p. xii, it is stated, "There are two original portraits of him, painted by Smybert in 1737. One of these portraits, in the possession of Mrs. William B. Richards of Boston, is perhaps among the best of Smybert's efforts." This is portrait No. 1. And on p. xv, "There is a portrait of Judge Lynde, by Smybert, in the possession of Dr. F. E. Oliver of Boston, and also one of Madame Lynde, by the same artist, both painted about the year 1735." These two quotations are in conflict as to the date of the pictures, 1737 being the right date for No. 1 and perhaps for No. 2. The statement that Smibert painted Madame Lynde is incorrect, as that portrait is by an unknown artist, about 1705.

Portrait No. 2 descended through Mary Lynde, daughter of the subject, who married Andrew Oliver, to Dr. Fitch E. Oliver, who owned it in 1867, and whose son Charles E. Oliver inherited it. He sold it in August 1925 to the present owner, the Essex Institute in Salem, Mass. It is decidedly inferior to No. 1 and this has led Mr. Alan Burroughs, in *John Greenwood in America, 1745–1752* (1943), p. 31, to say that No. 2 cannot be a replica by Smibert but must be called a copy by John Greenwood, probably painted after Lynde's death in 1747: "The two portraits of Benjamin Lynde, Sr. . . . are obviously not by the same artist, though both have been attributed to Smibert . . . When Greenwood made the copy is uncertain." He makes this judgment on technical grounds.

It is possible that he may be right, but if it was painted before 1748 it is highly improbable that the Lynde family would have turned to anyone other than Smibert, and if between that date and 1756 it might have been painted by Nathaniel Smibert, or possibly by John Smibert's nephew, John Moffatt. At the present writing I do not find it possible to make any definite attribution.

Reproduced: Catalogue of Portraits in the Essex Institute (Salem, Mass., 1936), no. 180.

BENJAMIN LYNDE, JR.

Subject: Benjamin, son of Judge Benjamin and Mary (Browne) Lynde of Salem, born Oct. 5, 1700, died at Salem, Oct. 9, 1781. He was graduated from Harvard in 1718, and entered on the practice of law. Member of the Council in 1737; judge of sessions and common pleas; succeeded his father as chief justice in 1745. He presided at the trial of Captain Preston in 1770 for giving the order that caused the Boston Massacre. He resigned as chief justice in 1772. In 1774 he was one of the signers of the Salem address to Gen. Thomas Gage.

Size: H. 29½ in.; W. 24¾ in.

Date: c. 1738?

Description: The head and bust of the subject are shown against a shaded background within a clearly defined oval, three-quarters front, the right shoulder towards the spectator, the head turned nearly full front. He wears a short gray wig, brown coat, unbuttoned, black-and-white brocaded waistcoat, and a scarf in the steenkirk style which went out of fashion in the 1730's. The end of the scarf is tucked through a buttonhole of his coat. In pose and countenance the portrait clearly resembles that of the subject's father, but the figure is stiff, the fabrics are not well painted, and the characterization is decidedly inferior to that in the portrait of the elder Lynde. This inferiority has led Mr. Alan Burroughs to attribute this portrait, like that of Benjamin Lynde, No. 2, to Nathaniel Smibert rather than to his father (see *Art in America*, April 1943). It is true that the portrait is distinctly characteristic of Nathaniel, strongly resembling that of Dorothy Wendell in pose and manner of treatment, but it is difficult to accept the attribution because the subject appears to be a man in his thirties, or at most forty, which means that he must have been painted while Nathaniel Smibert was still a small boy, whereas he would have been in the middle fifties by the time that Nathaniel could have executed this picture. The attribution, therefore, is still an open question.

Owner: This portrait, with that of Benjamin Lynde, Sr., No. 2, descended to Dr. Fitch E. Oliver of Boston, whose widow sold them about

1910 to the late Frederick Moseley of Boston, who was also descended from the Lyndes. The present owner is Mrs. F. S. Moseley.

Reproduced: It is stated in *The Diaries of Benjamin Lynde* that a copy was owned by Samuel H. Russell of Boston.

Mrs. Fitch E. Oliver also had a copy of this portrait made in 1910 when she sold the original to Mr. Moseley. Winsor, II, 558. *Diary of Benjamin Lynde, Jr.,* p. 129. *Massachusetts Law Quarterly,* vol. XXII (January 1937). F.A.R.L. photo. Sibley's *Harvard Graduates,* vol. VI, opp. p. 250.

References: Diaries of Benjamin Lynde, p. xx. *P. F. Mass.* 1359.

COL. WILLIAM PEPPERELL

Subject: William Pepperell, born 1646; died 1734. A Boston merchant; Justice of the Peace 1690–1725; Judge of the Court of Common Pleas of the Province of Massachusetts Bay, 1694–1702, 1708–1720. Lieutenant-Colonel of Militia.

Size: H. 30 in.; W. 23 in.

Description: The head and bust of the subject are shown against a plain background, half front, the right shoulder towards the spectator, the head turned right, three-quarters front. The right hand holds, awkwardly, a small open book. The face is full, florid, and strongly characterized. The subject wears a brown wig; white stock and long, straight Blenheim tie; and a dark brown robe, faced with terra cotta. The portrait is commonly attributed to Smibert, but is not characteristic of him. Pepperell would have been about 84 years old when Smibert reached Boston in 1729. While the portrait shows an elderly man, he might easily be twenty or twenty-five years younger than that. Both the apparent age of the sitter and the characteristics of the picture support the opinion that it is the work of an unidentified limner who was working around Boston between about 1690 and 1715.

Owner: The portrait is said to have been left to Pepperell's daughter, Dorothy Pepperell Prescott, and in 1894 to have been owned by her great-great-granddaughter, Millicent Jarvis, of Jamaica Plain, Mass., from whom it was acquired by the present owner, Admiral Reginald R. Belknap, Newport, R. I.

Exhibited: Loan Exhibition of One Hundred Colonial Portraits, Museum of Fine Arts, Boston, 1930. Century Club, New York, summer of 1949.

Reproduced: Bolton, II, 437. *Catalogue, Loan Exhibition of Colonial Portraits* (Boston, 1930), p. 69, as by Smibert.

PERKINS CHILDREN (JOANNA AND ELIZABETH?)

Subject: Two small children whose identity is uncertain, listed under these names in *Historical Records Survey: American Portraits Found in Massachusetts,* no. 1661, and attributed to Smibert(?). Augustus T. Perkins listed them as belonging to the Loring family, perhaps because the portrait was then owned by Francis C. Loring of Boston. At a later date the portrait was in the estate of William Powell Perkins, and the subjects were tentatively identified as Joanna and Elizabeth Perkins, born 1745 and 1747 respectively. Both identifications appear to be largely speculative.

Size: H. 25 in.; W. 25 in.

Date: If the above identification be accepted the picture might have been painted in 1748.

Description: Augustus T. Perkins wrote, "This work represents two children, a boy and a girl, said to be twins. They are dressed in white caps and robes." Granting that Perkins was describing this portrait, and the difficulty of guessing the ages of very small children in portraits, and recognizing that in the eighteenth century little boys and girls were dressed very much alike, I disagree with this description and should say that the two children are both girls, perhaps four and two years of age. They are seated towards each other on a couch, half front, their heads turned respectively right and left, nearly full front, a basket of flowers between them. They wear white caps and long white dresses. The older child, on the spectator's left, holds two cherries in her right hand while the left hand rests on the basket. The younger child holds a rattle with silver bells in her right hand, to which is attached a long ribbon in two strands which she holds with her left hand. The attribution of the portrait to Smibert is open to question, though it is commonly made.

Owner: Owned in 1878 by Francis C. Loring; in 1922 by the Misses Loring; later by the estate of William Powell Perkins; in 1938 by Paul M. Hamlen of Boston; in 1942 by Mrs. Daniel K. Catlin of St. Louis, Mo.

Reproduced: Alan Burroughs, *Limners & Likenesses,* no. 30, as by Smibert. F.A.R.L. photo.

References: Bolton, listed as "Unknown Sitters, Portraits of Children," in his article on Smibert in *The Fine Arts,* XX, 42 (August 1933). Alan Burroughs, *Limners and Likenesses,* pp. 38–39. P. F. Mass. 1661, as Joanna and Elizabeth Perkins.

JOHN RINDGE

Subject: John, son of Isaac and Elizabeth (Dutch) Rindge of Ipswich, Mass., born 1695; removed to Portsmouth, N. H., about 1710, where he died, November 6, 1740. Married Ann, daughter of Jotham Odiorne of Portsmouth. Merchant; member of the Provincial Assembly; Commissioner to Great Britain to settle the boundary dispute between Massachusetts and New Hampshire.

Size: H. *c.* 30 in.; W. *c.* 24 in.

Date: The late seventeen-thirties.

Description: The subject is shown within painted spandrels against a dark background, nearly full front, with his right shoulder slightly advanced. He wears a full wig, one knotted end of which falls in front of his right shoulder; a long, straight tie; and a sage-green velvet coat. The picture is attributed to Smibert but has been so heavily repainted that the correctness of the attribution is difficult to determine. Furthermore, the fact that the subject spent some time in Great Britain suggests the possibility that the picture may have been painted there.

I have not seen this picture and the foregoing description is based on information and a photograph at the Frick Art Reference Library.

Owner: In the nineteen-thirties the portrait was owned by Miss Helen Keeling Mills, Kent, Conn., to whom it had come by bequest from a cousin, Miss Mary Tilotson Stone, New York. After the death of Miss Mills in 1939 it passed to the present owner, Mrs. Robert Brumbacher, Salt Lake City, Utah.

Reproduced: F.A.R.L. photo.

CAPTAIN JOHANNES SCHUYLER AND HIS WIFE

This double portrait of Captain Johannes and Elizabeth (Staats) Schuyler, now in the possession of the New York Historical Society, was attributed to John Smibert in an article by William Sawitzky in the Society's *Quarterly Bulletin* (vol. XVIII, no. 2, July 1934) entitled "Portrait of Captain and Mrs. Johannes Schuyler; a hitherto unrecognized work of John Smibert," and that attribution is repeated in the *Catalogue of American Portraits* of the New York Historical Society, pp. 268–269.

Mr. Sawitzky argues that "in draughtsmanship, color, brushwork, and small mannerisms" it is characteristic of Smibert. The difficulty of explaining how Smibert, who never visited New York, much less Albany, where Schuyler lived, could have painted the latter person and his wife, is met by pointing out that Mrs. Schuyler's youngest son by her first husband, Jacob Wendell, had settled in Boston, where he prospered and left a numerous and distinguished progeny. Mr. Sawitzky's surmise is that Captain and Mrs. Schuyler made a journey to Boston to see Jacob Wendell, soon after Smibert's arrival, and were there painted by him, about 1730. There is, however, no record of such a journey, and, while not impossible, it is highly improbable that one was made.

Mr. John Hill Morgan had earlier suggested that it had been painted about 1723 by Evert Duyckinck III of New York (*Early American Painters*, 1921, pp. 32–34). Mr. Morgan later changed his attribution of the portrait to John Watson in his monograph, *John Watson, Painter, Merchant and Capitalist of New Jersey, 1685–1768* (1941), reprinted from the *Proceedings* of the American Antiquarian Society for October 1940, reproducing two portraits which he had authenticated as the work of John Watson, namely those of Gov. Burnet and of Gov. Lewis Morris. The manner of painting of both of these, but especially of the latter, strongly resembles that of the portrait of Johannes Schuyler. Inasmuch as John Watson was frequently in New York he might well have been employed to paint the Schuylers, which he could have done at an earlier date than 1730, since he reached Perth Amboy from Scotland at least as early as 1714. Johannes Schuyler's costume and the apparent ages of both Mr. and Mrs. Schuyler suggest a date about 1720 as the period when they were painted.

The attribution to John Watson rests on a good deal more secure foundation than the attribution to John Smibert.

Reproduced: New York Historical Society, *Quarterly Bulletin,* vol. XVIII, no. 2 (July 1934), and *Catalogue of American Painting* (1941), p. 269.

REV. WILLIAM SHURTLEFF

Subject: William, son of Captain William and Suzannah (Lothrop) Shurtleff; born at Plymouth, April 4, 1689; died at Portsmouth, N. H., May 9, 1747. He was graduated from Harvard in 1707; ordained, 1712, pastor of New Castle, N. H., where he remained until 1731/32. Pastor of the South Parish, Portsmouth, N. H., from 1733 until his death. Married Mary, daughter of Theodore Atkinson.

Size: H. 30 in.; W. 25 in.

Description: The head and bust of the subject are shown almost full front, his right shoulder slightly advanced, against a brown background above spandrels in the lower corners. He wears a white wig, black coat and gown, and clerical bands. The portrait has been repainted, and although attributed to Smibert, does not appear to be his work. Possibly by John Moffatt.

Owner: Massachusetts Historical Society, Boston, given September 29, 1836, by Mrs. Susan Parker and Mrs. Lucretia Lyman. See M.H.S. *Proc.,* 1st Ser., II, 55.

Reproduced: A copy was painted in 1879 by Mrs. L. A. Bradbury for the South Church in Portsmouth.

An idealized version is reproduced in the *Century Magazine* for July 1893, p. 388, and in B. Shurtleff, *Descendants of William Shurtleff* (1912), I, 8.

C. K. Shipton, Sibley's *Harvard Graduates,* V, 396.

JOHN SMIBERT? SO-CALLED SELF-PORTRAIT NO. 1

Size: H. 49 in.; W. 39 in.

Date: 1728? At Rome?

Description: The subject is a man of about forty years, shown seated, three-quarters front, his right shoulder advanced, his head turned right nearly full front. He wears a long gray wig, a brick-red cloak or dressing gown, and breeches, below which appear the tops of his gray stockings. His right arm is held across his body, the forefinger pointing to the background at the spectator's right, a gesture frequently employed by Smibert. The background shows distant hills with nearer pyramids and palm trees (similar to the background in so-called Self-Portrait No. 2), the type of background often used to suggest an Italian setting. The subject's features sufficiently resemble those shown in Smibert's undoubted portrait in his "Bermuda Group" to suggest the possibility that the two heads may represent the same individual at about the same period in life, if allowance is made for the wig and more formal costume in the portrait under discussion, as compared with the informality of Smibert's appearance in the "Bermuda Group." They also sufficiently resemble the features of the man shown in No. 2 to allow the possibility that the two pictures represent the same individual, the first in serious mood, the second jocosely.

Owner: This portrait was sold by Christie, Manson & Woods, London, June 27, 1927. In the sales catalogue it was listed as "No. 126, Portrait of a gentleman in a brown dress, pointing to a pyramid." It was bought by Leger and Son for ten guineas, and was soon after shipped to this country.

Christie, Manson & Woods, who on the same date also sold the portrait listed as Self-Portrait No. 2, stated that they had acquired both pictures from a dealer who said that they came from an old house in Kent. Beyond that no information is available.

Owned in 1934 by Julius Weitzner, New York.

Reproduced: Parnassus, vol. IV, no. 4 (April 1932).

JOHN SMIBERT? SO-CALLED SELF-PORTRAIT NO. 2

Size: H. 37½ in.; W. 28½ in.
Date: On the back: *Jo. Smibert pinxit*
                           Romae, 1728
The portrait has been rebacked, but the above is said to be a careful copy of the inscription painted on the back of the original canvas.

Description: The subject is shown seated, half front, his left shoulder towards the spectator, his head turned to his left, nearly full front. He is dressed in a plaited shirt, unbuttoned at the neck, over which is a reddish-brown gown. The head, without a wig, is tied up in a blue silk kerchief, above which is his black cocked hat edged with gold braid. His right hand rests in his lap, holding an elaborate tobacco pipe with a very long, straight stem, while his left arm is held across his body, the forefinger pointing to the background, which shows distant woods and hills, a pyramid and two palm trees (similar to the background of So-called Self-Portrait No. 1), while in the middle distance is the small figure of a man riding a donkey, before whom stands an angel. These figures apparently represent Balaam and his ass, confronted by the angel, who, however, holds a musket instead of a sword. The face of the subject shows a long, straight nose with slanting nostrils, and wears a half-jovial, half-derisive appearance. The picture is clearly intended to convey some joke, for no painter would have shown a patron in such guise. If accepted as a self-portrait of Smibert, the figures of Balaam and the angel may have some humorous reference to the project of going to Bermuda, and the picture may have been painted for the amusement of the Rosa-Coronian Club.

This interpretation of the picture is regarded as dubious by good judges who question (1) whether it is a self-portrait by Smibert; (2) whether it may represent him but be by another hand; (3) whether it may represent another individual and be of continental European origin. There are at present no definitive answers to these questions, nor any satisfactory solution of the problem presented by the picture. I can go no further than to say that the interpretation of the picture which I have given is the most plausible one which I have been able to devise.

Owner: The Wadsworth Athenaeum, Hartford, Conn. This portrait, like that listed as Self-Portrait No. 1 was sold by Christie, Manson & Woods, London, on June 27, 1927. Both pictures had been acquired from a dealer who said that they came from an old house in Kent. This portrait was purchased by a dealer named Feldman, and later came into the hands of Leger & Son who shipped it to this country.

Exhibited: Yale University Art Gallery, "The Smibert Tradition," exhibition, October–November 1949.

Reproduced: Parnassus, vol. IV, no. 4 (April 1932).

CAPTAIN EDWARD TYNG

Subject: Edward, son of Edward Tyng, born in Boston 1688, died in Boston September 8, 1755. His father was appointed governor of Annapolis, N. S., but was captured by the French on his way to his post and taken to France where he died. Edward, Jr., was commissioned captain of the fortifications of Boston in April 1740. On June 18, 1744, news reached Boston that a French privateer from Cape Breton was cruising in Massachusetts Bay. Captain Tyng was dispatched against her in command of the snow-rigged vessel Prince of Orange, which had been built in 1740 at the expense of the Province, to protect the commerce and fisheries of the colony. On June 24 the two vessels met off Cape Cod, and Tyng captured his enemy without the loss of a man. In gratitude the merchants of Boston presented him with a great silver cup weighing one hundred ounces, of the type known as a "bishop," made by Jacob Hurd. It is one of the finest pieces of silverware ever made in Boston, and is now in the Garvan Collection at the Yale University Art Gallery. In 1745 Tyng commanded the frigate Massachusetts in the expedition against Louisburg.

Size: H. 49¾ in.; W. 40⅜ in.

Date: The portrait which is neither signed nor dated, was presumably painted either in the summer or fall of 1744, or after the return of the expedition from Louisburg, probably the latter, because the ship shown is a frigate and not a snow.

Description: Captain Tyng is shown nearly three-quarter length, standing against a dark background, half front, with his left shoulder towards the spectator, his head turned left nearly full front. He has a strong, well-modeled face, and wears a long gray wig, a long hanging scarf, and a light chocolate-brown coat over a handsome brocade waistcoat. His cocked hat with gilt edging is held against his left side by his arm, and his left hand holds a telescope. A sword hilt shows at his side. His right hand points to an opening in the background through which is seen a frigate under sail with a red ensign.

Opinions differ as to the painter of this handsome portrait. At the

Yale University Art Gallery it is attributed to "Unknown Painter" on the theory that it was painted in England. I know of no evidence that Tyng made a voyage thither in the late seventeen-forties, and the portrait appears to be a companion piece to that of Mrs. Tyng, definitely attributed to Smibert. Tyng's portrait has also been attributed to Blackburn. It could be his work only if painted in England, since Blackburn did not reach Boston until ten years after the episode which the portrait seems to celebrate, and only just before Tyng's death. No artist other than Smibert is known to have been in Boston in 1744 or 1746 who could have executed so fine a portrait, but it is not clearly characteristic of his style and is rather better than even the best of his known works. The name of the painter to whom it should be attributed remains, therefore, an open question.

Owner: The cup and portrait descended to Tyng's son, William, a loyalist, and were seized in 1775, but restored by order of the Provincial Congress, and descended in the family. Owned in 1902 by heirs of Rev. Timothy Hilliard, and later by his descendant, Miss Mabel Harlow of Boston, from whom it was purchased in 1929 by Francis P. Garvan and presented to the Yale University Art Gallery.

Reproduced: Bulletin of the Associates in Fine Arts at Yale University, vol. IV, no. 3 (October 1932), p. 149.

William Goold, *Portland of the Past*, with historical notes of Old Falmouth (1886), opp. p. 247, attributed to Blackburn.

UNIDENTIFIED WOMAN (MRS. CLARKE, SO-CALLED)

Subject: This portrait was formerly on loan at the Essex Institute, Salem, Mass., as representing a Mrs. Clarke, otherwise unidentified.

Size: H. 36½ in.; W. 28¼ in.

Date: Perhaps 1740 or later.

Description: The subject is an erect woman in her late twenties shown against a wall on the right and a dimly painted landscape on the left; nearly full front, her left shoulder advanced, her head turned slightly to her left. She has dark hair and eyes, and wears a blue-green dress with muslin trim, and a pink scarf thrown over her right shoulder. Her left arm is held across her body, the hand holding a flower. While the portrait shows some characteristics of Smibert's work, and has been attributed to him, the attribution, in my opinion, requires further support before being definitely accepted.

Owner: Mrs. David Murphy, New York.

Exhibited: Yale University Art Gallery, "The Smibert Tradition," exhibition, October–November 1949.

JOSHUA WINSLOW?

Subject: This portrait is supposed to represent Joshua, son of Edward III and Hannah (Moody) Winslow; born in Boston 1694; married

Elizabeth Savage about 1720; merchant and shipowner; died in Boston 1769.

Size: H. 25½ in.; W. 27¾ in.

Date: c. 1730?

Description: The subject is shown seated at a table, his body three-quarters front, his right shoulder towards the spectator, his head turned right, nearly full front. He wears a dark-red turban above his close-cut hair, a robe of the same color, and a shirt with ruffles, left unbuttoned at the neck. His right hand holds a quill pen and rests on a writing pad on the table before him. The background is dark, but through a window is a vista of a ship.

This portrait, with its companion piece representing the subject's wife, was in the last century stored for a long time in the attic of a member of the Winslow family, whence it was retrieved many years ago by the late owner, Arthur Winslow of Boston. Both pictures were in a dilapidated condition and were restored by a Polish artist then in Boston, and later (1945) by Alfred Lowe of the Museum of Fine Arts, Boston. Mr. Arthur Winslow, in his book of family records entitled *Francis Winslow* (1935), on pp. 61–62 assumes that the portraits represent Joshua Winslow and his wife, painted by John Smibert, because in the inventory of Joshua's estate, 1778, are listed:

> 2 Family Pictures Mr. Winslow & Wife 4.3.0
> 1 Gilt Picture Olde Mr. Winslow 2.0.0
> In the back parlor.

The picture of "Olde Mr. Winslow . . . In the back parlor" was undoubtedly that of Edward Winslow III (*q.v.*) by John Smibert, and it was a natural assumption that the two portraits found in the attic were the "Family Pictures" representing Joshua Winslow and wife, and that they were by the same artist.

The assumption, however, is not necessarily correct. The subject of the portrait looks rather younger than the thirty-six years which Joshua Winslow would have reached in 1730, the earliest year in which John Smibert could have painted him. The turban and shirt open at the neck are much more characteristic of Nathaniel Smibert's portraits than of his father's, and so is the painting of the eyes and mouth. William Sawitzky attributed the portrait to Nathaniel (probably on the basis of a photograph) and, in my opinion, that attribution has a good deal to support it, although it may be argued that the portrait and its companion piece have been so largely repainted that it is now impossible to form any decisive judgment on the subject.

If the portraits are by Nathaniel rather than by John Smibert they must have been painted between 1750 and 1756, in which case they must represent unidentified persons other than Joshua Winslow and his wife.

Owner: Mrs. Charles Cotting, Boston. In 1935 both pictures were owned by Arthur Winslow of Boston. At his death they were inherited by his daughter, Mrs. Charles Cotting, and are (1949) on loan at the Boston Athenaeum.

Reproduced: Arthur Winslow, *Francis Winslow* (1935), opp. p. 62. F.A.R.L. photo.

References: Arthur Winslow, *op. cit.,* pp. 61–62. P. F. *Mass.* 2509, attributed to John Smibert.

MRS. JOSHUA WINSLOW?

Subject: This picture is supposed to represent Elizabeth, daughter of Thomas and Margaret (Lynde) Savage; born in Boston, 1704; married Joshua Winslow 1720; died 1778.

Size: H. 35¼ in.; W. 27¾ in.

Date: c. 1730?

Description: The subject is shown standing, nearly full front, against a dark background, with a landscape background showing faintly to the left. She wears a dark blue-green dress, cut low, with white muslin trim at the bosom and sleeves. Her right hand hangs at her side; her left arm is held across her body, the hand raised to her bodice. She is a tall young woman with brown eyes, very dark hair, a curl of which hangs over her left shoulder, and a rather long nose.

The reasons for questioning the identification of the subject, and that of her husband in the companion portrait, are discussed under Joshua Winslow (*q.v.*). It should be added that Elizabeth Savage was painted as a girl of twelve or fourteen by an unidentified artist (see Clarke and Foote, *Jeremiah Dummer,* 1935, pp. 199–200) and in that portrait is shown with light-brown hair and a fair complexion. It seems hardly possible that the young woman shown in the portrait here discussed can be the same individual as that shown in the earlier portrait of Elizabeth Savage.

The pose and manner of painting closely resemble the portrait of Mrs. Peter Harrison (Appendix 4). Both portraits are reminiscent of John Smibert's portraits of women, but in both the anatomy of the neck and bosom is bad and the whole technique is inferior to that of John Smibert, but it may be argued that these deficiencies in the present portrait are the result of the extensive repainting it has undergone.

The problem presented by this portrait and its companion piece, whether they are by John Smibert or by his son Nathaniel, and whether they represent Mr. and Mrs. Joshua Winslow or unidentified individuals, is discussed under Joshua Winslow (*q.v.*).

Owner: Mrs. Charles Cotting, from the same source as that of the previous portrait.

Reproduced: Arthur Winslow, *Francis Winslow* (1935), p. 62. F.A.R.L. photo.

References: Arthur Winslow, *op. cit.,* pp. 61–62. P. F. *Mass.* 2500, attributed to John Smibert.

SECTION D

COPIES BY SMIBERT

Copies known to have been made by Smibert from originals in Italy or elsewhere.

CARDINAL BENTIVOGLIO BY VAN DYCK

Guido, Cardinal Bentivoglio (1579–1644). Half length, H. 30 in., W. 25 in. The full-length portrait of Bentivoglio in Florence was painted in 1623 by Anthony Van Dyck, then twenty-four years old, while the artist was Bentivoglio's guest in Rome, at a period when Van Dyck was under the influence of Titian. Smibert, during his residence in Florence in the course of his Italian sojourn, 1717–1720, copied the head and bust of this portrait. He brought his copy to America with his collection of copies of Italian pictures, and it remained his property until he died. When John Trumbull rented Smibert's studio in 1777–1778 he copied Smibert's copy. It is commonly stated that he later purchased Smibert's copy and gave it to Harvard College, because a vote of the Corporation on January 9, 1791, thanked Col. John Trumbull for "his present of a copy by the late Mr. Smibert of Boston from a portrait by Vandyck of Cardinal Bentivoglio." The Corporation evidently failed to realize that the gift was in reality Trumbull's copy of Smibert's copy. "The smooth, tight style is that of the youthful Trumbull, as is confirmed by an entry in Trumbull's manuscript catalogue of his works in the Yale Library, giving under the date of 1778, 'Copied from a copy by Mr. Smibert of Van Dyke's wonderful picture at Florence. Given to Harvard College 1789' " (*Harvard Portraits: a Catalogue of Portrait Paintings at Harvard University*, pp. 17–18). It is not known whether or not Smibert's copy is now extant.

THE CONTINENCE OF SCIPIO BY POUSSIN

In the manuscript "Catalogue of Pictures belonging to the Estate of the late Hon. James Bowdoin, Esq., bequeathed by him to Bowdoin College," is the following entry:

No. 3. Continence of Scipio Scipio restores to the Celtiberian Prince, Alluicius, his spouse, a captive in the Roman camp.

Painter unknown, Copy by Smibert, Original lost at sea.

This entry identifies the picture which is now in the Walker Art Building, Bowdoin College, as the copy by Smibert to which frequent reference has been made (see above, pp. 89–90, 124). It hung in Smibert's painting room until the house was sold and the contents dispersed after the death of his nephew John Moffatt in 1777, at which time James Bowdoin may have bought it. When the catalogue was written the compiler did not know that the original was by Poussin and he was mistaken in saying that it had been lost at sea. It was painted for Cardinal Barbarini in 1643; then was in the de Morville Collection, from which it passed to the great collection at Houghton in Norfolk, where it was in 1741, when Claude Dubosc engraved it. It was later acquired, with many other pictures from Houghton, by Catherine the Great, and was hung at the Hermitage in St. Petersburg. Smibert's copy was copied by Trumbull at Boston in 1778.

LUIGI CORNARO BY TINTORETTO

A portrait of Luigi Cornaro, copied from the original by Tintoretto in Florence. Smibert's copy is now in the Walker Art Building, Bowdoin College.

JAN VAN MONTFORT BY VAN DYCK

A portrait of Jan van Montfort, copied from the copy in the Uffizzi of the original by Van Dyck in Vienna. Smibert's copy is now in the Walker Art Building, Bowdoin College. Reproduced, *Art in America*, vol. XXX, no. 2, p. 111. It is highly probable that these two copies of well-known portraits were bought by James Bowdoin when the contents of Smibert's studio were dispersed.

CHARLES AND JAMES STUART BY VAN DYCK

Heads of Two Boys (Charles and James Stuart) from Van Dyck's portrait. Smibert's copy was copied by Trumbull at Boston in 1778. The present location of Smibert's copy is not known.

DANAË BY TITIAN

"Danaë and the Golden Shower." There are several versions of this picture by Titian. Smibert probably copied the version which was in the Farnese Collection and afterwards in the National Museum at Naples, but which may have been in Florence when he copied it. Smibert's copy was formerly owned by Bowdoin College but was sold in the nineteenth century. In 1915 it was owned by George Henry Hall, who bequeathed it in that year to Miss Jennie Brownscombe of New York. The present location of Smibert's copy is not known.

It is, apparently, to this picture that Copley referred when he wrote: "A naked Venus and Cupid at Smibert's is copyd from one of Titiano's in the possession of the Grand Duke which hangs over the celebrated

Titian Venus, but is by no means equil to it" (*Copley-Pelham Letters*, p. 340). Perhaps this is the picture which Trumbull copied and recorded as "Education of Cupid after Smibert after Titian in the Borghese Gallery, Rome."

MADONNA AND CHILD BY RAPHAEL

Mather Byles, in his poem, "To Mr. Smibert, on viewing his Pictures," perhaps refers to Raphael in his line, "Th' Italian master sits in easy state." In any case it is certain that Smibert had a copy of at least one picture by Raphael because Copley wrote to Henry Pelham, "I will refer you than [then] [to] the Coppy at Smibert's of the Holy Family, which although a Coppy from Raphael, is notwithstanding very different from his Painting" (see p. 122). Hagen, in his *Birth of the American Tradition in Art*, p. 45, identifies the original as Raphael's Madonna dell' Impannata, saying, "This is the only painting in the Medici collection that fits Copley's description of Smibert's copy of a holy family by Raphael."

HECTOR AND ANDROMACHE

This picture (H. 50 in., W. 40 in.) shows five full-length figures. Two women, Andromache and an attendant, are shown on the left; Hector and a soldier on the right; the child in the center being held out to Hector by Andromache. The two women are shown in costumes similar to those prevalent in England at the time that Smibert painted; the two men in what was supposed to be classical costume and armor. Some of the faces have been a good deal repainted. The picture, which was deposited on loan in 1921 at the Museum of Fine Arts, Boston, passed by descent to the present owners, Mrs. R. G. Fuller and Henry Fuller. On the back it bears a label, alleging it to be the work of Smibert. It is quite possible that it came from his studio and that it is a copy of a European painting, or, perhaps more probably, an original by him, perhaps after an engraving.

ANCIENT PHILOSOPHERS

When Charles Willson Peale visited Smibert's studio in 1768 he noted, among the unfinished pictures, one with "several heads painted, of the ancient philosophers, and some groups of figures, these were the last works of Smibert." Nothing more is known of this group of "Ancient Philosophers." One of the other groups may well have been that showing the "Bermuda Group."

JOHN ENDECOTT

In 1737 Smibert painted a copy (with some variations) of the original portrait of Governor Endecott which was painted by an unknown limner in 1665. Smibert's copy was given to the Massachusetts Historical Society, Boston, by Francis C. Gray, November 24, 1836.

DRAWINGS ATTRIBUTED TO SMIBERT

In the Walker Art Building at Bowdoin College, Brunswick, Maine, in the collection of drawings bequeathed to the College by James Bowdoin III, with his collection of portraits, are three drawings which have been attributed to Smibert. These were mentioned in an article on "Drawings by Old Masters at Bowdoin College Ascribed to the Northern Schools," by Frank Jewett Mather, Jr., in *Art in America*, vol. II, no. 11, p. 116 (February 1914). See *Descriptive Catalogue of the Art Collections at Bowdoin College* (1930).

These drawings are as follows:

Pastoral Scene and a Camp, a circular drawing in sepia, shaded with a brush, between concentric rings, the diameters of which are 6½ inches and 2¾ inches. The drawing appears to be a design either for a domed ceiling or for a circular dish. It is marked in pencil, by an unknown hand, "John Smibeth" (*sic*). The drawing appears, however, to date from the sixteenth century, and there is no good reason for attributing it to Smibert.

Fisherman and Boat. "The boat is drawn up to an inlet. Two men are in the boat, another is washing a net hanging over its side. A youth and a woman holding a child are standing on the shore by the boat. In the foreground at the right is a reclining man, near whom are several dogs. The view is seaward. Two angels are flying in the heaven, towards whom the gaze of three of the persons is directed" (*Catalogue*). On the back, in ink, an eighteenth-century hand has written "John Smibert." This is certainly not the artist's signature to his work, and the drawing appears to belong to an earlier period. If the handwriting is Smibert's, which is improbable, it might signify his ownership of the drawing. If the handwriting is by another it might signify either that the drawing had been in Smibert's collection, or that it was mistakenly attributed to him.

Grand Duke Cosimo III, a small oval crayon drawing, a biting caricature, showing the head of Cosimo III in profile, facing to the spectator's left (reproduced in *Antiques*, vol. XVIII, no. 3, August 1930). It is mounted on another sheet of paper of different texture on which is written, in ink, "Cosmo the 3rd, Grand Duke of Tuscany, from the life, by John Smibert," in small and rather elegant handwriting of the late eighteenth or early nineteenth century. Professor Hagen (pp. 49–51) thinks that it is not an original drawing by Smibert but a copy by him of a drawing by the Italian artist Alessandro Magnasco, whom he believes to have been in Florence at the time of Smibert's visit. He explains the inscription by assuming that it is incorrectly copied from an earlier one which has been trimmed off, and that some such words as "after a drawing by Magnasco," between "Tuscany" and "from the life," have been omitted. Professor Hagen's theory is highly ingenious but not very convincing. The Bowdoin drawings were purchased in France by James Bowdoin II, during his residence there, before his return to this country in 1809. If this drawing was included in that purchase, as Professor Hagen assumes, and if, before it came into James Bowdoin's hands, it bore an attribution to Smibert, Professor Hagen's theory becomes at least plausible. There is evidence, however, that a second copy of the same drawing was in James Bowdoin's collection when it was bequeathed to the College in 1813. The College sold it in 1850, and it was last heard of in 1915, when it was advertised for sale. It is not recorded whether it bore any inscription. The existence of *two* copies of this drawing raises some interesting questions and tends to invalidate Professor Hagen's theory. It is extremely unlikely that both would have been included in the collection which James Bowdoin purchased in France, and it would have been an equally extraordinary coincidence if that collection had contained a drawing of which Smibert had a duplicate in Boston. It would seem more probable that both copies were in Smibert's possession and that both were bought by James Bowdoin when he purchased other pictures from Smibert's studio at the time that its contents were dispersed. Even in that case it is still an open question whether either or both drawings were by Smibert or whether they were originals by Magnasco or copies from one by him. Although the inscription may record a tradition that Smibert drew Cosimo "from the life," its value as evidence is not great because it appears to date from a period approximately fifty years after Smibert's death. Furthermore, for reasons stated on p. 14, it is difficult to believe that Smibert, who unquestionably received favors at the hands of Cosimo, would have cared, or perhaps dared, to draw so biting a caricature of the senile Grand Duke "from the life."

SECTION E

CERTAIN OTHER PORTRAITS

In the course of a period which began as early as 1917 and ran into the nineteen-thirties certain dealers offered for sale at least sixteen portraits to which Smibert's name was attached (besides many others attributed to other artists of the colonial era), to which considerable publicity has been given and which must therefore be discussed in this place.

One of these pictures was called a portrait of Smibert by Peter Pelham; the others bore signatures of Smibert's name followed by the word *fecit* or *pinxit* and a date. The late Frank W. Bayley, in his *Five Colonial Artists of New England* (1920), reproduced in his chapter on Smibert the portrait attributed to Pelham (p. 343); eight portraits to which Smibert's signature was attached (pp. 347, 351, 385, 393, 395, 417, 419, 429); and the signature on one of them (p. 343). Most of the other portraits to which Smibert's signature is attached appeared after the publication of *Five Colonial Artists* but have been publicized elsewhere.

I have already pointed out (see above, p. 70) that although Smibert seems habitually to have signed and dated the portraits which he painted in England, as he did the "Bermuda Group" which he painted in Newport soon after his arrival in 1729, his signature has not been found on a single one of the portraits later than that date which appear to be indubitably his work, listed in Section A of this catalogue. It is, therefore, somewhat surprising that within a brief period so many of his signatures on portraits should have been, as Bayley wrote, "discovered in . . . recent years by the author of this book" (*op. cit.*, pp. 339–340).

These portraits are said to represent well-known persons of the period when Smibert worked in Boston, and it was, again, somewhat surprising that their existence had never been elsewhere recorded and had remained completely unknown until their "discovery" by the dealer, or group of dealers, who offered them for sale. They were, however, in most cases accompanied by a pedigree purporting to give their line of descent from the subject to the unnamed "heirs" from whom the portrait had been acquired, or they had confirmatory labels pasted on the back.

These pictures attributed to Smibert—like the many others purporting to be the work of other colonial artists—were at first accepted without question and were purchased by or for museums of high standing or by well-informed collectors. As the number of them increased, however, and it was observed that the accompanying pedigrees tended to fall into similar patterns and in all cases ended in a vague statement which never admitted of independent verification, suspicions developed as to the authenticity of the portraits in question, either as to the identification of the subject or the attribution to the painter, or both. In no instance known to me has other evidence come to light which substantiates the statements made in such a pedigree, and in some cases technical examination of the signature has shown it to have been added to the portrait at some recent time. In this group of portraits bearing Smibert's alleged signature, all the signatures appear to have the same character, with slight but significant variations from his genuine signature on the "Bermuda Group."

The result has been that few, if any, experts in the field of colonial art now accept the pictures in the following list as the work of Smibert. In their opinion, with which I concur, most of them are probably English portraits of the first half of the eighteenth century which have been imported into this country, to which Smibert's signature and a date have been added, and for which plausible pedigrees have been compiled to facilitate sale. It is impossible to say at what stage these proceedings took place in the passage to the market of these portraits attributed to Smibert, but, in my opinion, it was probably before they came into Bayley's hands for sale.

It is a disagreeable duty to discuss this unpleasant matter, and I regret the annoyance or pain which may be caused to owners who acquired one or another of these pictures in good faith, although some of them have already come to the same conclusions and have removed the portraits from their walls. But I cannot omit from this book all mention of pictures which have been given publicity as the work of John Smibert and my readers are entitled to a frank expression of my honest opinion as to their authenticity. I have, however, not disclosed the name of the owner in the case of such of these portraits as are in private hands.

PORTRAIT SUPPOSED TO REPRESENT JOHN SMIBERT, ATTRIBUTED
TO PETER PELHAM

This portrait (29½ × 24¼ inches) shows, within a dark-brown painted oval against a light-brown background, the head and bust of a pallid old man with rather heavy arched eyebrows and brown eyes, who wears a brown coat and long steenkirk tie. If the portrait in fact represents Smibert it must have been painted not more than a year or two before his death on April 2, 1751, at the age of 63. The face shown, with its long, prominent nose with receding nostrils, dark eyes with heavy arched eyebrows, Cupid's-bow mouth, and dimpled chin, bears some resemblance to the only indisputable likeness of Smibert, his self-portrait in the "Bermuda Group," painted in 1729 when Smibert was forty-one, and also to the face shown in the two portraits tentatively called Self-Portraits No. 1 and No. 2, supposed to have been painted in Rome in 1728. Twenty years later, when he was ill and prematurely old, he might have looked like the old man in this portrait attributed to Pelham, but the resemblance is far too slight and uncertain to warrant acceptance of the portrait without support by sound historical evidence.

The portrait has been relined and on the back of the canvas, in block letters in ink, is the following inscription:

Portrait of my friend Smibert drawn by P. Pelham
Jahleel Brenton.
Copied from the original inscription on the back
of this picture by
J. Oliver
Liner
New York.

Jahleel Brenton, the younger, who must be the person whose name is attached to this statement, in 1732 inherited the property of his uncle of the same name, and died in 1769. He was a person of importance in Newport who might naturally have seen something of Dean Berkeley and his party and who might have formed a friendship with Smibert during the latter's stay of nine months in Newport. But, aside from this inscription, no evidence of such a friendship has come to light, and it would seem unlikely that so brief an acquaintance would have been sufficiently valued by Brenton to lead him to commission Pelham to paint this picture twenty years later; and if Pelham painted Smibert from any other motive than on commission from Brenton the overwhelming probability is that he would have done so for Smibert's family, who would not have been at all likely to dispose of it before the death of Smibert's last surviving son. Therefore, only indisputable evidence of the authenticity of the inscription would give adequate grounds for accepting it. But the present inscription is avowedly a copy of a statement alleged to have been written or painted on the back of the original canvas, and there is now no way of verifying the authenticity or, indeed, the existence of that alleged statement. The inscription, therefore, cannot be accepted as affording satisfactory evidence either that the portrait is by Peter Pelham or that it represents Smibert.

When the portrait was purchased by the late Thomas B. Clarke, of New York, about 1922, a pedigree for it was furnished in a written statement dated January 4, 1922. According to this statement, both this portrait and that of Dean Berkeley which, signed by Smibert and dated 1728, was purchased in 1917 by the Worcester Art Museum, hung in the Brenton house at Newport when the house and contents were purchased in 1800 by Ebenezer Burrill. Soon afterward Mr. Burrill removed the two portraits to New York, and they passed to his son, Alfred Mansfield Burrill, who died in 1869, and were the property of the latter's heirs until sold by them some fifty years later. The pedigree is confused as to the members of the Brenton family who owned the picture before 1800, and does not disclose the names of the "heirs" of A. M. Burrill who owned the pictures after the latter's death. It is, therefore, not possible to authenticate the accuracy of the statement made in the pedigree, which, in my opinion, cannot be accepted as reliable, in the lack of supporting evidence.

An X-ray photograph of the portrait does not sustain the opinion that the brushwork is that of Peter Pelham, and the costume appears to be too early for the period of 1750. The long steenkirk tie had gone out of fashion before that date in favor of ruffles. It is true that old men continued to wear it after it was outmoded, but Smibert is shown wearing ruffles as early as 1729 in his self-portrait in the "Bermuda Group," and it would seem unlikely that he would have reverted to the older fashion twenty years later.

In view of these considerations, and lacking any indubitable evidence that the portrait either represents Smibert or is by Pelham, I do not feel justified in accepting either claim for it.

The portrait passed, as a picture of Smibert by Pelham, with the collection of Thomas B. Clarke into the hands of the present owner, the A. W. Mellon Educational and Charitable Trust, Washington, D. C.

Reproduced: Bayley, p. 343.

DEAN GEORGE BERKELEY (SO-CALLED)

This portrait is owned by the Worcester (Mass.) Art Museum which acquired it in 1917 from Frank W. Bayley as a portrait of Berkeley. Size: H. 30 in., W. 25 in. It is signed on the lower right side of the picture:

Jo. Smibert f.
1728

The subject is shown within a painted oval, nearly full front, against a very dark background. He wears a gray wig, cassock, girdle, black silk gown, and bands. The face does not strongly resemble that of Berkeley as shown in the Bermuda Group. A label on the back reads, "This portrait of Bishop Berkeley painted by Smybert in 1728 was restored by Henry Ferguson of New York City in 1896."

The pedigree given for the portrait is the same as that given for the portrait alleged to represent Smibert as an old man and attributed to Peter Pelham (*q.v.*). The portrait of Berkeley is said to have been the property of Jahleel Brenton, Sr., who died in 1732, bequeathing it to his nephew, Jahleel Brenton, who died in 1769. Both of these pictures are supposed to have been acquired about 1800 by Ebenezer Burrill (1763–1839) who took them to New York, and to have been purchased from the latter's heirs. This pedigree does not coincide at all points with information provided by Charles Henry Hart, who appears to have owned this portrait before Frank Bayley sold it, and neither statement has been confirmed. In my opinion the pedigree given for the picture is very questionable.

The picture does not appear to be the work of Smibert, but, in my opinion, seems to be of more recent origin, perhaps the work of a painter skillful in imitating the style of the middle of the eighteenth century, and the signature appears to be a later addition. This is the present opinion of the authorities at the Worcester Art Museum who, since 1943, have listed the portrait as "Unknown Man by an Unknown Artist."

Reproduced: (As a portrait of Berkeley by Smibert) *Worcester Art Museum Bulletin* (October 1917), p. 45. Dunlap, I, frontispiece. Bayley, p. 347. *Antiques*, XVIII, 118 (August 1930), article by F. W. Bayley. F.A.R.L. photo.

Exhibited: (For purposes of comparison with Smibert's work), Yale University Art Gallery, "The Smibert Tradition," exhibition, October–November 1949.

DR. DEAN GEORGE BERKELEY (SO-CALLED)

A portrait supposed to represent Dr. Berkeley was included as item number 13 in a collection of pictures made by Mr. Frank Bulkley Smith of Worcester, Mass., which was sold by the American Art Association, New York, in 1920. It was bought by Seaman, acting as agent, for six hundred and fifty dollars. Mr. Smith had acquired it in 1917 from Mr. E. R. Lemon, the former owner of the Wayside Inn, Sudbury, Mass. Its earlier history is not known, but a paster on the stretcher read, "Bought from the old Berkeley home outside Newport, R. I.–'Westward the course of empire.'"

Charles Henry Hart made an examination of the portrait and wrote of it, "Doubtless a contemporaneous replica of the canvas in the Worcester Art Museum, which is signed and dated Jo. Smibert, fc., 1728. It is an extremely good example of Smibert at his best, and particularly interesting from the close relations that existed between the subject and the painter." The present location of this picture has not been traced but a reproduction of it does not warrant acceptance of Mr. Hart's statement. It is very questionable whether the portrait is Smibert's work, and the person whom it represents, though he bears some resemblance to Berkeley, is shown as an older and heavier person than the subject of Smibert's authentic portraits of Berkeley.

Reproduced: F.A.R.L. photo.

MRS. GEORGE BERKELEY

F. W. Bayley reproduced in *Five Colonial Artists of New England* (1929), p. 351, a portrait supposed to represent Mrs. George Berkeley, and signed *Jo. Smibert fecit.* The subject, however, does not at all resemble Mrs. Berkeley as portrayed in the large picture of Dean Berkeley and his entourage, and the portrait does not look like Smibert's work, in spite of the signature which, in my opinion, appears to be a later addition. The portrait was shown in 1925 as a representation of Mrs. Berkeley by Smibert at the Copley Gallery, Boston. Later it was owned by Hiram Burlingham. It was sold for forty-five dollars in the Stanford White and Others Sale, American Art Association, Anderson Galleries, Inc., March 23, 1934, at which time it was purchased by the Fellows of Berkeley College, Yale University, to which it now belongs. The authorities at Yale University do not now consider the portrait to be either a representation of Mrs. Berkeley or by Smibert.

STEPHEN DE LANCEY

This portrait has been reproduced as a painting by Smibert in *Art in America*, IX, 54 (December 1922), and in the *American Magazine of Art* (June 1928), p. 297, and is discussed in C. K. Bolton's *Portraits of the Founders* (1929), III, 755–757, 945. It was purchased about 1921 by the late Thomas B. Clarke of New York, and was attributed to Smibert when it passed with Mr. Clarke's collection into the hands of the A. W. Mellon Educational and Charitable Trust, Washington.

The portrait is signed *J. Smibert, fecit 1734* in gray script, on the right side abreast of the shoulder, and when the portrait was purchased by Mr. Clarke it bore a label pasted on the back with the inscription, "Portrait of my father by Smibert. James De Lancey." Nevertheless it cannot, in my opinion, be accepted as Smibert's. Smibert never painted in New York, and there appears to be no record that Stephen De Lancey visited Boston during the period of Smibert's activity. The portrait is certainly not in Smibert's usual manner, but appears to be of Anglo-Dutch origin. Virgil Barker, in an article in *The Arts*, XIII, 277 (May 1928), says of the portrait: ". . . its brushwork and way of seeing are so inconsistent with his [Smibert's] authenticated manner . . . that another authorship must be considered." Other critics share Mr. Barker's views.

In view of these considerations, and of doubts as to the authenticity of both the signature and the label, the attribution of the portrait to Smibert cannot, in my opinion, be accepted.

REV. ALEXANDER GARDEN (SO-CALLED)

This portrait is reproduced in the Brooklyn Museum *Catalogue of Exhibition of Early American Paintings* (Brooklyn, 1917), opp. p. 81, and in Bayley's *Five Colonial Artists of New England*, p. 385, as the portrait of Rev. Alexander Garden, an Anglican clergyman, by Smibert. It is very obscurely signed with what appears to be the letters *J. S.*, followed by the date 1734.

The claim that the portrait represents Rev. Alexander Garden appears to be without foundation. Appleton's *Biographical Encyclopedia* says that a clergyman of that name was born in Scotland about 1685, came to America in 1719, and served as rector of St. Philip's Church, Charleston, S. C., and commissary for the Bishop of London until shortly before his death in Charleston in 1756. He traveled in the northern colonies in 1735, but the portrait bears no indication, other than quite recent labels, that it represents him, and is accompanied by no pedigree to support the identification. It represents a man who appears to be younger than Garden would have been in the 1730's, and, although he wears a rather high, black waistcoat, he has also a light brown coat, a most unusual costume in which to depict a clergyman of the period. Furthermore, the costume is that of the 1750's rather than that of twenty years earlier. For these reasons the identification of the subject as Rev. Alexander Garden must be regarded as highly questionable.

The signature, in black paint, appears to have been at some time in the past superimposed on the original paint. Even if it were contemporary with the picture, it would be difficult to accept it as Smibert's. The crudely painted letters *J. S.* are almost illegible and do not appear to be shaped as Smibert shaped them in his authentic signatures, and no other portrait by him is known to have been signed by initials only, rather than *Jo: Smibert*. The date is also difficult to decipher, but is probably correctly read as 1734. Smibert was never in South Carolina, and if Alexander Garden was painted by him Garden must have visited Boston. There appears to be no record of his having done so, although it is possible that Boston was included in his northern itinerary of 1735; and, if he had reached Boston and had been painted before March 25, the portrait might have been dated 1734 (Old Style). The style of painting, however, does not appear to be that of Smibert. For these reasons the attribution to Smibert must, in my opinion, be set aside.

The portrait was purchased from a New York dealer in November 1916 by the late Thomas B. Clarke of New York, and was attributed to Smibert when it passed with his collection to the A. W. Mellon Educational and Charitable Trust, Washington.

MRS. WILLIAM GREENE

This portrait was reproduced as Smibert's in Bayley's *Five Colonial Artists of New England*, p. 393, and was exhibited at the Exhibition of American Portraiture, 1750–1850, Rhode Island School of Design, Providence, December 1936, and at the Corcoran Gallery of Art, Washington, D. C., November 1937–March 1938. It is signed *Jo. Smibert pinx 1734*. The genuineness of the signature, however, appears to be open to question; the pedigree of the portrait has not been disclosed; and the manner of painting is more sophisticated than is usual with Smibert. In my opinion the portrait looks like a rather superior example of English portraiture of the mid-eighteenth century.

JEREMIAH GRIDLEY (SO-CALLED)

Subject: This portrait is said to represent Jeremiah Gridley who was born in Boston March 10, 1705; was graduated from Harvard 1725; colonel in the militia; Grand Master of Masons in North America; Attorney General for the Province 1742–1767; died in Brookline, Mass., September 10, 1767.

Size: H. *c.* 30 in.; W. *c.* 25 in.

Date: Signed, *Jo. Smibert fecit 1731*, in red paint, lower right edge of picture.

Description: The head and bust of the subject are shown against a shaded background above small spandrels in the lower corners, half front, his right shoulder towards the spectator, his head turned to his right nearly full front. He wears a full bob wig, steenkirk tie, and brown coat.

Owner: Harvard University Law School, Cambridge, Mass., to which it was presented in 1928 by the same group of alumni that, about the same time, gave the Law School the portrait of Benjamin Pratt (*q.v.*).

Reproduced: Bayley, p. 395. *Massachusetts Law Quarterly,* vol. XIV, no. 2, p. 42. *Catalogue, Loan Exhibition of One Hundred Colonial Portraits,* Museum of Fine Arts (Boston, 1930), p. 42. F.A.R.L. photo.

Note: The identification of the subject is open to question because no satisfactory pedigree has been provided; he appears to be an older man than Gridley would have been in 1731 (about twenty-six years) and the wig and steenkirk tie suggest an earlier date. The genuineness of the signature is also open to question. It is true that Alan Burroughs (*Art in America,* XXX, 114) says of it, and of the similar signature in red paint on the portrait of William Tailer (*q.v.*), "Since the signature in Gridley's portrait appears to be an integral part of the thin and slightly worn background, both must be considered genuine." A recent technical examination of the signature on the Tailer portrait, however, made by Sheldon Keck of the Brooklyn Museum, led to the conclusion that the signature on that portrait "is definitely later, probably over 150 years later—than the original paint underneath," which by implication invalidates Mr. Burroughs' statement.

In any case I find myself unable to accept Mr. Burroughs' opinion, and question both the identification of the subject and the attribution to Smibert. In my opinion the portrait is probably of English origin.

GOV. JOSEPH JENCKES

Joseph Jenckes (1656–1740) held various offices in Rhode Island, and was governor 1727–1732.

A small portrait (oval, H. 10 in., W. 8 in.) was exhibited at the Pennsylvania Academy of Fine Arts, Philadelphia, in 1926, as a representation of Governor Jenckes, painted by Smibert, and signed *J. Smibert fecit, 1729.*

On the back of the portrait is a piece of old tape on which is written, "Joseph Jenckes, aetatis 73—given by him unto Governor Ward." This picture is said to have descended from Governor Richard Ward of Rhode Island to a Mary S. Ward, and subsequently to have been purchased for the Burlingham collection of early American portraits.

I have not seen this picture and know of it only from reproductions and notes in the Frick Art Reference Library and in the Rhode Island Historical Society's *Collections,* vol. XXVII, no. 3 (July 1934). I, therefore, reserve judgment on it, but, in my present opinion, the alleged pedigree for the portrait is too unreliable to establish the identification of the subject as Governor Jenckes; the manner of painting is not in Smibert's usual style, no other picture by him is known in so small a size, and his customary signature was *Jo: Smibert* rather than with the initial *J*. In the absence of better evidence than I have seen I cannot accept this portrait as either a representation of Governor Jenckes or as the work of Smibert.

LIEUT. GOV. SPENCER PHIPS

This portrait has been supposed to represent Spencer Phips, nephew and heir of Sir William Phips; born at Byfield, Mass., 1685, was graduated from Harvard College in 1703, and was Lieutenant Governor of Massachusetts from 1731 to 1757, in which latter year he died. It is signed *Jo. Smibert fecit 1740*. It has been reproduced as a portrait of Phips by Smibert in Bayley's *Five Colonial Artists of New England*, p. 417, in an article by F. W. Coburn in *Art in America*, vol. XVII, opp. p. 182 (June 1929), as "Spencer Phipps"; and in *Catalogue, Loan Exhibition of One Hundred Colonial Portraits*, Museum of Fine Arts (Boston, 1930), p. 70.

When purchased by the present owner the portrait was accompanied by a pedigree which traced the previous ownership to a Miss Elizabeth Degan, from whom it was said to have been acquired by a dealer. This pedigree is the same as that given for a portrait supposed to represent Sir William Phips, attributed to Thomas Child. The authenticity of the latter portrait, and of the pedigree, is discussed on p. 113 of *XVII*[th] *Century Painting in New England, a Catalogue of an Exhibition Held at the Worcester Art Museum, 1934* (printed 1935). The unsatisfactory character of the pedigree as connected with the portrait of Sir William Phips is there pointed out, and the same applies to the portrait supposed to represent Spencer Phips. The signature is also open to question.

Under these circumstances neither the identification of the subject nor the attribution to Smibert, can, in my opinion, be accepted. The portrait is, perhaps, one of contemporary English origin.

BENJAMIN PRATT (SO-CALLED)

Subject: This portrait is said to represent Benjamin Pratt, who was born at Cohasset, Mass., March 13, 1710; was graduated from Harvard 1737; married Isabella Auchmuty; represented Boston in the General Court; and was Chief Justice of the Supreme Court of New York from 1750 to his death on January 5, 1763.

Size: H. *c.* 30 in.; W. *c.* 25 in.

Date: Signed, lower right, *Jo. Smibert fecit 1741*.

Description: The subject is a rather slender man in middle life, shown within painted spandrels against a dark background, half front, his right shoulder towards the spectator, his head turned right nearly full front. He wears a dark coat, full bob-tailed wig, and long steenkirk tie with fringed ends.

Owner: Harvard University Law School, Cambridge, Mass., to which it was presented in 1748 by the group of alumni who also gave the Law School the portrait of Jeremiah Gridley.

Reproduced: Bayley, p. 419, as a portrait of Pratt by Smibert. *Art in America,* vol. XVII, opp. p. 1182. *Harvard Alumni Bulletin,* vol. XXXI, no. 18 (January 31, 1929). *Massachusetts Law Quarterly* (September 1930). Townsend, *The Auchmuty Family* (1932), p. 26. F.A.R.I. photo.

Note: A label on the back reads: "Chief Justice Benjamin Pratt, Property of Dr. Samuel Auchmuty, Rector of Trinity Church; left in my care, Lambert Moore, Clerk of Trinity." Samuel Auchmuty, of Trinity Church, New York, was Pratt's brother-in-law. This label, if genuine, would provide satisfactory identification of the subject, but it is open to question in the absence of other evidence. In my opinion, therefore, the identification of the subject is doubtful. He is shown as an older man than Pratt would have been in 1741 (thirty-one years of age), and he wears a wig and tie in fashion two decades earlier. Nor is the manner of painting characteristic of Smibert. The signature is also questionable. The Conservation Department of the Fogg Art Museum, Harvard University, says of it, "The paint of the signature covers the crackle and the abrasion of the gray background, which can be seen through the transparent resinous paint of the signature, and this would indicate that the signature is of later date than the painting." They believe it to be an English portrait of the early eighteenth century, by an unidentified artist, and in that opinion I concur.

JOHN READ

A portrait supposed to represent John Read who was born 1680, graduated from Harvard 1697, was admitted to the bar 1708, became attorney general, and died 1751, is owned by the Addison Gallery, Andover, Mass. It is signed *Jno. Smibert fecit 1738,* and has been reproduced as his work in *Creative Art,* vol. XI, no. 1 (July 1931); in the *Catalogue of the Permanent Collections,* Addison Gallery of American Art (1931); in Sibley's *Harvard Graduates,* IV, 370; and in the *Massachusetts Law Quarterly,* vols. XVI (1930), XXII (1937). It is also listed in *P. F. Mass.* The signature, however, appears to have been superimposed on the original paint, and, in my opinion, cannot be accepted as genuine; the portrait does not look much like Smibert's work; and the pedigree given for the portrait is not satisfactory. I, therefore, find it impossible to accept either the identification of the subject or the attribution of the portrait to Smibert.

Owner: The Addison Gallery, Andover, Mass., purchased in 1930 from Frank W. Bayley. The American Antiquarian Society, Worcester, Mass., owns what is described as a copy of a letter written by Bayley to Mrs. R. M. DeForest of New York, reading in part: "February 7, 1930 . . . I have today sold the Smibert portrait of John Reed [*sic*] for your account." The portrait is not now exhibited as representing John Read or as the work of Smibert.

Exhibited: Yale University Art Gallery, "The Smibert Tradition," exhibition, October–November 1949 (for purposes of comparison).

GOV. WILLIAM SHIRLEY (SO-CALLED)

This portrait, supposed to represent Gov. William Shirley, shows the head and bust of a middle-aged man wearing a large brown wig, a white shirt with steenkirk tie, and a red robe. The costume is that prevalent about the end of the seventeenth and the beginning of the eighteenth century, many years earlier than the period from which the portrait is supposed to come. The portrait is signed *Jo. Smibert ft Ao 174[8?]* in black script on the right side of the picture abreast of the shoulder. The signature resembles those by Smibert known to be authentic and does not appear to have been recently added to the portrait, but it is difficult to reconcile the signature and date with the period represented by the subject's costume.

Shirley was born in England in 1693; came to Boston in 1734; and was governor from 1741 to 1745. He lived in Boston at various periods thereafter, and died in Roxbury in 1771. Smibert painted a portrait of him after his return from the siege of Louisburg in 1745, from which Pelham made a mezzotint in 1747 (see Section B). The portrait from which Pelham made the mezzotint cannot now be located, but it was not the picture in question, since it represents Shirley at three-quarter length, out-of-doors, in a quite different costume, and the face shown in the engraving is not that of the man in the portrait under discussion.

This portrait was bought by the late Thomas B. Clarke of New York and passed with his collection into the hands of the A. W. Mellon Educational and Charitable Trust, Washington, D. C. When Mr. Clarke purchased it, it was accompanied by an unsigned handwritten memorandum stating that it came from Shirley's descendants. A typewritten pedigree also accompanied the picture, but its accuracy is open to question. In view of the lack of resemblance of the subject to the representation of Shirley in Pelham's mezzotint, and to the discrepancy of a quarter of a century or more between the date of the costume and the supposed date of the portrait, the identification of the subject with Shirley is very difficult to sustain. In my opinion the portrait is probably an English picture of the period of Sir Godfrey Kneller, to which the signature and date have been added at some time in the past. It was exhibited as a portrait of Shirley by Smibert at the Philadelphia Museum of Art, 1928, and at the San Francisco Fair, 1939.

LIEUT. GOV. WILLIAM TAILER (SO-CALLED)

This portrait is reputed to represent William Tailer (1676–1732) who was Lieutenant-Governor of Massachusetts in 1711, and again in 1730, and has been reproduced as by John Smibert in Bayley's *Six Colonial Governors of Massachusetts* (n.d.) and *Five Colonial Artists of*

New England, p. 429, and in *Catalogue, Loan Exhibition of One Hundred Colonial Portraits*, Museum of Fine Arts (Boston, 1930), p. 87. It has been repeatedly exhibited elsewhere. It is signed *Jo. Smibert, pinx, 1730*, in red letters under the edge of the table at the left side of the picture. Alan Burroughs in *Art in America*, XXX, 114, says of the signature, and the very similar one on the portrait of Jeremiah Gridley (1731; *q.v.*), "Since the signature on Gridley's portrait appears to be an integral part of the thin and slightly worn background, both must be considered genuine." I disagree with that opinion. Smibert did not sign in that way any portrait which can unquestionably be attributed to him, and the signature on this portrait alleged to represent Tailer appears to have been superimposed on the original paint, and then rubbed down to remove the appearance of newness. Sheldon Keck of the Brooklyn Museum concludes his report of a recent technical examination of the signature with the statement that the signature "is definitely later, probably over 150 years later—than the original paint underneath." In my opinion the portrait does not represent William Tailer, and is probably of much more recent origin, the work of a painter very skilful in imitating the style of the middle of the eighteenth century.

Exhibited: (for purpose of comparison with Smibert's work) Yale University Art Gallery, October–November 1949.

JOHN TAYLOR

A photograph of this picture of a boy with a deer is included with photographs of portraits by Smibert at the Frick Art Reference Library in New York, and the original is said to be signed *Smibert, 1743*. The subject is said to be John Taylor, born in Bath, England, in 1738, died 1806. Labels read, "John Taylor, Esq. grandfather of Dr. Taylor Gordon," and "This picture was presented as a gift to Gordon Stonehouse Hughes by his grandfather, Dr. Taylor Gordon." It was purchased by the Ehrich Galleries, New York, 1921, and was sold to the Sears Academy of Fine Arts, Elgin, Illinois, December 12, 1922. I have not seen the original picture but the whole manner of painting is so different from Smibert's that, in spite of the signature, I cannot accept the painting as his. In my opinion it is by another hand.

OXENBRIDGE THACHER

This portrait has been exhibited as representing Oxenbridge Thacher II by Smibert at the Exhibition of American Paintings, San Francisco, June–July 1935; at the Union League, New York, January 1937; at the National Gallery of Art, Washington, 1941, and elsewhere. It has been reproduced in *Art News* (July 12, 1930); *International Studio* (August 1930); and *Antiques* (September 1930); and was referred to by William Sawitzky in the New York Historical Society's *Bulletin*, vol. XVIII, no. 2, p. 33 (July 1934).

It is signed and dated *Jo. Smibert fecit 1731*. The genuineness of the signature, however, appears to be open to question, and the pedigree of the portrait, except in its opening stages, is the same as that given for the portraits said to represent Jeremiah Dummer and his wife, as recorded and discussed in *XVIIth Century Painting in New England, a Catalogue of an Exhibition Held at the Worcester Art Museum, July and August, 1934* (printed 1935), p. 72. The reasons there stated for regarding the pedigree as unsatisfactory in the case of the alleged Dummer portraits apply equally to this portrait supposed to represent Oxenbridge Thacher. Therefore both the identification of the subject and the attribution to Smibert must, in my opinion, be rejected.

LADY WARREN (SO-CALLED)

Among the pictures in the collection of American portraits made by the late Thomas B. Clarke of New York, now the property of the A. W. Mellon Educational and Charitable Trust, Washington, D. C., is a portrait said to represent Susannah De Lancy, wife of Sir Peter Warren. It is signed and dated: *Jo. Smibert, fecit 1746.* The picture dates from the period when Smibert painted, but is not particularly characteristic of his work. The identity of the subject is open to question, owing to the unsatisfactory character of the pedigree furnished for the picture in a handwritten memorandum signed with a signature reading "R. M. de Forest" and dated July 1, 1924, presumably at the time that Mr. Clarke purchased the portrait. It has not proved possible to verify the accuracy of this pedigree. Furthermore, the signature on the portrait clearly appears to have been superimposed on the original paint. The picture, therefore, cannot, in my opinion, be accepted either as a representation of Lady Warren or as an authentic painting by Smibert, although it has been exhibited as such at the Century Association in New York, 1925, and at the Inaugural Exhibition, Philadelphia Museum of Art, 1928.

Appendices

APPENDIX 1

The Dates of John Smibert's Birth and Death as Recorded in his Epitaph.
Most of the biographical dictionaries give 1684 as the year of John
Smibert's birth, an error which goes back to Walpole's *Anecdotes of
Painting in England*, and until very recently all notices of him in which
the year 1688 is correctly given have been incorrect as to the day or
month. The dates for his birth, marriage, and death are, however, to be
found in the draft of a Latin epitaph for the gravestone which his widow
proposed to erect over his grave in Boston. Copies of this epitaph are
in the British Museum (Add. Mss. 23,275, fol. 49–50) and in the Chamberlain Collection, Boston Public Library, and the entire epitaph is
printed in the *Proceedings* of the Massachusetts Historical Society,
XXXXIX, 39, in Worthington Chauncey Ford's article on "The Smibert-Moffatt Letters." An English translation will be found in Chapter
VIII. The original Latin is as follows:

EPITAPH

Quis Desiderio sit Pudor, aut modus
Tam Chari Capitis?   Hor:

In Tumulo hocce contiguo Conditur quicquid caducum et mortale
habuit, Vir Optimus Joannes Smibert Pictor celeberrimus cujus in Arte
sua Laudes debitas, etiam Italia, picturae alma Nutrix, olim agnovit.
In Brittania vero, Superiorem haud temere invenies, Æquales minime
multos. Quin mirum, igitur, si in America, quam, Salutis gratia, Natali
praetulit solo, ne vel Æmulum invenit aut reliquit: Quorum argumenta
diutina, ex Sententia optimorum Judicum, Imagines plurimae, multa cum
Arte et Scientia, Manu sua eleganter depictae.
Sed quanta quanta sit haec Laus, opposita tamen Moribus suis eximiis,
prope nulla est. In his enim colendis maxime studium Operamque foeli-
citer collocavit, Qui in omni Vitae Statu verae et infucatae Virtutis
Examplar editit. Hominum nempe, Communitatis, Membrum inprimis
dignum, si quidem hoc efficitur, Vitae, Solertiâ Integritate immaculatâ,
Indole placidâ, benignâ et humanâ unà cum Morum Facilitate et Sim-
plicitate jucundâ atque ingenuâ. Maritus, Parens, amantissimus; officiorum
in suos quosque Observantissimus; Amicus, porro, sincere Benevolus,
Fidus, Constans, Coronidis denique loco, Is, cujus universa Vita praedi-
cabat. Animum intime imbutum Reverentia et Charitate in DEUM O.M.
Cujus Cultur assiduus devotissimusque extitit, nec non Vera Fide et Spe

Vivida in Christum Jesum: Quibus Animam piam Suffultus, Deo, qui dedit, Tranquillus et Laetus, reddidit, IV° Non: Aprilis, Anno Ærae Christianae Vulgaris M, DCC, LI.

Natus erat Edinburgi Britannorum Septentrionalium IX° Kal. Aprilis Anno M, DC, LXXX, VIII, Parentibus honestis Oriundus. Uxorem, quam charam semper habuit, utpote vere piam et amandam, nunc, proh dolor! viduam maerentem, duxit III°. Kal. Augusti, Anno M, DCC, XXX, Mariam, Filiam natu maximam Reverendi Doctique Viri, olim Vita functi, Nathanaelis Williams, Bostoniensis: Cujus Conjugii Proventus Septem Filii, duaequae Filiae, quorum Filii quatuor, duaeque Filiae, in eodem cum Patre requiescunt Tumulo; Caeteri Supersunt.

Lector, si Talem amare et imitari possis, Beatus evades.

It will be noted that this epitaph says: *Natus erat Edinburgi . . . IX° Kal. Aprilis Anno M, DC, LXX, VIII . . . duxit III° Kal. Augusti, Anno M, DCC, XXX, Mariam Filiam . . . Nathanaelis Williams . . . Animam . . . Deo reddidit IV° Non. Aprilis, Anno . . . M, DCC, LI.*

Mr. Ford did not translate these dates from the Roman calendar into the English, and it apparently occurred to no one else to do so until Mr. Charles K. Bolton printed a note on "John Smibert's Date of Birth" in the *New England Quarterly*, vol. XII, no. 2 (June 1939), pp. 375–376. In his note Mr. Bolton states that, while he was puzzling over them, Mrs. Claude A. Pifer referred him to a table for making such transference of dates. Taking first the date of Smibert's death, it worked out to April 2, 1751, which is confirmed by three contemporary newspapers. The date of marriage worked out to July 30, 1730, as given in the twenty-eighth volume of the *Boston Record Commission Report*. The same method, applied to the date of birth, becomes March 24, 1688. This fits with the child's baptism on April 1, when eight days old. Mr. Bolton, however, does not note the curious fact that the date of birth is given New Style while those of marriage and death are Old Style: the explanation is that in Scotland the New Style calendar was adopted in 1600, whereas in England and the colonies it was not adopted until 1752.

APPENDIX 2

Note on Dr. Williams Smibert.

The eldest son of John and Mary Smibert is recorded in the printed *Report of the Records Commissioners of the City of Boston* as William, born January 29, 1732/3. Since in later life he was known as Williams, he was presumably given his mother's family name in baptism, and either the original recorder or a later copyist made the natural error of dropping the final *s*.

After serving an apprenticeship with a merchant he took up the study of medicine, which had been one of the several activities followed by his maternal grandfather. He entered Master Lovell's Grammar School in 1743, but did not go to Harvard. Sometime in the seventeen-fifties he went to Edinburgh, where he had numerous relatives to welcome him, and in 1762 he took the degree of Doctor of Medicine at the University of Edinburgh, being recorded as "Williams Smibert, Massachusetensis."[1] He submitted for his degree a thesis written in Latin, *Dissertatio Medica Inauguralis de Menstruis Retentis*, of which a printed copy is in the library of the College of Physicians in Philadelphia. The title page of this dissertation is as follows:

DISSERTATIO MEDICA

INAUGURALIS

DE

MENSTRUIS RETENTIS:

QUAM,

ANNUENTE SUMMO NUMINE,

ACADEMIAE EDINBURGENAE PRAEFECTI;

NEC NON

AMPLISSIMI SENATUS ACADEMICI CONSENSU,

ET NOBILISSIMAE FACULTATIS MEDICAE DECRETO:

PRO GRADU DOCTORATUS,

SUMMISQUE IN MEDICINA HONORIBUS ET PRIVILEGIIS

RITE ET LEGITIME CONSEQUENDIS,

[1] *List of the Graduates in Medicine of the University of Edinburgh from MDCCV to MDCCCLXVI.* Dr. Thomas Bulfinch of Boston, the second of that name, had taken the same degree at Edinburgh in 1757, probably the first man from New England and perhaps the first in the American colonies to do so. He had returned to his native Boston to practice medicine and may well have been one of the influences which led Williams Smibert to follow the same path.

ERUDITORUM EXAMINI SUBJICIT
WILLIAMS SMIBERT
MASSACHUSETENSIS IN NOVA ANGLIA.
AD DIEM 25 OCTOBRIS, HORA DUODECIMA MERDIANA.
MISERA PROFECTO, ET INIQUA FOEMINARUM CONDITIO, UT, QUAE HUMANI
GENERIS CONSERVATRICES, A NATURA, DESTINATAE SINT, EAEDEM, MORBIS
MAXIME OBNOXIAE, EFFINGERENTUR.
EDINBURGI:
APUD HAMILTON, BALFOUR, & NEILL,
M,DCC,LXII.

This dissertation runs to forty-two pages, and contains a quotation from Martial and a reference to "my friend, John Morgan of Philadelphia, who is diligently pursuing his studies in this school and who has related to me a case singularly worth remembering." The dissertation is also of interest for the light it throws upon his relations with John Moffatt, his father's associate in the "colour shop" in Boston, and with Dr. Thomas Moffatt of Newport. It will be remembered that these Moffatts were sons of Alison, John Smibert's older sister for whom he named his own first-born child. They were therefore Williams Smibert's first cousins, although Thomas was at least thirty years and John at least twenty-five years older than he was. The dedication, which is as follows, is a grateful recognition of what they had done for him, pointing out that John had been as a father to him after his own father's death.

AMICO SUO INTEGERRIMO,
CONSOBRINO AMANTISSIMO,
JOANNI MOFFATT,
VIRO, NON TITULIS, SED VIRTUTE, ORNATISSIMO:
QUI, EXTINCTO PATRE, PATERNO VERE ANIMO,
SE SUAQUE,
A PUERILIBUS ANNIS, CURAVIT, FOVIT, CUSTODIVIT:
NEC NON,
FRATRI EJUSDEM,
VIRO SPECTABILI, ERUDITISSIMO,
THOMAE MOFFATT, M. D.
STUDIORUM SUORUM RECTORI INCORRUPTISSIMO,
FAUTORI BENIGNISSIMO,
MAXIMORUM BENEFIFIORUM MEMOR:
HUNC PRIMUM LITERARUM LABOREM,
PRO DEBITA UTRIQUE PIETATE
DICATUM VOLUIT
WILLIAMS SMIBERT

After his graduation at Edinburgh in the fall of 1762 Williams Smibert returned to Boston and set up practice in the house in which he had been born, which still contained his father's art collection and the "colour shop" run by John Moffatt. He lived there, the last surviving child of Mary and John Smibert, until his death shortly before the Revolution, and he bequeathed the property to John Moffatt. Neither man is recorded as having married.

The only item which has come to light which gives any information about this later period of his life is a letter from him to the same John Morgan of Philadelphia[2] to whom he referred in his dissertation. It was found in the correspondence of Dr. Morgan which had been given to the Library of the College of Physicians in Philadelphia, and has been printed, with notes, in the *Annals of Medical History*.[3] It runs as follows:

My friend Mr. Marshall has just sent me word he sets out for Philadelphia at 11 o'clock, it is now 10—a warning so short allows me time just to salute you, to inquire after your health & welfare, and to assure you that tho' I am a negligent correspondent, I am not a forgetful friend—how are you going on at Philadelphia? does the number of your students increase? do they yet begin to see their former errors & relish the regular attainment of Science? did I not know their motives & strange infatuation I should be amazed at their not taking the only advantage they have in America, & send their sons from hence to your college, rather than train them up in ignorance and presumption—but this will ever be the case while they are taught to believe compleat medical knowledge is to be acquired in a few months under the tuition of a retailer of drugs[4]—Martial [*sic*] will give you an account of them— Has any new medical publication appeared among you that is ingenious and clever—have you seen Alexander's Essays on the external application of Antiseptics in putrid diseases, on the doses and effects of medicines, and Diuretics & Sudorifics[5]—I am pleased & edified by them—his manner of writing is pretty, & the choice of his subjects interesting— get the book, if—[top of sheet torn off]—it—There is one Smith [several words removed by tear referred to above] one half is taken up in

[2] Dr. John Morgan, 1735–1789, a distinguished physician. He was Medical Director of the Continental Army and founder of what is now the Medical School of the University of Pennsylvania. A portrait of him by T. S. Duché is in the Historical Society of Pennsylvania.
[3] "A letter from Dr. Williams Smibert, of Boston, to his former fellow-student at Edinburgh, Dr. John Morgan of Philadelphia, written February 14, 1769," by W. B. McDaniel, 2ᵈ, *Annals of Medical History*, 3ᵈ Ser., vol. I, no. 2 (March 1939), pp. 194–196.
[4] Footnote by McDaniel (see note 3, above): "One suspects that Smibert may have had in mind here his elder colleague Silvester Gardiner. Viets, *A Brief History of Medicine in Massachusetts*, says that Gardiner, who was the proprietor of several very profitable apothecary shops, 'was not quite so much a physician as he was a business man'. But the practice of which Smibert complains was of long standing, of course, and nearer the rule than the exception."
[5] Footnote by McDaniel: "Alexander William. *Experimental Essays on the Following Subjects: 1. On the External Application of Antiseptics in Putrid Diseases, etc.* London, 1768."

metaphysical disquisitions to very little purpose, and the substance of the other half is borrowed chiefly from Dr. Whytt [6]—was time allowed me I could name others—as to the news or politicks of this place, I know nothing about them, my being so connected with both parties renders it impolitic in me to declare my sentiments on one side or the other, I therefore slide silently between them with [-out] offending either, wishing sincerely for perfect unanimity & brotherly love—pray make my compliments to Mrs. Morgan, to the Batchellor Lunen (if he still remains so) and to Shippen—Let me hear from you by Marshalls return, and believe, that notwithstanding my long and faulty silence that I am still your friend & very humble servant.

W Smibert

Boston 14 Feby 1769—Thermometer now at 10—

This letter suggests that Williams Smibert inherited some of his father's characteristics; that he was a quiet person, averse to professional wire-pulling and uninterested in the heated political controversies of the time—and a poor correspondent. In his will, dated January 17, 1770, he calls himself a "Doctor in Physic" and directs that his body is

to be placed in the Family Tomb with my Parents & their Offspring, being the last that survived them. With regard to my worldly goods & Estate, all my Real Estate viz Houses and lands in Queen Street, Lot of land in New Boston, Hill in Roxbury which my Father purchased of Daniel Whitney, also the whole of my Personal Estate I hereby devise and bequeath unto my Cousin Mr John Moffatt of Boston, Painter, in gratitude to him for that uncommon Friendship and truly Paternal Affection he has shown towards me throughout the whole of my life.

He appointed Moffatt as executor, and the will was witnessed by John Ewing, Jr., Thomas Walley, and Thomas Russell. The date of his death is not recorded but it must have occurred early in 1774, for papers of administration for the "Estate of Williams Smibert, of Boston, Physician" were granted on January 28 of that year.[7]

[6] Footnote by McDaniel: "It is probable that both Smibert and Morgan studied under Dr. Robert Whytt at Edinburgh."
[7] Probate Court Records (Middlesex County, Mass.), 73, 382–384.

APPENDIX 3

John Moffatt's Will and Inventory of Estate.

Williams Smibert at his death in 1774 bequeathed all his property to his much older cousin John Moffatt. Moffatt died, probably past seventy years of age, between July 9, 1777, the date of his will, and November 21, 1777, when it was probated. He describes himself as "John Moffatt of Boston in the County of Suffolk and the State of Massachusetts Bay, Painter," says that he is "weak and infirm of body" and indicates that he had left his own house to be cared for in his last illness by Mrs. Suriah Waite. The important items in the will are as follows:

Item. I hereby manumit, liberate and set free my Negro man Lincoln. I also give, devise & bequeath unto the said Lincoln Fifty Acres of Land in Ashburnham (to be taken out of my Lands there at the Discretion of my Executor) to be holden by him his Heirs & Assigns forever.

Item. I give unto Mʳˢ Suriah Waite of Boston aforesaid Widow, all such of my Household Furniture, as I brought with me to her House, & which she is now in the Possession of in Token of my Esteem & Respect for her.

Item. I give unto Belcher Noyes of said Boston Esqʳ, whom I have appointed Executor of this my Will, the Sum of Fifty Pounds for his trouble in executing the same.

Item. All the Rest and Residue of my Estate both Real Personal and mixt, whatsoever & wheresoever the same is, shall or may be found, I give, devise & bequeath unto my Brother Thomas Moffatt, if he shall return to Boston within three years after my Decease . . . But in Case my said Brother Thomas Moffatt should not return to Boston within three years of my decease Then & in That case I give devise & bequeath . . . same . . . unto my good Friend the said Suriah Waite.

Since Thomas Moffatt, then an old man of seventy-five years living in London, never returned to America, the property passed in due course to Suriah Waite, who by that time had become Suriah Thayer.

Belcher Noyes, as executor, in September 1779 filed an inventory of Moffatt's estate which is now almost illegible, but in which, in addition to the usual household articles, the following items appear:

1 large double House with out-houses, Queen Street, Boston . . . . £2500.
1 Lott of Land—W. Boston . . . . . . 30.
Fourteen Acres of land Roxbury . . . . . 400.
Library . . . . 71.
Twenty-two Past board books with Various Drawings . 49.13.1
Six large Pictures . . . . £ 40.
Twenty (?) Ditto smaller sorts . . . . . . [illegible]
Pictures from [illegible] to 64 . . . . . . [illegible]
A parcel of Heads etc. in Plaister of Paris . . . . 4.

This list would indicate that a large part of Smibert's art collection, if not its entirety, was still in the house, but adds nothing to our knowledge of its contents.

On September 22, 1785, Noyes filed an Executor's Account, in which it appears that the estate included lands in Ashburnham and Williamstown, Mass., on which he had paid taxes; that he had paid the Negro Lincoln £18.18.0, perhaps in lieu of the fifty acres of land bequeathed him; and that the house on Queen Street had been rented, for under "rent received for the Mansion House," beginning March 31, 1779, appear the names of a number of short-term tenants, including:

of John Trumbull for the Chamber to Nov. 16, 1779,
In Old Emission Currency, £61.6
of Mather Brown the Upper Chamber to Feb. 16, 1780   £ 8.14 [1]

[1] For Moffatt's will see Suffolk County Probate Court, LXXVI, 518–520; for inventory, LXXVIII, 418–420; for Executor's Account, LXXXIV, 554–558.

APPENDIX 4

Notes on Nathaniel Smibert and Catalogue of Portraits Attributed to Him.

Nathaniel, the third son of Mary and John Smibert, was born in Boston, January 20, 1734/35, and died there November 3, 1756. The only known reference to him during his lifetime is found in his cousin John Moffatt's letter to Arthur Pond, dated December 28, 1752 (see p. 104), in which Moffatt reports that Smibert left three sons of whom "the Second [1] inclines to Painting & seems to me of a Promising Genius." All our other information regarding Nathaniel Smibert, aside from the portraits which he left, is derived from obituary notices in the Boston papers, from a Latin elegy on him, from a letter written by him to Peter Harrison in July 1756, and from an account of him in a letter written by Judge Cranch more than half a century after Nathaniel's death.

In the *Boston Gazette* for Monday, November 8, 1756, appeared a twenty-eight-line obituary reading:

Last Wednesday in the Afternoon, died here, after a short illness, in the 22[d] Year of his Age, Mr. NATHANIEL SMIBERT, second Son to the late Mr. *John Smibert,* of this Town: He was a young Gentleman possessed of all those amiable Qualifications that endear or sweeten Life: From his Cradle, he wore the Marks of unaffected Virtue and Goodness; and thro' the whole Course of his Life, exhibited the most unexceptionable Pattern of filial Piety: In his Duty towards GOD, he was constant and devout; in his Opinions of Religion, modest; and in his Searches after Truth, indefatigable: His Manners were soft and engaging; his Friendship sincere; his Affections kind; and his Conversation lovely: He had the highest Reverence for Virtue, tho' in Want and Rags; and a Soul nobly disposed to relieve the Distresses of the Poor. His scholastic Acquirements were no less great, than his natural Endowments of Mind: For tho' *Painting* was his peculiar Profession; yet he was more or less acquainted with almost every Science: and had Heaven permitted him Life, seemed capable of improving himself in Art: His Constitution being naturally tender and delicate, subjected him to a Thousand Infirmities; all which he bore with the same Tranquility and Patience, as at his Maker's Fiat he resigned up Life. Happy they have called him Son! Happy the Youth that shall copy his Example! .... His Remains are to be inter'd this Evening.

[1] As the brother who came between Williams and Nathaniel Smibert had died young, Nathaniel, at the time of writing, was his father's second surviving son.

In the *Boston News-Letter* of November 11, 1756, is a similar notice:

NATHANIEL SMIBERT.—On Wednesday last departed This Life after a short Illness, and last Evening was decently inter'd, Mr. NATHANIEL SMIBERT, in the 22ⁿᵈ Year of his Age. He was the second Son of the late Mr. *John Smibert*, Painter, in which Business he succeeded his Father, and bad fair to equal him in his justly admired Skill. The amiable qualifications of this lately esteemed, and now, much lamented Youth, are more than can conveniently or prudently be mentioned on this Occasion. . . . His natural Ingenuity was remarkably promising, and though he had not the Advantage of an Academical Education, yet he had made such Progress in the dead and living Languages, and in many of the Arts & Sciences, as would be esteemed to deserve the Honours . . . . He had no Relish for the Scenes of high Mirth and Gaiety, but chose those Pastimes which improve the Thought and left an Agreeable Reflection.

Six months later, May 2, 1757, the *Gazette* published a Latin elegy with the heading

NATHANIEL SMIBERT—The following wrote to a Friend of the person so justly celebrated, would have been made Public sooner, had the author permitted it: yet 'tis hoped the Merit and Memory of the deceased, will sufficiently atone for its Appearance now.

The elegy was also printed in an octavo four-page leaflet, without the introductory note and with certain typographical errors in the *Gazette* corrected, under the title

In obitum magnae spei juvenis
Nathanaelis Smiberti,
Hartford, Connecticutensium, 1757
Jo. Beveridge.

The author, John Beveridge, was a Scot who had taught in Edinburgh, had emigrated to New England in 1752, and had taught for five years in Boston before moving to Hartford, and later to Philadelphia, where he died in 1767. In 1765 William Bradford, of the last-named town, published Beveridge's *Epistolae Familiares et Alia quandum Miscellanea*, on the title page of which Beveridge describes himself as "Professor of Languages in the Academy of Philadelphia." Beveridge evidently had a faculty for turning out Latin verse for his collection includes more than forty poems addressed to various friends, among them John Lovell, the Boston schoolmaster under whom he had served, Rev. Jonathan Mayhew, Governor Shirley, and other Bostonians. The elegy on Nathaniel Smibert is included in this volume and the "Friend" to whom it was "wrote" is indicated in the address "Ad Sam. Quincaeum, M.A." (Samuel Quincy). The poem is as follows:

O Quem futurum pectore finxeram,
Nuper peremptum funere lugubri
Natum, cecidit quem dolosa,
Dextera nil miserantis Indi! [2]

Eheu! dolores quot mihi concitat?
Longinqua quos non imminuat dies.
Sed quid querelas fundo vanas?
Sic voluit Pater ille Summus.

Ferale sedquit mens iterum mihi
Praesagit? Aut quis Jam gemitus meas
Invadit aures? cui paravit
Exsequias Libitina tristes?

Magni Parentis progenies bona
Effertur, olim te tibi Charior,
*******, Smibertus beata
Elysios petit umbra Campos.

Spectandus, (eheu!) nunquam alias mihi
Plorandus autem flebilibus modis.
Ignosce, quaeso, fas amici
Imbre pio cineres rigare.

En cerno quanto vividus impetu,
Praerupta Pindi culmina scanderet!
Et arte quâ plectrum moveret,
Cum caneret fidibus canoris.

En picta vivis tela coloribus,
Fatetur ipsam pendula Imaginem
Quumcunque tentaret peritus
Lina suis animare fucis!

Hunc nuda virtus, hunc fidei pius
Ornavit ardor, sanctaq [ue] veritas,
Pudorque. Spes nostras caducas,
O dubias, facilesque tolli!

Non hunc Juventas, non animi vigor,
Non ars Medentûm, vota nec omnuim
Sincera, non artes Minervae
Expediunt Acherontis undis.

[2] "The Author had an only Son not long since killed by the Indians."

At tanta vis mî si foret enthea,
Aut so modorum, si Citharae sciens
Essemve, virtutes in altum
Non humili eveherum Camoena.

Sed quid? Lupinos, purpureas rosas,
Calthasve quamvis bruma necaverit,
At vere vitales sequente
Depositos revocant honores

Sic sic caducos nos licet occupet
Vis dura fati, mox renovabimur
Et busta spernemus beati
Nonquam iterum posituri honores.

Haec quum profarer, vellere visus est
Smibertus aurem, talibus admonens:
Insane, caelestes voluptas
Nulla capit peritura mentes:

Ut nec dolores, qui miseros viros
Vexant acerbi; define mollium
Ergo querelarum; precabar
Magna prius, meliora dantur.

Vitae perennis Gaudia me manent
Aeterna, spes & fallere nescia:
Fatoq [ue] major, per omne
Sacra TRIAS reparabit oevum.

Quin sacra Patri, sacraq [ue] Filio,
Sanctoq [ue] pangas Carmina Flamina,
Qui me redemptum sempiternae
Faucibus eripuere mortis.

JOHN BEVERIDGE. Hartford, Connecticutensium, 1757.

Beveridge may have had Nathaniel Smibert as a pupil, though it is more probable that he had known him as the friend of the son whom he laments, but it is evident that Nathaniel had impressed him as an attractive and promising youth. Unfortunately his elegy tells us very little about its subject. From the first stanza we learn that the author himself had recently lost a son killed by the Indians, and now, he says (stanza 4), "Smibert, the promising offspring of a distinguished parent, once dearer to you than your own self, is taken away." Stanza 6 recalls "with what great power he scaled the rugged heights of Pindus," which

NATHANIEL SMIBERT

presumably refers to his talent as a painter, "and with what skill he employed the plectrum when he sang with the melodious lyre," which indicates that he was fond of music, as his father had been. Stanza 7 bids us "See, the canvas hanging there, painted with brilliant colors, speaks forth his very image when, in skilful manner, he sought to enliven the linen with his own features," which clearly indicates that Nathaniel had painted a self-portrait which Beveridge had seen. The remainder of the poem consists of conventional classical exclamations of grief and of pious meditations on the joy of the redeemed in heaven.

Making due allowance for the eulogistic quality of obituary notices and elegies it seems clear that Nathaniel was an amiable youth of quiet disposition, and the few portraits which can definitely be assigned to him are creditable pieces of work for one so young. That he ever painted any portraits would doubtless have been long since forgotten had not a letter, written more than half a century after Nathaniel's death by Judge William Cranch of Washington to William Dunlap, led the latter to include his name in his *History of the . . . Arts of Design in the United States*, published in 1834. Judge Cranch wrote:

There was a young painter in Boston, the particular friend of my father, about the year 1755, whose name should not be omitted in the list of American artists, as he bid fair to be one of the first of the age. His name was Nathaniel Smibert. I have an original letter of friendship from him to my father (the late Judge [Richard] Cranch [1726–1811] of Quincy, in Mass.), dated 'Boston, August 5, 1755,' and a copy of my father's answer, in which he says, 'When I consider the ease with which your hand improves the beauty of the fairest form, and adds new charms to the most angelic face, I do not wonder that your riper imagination should fly beyond your pencil, and draw the internal picture of your friend so much fairer than the original.'

In a letter from my father to the late Dr. John Eliot, of Boston, dated 'Quincy, July 20th, 1809' he says, 'Mr. Nathaniel Smibert, whom you mention, was one of the most amiable youths I was ever acquainted with: *but he came forth as a flower and was cut down.* I cannot now, after an interval of more than fifty years, recollect the time of his birth or his death. I remember that Mr. Peter Chardon, who took his degree in 1757, was then one of our acquaintance: and I think Mr. Smibert died about that time. I do not recollect that he left any writings. He received his grammar instruction under the famous master John Lovell but did not proceed to a collegiate education. He engaged in his father's profession of painting, in which he emulated the excellencies of the best masters; and had his life been spared he would probably have been, in his day, what Copley and West have since been, *the honor of America in the imitative art.* I remember that one of his first portraits was the picture of his old Master Lovell, drawn while the terrific impressions of the pedagogue were still vibrating on his nerves. I found it so perfect a likeness of my old neighbor that I did not wonder when my young friend told me that a sudden undesigned glance at it had often made him shudder.'[3]

Nathaniel did, in fact, enter the grammar school in 1744, probably graduated in 1750, and painted the portrait of Lovell within a year or two, when he was about seventeen years old. John Moffatt's statement in the letter quoted on p. 104 indicates that Nathaniel had begun painting at about that age and it is reasonable to assume that John Smibert had awakened his son's interest in art still earlier and had given him instruction. John Smibert's friend and near neighbor, Peter Pelham, though he survived Smibert by only eight months, could have given Nathaniel some pointers about both painting and engraving. Pelham's stepson, John Singleton Copley, was three and a half years younger than Nathaniel, but in view of his precocious interest in art, Dunlap had some grounds for saying that, "It is further, very probable, that Copley was the companion, the friend or the fellow-student of the younger Smibert."

The questionable part of Dunlap's statement is contained in the words "fellow-student." Nathaniel Smibert must have been well ahead of Copley in Master Lovell's grammar school, neither youth entered Harvard College, and if Dunlap meant "fellow-student in art," we are led to ask under whom they could have studied in Boston after the death of John Smibert and Peter Pelham. Both youths must have looked carefully at the score and more of portraits painted by Robert Feke during his prolonged second visit to Boston in 1748, which represented the latest fashion in art, and they must both, as boys, have had a speaking acquaintance with him. Aside from Feke's professional interest in painting, in common with Smibert and Pelham, it is certain that he was acquainted in Newport with Dr. Thomas Moffatt, Smibert's nephew and the brother of his business associate, John Moffatt, and that he frequented Smibert's home in Boston during his visits of 1741 and 1748. It is wholly improbable that Feke would not also have seen something of Peter Pelham, the stepfather of Copley. But Feke, though he clearly influenced some of the earliest portraits by Copley, as he did those by John Greenwood, could hardly have given any of these youngsters any formal instruction.

The only other painters working in Boston in the later seventeen-forties and until Blackburn's arrival about 1754, were Joseph Badger, the house painter, who executed crude though often vigorous portraits, and young Greenwood, who was only a little more than five years older than Nathaniel and who went to Surinam in 1752, and never returned to Boston. Badger may be dismissed from consideration,[4] but the portrait of Edward Bromfield, Jr., formerly attributed to John Smibert but now

[3] Dunlap (ed. of 1918), I, 28–29.
[4] Lawrence Park, however, thought it probable that Badger gave some instruction to Copley at the beginning of the latter's career. See Park, *Joseph Badger* (Boston, 1918), pp. 5–6.

Ezra Stiles, by Nathaniel Smibert

assigned to John Greenwood, suggests that Greenwood may have influenced Nathaniel Smibert. Greenwood is said to have begun painting portraits of his friends about 1742, at the early age of fifteen. The portrait of Edward Bromfield, Jr., cannot have been painted later than 1746, for he died in that year, aged twenty-three years. It thus falls within Greenwood's active period in Boston, and it gives plenty of evidence that Greenwood was influenced by John Smibert. But it also so markedly resembles some of Nathaniel Smibert's portraits of men, notably that of Ezra Stiles, that it might be taken for Nathaniel's work were it not that Nathaniel was less than twelve years old when Bromfield died. This indicates that when Nathaniel began to paint, at about sixteen years of age, he imitated the style of Greenwood, who was by that time in full career as a painter.[5]

Nathaniel's portrait of Ezra Stiles—his best work—also shows the influence of imported engravings, since the pose of the subject resembles that of John Smith in Kneller's portrait (now in the National Portrait Gallery, London) which was available in mezzotint. His portrait of John Lovell is also similar to Thomas Gibson's portrait of George Vertue, painted in 1723, and engraved by Vertue himself. In view of John Smibert's acquaintance with Vertue it would seem entirely probable that a print of this engraving might have been available for Nathaniel.

Nathaniel's portraits of women are more like those by his father than are his portraits of men. The picture of Mrs. Peter Harrison, for example, is reminiscent of John Smibert's portraits in the tilt of the head and general presentation, though quite inferior to his work in the anatomy of neck and bosom.

Of the fourteen portraits listed in the following Descriptive Catalogue we have satisfactory evidence that Nathaniel Smibert painted the portraits of Ezra Stiles, John Lovell, and Dorothy Wendell, and that there was a self-portrait. The portraits of the two younger Hall sisters (Mary Hall II, and Sarah Hall II) and of Peter Harrison and Mrs. Harrison can, I think, also be attributed to him with complete assurance on account of the date, 1756, when all four must have been painted, perhaps his latest works. And in both families there was an old tradition that the pictures were painted by "Smybert." That was correct, but, with the passage of years, it was natural enough that the youthful and little known Nathaniel should have been forgotten, and the name should have been mistaken to be that of his much more famous father.

The remaining portraits have been attributed to him by myself or others on grounds of style or probable date. These attributions are expressions of my present opinion, with which other critics may not agree, and which I hold subject to change.

The attribution to John Smibert of the portraits of Benjamin Lynde,

[5] For attribution of the portrait of Edward Bromfield, Jr., see Alan Burroughs, *John Greenwood in America* (Andover, Mass., 1943), pp. 31–33, and *Harvard Portraits*, 29–31. The portrait is reproduced in both publications.

Sr., No. 2 (*q.v.*), of Benjamin Lynde, Jr. (*q.v.*), and of Mr. and Mrs. Joshua Winslow (*q.v.*, Section C of Descriptive Catalogue) is open to question and it is possible that two or more of them may be the work of Nathaniel. The portraits of Rev. Charles Chauncy and Rev. Nathaniel Henchman are so much alike in certain details as to indicate that the same hand painted both, but there is no certain evidence that the hand was Nathaniel's, though I think that it probably was.

It seems clear that Nathaniel Smibert was an engaging youth, loved and admired by his friends, whose early promise of distinction unhappily never came to fulfilment. But his few surviving pictures afford small grounds for believing that he could have kept pace with his friend Copley, who, in turn, was painting his earliest portraits when Nathaniel died.

DESCRIPTIVE CATALOGUE OF PORTRAITS
ATTRIBUTED TO NATHANIEL SMIBERT

REV. CHARLES CHAUNCY

Subject: This portrait was purchased from the Chauncy family in 1847 by President Quincy of Harvard and others, and was presented to Harvard College as a portrait of its second president, Rev. Charles Chauncy, who was born in England in 1592, was president of the College 1654–1671/72, and who died in Cambridge 1671/72. It bears on the back a Latin inscription identifying the subject, and giving the date of painting, in which one figure is illegible, but the date intended was probably 1638.

This inscription, which is obviously later than the portrait, cannot be accepted as authoritative, but is the record of a mistaken opinion, since the portrait clearly dates from a period a hundred years later than that in which the first Charles Chauncy lived. The wig, costume, and manner of painting are those of the middle of the eighteenth century. The portrait, therefore, probably represents the great-grandson and namesake of the first Charles Chauncy. He was born in Boston January 1, 1705, and died there February 10, 1787. He was graduated from Harvard in 1721 and was the distinguished minister of the First Church from 1727 until his death. Even this identification of the subject, however, is open to some question because the face so little resembles that of the later Charles Chauncy as painted in his old age by McKay (*Harvard Portraits*, p. 41).

Size: H. 34½ in.; W. 28¾ in.

Date: Between 1750 and 1756.

Description: The subject is shown seated in an armchair, three quarters' front, his right shoulder towards the spectator, his head turned slightly right, nearly full-front, against a brown background. He wears a wig, a black coat over which is a golden-brown banian, or morning robe, white bands at the neck, and plain wrist bands. The pose, especially the way in which the hands hold an open book in his lap, strongly resembles that shown in the portrait of Rev. Nathaniel Henchman (*q.v.*).

Lawrence Park believed the portrait was painted by Smibert about 1735. The style, however, is not typical of John Smibert. It suggests rather the style of Nathaniel Smibert, the son of John, who could have painted it only in the years between 1750 and 1756 . . . At this time Charles Chauncy, the theologian and great-grandson of the President, was forty-five or fifty years of age . . . about the age of the subject of the portrait. The yellow and pink coloring in the robe and face is more characteristic of Nathaniel than of John Smibert, whose tones, as well as forms, were usually strong and full-bodied.[1]

Owner: Harvard University.

Reproduced: A copy belongs to the Harvard Club of New York. The head was engraved for the *New England Historical and Genealogical Register,* April 1865. *Harvard Graduates' Magazine* (December 1907), p. 248. Bolton, II, 551. *Harvard Portraits,* p. 39.

MRS. FRANCIS CLARKE

Subject: Deborah, daughter of Bartholemew and Hannah (Clarke) Gedney; born January 3, 1673 (?); married Francis Clarke, 1701; died ? Their daughter married William Fairfax of Virginia, who for a time held a government post in Salem, and her son, Bryan, later sixth Lord Fairfax, was born in Salem.

Size: H. 21 in.; W. 16 in.

Date: c. 1752–1753?

Description: The subject is an old woman facing nearly full front, against a shaded background. A little of her gray hair, parted in the middle, shows beneath her white coif, or widow's cap, which is tied under the chin by a black bow and is covered by a black hood. The pose is similar to that of Mrs. Margaret Sewall in the portrait by John Smibert, but the face is not so well modeled. The portrait has been attributed to John Smibert but is more likely to have been done by his son Nathaniel, to whom it is attributed by William Sawitzky and Alan Burroughs.

Owner: Essex Institute, Salem, Mass., the gift of the heirs of Mary C. Anderson, 1880.

Exhibited: Essex Institute.

Reproduced: Bayley, p. 371. Alan Burroughs, *Limners and Likenesses,* fig. 29.

References: Catalogue of Portraits in the Essex Institute, no. 44, p. 371. *P. F. Mass.* 81, attributed to John Smibert.

MRS. MARY DAVIE

Subject: Mary, probably daughter of John Mirick, born on or about June 3, 1635. She married three times, her third husband being George Davie (or Davis), a sea captain and a pioneer in the settlement of Wiscasset, Maine. After his death she lived in Charlestown, Mass., until her extreme old age, which she spent in Newton, where she died in 1752 at the age of 117 years. She is alleged to have had nine children, forty-five grandchildren, two-hundred great-grandchildren, and eight-hundred great-great-grandchildren.

Size: H. 13 in.; W. 9½ in.

Date: 1752, or a little earlier.

[1] *Harvard Portraits,* pp. 38–39.

Description: Only the head is shown of a very aged and withered woman, who wears a white cap tied under her chin.

Time has touched the colours with a clay-like, dingy tinge; from her great age the face is wrinkled and rugged; the features are strongly delineated, the eyes blue and smiling, the lips full and rosy, the forehead honest and open; & a white plain cap surrounds the head, face and chin, which gives a death-like look to the picture as though it had been taken from some living being, who had already entered the valley of the shadow of death; yet the expression is benevolent; but, if the original was ever handsome, this is a sad memorial of withered beauty.[2]

The portrait is said to have been painted in response to a request made by Governor Belcher to Judge Paul Dudley, after a visit to Mrs. Davie near the end of her life, that he would arrange to have her painted "by Smibert." The lack of skill shown in the picture, and the fact that John Smibert had ceased to paint about 1748 and had died in 1751, leads Mr. Alan Burroughs to set aside Governor Belcher's request as "implausible" and to attribute the picture to Greenwood.[3] This is to overlook the possibility that Belcher was referring not to John Smibert but to Nathaniel, who was on the threshold of his brief career. The clumsiness of the painting makes it more likely, in my opinion, that it is one of his earliest attempts at portraiture, rather than the work of Greenwood who, between 1750 and 1752, was painting with greater skill.

Owner: Massachusetts Historical Society, Boston. In the eighteenth century the portrait was owned by a Mrs. Skinner of Marblehead, who gave it to Rev. William Bentley of Salem, who in 1801 gave it to the Massachusetts Historical Society.

Bentley wrote in his *Diary*, September 29, 1798: "I was favored from Madam Skinner of Marblehead, with a likeness of *Mary Davis*, which had this paper accompanying it. 'The effigie of Mrs. Mary Davis aged 117.' . . . By a notice on the canvas, 1962, probably 1662, that might be the year of her arrival, for the settlement on the Kennebec at Wiscasset Point was in 1663, under one George Davie, whose children write Davis." In January 1801, Bentley gave the picture as recorded in M.H.S. *Proc.*, I, 139, ". . . the Portrait by Smibert, of Mary Davis, who died at Newton, 1752, aged 116. From Rev. William Bentley."

Reproduced: Bolton, II, 381. A. Burroughs, *John Greenwood in America*, p. 29.

References: Bolton, II, 379–81, 638. *P. F. Mass.* 577.

MARY HALL II

Subject: Mary, daughter of Hugh Hall III and his wife Elizabeth Pitts of Boston, born October 3, 1736; died May 13, 1757, on the day set for her wedding.

[2] Jackson, *Newton*, p. 267.
[3] A. Burroughs, *John Greenwood in America*, pp. 28–29, 59, 64.

Size: H. *c.* 29 in.; W. *c.* 24 in.

Date: 1756.

Description: I have seen only a small snapshot photograph showing this portrait, which appears to be a companion piece to the portrait of the subject's sister, *Sarah Hall II* (*q.v.*). They are similarly framed and the owner says that the two pictures are "alike enough to be twins." The subject is shown nearly full front, her head turned slightly to her right.

There are no grounds for questioning the identity of the two sisters, whose mother, Mrs. Hugh Hall, and aunts, Mary Hall I and Sarah Hall I (*qq.v.*), were painted by John Smibert. The portraits of the younger Mary and Sarah also bear old labels attributing them to "Smibert," but both the age of the subjects and the manner of painting are convincing evidence that they are the work of Nathaniel rather than of John Smibert.

Owner: Mrs. R. Roller Richardson. Mary Hall dying unmarried, her portrait, with that of her sister Sarah, passed to Sarah's daughter, Mary Clark, later Madam Baury, wife of Louis Baury de Bellerive. From Madam Baury the portrait of Mary Hall descended to Madam Baury's son, Rev. Alfred L. Baury, of Newton Lower Falls, Mass., and ultimately to Madam Baury's great-granddaughter, the late Mrs. Thomas E. Jansen, and that of Sarah Hall to Mrs. Baury's cousin, Mary Baury Jackson, wife of Robert C. Rathbone. Mrs. Rathbone, dying childless, left the portrait of Sarah Hall to her cousin Mrs. Jansen, on condition that she should give the portrait of Mary Hall to Mrs. Jansen's sister, the present owner, Mrs. R. Roller Richardson, 135 North Orange Drive, Los Angeles 36, California.

SARAH HALL II

Subject: Sarah, daughter of Hugh Hall III and his wife Elizabeth Pitts of Boston; born February 2, 1738, married (1) Elisha Clark of Middletown, Conn., (2) Wensley Hobby; died August 3, 1801, at Middletown.

Size: H. 29½ in.; W. 24½ in.

Date: 1756.

Description: The subject is a young woman, shown against a dark background within spandrels, half front, her right shoulder towards the spectator, her head turned to her right three-quarters front. She has brown hair, in which a string of pearl beads is entwined, hazel eyes, and a fresh complexion. She wears a golden-gray satin dress with white muslin trim. The portrait appears to be a companion piece to that of her sister, Mary Hall II (*q.v.*).

Owner: Thomas E. Jansen, Dedham, Mass. For the line of descent see under Mary Hall II.

PETER HARRISON

Subject: Peter, son of Thomas and Elizabeth (Denison) Harrison, born in York, England, June 14, 1716; died in New Haven, Conn., April 30, 1775. He and his older brother Joseph emigrated to Newport, and from being sea captains set up as merchants and prospered. On June 6, 1746, he married Elizabeth Pelham, after eloping with her to Hampton Falls, N. H. He studied architecture as a gentlemanly avocation and drew the plans for the Touro Synagogue, the Redwood Library, and the Market House in Newport; for King's Chapel in Boston; for Christ Church in Cambridge, Mass.; and, probably, for St. Michael's Church in Charleston, S. C.

Size: H. *c.* 30 in.; W. *c.* 25 in.

Date: 1756.

Description: The subject is shown half front, in a painted oval, against a shaded background, his right shoulder towards the spectator, his head turned right nearly full front. He has gray eyes and a long, straight nose. He wears a white neckband, brown coat and waistcoat, and a short white wig with four horizontal curls on its lower half.

This portrait and its companion piece representing Mrs. Harrison have been attributed by family tradition to John Smibert, and it has been assumed that they must have been painted in June 1746 when the couple passed through Boston on their homeward way after their marriage in New Hampshire. Neither portrait, however, is characteristic of John Smibert; Harrison's wig and tucked-in neckscarf belong to a style a decade later than that of their marriage; and Mrs. Harrison appears to be a woman in her thirties. In the family archives is a memorandum by Miss Elizabeth F. Thomas, a great-aunt of the present owner, which states, "We have a letter from Nath. Smibert to Peter Harrison dated July 29, 1756." This letter has been lost, but there is no reason to doubt the accuracy of the memorandum. There is no conceivable reason why Nathaniel Smibert should have written to Harrison in 1756 (only a few months before his own death) except in regard to a commission to paint these portraits, and the presence in Newport of Nathaniel's (much older) cousin, Dr. Thomas Moffatt, was sufficient reason for visiting Newport. Moffatt, who was a close friend of the Harrisons, may well have secured the commission.

The portrait of Peter Harrison is entirely characteristic of Nathaniel's style in the few portraits which are with assurance attributed to him: compare the painting of eyes and mouth, and of the neckband, in the portraits of John Lovell and Ezra Stiles; and the date 1756 is satisfactory for Peter Harrison's costume and for the age at which he and his wife are represented. Since Nathaniel died soon afterwards, on the threshold of his career, it was quite natural that within a generation the entirely correct attribution of the portraits to "Smibert" should have been incorrectly supposed to refer to the forgotten youth's well-remembered father. Both portraits were rather badly damaged in the early part of the nineteenth century, being taken off their stretchers, rolled up, and stored away as of negligible importance. They were retrieved about the middle of the century, and have more recently been skillfully restored, without being so much repainted as to obscure their original characteristics.

Owner: Maurice P. Van Buren, New York, to whom the portrait, with its companion piece, has come down by descent from the subject's youngest daughter.

Reproduced: A copy, with variations, by Louis Sands, was presented to the Redwood Library, Newport, in 1869. Updike, *History of the Episcopal Church in Narragansett,* II, 326. Dunlap, III, opp. p. 318, as by John Smibert. *Bulletin of the Society for the Preservation of New England Antiquities,* vol. VI, no. 2, serial no. 13, Article by Samuel F. Batchelder. Carl Bridenbaugh, *Peter Harrison, First American Architect* (Chapel Hill, N. C., 1949), opp. p. 30. F.A.R.L. 38549.

MRS. PETER HARRISON

Subject: Elizabeth, daughter of Edward and Arabelle (Williams) Pelham of Newport, R. I.; born 1721, married Peter Harrison in 1746; died 1784.

Size: H. 30 in.; W. 25 in.

Date: 1756.

Description: The subject's head and bust are shown nearly full front against a shaded background, her head turned slightly to the left. She has brown hair, a curl of which falls on her right shoulder, and large gray eyes. She wears an olive-brown dress with the usual white muslin trim in the bodice. In pose and general character the portrait resembles the work of John Smibert, but is less skilfully painted. For its attribution to Nathaniel Smibert see discussion of the portrait of the subject's husband.

Owner: Maurice P. van Buren, New York.

Reproduced: Copy by Louis Sands in Redwood Library, Newport, R. I. Updike, *History of the Episcopal Church in Narragansett,* II, 338. Bridenbaugh, Carl, *Peter Harrison,* opp. p. 31. F.A.R.L. 38550.

REV. NATHANIEL HENCHMAN

Subject: Nathaniel, son of Nathaniel and Anna (Greenwood) Henchman, born in Boston, probably on November 22, 1700, graduated from Harvard College 1717; minister at Lynn, Mass., from 1720 until his death, December 23, 1761. One of his children was Daniel Henchman, the Boston silversmith.

Size: H. 36 in.; W. 28 in.

Date: 1753–1755?

Description: The subject is shown seated half front against a light-brown shaded background, his right shoulder towards the spectator, his head turned to his right three-quarters front. He has brown eyes, a fair complexion, rather round face, and a cupid's-bow mouth. He wears a gray wig, somewhat askew, a black coat unbuttoned, a black waistcoat with three or four buttons unbuttoned at the waist showing a little of his white shirt, and a white neckcloth and ministerial bands. In his lap he holds an open Bible, his right hand in the act of turning a page over to that part of the book held in his left hand. The armchair in which he is sitting is badly drawn, being too small for him, and its top, behind his head, appears unfinished. It looks much like one of the two armchairs which frequently appear in portraits by John Smibert, to whom the picture has been attributed. The manner of painting, however, is not that of John Smibert, but does somewhat resemble that of his son Nathaniel. If that attribution is accepted the chair may represent a "property" which Nathaniel had inherited.

A similar chair appears in the portrait of Rev. Charles Chauncy, which strikingly resembles that of Henchman in pose and detail. In each picture the subject holds an open Bible in precisely the same manner, and the faulty drawing of hands and book is identical in each. The chief difficulty in assigning both pictures to Nathaniel Smibert is that in each one the subject appears rather younger than the fifty or more years which he must have reached to be painted by Nathaniel.

The portrait of Henchman is in the original frame.

Owner: M. Knoedler & Co., New York. A penciled memorandum on the back reading "5/1/44" presumably gives the date of acquisition by Knoedler. Nathaniel Henchman in his will left to his wife "my large picture, so long as shee shall be disposed to keep it," and to his daughter Anna "my small picture covered with glass." These pictures are listed in the lengthy inventory of a considerable property, reaching a total of £3000, as "The testator's large effigies, curtain and rod—£4.0.0" and "Small effigies—21.4." [4] The present portrait must be the one listed as "The testator's large effigies." In a later generation a Henchman married a Sewall and the portrait descended to Nellie L. Sewall, now Mrs. Bennett, of Burlington, Mass., who sold it to Knoedler.

Reproduced: Knoedler, *American Painting of the Eighteenth and Early Nineteenth Centuries* (1949), p. 1. Photograph by Knoedler & Co.

INDIAN PRIEST (SO-CALLED)

Subject: The picture shows a fine-looking American Indian, perhaps forty years of age, wearing a white shirt open at the neck, and with a blanket over his right shoulder, carried round his body beneath his left arm, and held together by his right hand. He is standing outdoors beside a tree. Nothing is known of the subject, date, or origin of the picture, nor is there anything to indicate that the Indian in question was a priest. The portrait is, however, an interesting picture of a New England Indian of the eighteenth century who had adopted something of the white man's civilization.

Owner: Bowdoin College, Brunswick, Maine. The picture belonged to the Bowdoin Collection which came in 1811 to Bowdoin College from the Estate of James Bowdoin III. The late Lawrence Park thought it might possibly be the work of John Smibert, but more recently William Sawitzky attributed it to Nathaniel Smibert. Of the two the latter is perhaps the more likely, but either attribution rests chiefly on the sup-

[4] Essex Probate Records, cccxxxviii, 472–474; cccxxxix, 259–265.

position that the Smibert studio was the most probable source from which James Bowdoin acquired the picture, with a number of others which he undoubtedly purchased when the contents of the studio were dispersed.

JOHN LOVELL

Subject: John Lovell, born in Boston June 16, 1710; died in Halifax, N. S., 1778. Graduated at Harvard 1728; usher at the Boston Latin School, 1729; succeeded Dr. Nathaniel Williams as "Master" of the school in 1734, which position he held till 1776. He delivered the first public address in Faneuil Hall, 1743, on the death of the donor, Peter Faneuil. He was a loyalist, and left Boston with the British troops in 1776.

Size: H. 28½ in.; W. 23½ in.

Date: c. 1750.

Description: The head and bust of the subject are shown within spandrels, against a shaded brown background, half front, his right shoulder towards the spectator, his head turned right, three-quarters front. He wears an olive-green turban, and a robe of the same color, lined with light brown, over a dark coat. He has a rather full face, dark-brown eyes, and dark but very narrow eyebrows, and appears to be about forty years of age.

The portrait has been attributed to John Smibert but the comment of Judge Cranch in a letter written in 1809 to Dunlap and quoted in the latter's *History of the Arts of Design*, I, 29, is authoritative for assigning it to Nathaniel (see pp. 261–262).

Owner: Harvard University. Alan Burroughs in *Art in America*, XXXI, 88 (April 1943), says that in 1846 the portrait which at some earlier date had been given to Harvard, was discovered "among the neglected rubbish of the College" by a committee of the Boston Latin School Association, which the next year obtained permission to have it copied. The copy is now in the Assembly Hall, Boston Latin School, Boston. See *Harvard College Papers*, 2ⁿᵈ Ser., XIV, 181.

Reproduced: Copy, Boston Latin School. Winsor, II, 401. Dunlap, I, 22. *Catalogue, Loan Exhibition of One Hundred Colonial Portraits*, Museum of Fine Arts (Boston, 1930), p. 53.

References: Dunlap, I, 29. *Harvard Portraits*, p. 89. M.H.S. *Proc.*, XVI (1878), 399. *P. F. Mass.* 1938.

NATHANIEL SMIBERT, SELF-PORTRAIT

That Nathaniel Smibert painted a self-portrait is proved by stanza 7 in the Latin elegy by John Beveridge in which the author says, "See the canvas hanging there, painted with brilliant colors, speaks forth his very image when, in skillful manner, he sought to enliven the linen with his own features" (see above, p. 261).

No other written reference to it has been found, nor is it known whether the picture is still extant.

EZRA STILES

Subject: Ezra, son of Isaac and Keziah (Taylor) Stiles, born at North Haven, Conn., November 29, 1727; graduated from Yale College 1746; tutor at Yale; minister of the Second Congregational Church, Newport, R. I., 1755–1777; president of Yale College 1777 until his death on May 12, 1795.

Size: H. 28¾ in.; W. 25 in.

Date: The portrait has been relined but on the back of the original canvas was an inscription reading:

> *Effigies Ezra Stiles*
> *Aetat 29 a Nat. Smibert*
> *depicta Apr. 2ᵈᵒ 1756*

Description: The future president of Yale College is shown as a young man within painted spandrels, against a dark gray-green background, nearly half length, half front, with his left shoulder towards the spectator, his head turned left nearly full front. He wears a cap and robe of yellow brocade over a black waistcoat, the middle buttons of which are undone, allowing a glimpse of the ends of the white neckscarf. His right hand, which is awkwardly painted, holds against his body a book bound in light red. The face is pleasing and lifelike, with brown eyes and rather thin, level eyebrows.

The portrait has a marked similarity in pose and detail to Sir Godfrey Kneller's portrait of John Smith (1652?–1742), the London engraver, which Kneller painted in 1696 and of which Smith, twenty years later, made a mezzotint, dated 1716. George Vertue made a note of it: "Mr. John Smith mezzotint his picture by Sir Godfrey Kneller, done when he was younger and fatter & fuller fac'd than he now is. his picture now painted by Mr. Murray much more like him that [than] the print" (Brit. Mus. Add. Mss. 23076. p. 14). It is reasonable to suppose that John Smibert during his residence in London was acquainted with John Smith and that he may have imported a print of the engraving which Nathaniel used as the basis of his picture of Ezra Stiles.

Owner: Yale University. The portrait was given by Ezra Stiles to his son Isaac in 1793. In 1919 it was purchased from descendants by Anson Phelps Stokes and others, and was presented to Yale University. It now hangs in the Yale University Art Gallery.

Exhibited: Addison Gallery, Andover, Mass., November 1942. Worcester Art Museum, Exhibition of New England Painting, 1700–1775, February 17–March 31, 1943.

Reproduced: Old-Time New England, vol. XI, no. 2, opp. p. 55 (October 1920). F. F. Sherman, *Early American Painting* (1932). Alan Burroughs, *Art in America,* XXXI, 88–97 (April 1943).

Reference: Old-Time New England (Bulletin of the Society for the Preservation of New England Antiquities), XI, 55–56 (October–November 1920).

UNIDENTIFIED MAN

Subject: An unidentified man.

Size: H. 30 in.; W. 24 in.

Date: From the costume it may be assumed that the portrait was painted in the seventeen-fifties.

Description: The head and bust of the subject are shown nearly full front, above very small spandrels in the lower corners. He wears a white wig, stock, and ruffle, a yellowish brown coat and waistcoat, the latter unbuttoned. The portrait has been tentatively attributed to Robert Feke, or to John Smibert, but can hardly be by either. It may possibly be the work of Nathaniel Smibert.

Owner: Mrs. George E. Thompson of New Haven, Conn.; purchased at an auction in 1931. Nothing is known of its pedigree.

DOROTHY WENDELL

Subject: Dorothy, daughter of John and Elizabeth (Quincy) Wendell, born March 19, 1733; married Richard Skinner; died April 3, 1822.

Size: H. 29¾ in.; W. 24¾ in.

Date: Signed, lower left corner: N. [?] Smibert Pinx 175[5?].

Description: The subject is shown within painted spandrels against a shaded brown background, full front, her head turned slightly to her left. She has brown hair and eyes, and a pleasing and alert expression. She wears a gray-blue silk dress with a stiff laced stomacher, with a pearl-gray scarf over her right arm and an elaborate lace cap. About her neck is a long white shirred collar trimmed with lace. In her hair above her right ear is a black ribbon with a pearl ornament. A shadow-graph of the portrait shows that drapery over her shoulder has been painted out and that originally she was shown wearing earrings.

Owner: Mrs. Edward B. Alford, Brookline, Mass.

Reproduced: Catalogue, Loan Exhibition of One Hundred Colonial Portraits, Museum of Fine Arts (Boston, 1930), p. 96.

Reference: M.H.S. Proc., XVI (1878), 399.

Bibliography

Abbreviations used in the Notes and Catalogue

Bayley: F. W. Bayley, *Five Colonial Artists of New England* (Boston), 1929).

Bolton: Charles K. Bolton, *Portraits of the Founders*, 3 vols. (Boston, 1919–1926).

Champlin & Perkins: Champlin & Perkins, *Cyclopedia of Painters and Paintings* (1888).

DAB: *Dictionary of American Biography* (New York, 1928–1936).

DNB: *Dictionary of National Biography* (London, 1921–1922).

F.A.R.L.: Frick Art Reference Library, New York. The number which follows the initials is that of the photograph of the portrait in question when taken by a member of the Library's staff. When the initials are followed by the abbreviation "photo." the photograph is from another source.

M.H.S. *Proc.:* Massachusetts Historical Society, *Proceedings*.

N.E.H.G.S. *Register:* New England Historic Genealogical Society, *Register*.

P. F. Mass.: *American Portraits, 1620–1825, Found in Massachusetts*, Historical Records Survey, W.P.A. (Boston, 1939, mimeographed). The number following the initials is that of the picture listed.

Vertue: *Vertue Note Books*, Walpole Society (London, 1930–1947), see Bibliography.

Winsor: Justin Winsor, ed., *Memorial History of Boston*, 4 vols. (1881).

BIBLIOGRAPHY

Primary sources of information about Smibert and his paintings are listed below in order of publication. Secondary references to him in biographical dictionaries of artists, and elsewhere, are not included, since they are only brief and frequently inaccurate summaries of information based chiefly on Walpole and Dunlap. Minor references to him or to his paintings in recent publications have been cited in the text and footnotes. For further reproductions ot his works, see the *A.L.A. Portrait Index* (1906), under the names of the sitters.

The Walpole Society in England has printed, *in extenso*, the notes made over a period of forty years by the antiquary and engraver George Vertue, in the following volumes of its annual publication (Oxford University Press):

XVIII (1930),	*Vertue Note Books* I		
XX (1932),	"	"	" II
XXII (1934),	"	"	" III
XXIV (1936),	"	"	" IV
XXVI (1938),	"	"	" V
XXIX (1947),	"	"	" VI, Index.

The volume cited as Vertue III, which presents the part of the notebooks dealing with Vertue's contemporaries, contains all of Vertue's references to Smibert, which are the ultimate source for almost all the information we have about his London career.

Horace Walpole, *Anecdotes of Painting in England*, ed. Ralph M. Wornum (1862), II, 673. First published 1762–1767 and until recent years the only available source of information about Smibert's career in Great Britain. Walpole's information was wholly derived from Vertue's notes, which he skillfully wove into a one-page account of Smibert, but he did not use all of Vertue's references to him and is inaccurate in some of his statements.

W. Dunlap, *A History of the Rise and Progress of the Arts of Design in the United States* (1894), revised ed. by Bayley and Goodspeed (1918), with many corrections. The earliest American account of Smibert, based on Walpole, but with much space given to Dean Berkeley. Some information about Smibert's American career, and the earliest account of his son Nathaniel.

William H. Whitmore, "The Early Painters and Engravers of New England," M.H.S. *Proc.*, IX, 197–216 (May 1866).

Augustus T. Perkins, M.H.S. *Proc.*, XVI, 392–399, 474–475 (December 1878), and XVII, 94–97 (May 1879). Whitmore and Perkins had little information about Smibert's career, but give the earliest lists of portraits attributed to Smibert and Blackburn, though with a number of mistaken attributions.

J. Winsor, *Memorial History of Boston* (1881), vol. II, Smibert's signature, and map locating his residence.

W. Updike, *History of the Episcopal Church in Narragansett, R. I.*, (1807), chapter by H. Bull on Trinity Church, Newport. An account of the arrival of Dean Berkeley's party in Newport and episodes of their stay there. Reproductions of several of Smibert's portraits.

Walter K. Watkins, "The New England Museum and the Home of Art in Boston," *Bostonian Society Publications*, second series, vol. II (1917). An account of Smibert's residence in Boston.

Lionel Cust, article on Smibert, *Dictionary of National Biography*.

George F. Dow, *Arts and Crafts in New England, 1704–1775, Gleanings from Boston Newspapers* (1927). For Smibert advertisements.

F. W. Coburn, "John Smibert," *Art in America*, vol. XVII, no. 4 (June 1929), pp. 175–187.

F. W. Bayley, *Five Colonial Artists of New England* (Boston, 1929), pp. 335–437. Contains forty-nine reproductions, but with numerous questionable attributions and mistaken identifications.

T. Bolton and H. L. Binsse, *The Antiquarian*, vol. XV, no. 4 (October 1930).

T. Bolton, "John Smibert: Notes and Catalogue," *Fine Arts*, XX, 11–15, 39–42 (August 1933). List of paintings attributed to Smibert.

T. Sizer, article on Smibert, *Dictionary of American Biography*. The first account of Smibert in brief space which is both adequate and accurate; detailed bibliography.

Alan Burroughs, *Limners and Likenesses* (Cambridge, 1936), pp. 34–41.

O. Hagen, *Birth of the American Tradition in Art* (1940), pp. 40–63.

Alan Burroughs, "The Development of John Smibert," *Art in America*, XXX, 111–121 (April 1942). An excellent discussion of Smibert's style.

Alan Burroughs, "Paintings by Nathaniel Smibert," *Art in America*, XXXI, 88–97 (April 1943).

J. T. Flexner, *American Painting: First Flowers of our Wilderness* (New York, 1947), chap. V.

Index